PASSIONATE HISTORIES

MYTH, MEMORY AND INDIGENOUS AUSTRALIA

PASSIONATE HISTORIES

MYTH, MEMORY AND INDIGENOUS AUSTRALIA

Edited by Frances Peters-Little,
Ann Curthoys and John Docker

ANU
THE AUSTRALIAN NATIONAL UNIVERSITY

E PRESS

ANU E PRESS

Published by ANU E Press and Aboriginal History Incorporated
Aboriginal History Monograph 21

This title is also available online at: http://epress.anu.edu.au/passionate_histories_citation.html

---

National Library of Australia
Cataloguing-in-Publication entry

Title: Passionate histories : myth, memory and Indigenous Australia / edited by Frances Peters-Little, Ann Curthoys and John Docker.

ISBN: 9781921666643 (pbk.) 9781921666650 (pdf)

Series: Aboriginal history monograph ; no. 21

Notes: Includes bibliographical references.

Subjects: Aboriginal Australians--History.
            Aboriginal Australians--Social life and customs.
            Mythology, Aboriginal Australian.
            Australia--History.

Editors: Peters-Little, Frances, 1958-
            Curthoys, Ann.
            Docker, John.

Dewey Number: 994.0049915

Contacting Aboriginal History
All Editorial enquiries: Editor, Aboriginal History, Australian Centre for Indigenous History, Coombs Building, ANU 0200. Sales and subscriptions thelma.simms@anu.edu.au

Aboriginal History Inc. is a part of the Australian Centre for Indigenous History, Research School of Social Sciences, The Australian National University and gratefully acknowledges the support of the History Program, RSSS and the National Centre for Indigenous Studies, The Australian National University.

WARNING: Readers are notified that this publication may contain names or images of deceased persons.

ANU E Press: All correspondence should be addressed to:
ANU E Press, The Australian National University, Canberra ACT 0200, Australia
Email: anuepress@anu.edu.au, http://epress.anu.edu.au

Cover image: *History's like water*, photography by James Henry Little.

Cover design and layout by ANU E Press

Contents

Dedication vii
Acknowledgements ix
Notes on Contributors xi
Foreword xix
  Ian Thorpe

Introduction 1
  Frances Peters-Little

Part one: massacres

1. The country has another past: Queensland and the History Wars 9
  Raymond Evans

2. 'Hard evidence': the debate about massacre in the Black War
in Tasmania 39
  Lyndall Ryan

3. Epistemological vertigo and allegory: thoughts on massacres,
actual, surrogate, and averted – *Beersheba, Wake in Fright,
Australia* 51
  John Docker

Part two: myths

4. Remembering the referendum with compassion 75
  Frances Peters-Little

5. Idle men: the eighteenth-century roots of the Indigenous
indolence myth 99
  Shino Konishi

6. 'These unoffending people': myth, history and the idea of
Aboriginal resistance in David Collins' *Account of the English
Colony in New South Wales* 123
  Rachel Standfield

7. Demythologising Flynn, with Love: contesting missionaries
in Central Australia in the twentieth century 141
  David Trudinger

Part three: memory and oral history

8. Paul Robeson's visit to Australia and Aboriginal activism, 1960 163
   Ann Curthoys

9. Using poetry to capture the Aboriginal voice in oral history transcripts 185
   Lorina Barker

Part four: identity, myth and memory

10. Making a debut: myths, memories and mimesis 205
    Anna Cole

11. Identity and identification: Aboriginality from the Spanish Civil War to the French Ghettos 219
    Vanessa Castejon

12. Urban Aboriginal ceremony: when seeing is *not* believing . . 229
    Kristina Everett

13. *Island Home Country*: working with Aboriginal protocols in a documentary film about colonisation and growing up white in Tasmania 247
    Jeni Thornley

Part five: the Stolen Generations

14. Reconciliation without history: state crime and state punishment in Chile and Australia 281
    Peter Read

15. Overheard – conversations of a museum curator 299
    Jay Arthur, with Barbara Paulson and Troy Pickwick

16. On the significance of saying 'sorry': Apology and reconciliation in Australia 309
    Isabelle Auguste

We dedicate this book to

JAMES OSWALD LITTLE

Descendant and elder of the Yorta Yorta and the Yuin/Monaro peoples

Acknowledgements

This volume of essays has truly been a collaborative effort. We thank Ian Thorpe for writing the foreword, and we are honoured and excited to receive his support. We owe Sue Ballyn a special debt. As Director of Australian Studies at the University of Barcelona, she hosted a conference entitled Myth, Memory, and History, in June 2008. We thank her not only for organising such a pleasurable and stimulating event, but also for supporting our proposal to produce this volume, based in part on the conference papers. Earlier versions (in some cases *much* earlier versions) of some of these papers (those by Jay Arthur, Isabelle Auguste, Lyndall Ryan, Kristina Everett, Peter Read and Anna Cole) have been published in the Centre's journal, *Coolabah*, vol 3, 2009, and we thank Sue for permission to publish these revised versions here.

We also thank Peter Read at Aboriginal History Inc for supporting this project from the beginning, and James Little for the cover image.

We would especially like to acknowledge all our contributors, for being easy to work with and joining in the spirit of the volume. Their 'passionate biographical notes' indicate their variety and commitment, and we are proud and delighted to have been able to draw together such a talented and dedicated group.

Finally, we enjoyed producing this volume, over many a long coffee in Glebe and Balmain coffee shops, and we trust that you, our readers, will enjoy reading it.

Notes on Contributors

Jay Arthur: I am passionate about telling histories as three-dimensional stories, that is, as an exhibition. The kind of exhibition I am interested in is one that is not solely about the objects, but about the way in which people move through that physical space to relate to the objects and the context in which these objects are placed. The National Library of Australia's 'Treasures' exhibition could have been held in a basketball court with the items laid on card tables and people still would have queued all night to see Jane Austen's letter or Beethoven's handwritten score. The kind of exhibition I am interested in is one that has an idea behind it that provides the activating principle. It may be an intellectual concept, or it may be an emotional response. I want to create an 'artwork' or an 'academic article' that people can enter in real time and space. Have I ever done something like that that I was satisfied with? Not at all. Each new project lures me on with its possibilities and I leave it at the end, as from an unsatisfactory relationship, with the good memories obscured by the final failure. The joy is in the pursuit of the imagined creation. My most recent exhibition is *From Little Things Big Things Grow: Fighting for Indigenous Rights 1920-1970*, which focuses on a group of activists, both Indigenous and non-Indigenous, who fought for the human rights of Indigenous Australians in that period. I have also been passionate about producing *The Default Country: a Lexical Cartography of Twentieth Century Australia* (2003), the book developed from my PhD thesis; and *It's a Dog's Life! Animals in the Public Service,* a National Archives of Australia exhibition which toured from 2004–2009.

Isabelle Auguste: I am from Reunion Island, a French territory in the Indian Ocean. My interest in Indigenous history and politics began in 1997 when I was an exchange student at the University of Minnesota. I followed some general Native American History as well as some Dakota and Ojibwa history and culture courses. I wrote my Master dissertation on 'Gaming and Sovereignty, the Impact of Native American Gambling on Indian and Non-Indian Societies'. I became interested in the situation of Indigenous people in Australia in 1999 and have devoted my last ten years trying to learn more about the place of Aboriginal and Torres Strait Islander people in Australian society. My thesis, defended in 2005, looked at the issue of Indigenous self-determination in Australia. Based on the United Nations Declaration on the Rights of Indigenous Peoples, it is a study of more than 30 years of Indigenous policy at the federal level and struggle for Indigenous rights. In 2007, I received a Lavoisier award from the French Department of Foreign and European Affairs to conduct some postdoctoral research on Reconciliation in Australia. I was a visiting fellow in

2007–2008 at the Australian Centre for Indigenous History, Research School of Social Sciences, Australian National University. I am now a lecturer and researcher at the University of la Réunion. My first book *L'Administration des Affaires Aborigènes en Australie depuis 1972, l'autodétermination en question* was published by l'Harmattan (Paris) in the Collection Lettres du Pacifique in 2008.

Lorina Barker: I am a descendant of the Wangkumara and Muruwari people of western New South Wales and am currently a PhD candidate researching family/community history at the University of New England. I also team-teach in Australian History in the School of Humanities at UNE. I am passionate about family/community history and I specialise in oral history and am particularly interested in the way in which Aboriginal history has been recorded. More importantly, my main interest is in the process of remodelling research methods and techniques so that they readily apply to, and are culturally appropriate for and accessible to my family and community, the core audience for my research. My recent research publications (including this chapter) focus on the interview and transcription processes of oral history research. In particular, I focus on the relationship dynamics between interviewer and interviewee and the cultural context that surrounds oral history methodology, especially when conducting research with Aboriginal people who are family/community members. I published '"Hangin' Out" and "Yarnin': reflecting on the experience of collecting oral histories", in *History Australia,* 2008. My 2009 keynote address at the second Australasian Narrative Inquiry Conference, UNE highlighted the largely undocumented history of Aboriginal people's contributions to the shearing industry in New South Wales, especially the role of Aboriginal men as shearers and rouseabouts. As part of the presentation I screened my short film, *A Shearer's Life: Introducing the Barker Brothers,* to demonstrate how visual media can be used to convey people's lived experiences and history.

Vanessa Castejon: I work in CRIDAF: Centre de recherches interculturelles sur les domaines anglophones et francophones, Université Paris 13. For many years now, I have been working on Aboriginal self-determination, treaty claims, and sovereignty as opposed to so-called solutions proposed by the Australian government to Indigenous people. I have been studying Australian institutional racism. I also worked on the recognition of Indigenous rights on an international scale, working on the declaration of the rights of Indigenous peoples as well as the United Nations Working Group on Indigenous Peoples and the creation of a global Indigeneity. I have also written on the image of Indigenous people outside Australia, focusing on France (concentrating on the Musée du Quai Branly). My publications include 'Une conciliation nécessaire après la Réconciliation? L'Etat des affaires autochtones en Australie en 2006', in Maryvonne Nedeljkovic (ed), *Conciliation and Reconciliation; Volume One: Strategies in the Pacific* (2008); *Les Aborigènes et l'apartheid politique australien* (2005); 'L'identité aborigène sous les gouvernements d'Howard: un retour aux définitions imposées de l'Aboriginalité?', *Le Mensuel de l'Université*, 20 (2007); and 'The Exoticism of the Musée du Quai Branly: a French Perspective on Aboriginal Australia', in Renata Summo-O'Connell (ed), *Imagined Australia, Reflections around the Reciprocal Construction of Identity between Australia and Europe* (2009).

Anna Cole: I am a researcher, writer, and sometimes film-maker and currently a Visiting Fellow in the Anthropology Department, Goldsmiths College, University of London. Prior to moving to London, I was a Post-doctoral Research Fellow with the Centre for Public Culture and Ideas at Griffith University, Queensland. I work in the area of historical anthropology, embodied knowledges, and the gendered politics of colonialism. I am finding out, as the women's liberation movement of the 1970s put it, how 'the personal is political' and how my own story of migration and assimilation relates to the colonisation of Australia past and present. Recent publications include 'The Marked Body', in Ivan Crozier (ed), *A Cultural History of the Human Body in the Modern Age: volume 6* (2009); 'Dancing with the Prime Minister', *Studies in Australasian Cinema* (2008); and (with Anna Haebich), 'Corporeal Colonialism and Corporal Punishment: a cross-cultural perspective on body modification', in *Social Semiotics* (2007).

Ann Curthoys: I loved History at school in Newcastle, where I grew up, and majored in it in my BA degree at the University of Sydney in the 1960s. At Macquarie University in 1973, I completed my PhD on racism and race relations in colonial New South Wales. Since then, I have followed many intellectual passions – histories of feminism, popular culture, television and journalism, Australian politics, Chinese-Australian immigration, and especially the relations between Indigenous and non-Indigenous people. I am also passionate about historical theory and method, and the public practices of history. In recent years, I have been seeking ways to understand Australian history that bring Indigenous-non-Indigenous relations into the centre of the story, within the wider frameworks of transnational and British imperial history. I am an Australian Research Council Professorial Fellow at the University of Sydney. My publications include *Freedom Ride: A Freedomrider Remembers* (2002); (with John Docker) *Is History Fiction?* (2010; 1st edition 2005); (with Ann Genovese and Alexander Reilly) *Rights and Redemption: History, Law, and Indigenous People* (2008); and (with Ann McGrath) *How to Write History that People Want to Read* (2009).

John Docker: I am a cultural historian, which I feel gives me a licence to wander. Over the decades I have been interested in literary and cultural theory, popular culture, postmodernism and poststructuralism, monotheism and polytheism, diaspora, historiography, Jewish identity, and Gandhian non-violence. I have always written personally, mixing theory and analysis with life stories and family history, and am currently writing an intellectual autobiography, *Growing*

Up Communist and Jewish in Bondi: Memoir of a Non-Australian Australian. Since the middle 1980s, I have written critiques of Zionist nationalism and settler colonialism, and recently have been reflecting on partition in Palestine and India, and Martin Buber's idea of a bi-national Palestine. I have devoted the last several years to genocide and massacre studies. Raphaël Lemkin suggested in his originating definition in 1944 that genocide is constitutively linked to settler colonialism. I am passionately critical of settler colonialism, whether in Israel or Australia. I am an adjunct Professor at the University of Sydney and the Australian National University. My most recent books are (with Ann Curthoys) *Is History Fiction?* (2005, 2010) and *The Origins of Violence: Religion, History and Genocide* (2008). In press is an essay entitled 'The origins of massacres', in Philip Dwyer and Lyndall Ryan (eds), *Theatres of Violence: Massacre, Mass Killing, and Atrocity in History* (2010).

Raymond Evans: I have been a practising historian for 45 years and a publishing one for 38 of these. My research has ranged over many aspects of Australian social and cultural history in this time but the core of my studies has centred on race relations, particularly indigenous/incomer contact studies and the predominant patterns of conflict these have engendered. I have grown especially interested in investigating not simply the intensity of such encounters but also the patterns of denial that have accrued around them to create a mythical webbing of camouflage, supporting an 'innocent invaders' syndrome of nationalistic 'explanation'. My most recent publications include *A History of Queensland* (2007), *Radical Brisbane: An Unruly History* (2004) and the chapters '"Pigmentia": racial fears and white Australia' and '"Plenty Shoot 'em": the destruction of Aboriginal societies across the Queensland frontier', in A Dirk Moses (ed), *Genocide and Settler Society: Frontier Violence and Stolen Indigenous Children in Australian History* (2004).

Kristina Everett: I hold a PhD in anthropology and am committed to classical ethnography as my research practice. I work in the Department of Indigenous Studies, Warawara at Macquarie University. My work at Warawara is focused on co-ordinating undergraduate and post-graduate Indigenous Studies programs drawing from models of best practice internationally and nationally. As well as a keen research interest in Indigenous education and inclusive curricula, I am also vitally concerned with social justice issues surrounding cultural revival and rejuvenation. My three favourite recent publications are 'Welcome to Country ... not', *Oceania* (2009); 'Affecting change through assessment: improving Indigenous Studies programs using engaging assessment', <http://www.ojs.unisa.edu.au> (2008); 'Too Much Information: when the burden of trust paralyses representation', in Peter Read, Frances Peters-Little and Anna Haebich (eds), *Indigenous Biography and Autobiography* (2008).

Shino Konishi: I am a descendant of the Yawuru people of Broome, Western Australia, and became passionate about history when I was a student at the University of Sydney and first read early explorers' descriptions of Aboriginal people. My PhD critically examined eighteenth-century ethnographic accounts of Aboriginal men, and I have since developed an interest in contemporary representations of Indigenous masculinity in politics and film. In late 2009 Maria Nugent and I co-convened a conference called 'Baz Luhrmann's *Australia* Reviewed: History, Film and Popular Culture' at the National Museum of Australia, and I am preparing an article on David Gulpilil's character King George and paternal love. However, my enduring interest is in the history of cross-cultural encounters between Aboriginal people and Europeans, and I am in the early stages of a new project on the nineteenth century called 'Through travellers' eyes: foreign observations of Aboriginal people and British colonisation, 1800-1850'. I am a research fellow at the Australian Centre for Indigenous History at the Australian National University, and a new co-editor of the journal *Aboriginal History* with Maria Nugent. My recent publications include '"Wanton with plenty": questioning ethno-historical constructions of sexual savagery in Aboriginal societies' in *Australian Historical Studies* (2008), '"Inhabited by a race of formidable giants": French explorers, Aborigines, and the endurance of the fantastic in the Great South Land, 1803', in *Australian Humanities Review* (2008), and a special issue of *Borderlands* on 'Indigenous Bodies' which I co-edited with Leah Lui-Chivizhe and Lisa Slater (2008).

Barbara Paulson: I am a Mununtjali/Gungari woman. I am a curator in the Aboriginal and Torres Strait Islander program (ATSIP) at the National Museum of Australia. I have worked and lived in many Aboriginal communities around Australia in differing roles such as artist, arts worker, counsellor, youth worker. Knowledge gained and developed while within those communities and positions is the reference point I use in any role where I am a cultural liaison and/or educator. The subject of representing Aboriginal and Torres Strait Islander cultures is a personal one, with Knowledge attained from family, communities, research and from personal experience as an Aboriginal woman of contemporary life in Australia.

Frances Peters-Little: I am a descendant of the Kamilaroi and Uralarai nations. I am also a filmmaker, historian, musician and lead singer of the band 'The Preferred Models'. Although my main interests are writing about Aboriginal arts and media studies and making films about New South Wales Indigenous history and urban black politics, my first passion and probably my last love, is music. I have an MPhil in Australian Studies from the ANU and a BA in Communications from UTS. Currently I am a PhD candidate at the University of Sydney. My most recent publications are (with Ann McGrath and Ingereth Macfarlane) (eds), *Exchanging Histories*, a special issue of *Aboriginal History*

(2006); (with Peter Read and Anna Haebich) (eds), *Indigenous Biography and Autobiography* (2008); and *Vote Yes for Aborigines*, a one-hour documentary film I wrote and directed, broadcast on SBS TV, 27 May 2007.

Troy Pickwick: I am a Murri from Queensland, who completed both my undergraduate and post-graduate studies at the University of Technology, Sydney. I have worked as an academic at universities, in addition to being the team leader of the Aboriginal and Torres Strait Islander Unit in the Australian Federal Police. I have a strong interest in writing film scripts and am now currently working at the National Museum of Australia in Canberra.

Peter Read: I was in Chile the day the message came from the editors of this volume to provide a note on what I was most passionate about. By chance it was the day before the bones of Victor Jara, about whom I write in my article, were to be reburied. His remains had been recently exhumed for forensic analysis from the grave into which he had been so hurriedly bundled in the second week of September 1973. I went on the tumultuous march next day with the editors' request uppermost in my mind. Fifteen thousand people played, sang, danced, shouted and demonstrated all the way from Santiago's CBD to the General Cemetery: everybody seemed to know his music and often broke into spontaneous song. Some of Jara's songs were a bit arrogant, and I'm no supporter of any party waving the hammer and sickle. But I could join in the chorus echoing Jara's most famous song: 'El derecho de vivir en paz' – the right to live in peace. That is the basis of most other human rights, yet the one that Aborigines have been so consistently denied for so long, and the one that has been the mainspring of much of my writings.

I am an Australian Professorial Research Fellow, Department of History, University of Sydney. I intersperse my studies of the history of Aboriginal Sydney with interviews, with Dr Jackie Huggins, of the former members of the Council for Aboriginal Reconciliation, and with visits to research memory and memorialisation in post-Pinochet Chile. My publications include *Tripping over Feathers; Scenes in the Life of Joy Janaka Wiradjuri Williams: a Stolen Generations narrative* (2009); *The Stolen Generations* (1981); and (with Marivic Wyndham) 'Between the silence and the scream: recordings made at sites in the last days of Victor Jara' in R Bandt, M Duffy and D McKinnon (eds), *Hearing Places* (2007).

Lyndall Ryan: After a gap of nearly 30 years, I recently returned to my original research passion – the history of the Tasmanian Aborigines. In *The Aboriginal Tasmanians* (1981), I argued that they used guerilla war tactics to resist the British colonial invaders with some success, but I paid scant attention to settler activism, let alone uncorroborated stories of massacre. Armed with a more coherent approach to re-examine the sources, I made an astonishing new finding: that most Tasmanian Aborigines were killed in massacres before the official record of the Black War began in 1828. I then applied the same approach to the investigation of frontier violence in colonial Victoria 1836–1851 with similarly startling results. Massacre, it seems, was more widespread on the Australian colonial frontier before 1850 than most Australian historians of my generation had previously believed. Now I am part of a global project to investigate massacre on the colonial frontiers in North America, South Africa, Australia and Europe 1780–1820. Recent publications include: 'Massacre in the Black War in Tasmania 1823-1834: a case study of Meander River region, June 1827', *Journal of Genocide Research* (2008); 'Settler massacre on the colonial frontier in Victoria 1836-1851', in a collection co-edited with Philip G Dwyer, *Theatres of Violence: Massacre, Mass Killing and Atrocity in History* (New York: Berghahn Books, forthcoming 2010); and a monograph, *The Tasmanian Aborigines: A History* (Sydney: Allen & Unwin, forthcoming 2011).

Rachel Standfield: I am a historian of racial thought and indigenous histories of Australia and New Zealand. I recently completed my PhD at the University of Otago in New Zealand, entitled 'Warriors and Wanderers: Making Race in the Tasman World, 1769-1840', and my chapter in this collection is based on part of that work. I am a lecturer in the Centre for Indigenous Studies, Charles Sturt University, and am the 2010 CH Currey Memorial Fellow at the State Library of New South Wales, researching the career of William Thomas, Protector and Guardian of Aborigines in colonial Victoria from the 1830s to the 1860s. Having previously worked in policy development, including at the Aboriginal and Torres Strait Islander Commission, I remain passionate about the connection between politics, social justice and history. My most recent publication is 'Violence and the intimacy of imperial ethnography: the *Endeavour* in the Pacific', in Tony Ballantyne and Antoinette Burton (eds), *Moving Subjects: Gender, Mobility and Intimacy in an age of global empire* (2008).

Jeni Thornley: I am a documentary filmmaker. My films are personal, poetic works in the essay mode that explore ideas around memory and private and public histories. I love working with images as a way of telling stories and expressing ideas. Each film takes many years to make. Several of my films explore the impact of colonisation and neo-colonialism. I like to work collaboratively and cross-culturally. I produced my recent film *Island Home Country* (2008) as a DCA doctoral project (film and thesis) at the University of Technology, Sydney. Filming in Tasmania, where I was born, and working with Aboriginal protocols and Tasmanian Aboriginal community members, I learned a lot and am still learning, particularly around cross cultural issues and Indigenous knowledges. *Island Home Country* screened nationally on the ABC in 2008 and is distributed by the Education Shop with a Study Guide by the Australian Teachers of Media (2008). My other films include *To the Other Shore* (1998) a diary film about motherhood and psychoanalysis; the co-directed feature documentary and Penguin book *For Love or Money: a history of women and work in Australia* (1983) and *Maidens: four generations of an Australian family* (1978). Since 2002, I have been lecturing in documentary at the University of Technology, Sydney, focusing on documentary film's history, changing forms, and ethics. I also work as a consultant script editor, researcher and film valuer for Australian film archives and the Federal Government's Cultural Gifts Program.

David Trudinger: Having spent the first nine years of my life on an Aboriginal mission station, I have tried in the last nine years or so to not only understand that personal experience but see it in the wider and more important context of the encounter of Europeans with indigenous peoples here in Australia as well as elsewhere in the colonised world. So, with something less than impeccable timing, but at least with some passion, I commenced an academic career late in life. My 2004 PhD from ANU, 'Converting Salvation', examined missionary discourse and praxis in relation to Indigenous peoples in Central Australia during the 1930s and 40s. Since 2007 I have taught Australian, urban, cultural heritage, and oral history, as well as a course on war and propaganda in the twentieth century, at the University of the Sunshine Coast in Queensland. I presented at the 2009 Australian Historical Association Conference a paper entitled, '"Where strangeness and intimacy, distance and proximity coexist": some matters of power, control and (in)justice on a Central Australian mission station in the 1940s'. I have also published 'The language(s) of Love: JRB Love and contesting tongues at Ernabella Mission Station, 1940-46', in *Aboriginal History* (2007).

Foreword

IAN THORPE

In 2009, I gave a speech at the 'Beyond Sport Summit' in London on July 9. It was a speech that came directly from the heart expressing my passion for justice for the first Australians.

When I had written the speech, I had many things to consider, for example, it was a speech that was a collaboration of my understanding of issues being faced by Indigenous Australians from the leaders in this area who I respect and admire. I had read and heard too often about the injustice that Indigenous people face everyday and as importantly I had witnessed first hand the hardships experienced by my 'Brothers and Sisters', a term I do not take lightly and only with respect.

I was also representing people whose names I know who had lived through these atrocities, this was my biggest responsibility speaking out for those who have a voice but are all too often not heard. Therefore, I am delighted to have my speech published in this book so that it may reach a wider audience of historians who also share my commitment for justice for Australia's Indigenous people.

I strongly believe that one of the ways we can overcome social injustice in Australia is through education, and that a significant part of that education needs to be through understanding Australia's history. Without a firm understanding of the past we are at a loss to know why and explain how such injustices and inequalities exist.

I would like to congratulate all the contributors of *Passionate Histories: Myth, Memory and Indigenous Australia* for keeping your passion for indigenous history alive, and to wish the editors, Frances Peters-Little, Ann Curthoys and John Docker, every success with this wonderful collection of essays.

My speech: Australia's dirty little secret

'Ladies and Gentlemen, first may I thank you all for participating in this wonderful event. I am incredibly excited to be able to address you in regards to Beyond Sport. For me this is an ambiguous topic.

As you may or may not be aware I am indeed an Olympian. I am no longer competing as a swimmer. I do take pride in my achievements in the pool and the valuable insight and education it has allowed me to take on, as I travelled the globe throughout my career.

When we speak of athletes there is a great deal that we know, like what is required of them, for me that meant 30 hours of training a week. We do this training just so we have a sporting chance to fulfil our life long dreams.

My travels with my sport since I was a very young and shy 14 year old opened the world to me, I didn't realise at the time that this adventure would turn into a career beyond my wildest dreams.

I was the youngest male to ever represent Australia in swimming. By 15 I was the youngest-ever male world champion. At 16 I broke four world records in four days and at 17 I was Olympic Champion, I had fulfilled my life long ambition as a child. I quickly realised I was a child in an adult world.

It was the child in me that throughout my career questioned why? Why is it so? Why is it done that way and why is the world the way it is?

In my travels, competition took me to places where sometimes I was met with abject poverty, whilst I simply swum. Why was my life so blessed when others just by fate had less opportunity than I? I guess I witnessed at a very young age how sport is an international language, a language that transcended borders, boundaries, cultural ideology, politics and even socio economic disadvantage.

I have only discussed my career up to when I was 17. It is because when I was 18 I established my charity, 'Fountain for youth'. I didn't realise at the time that this may be my biggest accomplishment. An achievement not in the sense of doing something right, rather a stepping stone where my values that I had gained from sport could be transferred to something that is bigger than sport and in my opinion far more important.

That said, sport was what has made me who I am today and has afforded me the privilege to work beyond sport. My charity work didn't begin at 18, I was just 15 when I began working with those less fortunate than myself. It was those years that shaped my understanding of what charity was. It gave me an insight into the power of celebrity and sport, especially in sport mad Australia.

I realised my value to organisations trying to bring positive change lent enormous weight to these causes. I must say though this should be an outrage, because as an athlete I am not as qualified to comment on health or education as the health professionals and educators who daily tackle the big issues. In fact it is a bit disappointing that a teenager's opinion garnered more attention than those who had been working on their chosen causes before I was even born. This realisation of the opportunity that my voice and name could lend to an excellent cause was the simple foundation laid for my very own charity.

I continued to win medals, breaking world records and continued travelling around the world recognising the needs of people, particularly children, in many places I visited. By this time my charity had enough money raised to commit to larger projects, I sat at a board meeting and stated that I wanted to help the world's neediest children. I started to think of what impact my effort could have in places like Africa or South East Asia. I then visited some of the worlds neediest communities, places without access to planes and cars that seemed to be a world away … but now they were truly at my back door.

The communities that I visited had illiteracy levels at 93 per cent … that was staggering only seven percent of a populous being able to read and write. Up to 80 per cent of the children in these communities have serious hearing impairments because of 'glue ear'; middle ear infections neglected from infancy. These kids will never hear the teacher in front of them in a classroom … that is, if there is a teacher and indeed a classroom.

Malnourished mothers are giving birth to babies that are seriously underweight and this only gets worse throughout a life born into poverty. Here diabetes affects one in every two adults. Kidney disease is in epidemic proportions in communities where living conditions; primary healthcare and infrastructure are truly appalling. In this part of the world even the community leaders are afflicted by clusters of chronic illness. Syndrome X, the doctors call it, diabetes, renal disease, strokes, hypertension, cancer and heart disease. Some people die with four or five of these chronic illnesses.

Rheumatic heart disease among the children in these places is higher than in most of the developing world. But I was not visiting communities in the developing world, I was in the middle of Australia, remote, yes, but this is Australia, a country that can boast some of the highest standards of living of any nation in the world. How shocked I was that Syndrome X was afflicting so many of the 460,000 Indigenous people of my country. As a result of these chronic illnesses and conditions Aboriginal life expectancy has fallen 20 years behind the rest of Australia. For some of my fellow countrymen life expectancy had plunged to just 46 years.

Australia's grim record on health care for Indigenous people is by far the worst of any developed nation. Developed? How can a country be 'developed' when it leaves so many of its children behind? Australia has not provided its citizens with an equal opportunity for primary health care, education, housing, employment, let alone recognition and a life of dignity.

Now I don't expect you to just take my word for it. I am not a Doctor, I am simply an athlete. But ask Australian health professionals like Doctor Jim Hyde who says that while our nation has plenty of medical problems, only Indigenous Australians are facing a genuine health crisis.

The Governor of New South Wales, my home State, Professor Marie Bashir, an eminent Child Psychiatrist, has repeatedly pointed out the national disgrace of allowing the 40 per cent of Indigenous children under the age of 15 to put up with health problems found in no other developed nation. Patrick Dodson, winner of the Sydney Peace Prize and one of our greatest statesmen, identifies health as a human right for Indigenous Australians.

'Only the most urgent government action', said Australia's 'Father of Reconciliation', 'could change the inequality that has created this health tragedy in our own backyard'.

How could citizens with the greatest need be so under funded? If we were to indeed recognise the severity of this gross neglect, funding to these communities should be extradited.

A commitment to the first Australians is well within the means of my country, and this is what I find inexcusable. I am talking about an issue with a solution. For Australia to heal its wounds that have been weeping for 200 years we must not ignore the issue, we must start the healing.

Like many people in Australia I was completely unaware of the huge gap in health and education outcomes let alone the differences of life expectancy. I, as many had, made an assumption; Australia is a rich country, don't we throw a lot of money at that problem? It disgusts me to speak those words now but that was what I thought. This was not just my lack of knowledge of this area but it is echoed throughout my nation.

An Aboriginal health expert, Shane Houston says:

> Aboriginal people are viewed by too many in the Australian community as an unwelcome burden on the nation. Governments say they have spent a lot of money on Aborigines but where do you see the results in this squalor? So the mainstream concludes that Aboriginal health is a waste of money. It is all the fault of the poor blacks. My people are

somehow expected to just extricate themselves from this maze of life-threatening conditions. And if we can't manage to do that, then many white people will shrug and say our end is inevitable.

Visiting Aboriginal people, in their homes, their communities, on their land, has allowed me to listen and given me some idea of the problems that Aboriginal people face. I listened to the concerns of mothers and fathers for the betterment of their children. This unwavering strength, in the face of social injustice. Within these communities I witness poverty, despair and pain … but I also see hope … hope from those men and woman who want more for their children.

With the words of these people in my head, I became part of a campaign in Australia called; 'Close the Gap', it is quite simply a program that recognises the difference between Indigenous and non Indigenous life expectancy in Australia and the huge gaps in all of the factors like education, jobs and housing that leave Aboriginal people so deeply disadvantaged.

Close the Gap is a commitment that this difference is unacceptable. It was supported by the government and also the opposition. This is the kind of action that is required in Australia. The issue of Indigenous health and education goes beyond government, it is a fundamental right. I hope all sides of government continue to commit to this policy as a starting point and it is not another hollow promise that falls short.

Australia's Prime Minister, Kevin Rudd has said that it was 'devastating' that a new report by our productivity commission showed that Aboriginal people had made little progress to close those gaps since 2000. He said this was 'unacceptable' and 'decisive action' had to be taken. The truth is that none of the problems I have mentioned can truly be rectified until our government and my fellow Australians recognise the injustice faced by Aboriginal Australians and how they are denied so many human rights. This has been highlighted once again by what is called in Australia 'The Intervention', the Federal Government's takeover of 73 remote Aboriginal communities.

The Intervention was constructed by the previous government and has since been reported to have been assembled in the space of just one day. The irony is that Aboriginal people had been campaigning for decades about the living conditions and the neglect of their children within their communities. The programs to protect and nurture the children, had been grossly neglected and under funded by government over the last decade. What appears to be a political stunt and a grab for government control over Aboriginal people continues to this day under the new government.

Once more an Australian government has claimed it is doing its best for Aboriginal Australians by taking over their communities, appointing white managers, more government bureaucrats, promising all kinds of things, if Aboriginal people will just sign over their communities under 40-year leases to the Federal Government. And politicians wonder why Aboriginal people do not trust them. The truth is for over 200 years Australian governments have neglected and patronised Aboriginal people.

The Intervention is unlikely to provide any lasting benefit to Aboriginal people because it tries to push and punish them, to take over their lives, rather than work with them. One of Australia's oldest and wisest Aboriginal leaders, Galarrwuy Yunupingu says the only way forward is for Aboriginal communities in these remote areas to be led and organised by their own organisations. Assimilation will not work.

So in the work I do, the way I try to contribute through my organisation, Fountain for Youth, we work with Aboriginal teachers, health workers, parents and children, with the health services and the schools, to encourage people to believe that we can move forward together. We support pre-schooling, health education, literacy backpacks that let kids carry home reading for the whole family. And we use sport where we can to make a difference.

As a swimmer, who would have thought I would have ended up supporting Flipper Ball, junior water polo for little Aboriginal kids in the mining communities of Western Australia. As a swimmer, who would have thought I would be back at university studying psychology and at the same time working with young Aboriginal university graduates on a mentoring program to help get more kids to complete High School and go on with their studies. As a swimmer, maybe I was expected to just be satisfied with the gleam of those gold medals. But all sportsmen and women know the truth – there is something beyond sport.

There is the challenge of playing a part in the human family ... to contribute and make a difference. We can use sport and use our sporting status to improve the lives of children and whole communities in so many places. We can make it a fairer, safer playing field for everyone.

In 20 remote Australian communities and with thousands of Aboriginal children I know life will have some extra opportunities if I commit to work hard on this. I do intend to work hard at this for the rest of my life.

That is my promise to you – beyond sport!'

Introduction

FRANCES PETERS-LITTLE

This book was inspired initially by a conference, as many collections of essays are. The conference in our case was an Australian Studies conference held at the University of Barcelona in July 2008, organised by Sue Ballyn of the Australian Studies Centre there. The theme of the conference was Myth, Memory, and History. The papers delivered under this heading varied considerably, but a strong strand was Indigenous Australian history. John Docker, Ann Curthoys and I agreed afterwards that we would like to edit a collection of essays from the conference based on that theme. As we drew the papers together, however, we included some additional authors whose work fitted with our theme of myth, memory, and Indigenous history. Our initial nine contributors grew to 17. Our organising theme came to encompass not only the original emphasis on myth, memory and history but also the role of passion – engagement, commitment, compassion, emotion – in historical work. In different guises, this concern kept emerging.

Debates over how detached historians should be in their approach to understanding the past have been around for centuries.[1] These debates have been especially lively in Australia over the last ten years. In the midst of its 'history wars', author Keith Windschuttle said in a radio interview that 'the responsibility of the historian is not to be compassionate but to be dispassionate'.[2] Other Australian historians, however, have argued the opposite. Greg Dening, for example, has suggested that 'historians needed to be more compassionate if they wished to be able to fully represent the past'.[3] John Thompson has commented that 'Windschuttle's chosen instrument has been a scalpel, his methods forensic. He says the historian must be dispassionate'.[4] Also critical of Windschuttle's advocacy of being dispassionate is Aboriginal lawyer, Noel Pearson, who writes that 'Windschuttle's correction of the leftists'

---

1   In their book, *Is History Fiction?*, Curthoys and Docker comprehensively cover various philosophical views about history writing from Herodotus and Thucydides to the late 20th and early 21st century 'history wars'.
2   Keith Windschuttle made the statement during an interview with Tony Jones on *Lateline*, an ABC television program that went to air on 3 September 2003: <http://www.abc.net.au/lateline/content/2003/s938399.htm>
3   Dening 2000.
4   Thompson 1994.

distortion of history is a distortion in the opposite direction', and accuses him of inexplicable antagonism towards Aborigines, that is, that Windschuttle's history is not at all dispassionate.[5] Bain Attwood argues that it is possible to be passionate and dispassionate at the same time: 'a good historian should be passionate, compassionate and dispassionate in reference to as many of their historical subjects as they can'.[6]

As an Indigenous woman and historian who spends much time writing about Aboriginal history and Australia's colonial past, I find this discussion of whether one ought to be compassionate or not somewhat bewildering. It is a luxury I have not been afforded. As an Indigenous scholar I am constantly reminded that I have little or no alternative but to work within a European framework to try and explain our history and experiences; it is a construct that I have to both work within and resist at the same time. The whole basis for wanting to become a historian in the first instance comes from a place deep inside me, from a desire to understand, acknowledge and come to terms with what has happened to my ancestors, my culture and my land.

Being unable to extricate oneself from one's history is something that anthropologist Deborah Bird Rose has observed amongst many Aboriginal people. She argues that Aboriginal people find Westerners' sense of the past to be very odd; for Aboriginal people, the past and the present are linked indissolubly through place and belonging.[7] This point is very true for me as it is for many other indigenous people. For example, Maori author Linda Tuhiwai Smith has argued 'history is important for understanding the present' and that 'reclaiming history is a critical and essential part of decolonisation'.[8] Aboriginal historian Jackie Huggins has stated that 'her love of history stems from her displacement as an Aboriginal person and like most students [she] was fed on a diet of lies and invisibility about the true history of Australia'.[9]

The ideal of being dispassionate and 'objective' has led many non-Indigenous scholars to express doubts about the truth value of Indigenous stories about what happened in the past. Literary critic and historian Penny Van Toorn warns that we must never underestimate the extent of agency used in the making and deployment of Indigenous storytelling.[10] Historians Bain Attwood and Fiona Magowan point out that oral narratives are heavily reliant upon memory; 'life stories or subjective accounts', they suggest, are 'very often self-marked by their own particular motives, aspirations, attitudes and conscience'.[11] Also sceptical

---

5   Pearson 2009.
6   Attwood 2005. See also Gaita 2000, whom Attwood discusses.
7   Rose 1992: 16, cited in Curthoys and Docker 2005: 1.
8   Smith 1999: 29-30.
9   Huggins 1998: 120.
10   Van Toorn 2001: 3.
11   Attwood and Magowan 2001: xiv.

is literary critic, Adam Shoemaker, who contended in 2004 that there were very few Aboriginal historians, and that in their absence there have been many Black Australian literary views of history that ran the risk of over-compensating the bias of white interpretations.[12]

These ideas of distortion and over-compensation are very curious. Jackie Huggins points out that whites are more likely than Indigenous people to distort the reality of Australia's indigenous past, because many are still in denial over how they took the land off Aboriginal people in the first place.[13] And was Margaret Tucker overcompensating when she and others told their stories in the groundbreaking film *Lousy Little Sixpence*?[14] Were black activists of the 1970s overcompensating when Gary Foley and others permitted filmmaker Alessandro Cavadini to film their protests at the 'tent embassy' and told their stories about the plight of Aboriginal people and land theft in rural Australia?[15]

As these examples indicate, documentary filmmakers rather than academic historians have understood Indigenous history most compassionately. Film has been a most powerful historical medium. One wonders what would have happened if Western Australian parliamentarian Bill Grayden had not been accompanied by Doug Nicholls and his camera when he visited Aboriginal people in the Warburton Ranges in 1957.[16] In addition, what might we have known of Eddie Mabo's fight for his beloved Mer Island, if Trevor Graham had not made the film, *Mabo: Life of an Island Man*?[17] Eight years earlier, in 1981, Eddie Mabo had given a lecture about land ownership and inheritance on Mer Island to a group of academics at James Cook University, but it was Graham's film that moved so many people to understand the issues.[18] These are stories that were missing from the history books in our schools, but when Indigenous people eventually told them they changed the way the world viewed Indigenous

---

12   Shoemaker 2004: 130-132.
13   I interviewed Jackie Huggins for *Vote Yes for Aborigines*.
14   *Lousy Little Sixpence*, a film made by Alec Morgan, narrates early struggles for Aboriginal land rights and self-determination, and depicts the removal of Aboriginal children and their subsequent employment as domestic servants and labourers.
15   Alessandro Cavadini and Carolyn Strachan made the film *Ningla a Na* in 1972. This documentary records the events surrounding the establishment of the Aboriginal tent embassy on the lawns of Parliament House. It incorporates interviews with black activists, the work of the National Black Theatre, Aboriginal Legal Service and Aboriginal Medical Service, plus footage from the demonstrations and arrests at the embassy. Synopsis by *Street Smart Films*.
16   The Grayden film (colour/no sound) runs for 20 minutes and contained confronting images of Aboriginal poverty, starvation, injury, and disease in the Warburton and Rawlinson Ranges. Discussed in Ann Curthoys' chapter in this volume.
17   *Land Bilong Islanders* is a film that follows Queensland's Supreme Court to Murray Island, the centre of a legal battle that forever altered relationships between black and white in Australia. Synopsis by Ronin Films.
18   In 1981, Eddie Mabo gave a lecture at a Land Rights conference at James Cook University and 'spelt out what land ownership and land inheritance was all about on Mer Island', James Cook University's News and Media page: <http://cms.jcu.edu.au/news/archive/JCUPRD_031129>

history. For many years, Indigenous voices had struggled against the silence about Aboriginal history; eventually, through film and oral history, they were finally able to make themselves heard.

While some white historians are suspicious of Indigenous stories about the past, those involved deeply in oral history have been more welcoming of oral story telling. Paula Hamilton and Linda Shopes, for example, urge historians to make an extra effort to bring more oral histories into the public domain if they would like to make real progress towards the heart of matters.[19] Historian Linda Tuhiwai Smith adds an indigenous perspective, taking issue with those who think of indigenous oral narratives as an inferior form of historical practice. Writing, she says, 'has been viewed as the mark of a superior civilization and other societies have been judged, by this view, to be incapable of thinking critically and objectively or having distance from ideas or emotion'.[20]

I find it curious that any text-based historian would consider writing about Aboriginal people without ever engaging with them. I am at a complete loss to understand why any white historian might suppose himself or herself unmarred and unencumbered by his or her own white prejudices.

It seems to me that indigenous accounts of history do not have to be in conflict with the evidence supplied in white documentation, but if there *is* a discrepancy, then perhaps we could ask historians to be just as critical of white-authored documents as they are of Aboriginal oral accounts. I believe that one's responsibility as a historian is to seek knowledge of an indigenous viewpoint and lived experience, and to look for additional evidence that might support that view, or at least explain why it exists. Our aim should be not to undermine indigenous perspectives and squabble about whether Aborigines are 'accurate', but rather to understand their viewpoint with compassion, and at the very least, 'include' it, consider it. For me, the inclusion of Aboriginal voices as primary sources is an absolute must for understanding and practising Aboriginal history.

The essays in this book all deal with questions of truth, myth, memory, and passionately engaged history, though in very different ways. Several consider massacre myths, ranging from the idea that there were no massacres (Ray Evans, Lyndall Ryan, John Docker), to the idea that the first few years of contact were peaceful and massacres only came later (Rachel Standfield). Some chapters consider several other pervasive myths, such as the myth of Aboriginal male idleness (Shino Konishi) and the myth of Flynn of the Inland (David Trudinger). Sometimes, the memory of an historical event can be falsely interpreted as a myth, as I argue is the case for the 1967 Referendum to change the Australian

---

19   Hamilton and Shopes 2008: viii.
20   Smith 1999: 28.

constitution. Essays focus on memory and the practice of oral history as a way of learning more about Indigenous experiences in the more recent past (Lorina Barker), or of tracing the impact of visitors on the dynamics of race relations within Australia (Ann Curthoys). These themes, of myth, memory, and oral history, are all important for the creation and maintenance of identity, both Indigenous and non-Indigenous. Two contributors explore the ways in which engagement with Indigenous history affects their own sense of non-Indigenous identity (Vanessa Castejon and Jeni Thornley), while Kristina Everett discusses the emergence of new Indigenous identities in the Sydney region. Finally, all these themes are important in the history of the Stolen Generations, and the attempts by non-Indigenous Australians to acknowledge and reckon with that history. Isabelle Auguste, Jay Arthur and her co-curators Barbara Paulson and Troy Pickwick, and Peter Read all discuss different aspects of this continuing and complex process.

References

Attwood, Bain and Fiona Magowan (eds) 2001, *Telling Stories: Indigenous History and Memory in Australia and New Zealand*, Allen & Unwin, Sydney.

— 2005, *Telling the Truth about Aboriginal History*, Allen & Unwin, Sydney.

Curthoys, Ann and John Docker 2005, *Is History Fiction?*, University of New South Wales Press, Sydney.

Dening, Greg 2000, 'Challenges To Perform: History, Passion and the Imagination', a paper given at the Challenging Australian History: Discovering New Narratives conference at the National Library of Australia, 15 April 2000, Canberra, accessed 23 May 2010: <http://www.nla.gov.au/events/history/papers/Greg_Dening.html>

Gaita, Raimond 2000, 'Guilt, shame and the collective responsibility', in *Essays on Australian Reconciliation*, Michelle Grattan (ed), Bookman Press, Melbourne.

Hamilton, Paula and Linda Shopes (eds) 2008, *Oral History and Public Memories*, Temple University Press, Philadelphia.

Huggins, Jacquie 1998, *Sister Girl: The Writings of an Aboriginal Activist and Historian*, University of Queensland Press, St Lucia, Queensland.

Pearson, Noel 2009, *Up from the Mission*, Black Inc, Melbourne.

Peters-Little, Frances 2006, *Vote Yes for Aborigines*, documentary film, Ronin Films, Canberra.

Rose, Deborah Bird 1992, 'Hidden histories', *Island* 51:14–19.

Shoemaker, Adam 2004, *Black Words White Page: Aboriginal Literature 1929–1988*, ANU E Press, Canberra.

Smith, Linda Tuhiwai 1999, *Decolonizing Methodologies: Research and Indigenous Peoples*, University of Otago Press, Dunedin.

Thompson, John 1994, 'The Historian's Conscience – Reviews', *The Age*, 13 November 1994, accessed 17 July 2010: <http://www.theage.com.au/articles/2004/11/12/1100227566160.html?from=storyrhs>

Van Toorn, Penny 2001, 'Indigenous life writing, tactics and transformations', in *Telling Stories: Indigenous History and Memory in Australia and New Zealand, Bain Attwood and Fiona Magowan* (eds), Allen & Unwin, Sydney.

Part one: massacres

1. The country has another past: Queensland and the History Wars

RAYMOND EVANS

Politicised history is a panacea, comforting the bereft, treating us, again and again, to the same consoling myths.

Iain Sinclair[1]

As poet/performer Leonard Cohen would have it, 'Everybody knows the war is over/ Everybody knows the good guys lost':[2] but when it comes to such consideration of the so-called 'History Wars' in Australia, the outcome is arguably not so cut and dried. It is possible to suggest that although an academic orthodoxy, emphasising a predominant tale of conquest migration and the multiple consequences of dispossession, comprehensively won that war intellectually, it failed to do so culturally. The neoconservative challenge that posits a benign Australian exceptionalism in the global saga of colonisation, and which comes more from outside the history profession than within it, largely held the fort by controlling the operation of the drawbridge. The doubters and deniers of searing colonial origins were granted unimpeded media access and political endorsement, while the so-called 'black-armband' historians were left, exposed and vilified, suffering death by a thousand column-inches. As Lyndall Ryan put it in her 2003 article, pointedly titled, 'Reflections by a target of a media witch hunt':

> Witch hunts follow a well laid out pattern. They usually begin with advanced warning ... that a target has been identified ... any response is dismissed as unsatisfactory and the reputation of the target is then ripped to shreds by print media columnists.

1   Sinclair 2009: 6.
2   Cohen and Robinson 1988: track 8.

In Ryan's case, a public furore, extending over six months, led in her words 'to calls by print media journalists … asking when I would resign my position at the university and then to the Vice Chancellor … asking when I would be sacked for shonky scholarship'.[3]

Perhaps the Australian media adopted the term 'wars' to designate this debacle because all can then be deemed 'fair' within them. There is, of course, a delicious irony in calling certain analytical differences 'wars', while simultaneously denying that repetitive physical conflicts embedded in our history, in which many thousands of people died, can ever be typified by such an excessive term. Yet, beyond this, the label 'History Wars' might be more appropriately replaced by that of 'Media Circus'. The Windschuttle campaign was conducted by much of the mainstream media with all the trappings of a moral crusade or, perhaps, a moral panic: the communal good had been assailed; a conspiracy to defraud had been exposed; the miscreants had been identified and public humiliation duly awarded. Righteous reckonings were recommended. Though some of the scholars embroiled in the argument attempted to play fairly by the rules of academic debate, the surrounding parameters of the discourse were already fatally flawed. Invariably, the good of the nation – and an equally fervent proclamation of 'the Australian Good' – were prioritised above the integrity of the discipline itself. History was cast as the hand-servant of Australia's national honour: its role of celebrating 'a story of achievement against overwhelming odds' was encouraged and applauded; its delinquent straying into the realm of negative critique denounced as disloyal and deceptive.[4] The beast of Australian history, as John Howard averred in his 2006 'Tribute to *Quadrant*', displayed 'the fangs of the Left' and required, by implication, appropriate muzzling.[5] The history profession's responsibility to promote and defend free-ranging research that may take any scholar in any direction on the trail of evidence on any subject – particularly in a publicly unpopular direction – was thereby severely compromised.

Secondly and probably most vitally, the debate was cast from the outset by its initiator as not so much about interpretive disagreement as an assault upon the scholarly integrity of certain individuals. A 'major academic deception', in Keith Windschuttle's estimation, had been exposed.[6] The campaign was personal and the personal was political. Frontier conflict historians, much like most historians, had not simply made small transcriptive or interpretive errors across long careers of research but had, under the guise of scholarship, purposely lied to the nation, to their colleagues and to generations of unsuspecting students.

---

3   Ryan 2003: 106–107.
4   Rutherford 2000: 7–10; Brawley 1997.
5   Howard 2006: 23.
6   Clark 2008: 4.

They had done so systematically and cabalistically in order to fulfil a subversive ideological agenda. A number of 'referencing errors (in works up to thirty years old)' were nationally calibrated into a terrible ascription of guilt as, in a process akin to Chinese whispers, a conspiracy to defraud and mislead was unmasked and amplified.[7] The leftward-leaning 'doyens of Australian history', as Janette Albrechtson of *The Australian* explained in 2006, had been exposed to public censure 'for telling fibs about so-called massacres'.[8]

The entire process bears very little resemblance to traditional academic debates, such as the earlier Botany Bay or *Convict Workers* disputes, or even the more spirited interchanges concerning gender's role in Australian history. As Ryan herself recognised, Windschuttle's attack:

> was not premised on the basis of conscientious counter-interpretation or the simple discovering of empirical error. Rather it constituted a relentless accusation ... of lying. I cannot recall a single other example of such an assault in the entire corpus of Australian historiography. Even Malcolm Ellis accused Manning Clark only of consistent error rather than of outright charlatanism.[9]

Historical debunking had morphed into a process of forensic proof-reading for the purpose of wounding *ad hominem* attack. As Windschuttle's own writings demonstrate, and as he himself has more recently (and embarrassingly) experienced, it is easy enough to make mistakes.[10]

The history profession itself was initially caught flat-footed by such blatant character assassination. To the small sectors of 'black-armbanded' and 'white blindfolded' historians who engaged in the conflict might be added a third and much larger category, the 'white arms-folded' historians who chose to stand resolutely apart. Aboriginal scholars largely recoiled from a painful squabble about what appeared as blatantly obvious. In the hurley-burley of reining in the so-called 'excesses' of the race conflict historians, it seemed for a time to escape general notice that some central premises and methodologies of the profession, such as the principle of defending independent research, were also being assailed. Politics, populism and patriotism threatened to overwhelm established process. The subsequent appearance of the multi-authored *Whitewash*, Stuart Macintyre and Anna Clark's *The History Wars*, and Bain Attwood's *Telling the Truth About Aboriginal History*, as well as a plethora of critical articles, have more or less demolished the scholarly *bona fides* of Windschuttle's writings and those of his various published supporters from an intellectual point of view. Attwood, for

---

7   Bonnell and Crotty 2004: 430.
8   Albrechtson 2006.
9   Ryan 2003: 106.
10   Simons 2009; Taylor 2009: 197, 216–225.

instance, concludes that Windschuttle's 'poor and faulty' polemical intervention is 'essentially irrelevant in scholarly terms'.[11] James Boyce's two shorter pieces in *Whitewash* and *Island* magazine alone appear sufficient to devastate the shaky empirical and interpretative underpinnings of what he dubs 'that shameful, heartless and uniquely bad book', *The Fabrication of Aboriginal History*.[12] In his masterly *Van Diemen's Land*, Boyce argues that Ryan and Henry Reynolds, far from exaggerating the Tasmanian Aboriginal death-rate from white violence, have 'actually moderated, not increased previous estimates'. Boyce finds himself more in agreement with 'most nineteenth century historians' who concluded that '[m]assacres were … likely to have been commonplace. Equally horrific, and almost unscrutinised [he continues] were the government-sponsored ethnic clearances of the west coast *after* the fighting was over'.[13] One could, as I hope this essay will demonstrate, say precisely the same for colonial Queensland.

Yet, as right-wing assault has withered, much of the mainstream media have maintained vigilant damage control as gate-keepers on that strategic bridge, spanning Australia's yawning chasm between elite, scholarly discourse and mass perception of the past. In the general public mind, it is down in this chasm that the black arm-banded historians largely remain, precisely where they were sacrificially hurled in 2002: And, so it is still widely held, good riddance to them!

The 'insistently political'[14] tone of the debate – indeed, its plain nastiness – appears crucially connected to its examination of foundational moments, to the moral calculus of settler colonialism on which the nation's origins are based. Much therefore appears to be at stake. In a sense, the embarrassments, silences and obfuscations that once attended the awkward matter of convict origins across several generations have now been exclusively focused on that twin shame of origination – the story of dispossession and sequestration that converted Aboriginal lands into British ones as settlement progressed. Australia's substitute founding myth, the Anzac legend sees public service, to a marked degree, in diverting attention from this country's 'darkling plains'[15] to the grim cliffs and beach-heads of Gallipoli. It is probably no coincidence that the various Howard governments revitalised Anzac reverence (first prompted by Bob Hawke's pilgrimage to the Peninsula in 1990) with the same degree of enthusiasm as they denounced the 'black-armband' reprobates. For in effect, Anzac and the frontier are obverse sides of the same interpretative coin. Anzac becomes the palatable rather than the distasteful story of national birth, where behaviours are apparently always ennobling rather than ignoble ones. Here,

---

11 Evans 2006: 24; Attwood 2005: 152.
12 Boyce 2003, 2004: 33.
13 Boyce 2008: 10–11.
14 Macintyre and Clark 2003: 221.
15 Evans et al 1993: 27.

the white Australian actors are portrayed as heroic and sacrificial rather than as potentially venal or cruel. The bloodshed of the real foundational saga is subverted and replaced by the glory and veneration attending the reticulated retelling of the Anzac blood-letting. The first story is as immersed in forgetting as the second is enmeshed in remembrance. The former is literally unspeakable; the latter liturgical. So that the latter, unfolding peculiarly upon a Turkish coastline, replaces the former, which explains, in considerable part, how migrant Australians came to inhabit what they now see as their own soil. This helps explain why it is invariably the race conflict historians and never the war historians who are freighted with the derisory 'black armband' label.

Historians have yet to construct a cartography of the selective trails of remembrance and forgetting in Australia's past. Furthermore, the labyrinthine pathways of denial and disclosure have as yet been scarcely entered. For a considerable time I have been fascinated by the cat-and-mouse games of revelation and suppression that investigation of the preserved records of the Queensland frontier continually throws up; and, in a recent essay, I concluded that denialism inheres within the very history that is now being denied. Suppression was often commensurate with commission and thus sedimented in the foundations of national culture.[16] But perhaps it is more complex than this. Although powerful patterns of denial run like coarse threads through the unfolding drama of Australian land-taking and, over time, come to predominate in the Australian psyche, their victory is always a shifting, tenuous and never total one. For there are, contemporaneously, so many sources that break that silence in order to thwart its intended conspiracy – the words of individual whistle-blowers, both named and anonymous, who need to enter their protests, sometimes stridently, sometimes cautiously; sometimes in small tangential voices, sometimes in persistent and unrelenting ones – against what was regarded in their time as well as our own as being both questionable and unjust: the uncompensated seizure of another's territory, the theft of children, the rape and sexual enslavement of women, the imposition of terror and the manifold, cursory killings of the original inhabitants. These are the kind of historical messengers that today's media love to shoot down. Yet even colonial children's literature, as historian Clare Bradford shows, was prone to declare that 'a war of extermination' was occurring on the frontiers of settlement.[17] In Richard Rowe's *The Boy in the Bush* (1869), the three child protagonists discover that '"civilization" peels off like nose-skin' in the Queensland tropics as ' "Christian" men, and even boys, are ready – eager – to shed blood like water'.[18] 'It is not pleasant to have to write about such things', Rowe admits:

---

16   Healy 2008; Evans 2008: 195–196.
17   Rowe 1869: 196 in Bradford 2001: 70.
18   Rowe 1869: 195 in Bradford 2001: 6.

but I must if I am to tell the whole truth about Australia … not one of the three felt the slightest scruple in shooting down a black, and then cutting off his head and hanging it *in terrorem* on a tree, as a game keeper nails a hawk to a gable.[19]

It is only when 'they get back from the Bush amongst their mothers, sisters … &c' that they are '*not* eager to talk about what they have done'.[20]

But, unlike Rowe's fictional children, there are other actors who openly defend themselves as perpetrators, invoking the cause of Empire and race as well as the entitlements of superior civilisation in justification of their deeds; or otherwise writing confessionally in later life in the hope of perhaps some form of release or absolution. Such writings are usually, though not exclusively, reserved for a later date than the deed itself when the chances of prosecution have faded or the repercussions of breaking with the white frontier code of silence are not so inhibiting.

Melbourne-born Christie Palmerston, the raffish North Queensland bushman, is of the former, more boastful kind in compiling an exploration diary that the *Queenslander* newspaper publishes in late 1883. It tells of how he and his 'sooty friend', one of his Melanesian servants, while blazing a track from Mourilyan Harbour near Innisfail to the Herberton tin-fields, encounter 'a big mob of Aborigines' near the North Johnstone River:

> coming down a creek towards us, armed with large swords and shields. 'Thank goodness they have no spears!' I muttered, for they looked a formidable lot … they could not have known the power of resistance the white man had, or they never would have advanced so openly … reason being a bit beyond these cute creatures, they had to be submitted to the usual ordeal. Their shields may answer very well for the purposes of their wars, but my rifle drilled them as easily as if they had been sheets of paper … my black companion did not understand the use of firearms, but carried a long scrub knife; he was an athletic fellow and fought like a demon. Between us we made terrible havoc before the enemy gave way.

In the aftermath of this assault on the Mamu people, Palmerston notices 'a little boy running away':

> I soon overtook him, and, laying the barrel of my rifle gently against his neck, shoved him over. He seemed struck with terror and amazement,

---

19 Rowe 1869: 196 in Bradford 2001: 40.
20 Bradford 2001: 6.

biting me, spitting and [shouting]. In my present garb I should have been an object of terror to a child of my own race – only a shirt and cartridge belt on, my legs bespattered with blood.

Palmerston here reveals himself stripped for aggressive action much like Native Police troopers about to affect a frontier dispersal. He next pitches camp 'close by the dead blacks'.[21] Although, as is usual in such accounts, the casualty rate is masked, Palmerston writes in a conscience-free, declamatory style and with a flamboyant openness, knowing he is not likely to be prosecuted by the Queensland colonial authorities for publicly self-confessed murder and child-abduction in a major newspaper. Significantly too, Palmerston is not so depicted in his *Australian Dictionary of Biography* entry, where he is described as being 'on unusually close terms with the Aboriginals whose allegiance he won by his firmness and skill as a shot'.[22] Archibald Meston, later to become Queensland's Southern Protector of Aborigines, protested against Palmerston's account, but only to question his prowess as a trail-blazer.[23] For Meston too would boast of the number of Aborigines he had killed at the Barron River and on Dunk Island.[24]

Writing in a more confessional mode, though at times lapsing into self-justificatory bluster, Dover-born butcher, Korah Halcomb Wills provides a similarly arresting insight into the mind-set of a white frontier perpetrator. Following the old colonial's death in England in 1896, his extraordinary document was eventually found in an attic in Woking, Surrey and transferred, via British Columbia, back to Queensland in 1986. One wonders whether such a manuscript would have survived if left behind in Bowen where much of the action occurs. Wills writes with minimal punctuation in a hurried, distracted, stream-of-consciousness manner as though unburdening himself of something unspeakable before dying. Yet there is also a brazen defensiveness in his account as it lurches between bravado and apologetics. After arriving in Bowen from Victoria in 1862, Wills recalls, many were the dispersing 'expeditions … I have been in and many are the curiosities that I have picked up in the camps of the Natives wild as they ever were, and perfectly rude and cannibles [sic] into the bargain'.[25] He particularly enjoyed:

---

21 Palmerston 1883: 557; Robinson 2008: 72.

22 Bolton 1974: 395–396.

23 *Brisbane Courier*, 30 July 1883.

24 Reid 2006: 146.

25 Wills, Korah 1895, 'Reminiscence', Brandon Papers [hereafter BP], Oxley Memorial Library [hereafter OML], OM75/75/3: 109.

the fish we used to find in some of the Natives 'Gunyahs' Crabs, Crawfish and Whitebait by dillybags-full (Buckets) oh the gorges we used to have at such times, that is all those who had the nerve or stomach to do so, and I must say that I revelled in it and so did the Black Native Police.[26]

The term 'dispersal', he cautiously explains:

was a name given for something not to be mentioned here, but it had to be done for the protection of our own hearths and Wives and families, & you may be sure we were not backward in doing what we were ordered to do and what our forefathers would have done to keep possession of the soil that was laying to waste and no good being done with it when we our own white people were crying for room to stretch our legs on ... we have got the Country and may we for ever hold it for we want it for the good of the whole civilized world ... we have risked our lives ... in arresting it from the savage.[27]

Though Wills admitted that 'in my time they were dispersed by hundreds if not by thousands', he reiterated that such 'dispersing ... must be done very much on the quiet'. At Bowen, in the 1860s, if reinforcements were required for a Native Police reprisal raid against the Juru and Bindal peoples, the Lieutenant — or from 1864 the Inspector — would 'resort to seeking for Volunteers, men who he thought he could trust for pluck and a quiettongue after all was over'. Wills was 'one of the first he used to drop in on' for he had been a member of the Victorian Volunteer Mounted Rifles before migrating to Queensland and being presented with a new Patent Terry's breech-loading rifle at a testimonial dinner in his honour at St Kilda. The Native Police Officer, Wills continued:

[would] select half a dozen fellows the staunchest he could find & press them into the service for the time being ... as Special Constables & put [them] under arms ... and off we would go for the scene of the outrage [meaning an Aboriginal attack on white enterprise or personnel] wheresoever it might be & to run the Culprits Down & disperse them...[28]

This combination of white vigilantes and black troopers was essentially illegal, as colonial authorities attempted to prevent the possibility of European witnesses being present at Native Police attacks on other Aboriginal peoples. Troopers themselves were unable to offer evidence until after 1884.[29]

---

26   Wills, 1895, 'Reminiscence', BP, OML, OM75/75/3: 154.
27   Wills, 1895, 'Reminiscence', BP, OML, OM75/75/3: 107.
28   Wills, 1895, 'Reminiscence', BP, OML, OM75/75/3: 106–107; *St Kilda Chronicle*, 23 August 1861.
29   Evans 2007: 139.

Yet Wills's account keeps returning to one particular 'dispersal' he attended, conducted with 'a few squatters and their friends', probably in the mid-1860s, not long after he had been elected as Bowen's Mayor. For there is something here, it would seem, that the ailing Wills needs to exorcise. He writes:

> the blacks had been playing up & killing a shepherd & robbing his hut when we turned out & run them to earth when they got on the top of a big mound & defied us & smacked their buttocks at us & hurled large stones down on us & hid themselves behind large trees & huge rocks but some paid dearly for their bravado. They had no idea that we could reach them to a dead certainty at a distance of a mile with our little patent breach loading "Terry's" when they were brought to bear on them some of them jumped I am sure six feet into the air...[30]

Closing in on 'one of these mobs of Blacks', Wills next:

> selected a little girl with the intention of civilizing & one of my friends thought he would select a boy for the same purpose & in the selection of which [sic] I stood a very narrow chance of being flattened out by a 'Nulla Nulla' from I presume the Mother of the Child I had hold of, but I received the blow from the deadly weapon across my arm which I threw up to protect my head and my Friend who has since been connected with the Government of the Colony & has held the high office of Chief Immigration Commissioner and protector of the Blacks ... in my time was a kidnapper to the hilt.[31]

Not content with his young trophy, however, Wills next decides to put his pork butchering skills into effect. 'I took it in my head', he writes:

> to get a few specimens of certain limbs and head of a Black fellow, which was not a very delicate operation I can tell you. I shall never forget the time when I first found the subject I intended to anatomize, when my friends were looking on, and I commenced operations dissecting. I went to work business-like to take off the head first, & then the Arms and then the legs, and gathered them together and put them into my Pack saddle and one of my friends who I am sure had dispersed more than any other man in the Colony made the remark that if he was offered a fortune he could not do what I had done. His name was Peter Armstrong a well known pioneer in the North of Queensland and pluck enough to face 100 blacks single handed any day as long as he had his revolver with him and his Rifle but that beat him he said.[32]

---

30   Wills, 1895, 'Reminiscence', BP, OML, OM75/75/3.
31   Wills, 1895, 'Reminiscence', BP, OML, OM75/75/3.
32   Wills, 1895, 'Reminiscence', BP, OML, OM75/75/3: 111–113.

On the following afternoon as his friends were bathing and fishing at 'the Lagoons' on the station, Wills was again hard at work nearby, divesting the severed limbs of their flesh. He continues:

> I got pretty well [on] with it until it became dark and I had to give up the unholy job, & we went back to the Station for supper & yarns, and pipes, and night caps of Whiskey before turning in … I had not been turned in long before I had such dreadful pains in my stomach that I thought I should have died & so did all my friends it was something awful until I could not speak for pain and my inside running out from me and I was quite unable to stop it and they all but gave me up for a dead-un … I managed to get over it … but was left very weak indeed. I believe it was a perfect shock to my system by doing such a horrible repulsive thing as I had been doing but I was not going to be done out of my specimens of humanity…[33]

With the bones and skull in his saddle bags, he then rides eighty miles back into Bowen with 'my little protegee [sic] of a girl … who rode on the front of my saddle … and crying nearly all the way'. As he nears the township, he meets 'different people who hailed me with how do and so on and where did you get that intelegent [sic] little nigger from'.[34]

Not long afterwards, Sir George Nares, the Arctic explorer visits Bowen and displays an Armstrong gun in the town. Not to be outdone, Wills exhibits, in his words:

> My Skull (pard-o-n my blackfellows [skull]) arms and legs to the disgust of many. I remember I had to cover them up with a flag, the Union Jack and if anyone wished to see what was under that flag they had to ask the favor of one of the committee who were afraid the Ladies might get a shock if they left it uncovered … it was a grand success in a monetary point of view & I think it was for the benefit of the [Bowen] hospital [of which Wills had been elected President of the Board in May 1864].[35]

In relation to the unnamed, stolen child, Wills tells others that he had 'picked her up in the Bush lost to her own tribe and crying her heart out'. And 'so', he continues, as if this were now the accepted story:

> I took compassion on her and decided to take her home & bring her up with my own children, which I did and even sent her to school with my own and when I went to Melbourne I took her there to place her at Boarding School with my eldest daughter [Georgiana] who was there

33 Wills, 1895, 'Reminiscence', BP, OML, OM75/75/3: 114–116.
34 Wills, 1895, 'Reminiscence', BP, OML, OM75/75/3: 116–117.
35 Wills, 1895, 'Reminiscence', BP, OML, OM75/75/3: 130.

but she took a severe cold and I had the Doctor to her who … said …
the climate was too cold for her and that she would be dead in less than
a month and he made me take her back again into her own climate when
he said I doubt if she will ever recover even there so I had to bring her
back again and she never lost her cold and eventually it carried her off,
so much for my trying to civilize the aboriginals.[36]

I have stayed at length with Korah Wills, allowing his graphically nonchalant
words to tell a story with little editorial intervention, as I wish to emphasise
both its exceptional and banal nature. Wills was a typical self-made colonial
male on the frontiers of settlement who stood unsuccessfully for the Queensland
Legislative Assembly in late 1866 against George Elphinstone Dalrymple,
another fervent frontier activist and a founder of Bowen. Wills served as
Bowen's mayor in 1865 and 1867, and was later elected as the mayor of Mackay
in 1876–1877. He corresponded with the Queensland Acclimatization Society
and was the proprietor of Bowen's largest hotel. By the early 1880s he owned
a string of Wills' Hotels throughout Queensland before retiring permanently
to England in 1886.[37] In London, he attended annual banquets of prominent
Queenslanders where he sat at table with such well-known planters as Charles
Rawson and Harold Finch-Hatton, leading squatters such as Arthur Hodgson,
Edward Weinholt and Oscar De Satge, and famous colonial officials such as Sir
George Bowen and Sir James Cockle. Here they listened to speeches, such as
that delivered by Sir Edward Sandys Dawes, who in June 1895, as Wills was
writing his startling memoir, spoke fondly to the assembly of former Queensland
Premier, Sir Thomas McIlwraith, who would entertain London dinner-guests
with stories of Aboriginal cannibalism and aver 'that he would undertake to
disperse an army of them with a stockwhip (laughter)'.[38]

Wills was thus no loner, outsider or gun- and knife-toting eccentric. He was
part of the land-holding establishment of Queensland and shared strong, elitist
views on, for instance, *fin-de-siecle* working class radicals whom he denounced
as 'low and scurrilous scum'.[39] Though he may, to our present ears, sound
exceptional, he was not. His opinions, and even his actions were largely within
the tolerated mainstream of his time. Bowen's newspaper, the *Port Denison Times*
advocated in 1867 the taking of 50 Aboriginal lives for every white casualty.[40]
Wills's conscienceless killing of Aborigines was replicated across the colony as
was his blatant child abduction activity, as Shirleene Robinson's recent book,
Something Like Slavery makes painfully clear. Even his corpse dissection was

---

36   Wills, 1895, 'Reminiscence', BP, OML, OM75/75/3: 117–118.
37   Frankland to Evans, 5 May 1986; Brandon to Frankland, 14 April 1986; *Brisbane Courier*, 24 June 1864,
2 August 1865, 6 July 1867.
38   Queenslanders at Dinner, June 1890–June 1895 (cuttings), BP, OML: 52–85.
39   Wills, 1895, 'Reminiscence', BP, OML, OM75/75/3: 209–210; *Brisbane Courier*, 11 September 1894.
40   *Port Denison Times*, 2 March 1867.

not particularly anomalous if we consider the skeletal collections of deceased Aborigines in museums throughout Europe, Britain and Australia. Three of the visiting scientists, Karl Lumholtz, Richard Semon and probably Amalie Dietrich, encountered Queensland settlers who offered to shoot an Aborigine for them so they might obtain the skull. Archibald Meston, the subsequent architect of Queensland's *Aboriginals Protection and Restriction of the Sale of Opium Act 1897*, wrote in 1887 to Edward Ramsey, the curator of Sydney's Australia Museum, 'Re skulls &c, skeletons of the festive myall! … At your prices I could have procured about £2000 worth in the last six years. I shall start on the warpath again! Hope to succeed in slaughtering some stray skeleton for you'.[41]

Wills's beliefs about blood and soil were also hegemonic as was his conception of what was implied in his time by the term 'civilising'. On his journey to Bowen in 1862, he had detoured to visit those shrines of pioneering sacrifice, Hornet Bank and Cullin-la-Ringo, sites of the Fraser and Wills massacres respectively. The deaths of Korah Wills' Victorian namesake, Horatio Wills and 18 others of his party had only just occurred in mid-October 1861, several months before the former's visit, and white reprisal activity was doubtlessly still continuing in the region. Horatio Wills had formerly been a settler of the Grampians of Western Victoria and had himself been involved, along with his workers, in the massacre of Aborigines. Emily Wills, Horatio's wife, wrote to her brothers in Germany just before Christmas 1861 that 300 blacks, 'Gins and all' had been slaughtered in retaliation: 'hunted like wild dogs', she added with undisguised relish. 'I hope you read your bibles often', her letter concludes.[42]

This then was the asymmetrical milieu of frontier destruction – of violent resistance and disproportional counter-killings – within which frontiersmen such as Palmerston and Korah Wills operated. It is a painful and distressing world for contemporary Australians to re-enter, for it reconnoitres the dark continent within the human spirit that the savage process of dispossession tends to draw out. The *Quadrant* day-trips to 'Fantasy Island' will continue to provide a welcome detour for many. Yet the only aspect of the phenomenon of Korah Wills that is truly exceptional is his compulsion for such detailed, self-incriminating disclosure, as his guilty words literally tumble over each other in their eagerness to escape his pen. Others in his time left less revealing fragments concerning reprisals they had attended. Overall these also reinforce Boyce's point that today's race conflict historians, if anything, provide a pale reflection of the struggle rather than embellishing or fabricating it. In 1865, for instance, EO Hobkirk, 'an old identity of South Western Queensland' was present at a mass killing of Aborigines on the Bulloo River after an Aboriginal

---

41   Lumholtz 1889: 373; Semon 1899: 266–267; Turnbull 2008: 231–232.
42   De Moore 2008: 122.

worker, described as a 'pet black boy', murdered John Dowling, the manager of Thouringowa Station. His brother, Vincent gathered a white posse to secure the culprit, but when local Aborigines would not provide information – to quote Hobkirk:

> Mr. Dowling then said, 'if you do not tell me I will shoot the lot of yous'. Still they remained silent. Mr. Dowling and the others then set to work and put an end to many of them, not touching the 'gins' and young fry. This I know to be true as I helped first to burn the bodies and then to bury them. A most unpleasant undertaking! But as I was only a 'Jackaroo' on 'Cheshunt' station at the time, I had to do what I was told.[43]

Vincent Dowling had earlier been a pioneering cattleman on the Upper Darling River in 1859. His head stockman, John Edward Kelly later provided graphic descriptions of atrocities visited by white settlers on the local Aboriginal peoples. 'We feel perfectly certain that we have not exaggerated one single statement we have made', Kelly concluded his account: 'We have seen the bones'.[44]

The memorably named John Charles Hogsflesh was working as principal mail contractor on the Palmer River track in October 1874, when he discovered the mutilated bodies of German goldminer Johann Straub, his wife Bridget and young daughter Annie. These two females were the first known white women killed by Aborigines in North Queensland. A massive reprisal, involving squads of Native Police troopers led by Second-Class Inspector Thomas Clohesy, Acting Inspector Tom Coward, Sub-Inspector Edwin Townshend and Acting Sub-Inspector Alexander Douglas, reinforced by white civilian volunteers, culminated in a large-scale massacre of Aborigines at Skull Camp.[45] One of these volunteers, WH Corfield wrote that any compunction he felt towards mercy during the operation evaporated when he thought of the 'outrages' committed on the German family.[46] But Hogsflesh, who was probably also German himself and 'unfortunately' sworn in as 'an Especial Constable', as he put it, later reported that although he 'was Pressent [sic] at the Skull Camp Massacre – it was nothing else – I was not a Participator. I could not do it'. If a book were written on the ill-treatment of North Queensland's Aborigines, he continued, it would represent 'one of the blackest pages in the History of Queensland'. 'I hope it never will [be written]' he added cautiously. For Skull Camp was, he maintained, basing his conclusion on 25 years frontier experience, 'only

---

43   Copland et al 2006: 77–78; Richards 2008: 67.
44   *The Stockwhip*, 22 April 1876; *Maryborough Chronicle*, 9 May 1876; Evans, R 2009: 10.
45   Richards 2008: 292–293.
46   Evans et al 1993: 52–53, 128.

one case. I could fill this sheet with similar. One is sufficient to Repeate. The sickening Details is best forgotten'.[47] Hogsflesh's letter to Queensland Premier, Boyd Morehead, was filed away, unanswered.

Writing in the *Cairns Post* in 1926, Michael O'Leary recalled how in the mid-1880s he camped at Skeleton Creek, near the Mulgrave River, where 'nearly every stump or tree had a nigger's skull as a trophy ... When we made camp, I strolled round and counted sixteen of these gruesome relics'.[48] Historian Timothy Bottoms believes this Golgotha was connected with the 'big "battue"' (a hunting term denoting a round-up for destruction) conducted near Cairns against the Yidinydji people in 1884–1885. One participant, Jack Kane later told anthropologist Norman Tindale how combined Native Police and colonists' raids, lasting a week, slaughtered Aborigines at Skull Pocket, along the Mulgrave River and at Woree. Tindale recorded in his diary:

> each man [was] armed with a rifle and revolver. At dawn one man fired into their camp [at Skull Pocket] and the natives rushed away in three other directions. They were easy running shots close up. The native police rushed in with their scrub knives and killed off the children. A few years later a man loaded up a whole case of skulls and took them away as specimens. [Kane added matter-of-factly,] 'I didn't mind the killing of the "bucks" but I didn't quite like them braining the kids'...[49]

There is a striking congruity in these abrasive stories that are told, almost calmly, by voices that echo from and relate back into a different kind of normalcy from our own. This is, I would contend, the normalcy of a world of undeclared ethnic warfare, fought pre-emptively and ferociously, with no declared rules of engagement or agreed parameters. It is a territorial, unscrupulous, terrorising, scrappy and dirty conflict, replete with genocidal incidents. In many areas it appears to have been fought almost to the finish – and these candid perpetrator and witness stories match in their flavour the accusatory reports of colonial whistle-blowers who in larger numbers write, mostly anonymously to the press, invariably fruitlessly to the Queensland government and with occasional, glancing success to the British Colonial Office or the Aborigines Protection Society. Indeed, it is possible to argue that in composite, the degree of colonial disclosure of frontier excesses occurring in Queensland more or less balances the on-going degree of stone-walling and denialism. Though there is usually an element of circumspection regarding the identity of involved personnel and other condemnatory details such as the precise number of Aboriginal casualties, the accumulated evidence unfolds a continually reiterated and virtually

---

47 Hogsflesh, John to Morehead, Boyd, 8 October 1889, Queensland State Archives [hereafter QSA], Col A595, in-letter 9567.
48 *Cairns Post*, 1 November 1926; Bottoms 2000: 122.
49 Bottoms 2000: 121–123.

inescapable story of desperate resistance and ruthless suppression. Although a cloak of secrecy and euphemism usually accompanied the illegal commission of individual or group killings and most participants wisely held their counsel, the cloak was porous. Sometimes perpetrators boasted, confessed or left cryptic clues regarding their actions. Sometimes those actions were witnessed by others and the private circulation of damning information was made public by a colonial whistle-blower. The principal source of a more disciplined silence was institutional in nature. It involved a colonial police service that not only did not investigate most violent Aboriginal deaths as crime scenes, but also actually took part in and often directed massacres. And it consequently involved a colonial legal service that played little part in extending the rule of law to frontier regions in relation to ubiquitous Aboriginal casualties at the hands of others. Though the potential for law enforcement was ever-present, imposing caution in the reportage of wrong-doing, it was rarely effected. The only non-Aboriginal ever executed for the murder of an Aborigine in Queensland was a Chilean sailor, Leonardo Moncardo, in 1892 for the killing of a Darwin Aboriginal child named Bob on a trading boat off Thursday Island. It was more of a work-place incident than a frontier one.[50]

For much of the nineteenth century therefore, the principal source of denialism concerning frontier violence was invariably official in origin and was, overall, out of step with virtually every other form of reportage on the subject. Disclaimers and rebuttals by the Queensland government regarding reported atrocities rarely appeared to be believed by the colonial press; but, aided by a swelling migrant population who usually seem to be unconcerned as to the fate of Aborigines, or openly hostile towards them, politicians and bureaucrats maintained a constant barrage of disavowal and repudiation. As the persistent Catholic activist for Aboriginal protection, Father Duncan McNab was informed by a Government Minister in November 1880, 'Nineteen-twentieths of the population ... care nothing about them, and the other twentieth regard them as a nuisance to be got rid of'.[51]

Even though Queensland from 1859 was a self-governing colony, responsible for its own internal order, its various governments were at pains to deflect criticism from Whitehall and avoid Colonial Office scrutiny and rebuke on matters of racial policy. Defending its international reputation in a British Empire that promoted civilised sanctity was crucial. Private reports of frontier atrocities reaching Britain were deflected by the Queensland authorities as being concocted and inauthentic. Reassurances were given that everything conceivable was being done to offer Aboriginal peoples just terms. For instance, in July 1865, the Queensland Executive Council assured the Colonial Office that, as well as its

---

50 Dawson 2005: 35.
51 Evans et al 1993: 79.

annual blanket distribution, 'medical assistance' and even 'grants of land' were being offered to Aborigines. 'The question of the general amelioration of their condition by founding special hospitals for them, and industrial schools for their children, has repeatedly engaged the attention of the Colonial Government and Parliament',[52] the report continued. The 'grants of land' in question were actually for Christian missionary societies who never availed themselves of the offer. The rest of the assurances were simply specious window-dressing. Official documentation in Queensland, rather than delivering the most dependable of interpretations to posterity, is probably the most suspect.

Official circumlocution was passed on down the line. For instance, during the overlanding expedition of Frank and Alexander Jardine from Rockhampton to Somerset at the tip of Cape York between August 1864 and January 1865, there were 11 encounters with various Aboriginal groups along the way and, in at least nine of these, Aborigines were killed.[53] Following an affray on 16 December 1864, the Government Surveyor accompanying the Jardines and four Native Police troopers reported that the brothers were 'attacked by some natives, whom they soon put to flight'.[54] The Jardine's private journal discloses more fulsomely that 'eight or nine' Aborigines were killed.[55] Two days later, in a more severe clash at the Mitchell River, the Surveyor, Archibald Richardson again writes of the over-mastered Aborigines, 'Many of them lost the number of their mess, but none of our party were hit'.[56] The Jardines, however, frankly disclose:

> The natives at first stood up courageously, but either by accident or through fear, despair or stupidity, they got huddled in a heap, in, and at the margin of the water, when ten carbines poured volley after volley into them from all directions, killing and wounding with every shot with very little return … About thirty being killed … [m]any more must have been wounded and probably drowned, for fifty-nine rounds were counted as discharged.[57]

It would, of course, be excerpts from Surveyor Richardson's diary that found their way to Britain, though even his tight-lipped reportage encountered official disquiet there.

A pattern of denial, however, was certainly gaining the upper hand throughout Australian society as Federation approached. Sir Horace Tozer, Queensland's

---

52 Queensland Executive Council to British Colonial Office, 4 July 1865, Public Records Office, Kew, Co 234/12, 57283.
53 Loos 1982: 252–253.
54 Hiddens 1994: 152.
55 Hiddens 1994: 48.
56 Hiddens 1994: 153.
57 Hiddens 1994: 50.

Agent General in London and a former Colonial Secretary, wrote in the *Empire Review* in 1901 that Aboriginal numbers had declined simply due to 'civilization and its vices'. Frontier deaths were the result of the 'tribal conflicts' of 'cannibals'.[58] George Frodsham, the Anglican Bishop of North Queensland, added poetically that Aborigines were dying out because they had 'shuddered at the approach of the stranger'. They were now 'flitting silently and quickly into the limbo of forgotten races'.[59] White agency apparently had little to do with it: Aborigines were so 'very low in the intellectual scale of humanity'[60] that all they could absorb was moral degradation. In short, they were, individually and collectively, killing themselves. Australian children's literature now also began to emphasise silence and concealment. Mrs Aeneas Gunn's *The Little Black Princess of the Never Never* (1905) was silent on frontier violence while Ethel Turner's *Seven Little Australians* was re-tooled between 1894 and 1900 to eliminate 'the shadow of ... sorrowful history' from the text.[61] Turner in 1894 had included the Aboriginal narrative of Tettawonga in her book, prefacing it with a reference to the 'nightmare' of 'evil' that white intrusion had brought. This section of text was excised from all subsequent editions. School *Readers* inculcated collective amnesia by presenting a land 'entirely empty of inhabitants' before the British arrival.[62] Federation poetry, celebrating the ethical *bona fides* of the new nation, trumpeted a theme of constant peace:

> We have no records of a bygone shame.
> No red-writ histories of woe to weep.[63]

claimed poet John Farrell; while Banjo Paterson in 'How the Land Was Won' reiterated:

> we have no songs of strife,
> Of bloodshed reddening the land.[64]

Yet it was, pre-eminently, the Queensland poet, Toowoomba-based George Essex Evans who earned Federation's title of Australia's 'patriotic poet'[65] by winning the prize for the best commemorative verse with his 'Commonwealth Ode'. In this poem, much admired by Alfred Deakin, Evans depicts Australia as a land 'empty, memoryless and unproductive' before the British arrival.[66] It then blossoms to become:

---

58   Tozer 1901: 183–184.
59   Frodsham 1915: 195, 213.
60   Creed 1905: 89.
61   Gunn 1905: 21, Turner 1894: 10 in Bradford 2001: 3–5, 15, 91.
62   Bradford 2001: 21–28.
63   Farrell 1887: 29; Hirst 2000: 21.
64   Evans 2002: 182.
65   Mackenzie-Smith 2001: 67.
66   Tiffin 1991: 71.

Free-born of Nations, Virgin white,
Not won by blood nor ringed with steel.
Thy throne is on a loftier height,
Deep-rooted in the Commonweal![67]

It is similar in tone to other poems Evans wrote, such as 'A Federal Song', 'Stand Forth, O Daughter of the Sun', 'An Australian Symphony' and 'The Women of the West', all extolling pioneering virtues and summoning the new nation into being. In sentiment, this was in basic conformity with the general literary industry of its time, intent upon fashioning a new kind of reality about Antipodean honour and innocence. Yet we might expect that Essex Evans, of all such writers, should have known better.

When Evans wrote his Ode in 1900, he was married to Blanche Hopkins, the sister of former Native Police Officer, Second-Class Sub-Inspector Ernest Eglinton.[68] Eglinton was based at the Boulia Native Police camp from 1878 to 1884, after which he became a local Police Magistrate. He was involved in numerous patrols across the inner Gulf region around Cloncurry and oversaw the near elimination of the Kalkadoon people. In early 1879 he carried out reprisals after Kalkadoons had ambushed and killed Russian cattleman, Bernard Molvo and three others of his party at Woonamo waterhole in Sulieman Creek, leading to 'constant shoot-outs' throughout that year.[69] He next avenged the killing of Native Police cadet, Constable Marcus La Poer Beresford and several of his troopers in January 1883, eventually fighting a battle against the Kalkadoons with an armed posse of white squatters in April.[70] One account claims that 'scores of blacks were killed'. Another settler, Robert Clarke, writing in 1901, offered an even higher casualty rate, with the Native Police 'in their glory shooting down everything'.[71] A memoir Eglinton wrote in 1920 about the 'exceedingly cruel' Kalkadoons mentions little of this. Most violence is from the Aboriginal side of the frontier (though sometimes caused by white cruelty and 'Gin-stealing'), while tales of Native Police 'ferocity and cruelty' are dismissed as a product of 'the gentle art of leg-pulling'.[72]

Significantly, George Essex Evans was himself located in the same region as his future brother-in-law in the early 1880s, having joined a surveying party that left Warwick on the Darling Downs for Dalgonally Station on Julia Creek, north-east of Cloncurry, in mid-March 1883. The surveyors, under the leadership of Gilbert Daveney and his cousin James Daveney Steele, were photographed

---

67   Evans 1900: 1–2; Byrnes and Vallis 1959: 40–41.
68   O'Hagan 1981: 446–447; Richards 2008: 233.
69   Loos 1982: 224; *Queenslander*, 8 March 1879.
70   Hillier, nd, '"If You Leave Me Alone…"', unpublished ms: 121.
71   Laurie 1959: 70; Armstrong nd: 128.
72   Eglinton, 1920, 'Pioneering in the North-West…', Mitchell Library, ms: 1–8.

during the long expedition heavily armed. One of the party sports a bandolier of bullets around his body. In a short recollection, entitled 'Memories of the Gulf', written in 1926, Steele records violent encounters with his 'blackboy' while at Dalgonally, adding darkly, 'Subsequently the Inspector of Native Police looked after him'.[73] The officer was probably Eglinton himself. Steele later acted as Best Man at the Burketown wedding of James Lamond, a Sub-Inspector of Native Police who, in 1885, would inform Frank Hann of Lawn Hill that '[t]he police have shot ... round this run alone over 100 blacks in three years'.[74]

It beggars belief that Essex Evans was somehow innocent of any knowledge of such concerted mayhem when he wrote his epochal tribute to the 'quiet continent' in 1900. He had, in effect, stretched poetic licence beyond its elastic limit. Further investigation shows that the poet published a humorous article entitled 'My Gulf Helmet' concerning his Cloncurry surveying experience under the pseudonym of 'Christophus' in *The Antipodean*, a literary journal he co-edited in 1894. In this he details his preparation to travel into 'the country of the rude and untutored Myall':

> I had an excellent outfit. We were going far from the haunts of civilization, amongst the savages of the North. 'It is well to be prepared', the Boss said. I was prepared. I was clad in a war-like and elegant costume. I wore long leather gaiters and long fierce spurs. Round my waist was strapped an empty but formidable cartridge belt ... in front of the saddle was a bulky valise and revolver in a strapped case. On the right of the saddle hung a tomahawk ... quite a group of little boys ... called me 'Lord Wolseley' ... My appearance was so military.[75]

The central thrust of the story concerns Essex Evans' overly large pith helmet. 'I could see nothing but green lining when I had it on', he writes; but he clearly required no such helmet to restrict his later vision.[76] His poetry championed aversion to any themes of negativity in the colonial story. 'An Australian Symphony', for instance, seeks to banish all 'mournful' cultural 'undertones' from the national refrain:

> These mangrove shores, these shimmering seas,
> This summer zone –
> Shall they inspire no nobler strain
> Than songs of bitterness and pain?

---

73   Steele 1926: 9–10.
74   Roberts 2005: 232; Slack 2002: 79, 81.
75   Evans 1894: 107.
76   Evans 1894: 107, 109–110, 112.

Evans demands that Australia's music requires 'a loftier tone':

> Her song is silence: unto her
> Its mystery clings.
> Silence is the interpreter
> Of deeper things.[77]

And, one might add, also the censor.

Such concealment became a dominant reflex during the twentieth century as a major psychological problem with national accountability was generated. Its effects were wide-ranging and, for most white Australians, inclusive and enduring. Convictism and colonialism were both spring-cleaned of telling stains for the consumption of these innocent invaders, as 'the Great Australian Silence' grew more pervasive. Aborigines themselves became a vanishing race in the wider Australian mind. The engine of this cultural amnesia remained principally institutional in nature as a selective process of forgetting was fostered both educationally and politically. Saying little or nothing about Aborigines and their fate was simultaneously saying much about British-Australians and their sense of self-worth. As the *Queensland School Reader* (Book six), studied by generations of students, fulsomely declaimed about George Essex Evans:

> His muse delights in imperialism – a true and lofty imperialism which, while ever ready to defend its own, does not glory in the smoke and scarlet of war, but prefers to extend its borders by the influence of righteous rule, and finds its ideals in Empire-builders such as Raleigh and Cook, Rhodes and Grey, and in the countless host of brave pioneers the world over, who have blazed tracks of civilisation across new countries, founded prosperous cities, and won in quiet heroism the splendid victories of Peace.[78]

In Queensland during this time most of the Native Mounted Police records disappeared. Although historian Jonathan Richards, who has painstakingly scoured the Queensland State Archives for all Native Police references, has recently concluded that, 'it is no longer acceptable to allege that there are no [such] records' and dismisses claims of missing files as 'conspiracy theories', it nevertheless appears clear that a vast culling of sensitive items has at some point occurred.[79] Most of the surviving records are scattered in departmental holdings other than that of the Police Department and Police Commissioner's Office where, all being above board, they should belong. The vast majority of these extant files are relatively innocuous Police Staff records, though even a

---

77 Evans 2009: 3.
78 Fowles 1913: 6.
79 Richards 2008: 207.

considerable number of these are also missing. Thus, although Richards' recently published *The Secret War* throws new light on the organisation and rationale of the Native Mounted Police Force and the career trajectories of certain of its white personnel, it usually pulls up short when it arrives at action in the field. This is because, as another researcher, Robert Jensen has found – and my own work over the years would corroborate – even though:

> collisions between police and native tribes were regularly reported … it is equally clear that only scattered remnants of these reports survive…

> [These are] largely preserved in the Department of the Colonial Secretary where they *do not* naturally belong, rather than where they *ought to have been* amongst the files from the Police Department.[80]

The most sensitive of such missing documents are the regular 'monthly reports' required from all officers, outlining the date and particulars of every collision and dispersal that had transpired while on patrol. Such orders were first released in 1861 and strongly reinforced by the 1866 Native Police Regulations that demanded both a field journal and duty diary be kept. Jensen states, 'evidence shows that the Government printer made a specific Native Police Officers Diary with columns for this purpose and … officers are on record for ordering these diaries'.[81] Given that some 85 Native Police camps operated between 1859 and 1900, for an average space of seven years apiece, there should ideally be over 7000 of these monthly reports in existence. Yet only a handful remain. It is like a huge jigsaw puzzle with most of the vital middle pieces removed. The challenge is to use these missing pieces like a musician uses silence.

As both Richards and Jensen conclude, 'incomplete … records … prevent us from being able to count the actual number of killing episodes' or the precise numbers killed.[82] Yet there may be a way of arriving at a roughly reliable estimate – or at least a defendable minimum – of Native Police killings between 1859 and 1898, when Queensland's *Aboriginals Protection and Restriction of the Sale of Opium Act 1897* became law. As stated above, we know from Richards' work that 85 camps were established in this time as well as the number of years that each one operated. Such camps reached a numerical peak of 42 during the 1870s when frontier relations in the north and west of Queensland intensified and troopers received breech-loading Snider Rifles that multiplied fire-power five times over the previous muzzle-loading Carbines. By the 1890s, the number of camps had fallen to 20, located largely in the Cape and Gulf. If we delete the Frome camp on the Palmer River that began in 1898 from our consideration, we have a total of 84 camps operating for an aggregate of some 596 years – or roughly seven years

80   Jensen, 2007, 'What Does the Archived Records Reveal…', unpublished ms: 2–3.
81   Jensen, 2007, 'What Does the Archived Records Reveal…', unpublished ms: 1.
82   Richards 2008: 207; Jensen, 2007, 'What Does the Archived Records Reveal…', unpublished ms: 4.

per camp.[83] From these camps, Native Police detachments conducted monthly patrols, visiting pastoral stations and mining fields in their ambit region and carrying out desultory dispersals of Aboriginal groups encountered in order to pre-empt or avenge depredations. Richards writes, 'usually between three and eight troopers were led by a European officer, although occasionally double detachments ... were worked by one or two officers. Sometimes, the patrols were continual'as in the case of the so-called 'Flying Detachments' set up in 1868.[84] As the 1864 Regulations candidly stated, 'the duties of the officers are never-ending; their presence is required everywhere ... all gatherings of aboriginals in the neighbourhood may be followed by the police, and disarmed and dispersed by force'.[85] Sometimes, too, more than one patrol might be underway in a region when more than one officer was present or when that region was in a state of enhanced alert. Yet, if we assume only one patrol per month, we are still looking at a potential aggregate of 7152 patrols. Let us strip this back further, however, to a rounded figure of 6000 patrols, in consideration of times of illness, desertion, flooding or other natural disasters when patrolling might be curbed; as well as to recognise any months in a year when a camp may have folded or not yet begun its operations. This would suggest an average of ten patrol reports per year rather than 12.

But how can we assess the number of collisions with Aborigines per patrol if the vast bulk of the monthly reports have gone missing? Luckily, a small number of these have survived among the Colonial Secretary's files and elsewhere, allowing one to compile a case study of such circuits from 1865 to 1884. From available data, I have collected 22 monthly accounts of rounds across areas of central and north-eastern Queensland, as well as in the Gulf country. These reports represent the activities of 11 Native Police Officers in eight regions across three decades. During these patrols, such Officers enumerate 57 collisions with or dispersals of Aborigines – an average of 2.6 such engagements per patrol.[86] Even if, for the sake of caution, we again drop this back to two dispersals on average per patrol, we still arrive at an aggregate projection of roughly 12,000 dispersals by Native Police alone between 1859 and 1897. How many Aborigines then were killed, on average in each dispersal? Mostly officers are careful not to enumerate such casualties with any precision, although various records do again provide an actual, though not necessarily an accurate figure. As researcher Alan Hillier comments, 'most of the deaths were never reported ... as the Native Police

83   Richards 2005: 349–351.

84   Richards 2008: 17: Hillier, nd, '"If You Leave Me Alone..."', unpublished ms: 263.

85   Hillier, nd, '"If You Leave Me Alone..."', unpublished ms: 320–321: Richards 2008: 45.

86   Blakeney, Carr and Nantes, 'Monthly reports: January–June 1866', QSA, Col A 127/2455; Paschen, 'Monthly report, June 1865', QSA, Gov/24; *Port Denison Times*, 16 June 1866; Loos 1982: 43; *Brisbane Courier*, 17 September 1872; Johnstone, 'Monthly report, March 1873', QSA, Col A 184/1430; Hillier, nd, '"If You Leave Me Alone..."', unpublished ms: 219–222, 245–246; Springsure Police Letter Book, 1866–73, QSA, A36–355; Armstrong nd: 136–145; *Courier Mail*, 25 January 2003; Fysh 1961: 144–147.

officers knew better than to send in reports that could [potentially] hang them'.[87] Furthermore, the Police Commissioner from 1864 until 1895, DT Seymour, had no desire to read detailed dispersal accounts. Hillier states, 'Seymour washed his hands of any violence. He maintained his role as overseer of operations, rather than becom[ing] involved in the murky world of [field] activities'.[88] Yet on the odd occasion that a casualty number is recorded, they range widely from high double figures (and sometimes even triple ones) during extended times of reprisal raiding to smaller group totals, ranging from three to 12 or so during more regular clashes.[89] Even if we once more play it incredibly safe here and suggest the extremely conservative figure of only two killed on average per dispersal, we find ourselves confronting an aggregate estimate of 24,000 violent Aboriginal deaths at the hands of the Native Police between 1859 and 1897 alone. This, of course, is only a mathematical speculation, but, I would suggest, one that deserves some attention and consideration. It is equally important that such an estimate be understood not only as a bare, debatable statistic but also as a sequential quotient of grief and pain. Furthermore, the surprisingly large figure does not include a prior decade of Native Police patrols and dispersals from 1849 to 1859, or indeed *any* of the private white settler or military assaults on Aborigines from 1824 that may have actually rivalled, in composite, Native Police attacks in their intensity. The maths grow increasingly disquietening. Whatever the overall figure may be – and it will remain forever speculative – it certainly dwarfs Reynolds' controversial 20,000 Aboriginal mortality estimate from frontier violence for the whole of Australia from 1788 to 1930.

Queensland's past appears then to be an ideal locale for burying the so-called 'History Wars' and for composing an epitaph to their essentially wrong-headed, viperish and irrelevant nature. The territory of Queensland equals above two-thirds the size of Europe and contained, pre-contact, arguably around 35 per cent of Australia's Aboriginal population. Its incoming settlers spread themselves across the continent's widest territorial range at a time when both Western weapons-technology and scientific racism were burgeoning. The pattern of frontier relations persisted there for almost a century.[90]

The past is always a puzzle that is never satisfactorily solved, but empirical investigation of Queensland's frontier, even more so than that of Tasmania, appears to disclose that so-called 'Black-Armband' historians, rather than fabricating and exaggerating a violent heritage, have probably down-played

---

87   Hillier, nd, '"If You Leave Me Alone…"', unpublished ms: 264.
88   Hillier, nd, '"If You Leave Me Alone…"', unpublished ms: 268; Thorpe 1985: 254–255.
89   See, for instance, Copland et al 2006: 70; Roberts 2005: 232–233; Loos 1982: 36–37, 41; Armstrong nd: 170–171; Richards 2008: 66–68; Hillier, nd, '"If You Leave Me Alone…"', unpublished ms: 60, 84, 109, 143, 162, 201; Evans et al 1993: 61, 63, 130–131, 375–378; Evans 2004: 156–157; Collins 2002: 213; de Moore 2008: 122.
90   Evans 2004a: 68–70, 2004b: 162–164.

it with a degree of cautious restraint. Even the self-incriminating perpetrator testimony points in this direction. The Queensland scene did not host any 'Nun's picnics'.[91] Rather it was a locale of fear and devastation. As well as an inordinately high Aboriginal death-rate from physical attack, above 1000 European, Asian and Melanesian mainland colonists died violently. Reynolds' estimate of fatalities, much derided for its alleged excessiveness, apparently requires radical upward revision; and, despite confident neoconservative assertions, official pronouncements on inter-racial matters in Queensland (at least) often seem to be the *least* likely of historical sources to be trusted. Concealment and disclosure about the nature of Imperial dispossession and colonial settlement are locked in an on-going dynamic tension throughout much of our history and this long serpentine dance of contestation requires urgent unravelling. The turn of the millennium was by no means the first time in this country that fervent denialism has mounted its brash and popular challenge.

Acknowledgements

My sincere thanks and appreciation for their thoughtful comments and practical help to Timothy Bottoms, Mark Cryle, Ann Curthoys, Leanne Day, Jacqui Donegan, Ernie Grant, Anna Haebich, Robert Jensen, Murray Johnson, Bill Kitson, Judith McKay, Jahara Rhiannon, Shirleene Robinson, Lyndall Ryan and Bill Thorpe.

References

Primary Sources

Blakeney, Carr and Nantes, 'Monthly reports: January–June 1866', Col A 127/2455, Queensland State Archives (QSA), Brisbane.

Eglinton, Ernest 1920, 'Pioneering in the North-West. A few Rambling Notes of Happenings in the Far North-West of Queensland 40–45 years ago', ms, Mitchell Library, Sydney.

Hillier, Alan nd, ' "If You Leave Me Alone, I'll Leave You Alone". Biographical Sketches, Reports and Incidents from the Myall Wars of the Queensland Native Mounted Police Force 1860–1885', unpublished ms.

Hogsflesh, John to Morehead, Boyd, 8 October 1889, Col A595, in-letter 9567, QSA, Brisbane.

91   Manne 2003: 299; *The Australian*, 16 December 2002.

Jensen, Robert 2007, 'What Does the Archived Records Reveal about the Reports of the Native Police Force?', unpublished ms.

Johnstone, 'Monthly report, March 1873', Col A 184/1430, QSA, Brisbane.

Native Police, Queensland, 'Monthly reports, January–June 1866', Col A127, in-letter 2455; June 1865, Gov/24; March 1873, Col A184, in-letter 1430, QSA, Brisbane.

Paschen, 'Monthly report, June 1865', Gov/24, QSA, Brisbane.

Port Denison Times, 1866, Queensland State Library, Brisbane.

Queenslanders at Dinner, June 1890–June 1895 (cuttings), Brandon Papers, Oxley Memorial Library, Brisbane: 52–85.

Queensland Executive Council, Brisbane to British Colonial Office, London, 4 July 1865, Co234/12, 57283, Public Records Office, Kew, United Kingdom.

Springsure Police Letter Book, 1866–73, A36–355, QSA, Brisbane.

Wills, Korah 1895, 'Reminiscence', Brandon Papers, OM75/75/3, Oxley Memorial Library, Brisbane.

Newspapers

The Australian

Brisbane Courier

Cairns Post

Courier Mail

Maryborough Chronicle

Port Denison Times

Queenslander

St Kilda Chronicle

The Stockwhip

Secondary sources

Albrechtson, Janet 2006, 'Asking the right questions: Geoffrey Blainey, Keith Windschuttle and co have undermined the progressive establishment', *The Australian*, 23 August 2006.

Armstrong, Robert nd, *The Kalkadoons. A Study of an Aboriginal Tribe on the Queensland Frontier*, William Brooks, Brisbane.

Attwood, Bain 2005, *Telling the Truth about Aboriginal History,* Allen & Unwin, St Leonards, New South Wales.

Bolton, GC 1974, 'Palmerston, Christie (1850? – 1897)', *Australian Dictionary of Biography*, vol 5, Melbourne University Press, Melbourne: 395–396.

Bonnell, Andrew G and Martin Crotty 2004, 'An Australian *"Historikerstreit"?'*, *Australian Journal of Politics and History* 50(3): 425–433.

Bottoms, Timothy 2000, 'A History of Cairns, City of the South Pacific, 1770–1995', unpublished PhD thesis, James Cook University, Queensland.

Boyce, James 2003, 'Fantasy island', in *Whitewash: On Keith Windschuttle's Fabrication of Aboriginal History*. Robert Manne (ed), Black Inc, Melbourne: 17–78.

— 2004, '"Better to be mistaken than to deceive": The fabrication of Aboriginal history and the Van Diemonian record', *Island* 96, Autumn: 9–37.

— 2008, *Van Diemen's Land*, Black Inc, Melbourne.

Bradford, Clare 2001, *Reading Race*: *Aboriginality in Australian Children's Literature*, Melbourne University Press, Melbourne.

Brawley, Sean 1997, '"A comfortable and relaxed past": John Howard and the "Battle of History"', *Electronic Journal of Australian and New Zealand History*, 27 April 1997, accessed 15 May 2010:

<http://www.jcu.edu.au/aff/history/articles/brawley.htm>

Byrnes, RS and Val Vallis 1959, *The Queensland Centenary Anthology*, Longmans, Green, London.

Clark, Anna 2008, *History's Children: History Wars in the Classroom*, University of New South Wales Press, Sydney.

Cohen, Leonard and Sharon Robinson 1988, 'Everybody knows', in *I'm Your Man*, produced by Leonard Cohen, CBS Records, CBS 460642.

Collins, Patrick 2002, *Goodbye Bussamarai: The Mandandanji Land War, Southern Queensland 1842–1882*, University of Queensland Press, Brisbane.

Copland, Mark, Jonathan Richards and Andrew Walker 2006, *One Hour More Daylight. A Historical Overview of Aboriginal Dispossession in Southern and Southwest Queensland*, Social Justice Commission, Toowoomba.

Creed, J Mildred 1905, 'The position of the Australian Aborigines in the scale of human intelligence', *The Nineteenth Century* 335, January: 89–96.

Dawson, Christopher 2005, *A Pit of Shame. Boggo Road's Executed Prisoners and South Brisbane Cemetery*, Boggo Road Gaol Historical Society, Brisbane.

De Moore, Greg 2008, *Tom Wills. His Spectacular Rise and Fall*, Allen & Unwin, Crows Nest, New South Wales.

Evans, George Essex ('Christophus') 1894: 'My Gulf Helmet', *The Antipodean. An Illustrated Annual*, George Robinson, London: 107–112.

— 1900, *The Secret Key and Other Verses*, accessed 15 May 2010: <http://www.telelib.com/words/authors/E/EvansGeorgeE/verse/SecretKey/commonwealth>

— 2009, 'An Australian Symphony', *Free Poetry E-Book: 6 Poems of George Essex Evans*, accessed 15 May 2010: <http://www.poemhunter.com/poem/an-australian-symphony>

Evans, Raymond 2002, 'White citizenship: nationhood and race at Federation', *Memoirs of the Queensland Museum* 2(2): 179–187.

— 2004a, 'Across the Queensland frontier', in *Frontier Conflict: The Australian Experience*, Bain Attwood and SG Foster (eds), National Museum of Australia, Canberra.

— 2004b, '"Plenty shoot' em". The destruction of Aboriginal societies along the Queensland frontier', in *Genocide and Settler Society: Frontier Violence and Stolen Indigenous Children in Australian History*, A Dirk Moses (ed), Berghahn Books, New York.

— 2006, 'Past imperfect/present tense', *Overland* 184, Spring: 23–27.

— 2007, *A History of Queensland*, Cambridge University Press, Melbourne.

— 2008, 'Done and dusted', in *Hidden Queensland, Griffith Review*, Spring: 183–198.

— 2009, 'Queensland, 1859: Reflections on the act of becoming', *Queensland Review* 16(1): 1–15.

—, Kay Saunders and Kathryn Cronin 1993, *Race Relations in Colonial Queensland: A History of Exclusion, Exploitation and Extermination*, University of Queensland Press, St Lucia, Queensland.

Farrell, John 1887, *How He Died and Other Poems*, Tuner and Henderson, Sydney.

Fowles, FWH 1913, 'George Essex Evans (1863–1909)', *Queensland School Reader* (Book VI), Department of Public Instruction, Brisbane.

Frodsham, George 1915, *A Bishop's Pleasance*, Smith Elder, London.

Fysh, Hudson 1933, *Taming the North*, Angus and Robertson, Sydney.

Gunn, Aeneus 1905, *The Little Black Princess of the Never Never*, Angus and Robertson, Sydney

Healy, Chris 2008, *Forgetting Aborigines*, University of New South Wales Press, Sydney.

Hiddens, Les (ed) 1994, *The Journals of the Jardine Brothers and Surveyor Richardson on the Overland Expedition from Rockhampton to Somerset, Cape York*, Corkwood Press, North Adelaide.

Hirst, John 2000, *The Sentimental Nation: The Making of the Australian Commonwealth*, Oxford University Press, Melbourne.

Howard, John 2006, 'A tribute to *Quadrant*', *Quadrant*, November 2006.

Laurie, A 1959, 'The Black War in Queensland', *Journal of the Royal Historical Society ofQueensland* 6(1), September.

Loos, Noel 1982, *Invasion and Resistance: Aboriginal-European Relations on the North Queensland Frontier 1861–1897*, Australian National University Press, Canberra.

Lumholtz, Carl 1889, *Among Cannibals. An Account of Four Years Travels in Australia and of Camp Life with the Aborigines of Queensland*, J Murray, London.

Mackenzie-Smith, John 2001: 'Two Queensland federation poets and the Red Page Razor', in *Our Federation. Brisbane: Patriotism, Passion and Protest*, Barry Shaw (ed), Brisbane History Group Papers, 18: 57–68.

Macintyre, Stuart and Anna Clark 2003, *The History Wars*, Melbourne University Press, Melbourne.

Manne, Robert (ed) 2003, *Whitewash: On Keith Windschuttle's Fabrication ofAboriginal History*, Black Inc, Melbourne.

O'Hagan, Margaret 1981, 'Evans, George Essex (1863–1909)', *Australian Dictionary ofBiography,* vol 8, Melbourne University Press, Melbourne: 446–447.

Palmerston, Christie 1883, 'From Mourilyan Harbour to Herberton', *The Queenslander*, 6 October 1883: 557.

Reid, Gordon 2006, *'That Unhappy Race': Queensland and the Aboriginal Problem 1838–1901*, Australian Scholarly Press, Melbourne.

Richards, Jonathan 2005, '"A Question of Necessity": The Native Police in Queensland', unpublished PhD thesis, School of Arts, Media and Culture, Griffith University, Brisbane.

— 2008, *The Secret War, A True History of Queensland's Native Police*, University of Queensland Press, St Lucia, Queensland.

Roberts, Tony 2005, *Frontier Justice: A History of the Gulf Country to 1900*, University of Queensland Press, St Lucia, Queensland.

Robinson, Shirleene 2008, *Something Like Slavery: Queensland's Aboriginal Child Workers 1842–1945*, Australian Scholarly Press, Melbourne.

Rowe, Richard 1869, *The Boy in the Bush,* Bell and Daldy, London.

Rutherford, Jennifer 2000, *The Gauche Intruder: Freud, Lacan and the White Australian Fantasy*, Melbourne Press, Melbourne.

Ryan, Lyndall 2003, 'Reflections by a target of a media witch-hunt', *History Australia* 1(1), December: 105–109.

Semon, Richard 1899, *In the Australian Bush and on the Coast of the Coral Sea: Being the Experiences and Observations of a Naturalist in Australia, New Guinea and the Moluccas,* Macmillan, London.

Simons, Margaret 2009, 'How Windschuttle swallowed a hoax to publish a fake story in *Quadrant*', Crikey, 6–8 January 2009, accessed 15 May 2010: <http://www.crikey.com.au/2009/01/06/how-windschuttle-swallowed-a-hoax-to-publish-a-fake-story-in-quadrant>

Sinclair, Iain 2009, 'Upriver', *London Review of Books* 31(12), 25 June: 5–10.

Slack, Michael 2002, 'The "Plains of Promise" revisited: a reassessment of the frontier in north western Queensland', *Journal of Australian Studies* 75: 71–83.

Steele, James Daveney 1926, 'Memories of the Gulf', *The Queensland Surveyor* 7(6), January: 9–10.

Taylor, Tony 2009, *Denial: History Betrayed*, Melbourne University Press, Melbourne.

Thorpe, William 1985, 'A Social History of Colonial Queensland. Towards a Marxist Analysis', unpublished PhD thesis, Department of History, University of Queensland.

Tiffin, Chris 1991, 'Metaphor and emblem: George Essex Evans's public poetry', *The Literary Criterion* 4(27): 61–74.

Tozer, Horace 1901, 'The coloured races of Australia', *The Empire Review* 1: 182–188.

Turnbull, Paul 2008, 'Theft in the name of science', *Hidden Queensland, Griffith Review*, Spring: 227–235.

Windschuttle, Keith 2002, *The Fabrication of Aboriginal History, Volume One: Van Diemen's Land 1803–1847*, Macleay Press, Sydney.

2. 'Hard evidence': the debate about massacre in the Black War in Tasmania

LYNDALL RYAN

The Black War in Tasmania 1823–1834, is widely perceived by historians as one of the best documented of all Australia's colonial frontier wars. Yet debate still rages about whether massacres were a defining feature and whether they accounted for the deaths of many Aborigines. As Keith Windschuttle has pointed out, this is an important debate because it reflects on the character of the Australian nation and the behaviour of its colonial forbears in seizing control of Aboriginal land.

This paper reviews the debate from its origins in 1835 to where it stands today. It largely concerns the issue of 'hard evidence' and how it was used. To explore the conduct of the debate and how the key protagonists used the available sources, methods and explanatory frameworks to make their case, the paper is divided into three historical periods: 1835–1870; 1875–1939; and 1948–2008. It finds that in the first period, the belief in widespread massacre dominated the debate, drawn from oral testimony from the victorious combatants. In the second period, the belief in massacre denial took hold, based on the dominance of archival sources and the doctrine of the self-exterminating Aborigine. In the third period the protagonists engaged in a fierce contest for control of the debate based on different interpretations of the sources. One side argues for massacre denial, based on the belief that more settlers than Aborigines were killed in the Black War while the other argues that in applying new methods of interpretation, the 'hard evidence' for massacre is now overwhelming and that its incidence was widespread.

The paper concludes that the concern with 'hard evidence' indicates that the massacre debate today is a microcosm of the wider debate about the impact of settler colonialism on indigenous peoples; and in particular about the humanity of the Tasmanian Aborigines. Above all it reflects the reluctance of many white Australians even today, to come to terms with incontrovertible evidence about our violent past and to seek reconciliation with Aboriginal survivors.

Introduction

In 2002, historian Keith Windschuttle claimed that, from his search for 'hard evidence' in his own 'exhaustive' reading of the sources relating to the Black War in Tasmania (1823–1834) he could find only rare incidents of massacre and that overall, more settlers than Aborigines were killed in the conflict.[1] In making this extraordinary assertion he was simply the latest in a long line of historians to enter the massacre debate which has dominated the historiography of the Black War since 1835.

The debate is central to understanding the wider debates about settler colonialism and how Australian historians have framed the past. How then did the debate begin, how did it develop and where does it stand today? To explore these questions, this paper selects for analysis the arguments made by the key participants, largely historians, who have shaped the debate over the last 174 years. To understand how they have used the available sources and methods and explanatory frameworks to make their case, the discussion focuses on three historical periods: the first from 1835 to1870 when the Black War was still vivid in colonial memory; the second from 1875 to 1939 when the ideas and beliefs of scientific racism dominated the debate; and the third period from 1948 to 2008 when competing views about settler activism and Aboriginal resistance almost took the debate to an impasse. In taking this approach the key components of the debate can be identified and their impact on the debate today can be assessed.

1835–1870

The massacre debate took off at the end of the Black War, when historians were confronted with the grim statistic that fewer than 250 Aborigines had survived. What had happened to the rest? If few Aborigines had lived in Tasmania at the war's outset, then how had they managed so effectively to terrorise the colonists for so long? If there had been many more, as many settlers had believed, how had their numbers declined so rapidly? Faced with this moral dilemma, historians looked for some explanations.

Henry Melville a radical journalist and newspaper editor set the parameters of the debate. Arriving in Tasmania in 1827, during the war's second phase, he quickly found employment on the colony's leading opposition newspaper. Some of his published articles and reports which were based on interviews with settlers in the war zones and discussions with the colonial elite in Hobart became the basis of his own account of the Black War, published in 1835.[2]

---

1 Windschuttle 2002: 131-166.
2 Mackaness 1965.

He was in no doubt that when the war escalated in late 1826, the Aborigines were 'massacred without mercy'. 'At this period', he wrote, 'it was common for parties of the *civilized* portion of society to scour the bush, and falling in with the tracks of the natives, during the night to follow them to their place of encampment, where they were slaughtered in cold blood' and that the effect of martial law, which was in operation from November 1828 to February 1832, 'was to destroy, within twelve months after its publication, more than two thirds of these wild creatures, who by degrees dwindled away till their populous tribes were swept from the face of the earth'.[3] But the conflict was far too fresh in popular memory for him to identify the perpetrators let alone the dates and locations of their awful deeds. The 'failure' to produce 'hard' evidence would lead a later generation of historians to ignore his conclusions.

The Quaker missionary James Backhouse, who made two extended visits to Tasmania in the later stages of the war between 1832 and 1834, was also in no doubt that the colonists had shot many Aborigines, 'sometimes through fear, and there is reason to apprehend, sometimes through recklessness'.[4] But he too was reluctant to offer 'hard evidence'. Rather he believed that the few surviving Aborigines should be grateful for the opportunity offered by the colonial government to adopt British ways and convert to Christianity. In this way, the settlers would be redeemed for their misdeeds.

John West faced a similar problem. A Congregational minister and journalist he arrived in Tasmania four years after the war had ended and quickly realised that it had been a defining moment in the colony's history. As a leading opponent of convict transportation and an ardent advocate of colonial self-government, he championed the colony's future at the expense of its violent past. In *The History of Tasmania* published in 1852, he was in no doubt that massacre had been practised during the Black War and suggested four different ways in which it had happened. But he did not believe that it was appropriate to identify known perpetrators and witnesses, let alone the dates and places where the mass killings took place:

It would be a waste of time even to condense, in the most succinct relation, all the incidents that occurred. Narrative is tedious by the monotony of detail, and the events themselves were recorded by those who witnessed them, with ominous brevity. Such crimes were of daily occurrence; perhaps sometimes multiplied by rumour, but often unheard and unrecorded ... the poet of the Iliad did not describe more numerous varieties, in the slaughter of his heroes.[5]

---

3   Mackaness 1965: 71, 79.
4   Backhouse 1967[1843]: 79.
5   Shaw 1971: 283.

He admitted that massacre had been an unfortunate component of the war, but he also believed that it was imperative the colonists must 'move on' from the horrors of the past to prepare for self-government. In this new environment, the Aborigines, who he now believed were on 'the brink of extinction', could be conveniently forgotten.[6]

James Bonwick disagreed. An evangelical schoolteacher, he arrived in Tasmania in 1842, eight years after the war had ended and like West, he was also surprised that war trauma continued to dominate the colonial psyche. He interviewed many colonists about their wartime experiences and when he moved to Victoria in 1849, collected more accounts from colonists who had left Tasmania in the mid 1830s and who were it seems, even more anxious than their counterparts who had remained in Tasmania, to testify about their involvement in some of the war's more shocking incidents. In *The Last of the Tasmanians*, published in 1870, he furnished in some cases enough clues for the reader to identify the informant, the date of the specific incident and the place where it happened. In all he mentioned 16 instances of massacre, with a combined loss of at least 300 Aboriginal lives. If any reader was in doubt that massacre was widely used to dispose of hundreds of Aborigines in the Black War, then Bonwick's account appeared to offer more than enough evidence to dispel it.[7]

At the end of the first period, the debate appeared to have been resolved in favour of widespread massacre. This is not surprising. The Black War was still a vivid memory for many colonists in Tasmania and Victoria and stories of massacre were pervasive in both colonies even if the actual details were difficult to obtain. By the time Bonwick's work was published in 1870 however, war trauma was beginning to fade and some colonists were disturbed that his book had generated international condemnation about the fate of 'the last of the Tasmanian Aborigines'. With Tasmania's violent past returning to haunt them, some colonists sought a new champion to make the past more palatable.

1875–1939

If the hour produces the man, then James Erskine Calder, the colony's former surveyor general, filled the breach. He had arrived in the colony at the height of the Black War in 1829 and through his survey work had helped fulfil the settlers' dream of transforming Tasmania into a vast sheepwalk. Anxious to restore the colony's tarnished reputation he searched for other sources of evidence that he believed would be more reliable than Bonwick's unnamed informants. He searched for the official sources of the war and located what he called the 'nineteen awful volumes' of papers in the vaults under the Colonial

---

6   Shaw 1971: 285.
7   Bonwick 1970[1870].

Secretary's Office in Hobart. They provided a very different story of the Black War. Instead of reports of massacres he found instead, numerous accounts of 'fictitious fights', which 'though still repeated by lovers of the marvelous and horrible, were found to be utterly false on investigation'.[8]

> I know of no trustworthy record of more than one, two, three or at most four persons being killed, in any one encounter. The warfare, though pretty continuous, was rather a petty affair, with grossly exaggerated details – something like the story of the hundred dead men, reduced, on inquiry, to three dead dogs ... Up to the time of their voluntary surrender ... the [Aborigines] not only maintained the ground everywhere ... they had by far the best of the fight; ... and as far as I can learn, at least five of the [settlers] dying for one of the [Aborigines].[9]

This finding led him to conclude that the Aborigines were responsible for their own demise. They had died, he contended, not from mass killings by the colonists, but from intertribal wars and 'the prevalence of epidemic disorders; which, though not introduced by the Europeans, were possibly accidentally increased by them ... and their own imprudence' in refusing to use European remedies to treat them.[10]

From that moment, massacre denial took hold. Based on the doctrine of Aboriginal self-extermination, Calder's work absolved the colonists from responsibility for the past. By the end of nineteenth century the massacre debate appeared to have been resolved in resounding victory for the massacre denialists. Their beliefs matched another aspect of the doctrine of Aboriginal self-extermination, the discourse of scientific racism which placed the Tasmanian Aborigines at the lower end of the human evolutionary scale. In this position, they were believed to have been far too primitive to withstand British colonisation. This discourse dominated scholarly research on the Tasmanian Aborigines until the outbreak of World War II. By then the Black War had been relegated to a melancholy footnote in Tasmania's colonial history and the Aborigines had simply 'faded away'.[11]

1948–2008

The debate was rekindled after the War by journalist Clive Turnbull in his powerful text, *Black War: the extermination of the Tasmanian Aborigines*. Written in the shadow of his experiences as a war correspondent in Europe and Asia, it was imbued with 'the long shadows of massacre remembrance' that had

8   Calder 1875: 7.
9   Calder 1875: 8.
10   Calder 1875: 25-27.
11   Giblin 1939: 20.

permeated his own family in Tasmania since the 1820s. It was also the first text to draw an analogue between the Nazis' attempts to exterminate the Jews and British attempts to exterminate the Tasmanian Aborigines. From his exhaustive search of the colonial newspapers as well as the official account of the Black War published in *British Parliamentary Papers*, Turnbull was in no doubt that massacre played a key role in the extermination of the Aborigines even though neither source offered hard evidence to support his case. He believed that 'the wiping out of the Aborigines began in earnest' in 1828 and that most massacres probably occurred during the martial law phase, between November 1828 and January 1832.[12] But the absence of 'hard' evidence of specific incidents left his account open to question. Perhaps his experience as a war correspondent enabled him to read between the lines.

The problem of evidence also concerned Brian Plomley, the editor of the Tasmanian journals of the conciliator, George Augustus Robinson.[13] As a physical scientist and imbued with the beliefs of scientific racism, he could not believe that massacres were widespread during the Black War even though Robinson had recorded several instances of them in his journal. He was particularly concerned that Bonwick's accounts of massacre, which were once again attracting international scholarly attention in the aftermath of the Holocaust, should be contested. In his *Annotated bibliography of the Tasmanian Aborigines*, published in 1969, he disputed

> Bonwick's uncritical acceptance of the stories told him by 'old hands' [which] has reduced their value considerably. Bonwick's statements, if not confirmed from primary sources, should largely be considered as suspect, and opened to doubt in great or small degree. Many of his informants had little or no understanding of the events they witnessed, if indeed they themselves witnessed them.[14]

As the leading scholar of the Tasmanian Aborigines, Plomley's extraordinary attack was taken very seriously by the next generation of historians like me. Embarking on my own research into the history of the Tasmanian Aborigines, I largely avoided Bonwick's work. In my own book, *The Aboriginal Tasmanians*, I argued that Aboriginal resistance rather than settler activism was the key feature of the Black War and believed that most Aborigines were probably killed in ones and twos although at four times the rate of the settlers. While I did record six instances of massacre, I did not believe that they had any real impact on the war's outcome.[15]

---

12 Turnbull 1965: 80, 97.
13 Plomley 1966.
14 Plomley 1969: 14–15.
15 Ryan 1981: 174.

Lloyd Robson, the leading historian of Tasmania, disagreed. Like Turnbull he was also a Tasmanian 'native son' and 'the long shadows of massacre remembrance' loomed large in his historical consciousness. In *A History of Tasmania Volume I*, he noted at least eleven incidents of massacre during the Black War and made special mention of an incident reported in great detail by a settler to a government inquiry in 1830 but which was quickly denied by two others. This kind of contested evidence he said, 'illustrates the difficulty of getting some of the truth about the war, for if ever there was a case of the victors writing history, this is it'. He was the first historian to contest the absence of hard evidence and to suggest that new methods were needed to interpret disparate data.[16]

His call for new methods fell on deaf ears. With the resurgence of the modern Aboriginal community in Tasmania and their claims for the return of 'stolen' land, historians whose families had arrived in Tasmania before the Black War became concerned to show that its outcome was not their fault. They argued that rather than settler activism, it was key Aboriginal leaders and government agents who had had betrayed the Aboriginal people into surrendering to a ruthless colonial governor. By the end of the 1980s the Black War was represented as an encounter between two well armed groups in which the settlers rather than the Aborigines were lucky to survive.[17]

In 1992, Brian Plomley re-enforced this emerging belief when he published *The Aboriginal/Settler Clash in Van Diemen's Land 1803-1831*. Designed as the last word on the Black War, the publication was an exhaustive survey of the colonial newspapers and official archival sources of the war. In presenting what he called the 'written record' as 'hard evidence', he expected that readers could now objectively reach their own conclusions about the conduct of the war:

So far as the official record is concerned, it is on the whole a factual one because it is based on statements by the magistrates of the various districts. The errors here lie chiefly in the exaggerations of the informants, who striving to present their cases in the best possible light claimed that larger bodies of Aborigines were involved, or were killed, and that greater damage was done.[18]

In adopting a class based approach to the official record, Plomley seemed unaware that some magistrates had much to hide about their violent attacks on the Aborigines and that some of the convict 'informants' might indeed have been telling the truth as they saw it. Nor did he convey much respect for the integrity of some of the contemporary newspapers such as the *Colonial Times*, which Melville had worked for, because they 'not only paid as much attention to rumour as to events, but commented freely upon the situation. Rumour

---

16   Robson 1983: 217.
17   Rae-Ellis 1981, 1988; Pybus 1991.
18   Plomley 1992: 7.

sometimes led a newspaper to proclaim atrocities in one issue and refute them in the next'.[19] He concluded that 'wanton attack and ill-treatment by the settlers was confined to a few individuals' and only sometimes 'by the mob', although he did acknowledge that the 'Ku Klux Klan type mob who hunted down and killed parties of Aborigines is on record in Robinson's journals, but as might be expected was never the occasion for comment.'[20]

Had he followed up GA Robinson's reports of massacre with accounts in the colonial press and settler reports in the official archives, he might have substantiated Robson's conclusion that it is the victors who write history. As it was, Plomley's unrivalled reputation as the leading scholar of the Tasmanian Aborigines elevated his conclusions and the methods he used to reach them to a realm beyond scholarly criticism. Sadly, in this case, it conferred on this particular work the status of an objective historical document.

In this guise it was then used without equivocation by several historians. In 1995 for example, Henry Reynolds used it as the key source of evidence for his argument that in the Black War 'the numbers [of Aborigines] actually killed by Europeans may have been less than is generally supposed', that the massacres that Robinson recorded along the Meander River 'were rare in Tasmania' and that 'the mortality rate on each side was more even: perhaps somewhere between 150 and 250 Tasmanians were killed in conflict with the Europeans after 1824 (with another 100 or 150 dying before that date), while they killed about 170 Europeans'.[21]

Reynolds' extraordinary conclusion inadvertently set the stage for Keith Windschuttle's entry into the debate in 2002. He also used Plomley's *Aboriginal/Settler Clash,* and then manipulated Reynolds' statistics to make the astonishing claim that twice as many settlers than Aborigines were killed in the war. He then further claimed that the settlers by virtue of their Britishness could not have engaged in the kinds of brutal and violent warfare that had been advanced by Robson and that most of the massacres noted by Robson and myself, were either exaggerations or outright fabrications.[22]

Windschuttle's idiosyncratic approach to the investigation of eleven alleged incidents of massacre was based on what is known as report discounting: the exclusion of every piece of known evidence except the one piece that denied it had happened.[23] Yet rather than shutting down the debate, as he had expected to do, he opened it up to new methods of investigation.

---

19   Plomley 1992: 8.
20   Plomley 1992: 9.
21   Reynolds 1995: 51, 79, 82.
22   Windschuttle 2002: 131–166.
23   Windschuttle 2002: 131–166.

Since then new methods and typologies of massacre developed by the French sociologist Jacques Semelin have been applied to investigating its possible incidence in the Black War. He argues that hard evidence for massacre is constrained by the fact that it tends to be carried out in secret, that the physical evidence is usually quickly removed, that no witnesses are intended to be present and that if they are, then they are usually afraid to speak out until long afterwards either to escape retribution from the perpetrators and/or prosecution by the authorities. He concludes that historians must employ new interpretive methods to understand the context of massacre and to look for disparate forms of evidence to comprise the hard evidence to make their case.[24]

There is no doubt that Semelin's methods have revolutionised the way historians investigate massacre on the Tasmanian colonial frontier today. Recent research into the Black War includes the investigation of specific incidents of massacre using a wide array of disparate evidence, a survey of the way the war was conducted in each particular phase and nuanced studies of the ways Aborigines and colonists in specific regions in colonial Tasmania experienced the conflict.[25] From these findings the view is emerging that massacre appears to have been used as a deliberate strategy by the colonial government to destroy targeted groups of Aborigines in particular areas of Tasmania during a specific phase of the Black War.[26]

Conclusion

In 2009, the massacre debate in Tasmania has turned full circle from its origins in 1835. The concern about 'hard evidence' that has bedevilled the debate from the outset now appears to have moved into a new trajectory. The most recent findings appear to offer the clearest explanation yet for the grim statistic that historians first confronted in 1834 that fewer than 250 Aborigines had survived the Black War.

The massacre debate is by no means settled. The impact of introduced disease still awaits resolution and Indigenous scholars have yet to enter the debate. Yet in its current trajectory it has opened up new understandings of how frontier wars were conducted and reported in colonial Australia before 1850 and in other comparable settler societies in the nineteenth century.[27] Whatever the findings that new research might reveal, the fate of the Tasmanian Aborigines will continue to attract international attention. For the terrible story of their

---

24 Semelin 2007.
25 Breen 2001; Boyce 2003, 2008; McFarlane 2003, 2008; Tardif 2003; Kiernan 2007; Madley 2008; Ryan 2006, 2008a.
26 McFarlane 2008; Ryan 2008b.
27 Keirnan 2007; Madley 2010; Ryan 2010.

near demise remains a microcosm of the wider story of the settler colonial encounter with indigenous peoples worldwide. In this story, the determination by so many historians to misunderstand what massacre is and the context in which it occurs has played a critical role in perpetuating massacre denial.

The massacre debate today is a microcosm of the wider debate about the impact of settler colonialism on indigenous peoples and in particular about the humanity of the Tasmanian Aborigines. Above all it reflects the reluctance of many white Australians even today, to come to terms with incontrovertible evidence about our violent past and to seek reconciliation with Aboriginal survivors. I would like to hope that this review of the massacre debate in the Black War in Tasmania will take Aboriginal and non-Aboriginal Australians closer to reaching that outcome.

References

Backhouse, James 1967[1843], *Narrative of a Visit to the Australian Colonies*, Johnson Reprint, London [Hamilton, Adams, and Co, London].

Bonwick, James 1970[1870], *The Last of the Tasmanians; or, The Black War in Van Diemen's Land*, Reprint Libraries Board of South Australia, Adelaide [Sampson Low, Son, & Marston, London]

Boyce, James 2003, 'Fantasy Island', in *Whitewash: On Keith Windschuttle's 'The Fabrication of Aboriginal History'*, Robert Manne (ed), Black Inc, Melbourne.

— 2008, *Van Diemen's Land*, Black Inc, Melbourne.

Breen, Shayne 2001, *Contested Places: Tasmania's Northern Districts from Ancient Times to 1900*, Centre for Tasmanian Historical Studies, Hobart.

Calder, James Erskine 1875, *Some Account of the Wars, Extirpation, Habits etc. of the Native Tribes of Tasmania*, Henn and Co, Hobart.

Giblin, Robert William 1939, *The Early History of Tasmania, vol. II: The Penal Settlement Era, 1804–1818, Collins, Sorell and Arthur*, Melbourne University Press in association in Oxford University Press, Melbourne.

Kiernan, Ben 2007, *Blood and Soil: A World History of Genocide and Extermination from Sparta to Dafur*, Yale University Press, New Haven.

Mackaness, James (ed) 1965, *The History of Van Diemen's Land From the Year 1824 to 1835 Inclusiveby Henry Melville*, Horwitz–Grahame, Sydney.

McFarlane, Ian 2003, 'Cape Grim', in *Whitewash: On Keith Windschuttle's 'The Fabrication of Aboriginal History'*, Robert Manne (ed), Black Inc, Melbourne.

— 2008, *Beyond Awakening. The Aboriginal Tribes of Northern Tasmania: A History*, Fullers Bookshop, Riawunna and the Community, Place & Heritage Research Unit, University of Tasmania, Hobart.

Madley, Benjamin 2008, 'From terror to genocide; Britain's Tasmanian penal colony and Australia's history wars', *Journal of British Studies* 47: 77–106.

— 2010, 'Massacre on the colonial frontiers in Tasmania and California: a comparative analysis', in *Theatres of Violence: Revisiting the Massacre in History*, Philip Dwyer and Lyndall Ryan (eds), Berghahn Books, New York.

Plomley, Norman James Brian (ed) 1966, *Friendly Mission: The Tasmanian Journals of G.A. Robinson 1829–1834*, Tasmanian Historical Research Association, Hobart.

— 1969, *An Annotated Bibliography of the Tasmanian Aborigines*, Royal Anthropological Institute of Great Britain, London.

— 1992, *The Aboriginal/Settler Clash in Van Diemen's Land 1803–1831*, Occasional Paper No 6, Queen Victoria Museum & Art Gallery Tasmania in association with the Centre for Tasmanian Historical Studies, University of Tasmania, Hobart.

Pybus, Cassandra 1991, *Community of Thieves*, William Heinemann Australia, Port Melbourne, Victoria.

Rae-Ellis, Vivienne 1981, *Trucanini: Queen or Traitor*, Australian Institute of Aboriginal Studies, Canberra.

— 1988, *Black Robinson: Protector of the Aborigines*, Melbourne University Press, Melbourne.

Reynolds, Henry 1995, *Fate of a Free People*, Penguin Books Australia, Ringwood, Victoria.

Robson, Leslie Lloyd 1983, *A History of Tasmania Volume I: Van Diemen's Land from the Earliest Times to 1855*, Oxford University Press, Melbourne.

Ryan, Lyndall 1981, *The Aboriginal Tasmanians*, University of Queensland Press, St Lucia, Queensland.

— 2003: 'Who is the fabricator?', in *Whitewash: On Keith Windschuttle's Fabrication of Aboriginal History*, Robert Manne (ed), Black Inc, Melbourne.

— 2006, 'Massacre in Tasmania: how can we know?', *Australia and New Zealand Law and History E-Journal*, Refereed Paper No 6: 1–21, accessed 10 May 2010: <http//www.anzlhsejournal.auckland.ac.nz/pdfs_2006/Paper_6_Ryan.pdf>

— 2008a, 'Chronological index: list of multiple killings of Aborigines in Tasmania; 1804–1835', in *Online Encyclopaedia of Mass Violence*, Jacques Semelin (ed), Social Sciences Po, Paris, accessed 10 May 2010: <http://www.massviolence.org/+-Tasmania-+?id_rubrique=6>

— 2008b, 'Massacre in the Black War in Tasmania 1823–34: a case study of the Meander River region, June 1827', *Journal of Genocide Research* 10(4): 479–499.

— 2010, 'Settler massacres on the Port Phillip Frontier, 1836-1851', *Journal of Australian Studies*, 34(3): 257-273.

— 2011, 'Massacre on the colonial frontier in Victoria: a comparative approach', in *Theatresof Violence: Revisiting the Massacre in History*, Philip Dwyer and Lyndall Ryan (eds), Berghahn Books, New York.

Semelin, Jacques 2007, *Purify and Destroy: The Political Uses of Massacre and Genocide*, Hurst & Company, London.

Shaw, Alan George Lewers 1971, *The History of Tasmania by John West*, Royal Australian History Society and Angus and Robertson, Sydney.

Tardif, Phillip 2003, 'Risdon Cove', in *Whitewash: On Keith Windschuttle's 'The Fabrication of Aboriginal History'*, Robert Manne (ed), Black Inc, Melbourne.

Turnbull, Clive 1948, *Black War: The Extermination of the Tasmanian Aborigines*, FW Cheshire, Melbourne.

Windschuttle, Keith 2002, *The Fabrication of Aboriginal History Volume I: Van Diemen's Land 1803–1847*, Macleay Press, Sydney.

3. Epistemological vertigo and allegory: thoughts on massacres, actual, surrogate, and averted – *Beersheba*, *Wake in Fright*, *Australia*

JOHN DOCKER

Massacres of Indigenous people are both remembered and not remembered, creating in white Australian consciousness a confused energy around the ways Indigenous history is understood.[1] Massacres occurred from the 1790s, early in British settlement of the continent, through the nineteenth century until well into the twentieth. Yet because this feature of Indigenous history is rarely faced directly or frankly, it emerges in popular culture indirectly, as in Freud's image of psychic unease, where that which is repressed will always find ways to disturb the surface of consciousness. What is feared is that one's society, if accused of having committed extreme violence, will suffer loss of honour among the nations. In this reading of Indigenous history I will look at what is *not* there, what is disregarded, minimised, and deflected.

In an essay on Edward Said, Ella Shohat uses the felicitous phrase epistemological vertigo to refer to how difficult it is for Jews, knowing themselves as a people of suffering and persecution, also to regard themselves as victimisers of others. It is a difficulty, she points out, that has been particularly posed in modernity by Zionist nationalism, whose aggressive settler colonialism in Palestine has made victims of both the Palestinians and also the Sephardim, the Arab Jews of the Middle East; and it is a vertigo, she reflects, that is also part of Euro-American historical consciousness, which cherishes an image of being anti-colonial since the nation foundationally gained its independence by freeing itself from imperial Britain. In each case, Shohat argues, the presence and civilisations of the Indigenous inhabitants, the Palestinians and the Native Americans in North America, are ignored or held to be of no account.[2] In similar terms, Ann Curthoys evokes the power of victimology in white Australian popular

---

1   McKenna 2002.
2   Shohat 1992: 134, also 140–141; Shohat 1988: 1–35; Shohat 2006: 201–232; Docker 2001: 141–142.

historical consciousness and mythology, subtended by an uneasiness and anxiety that one's society not be perceived as a perpetrator nation in relation to its Indigenous peoples.[3]

Epistemological vertigo and allegory are drawn to each other, allegory suggesting phenomena that cannot be faced directly, that are displaced into other representations. Here I will explore how such allegorical displacement works in Australian historical consciousness in relation to Indigenous massacres.

The texts I will focus on are Paul Daley's book *Beersheba: A Journey Through Australia's Forgotten War*, published in 2009, concerning events in Palestine in 1917–1918; Baz Luhrmann's wonderfully provocative film *Australia*, referring to history in Central and Northern Australia between 1939 and 1941, which was released in late 2008; and another remarkable film, *Wake in Fright*, made in 1971 by the Canadian director Ted Kotcheff, beautifully restored and re-released in 2009. I want to think about three scenes of massacres actual, surrogate, and averted. The actual scene is the Arab massacre by Anzac forces, Australians and New Zealanders, in late 1918 in the Bedouin village of Surafend in Palestine. The other scenes are fictional and involve the massacre of kangaroos in *Wake in Fright*, and, averted at the last moment, of cattle in *Australia*, reminding us that, in terms of environmental history, massacre can involve slaughter of animals. Massacre indeed is etymologically associated with animals; the word traditionally used in France for the butcher's chopping block, in the sixteenth century it gained its modern meaning, which then spread from France to England.[4]

I will regard the three scenes of massacre in my chosen texts as allegorical. In terms of method, what interests me in exploring these texts, whether they are works of history like *Beersheba* or films like *Wake in Fright* and *Australia*, is the play of genre, textual tensions and stresses, ambivalences, narratives and counter narratives, stray details, obfuscations, and oddities.[5]

I suggest that a haunting dyad, legible in all three texts in different ways, of heroic values and dishonourable massacre, helps to shape, destabilise and bring incoherence to, white Australian historical memory and consciousness. The haunting can never be resolved and will always require new, impossible, attempts to create an unambiguous narrative. The textual result is confusion, even discursive and aesthetic chaos.

---

3   Curthoys 1999: 1–18; also Docker 2008a: 113–144.
4   Levene 1999: 7–9; also Greengrass 1999: 69.
5   Docker 2008a: 92.

Massacre studies and world history

In the last several years I have been involved in genocide and massacre studies, 'world history' fields that are quite closely related, for both question and explore humanity at its limits; but they are also to some degree distinct.[6] Genocide as a mode of inter-group violence frequently involves massacre, yet massacres can be a more diffuse phenomenon, involving, for example, as Mark Levene suggests in the introduction to *The Massacre in History*, the actions of a single individual.[7] A feature of the field is what Jacques Semelin emphasises, the difficulty of explanation.[8] We need to know more why in massacres groups suddenly turn on their neighbours with whom there may have been friendly relations for many years; we ask why massacres occur at certain times and not others; we wonder how massacres can be both carefully thought out and yet exhibit emotion and frenzy of an almost erotic kind; why they frequently involve the most appalling atrocities, as in mutilation, dismemberment, disembowelling, cannibalism, the drowning of or setting fire to victims; we observe that massacres often involve molestation of women including kidnapping, disfigurement, and rape.[9]

There is also the 'world history' question of the relationship between European colonisation and massacre. Massacres, as Lyndall Ryan and Ray Evans discuss so well in their essays in this book, were an integral part of the colonising of Australia, a primary and characteristic mode of what late twentieth century international law would identify as ethnic cleansing. Lyndall Ryan challenges historiography to recognise how frequently massacres were deployed as a means of destroying and clearing from desired land the continent's Indigenous societies and peoples. Ray Evans points to the recurring methods of the coloniser perpetrators, that they simultaneously acted and concealed evidence as they acted, especially in the burning of bodies. Colonial massacres, Evans reflects, were accompanied by codes of secrecy and silence, or obfuscatory language and indirect references; key records were lost; perpetrators already were or might become important men of standing in colonial society, commercially and politically. We can also note that the colonising of the Australian continent from late in the eighteenth century was preceded by centuries of European colonisation elsewhere, creating a repertoire of methods and techniques that included massacre, and many colonisers, soldiers of empire, and imperial administrators moved between various colonies.[10] In these trans-empire and transcolonial terms, we can say that

---

6   Docker 2010.
7   Levene 1999: 1, 5.
8   Semelin 2003: 204, 208–209.
9   Semelin 2003: 208. For the massacres that frequently occur during partitions, see also Khan 2007; Pandey 2001.
10   Cf Lambert and Lester 2006: 24, note 94.

from 1492, taken as a collective, the European colonisers of other peoples' lands, around the world, when they considered there was a need, proved themselves practised massacrists.

European colonisation has involved slaughter of both humans and animals. A glance at North America is helpful here.

Peter Coates, in his essay in *The Massacre in History* on the melancholy fate of the wolf in United States history, suggests that massacres of unwanted humans and predator animals like wolves (and coyotes and mountain lions) were, in the European settlement of North America from the Puritan seventeenth century onwards, part of a single spreading process of invasion, conquest, and subjugation. Through the centuries of colonisation, he observes, the most notorious massacres of humans involved non-whites, the main victims being Indigenous peoples. In animal terms, biocide was practised on a wide scale, the destruction of multiple wild species. Between 1492 and 1900, an estimated 60 to 75 million buffalo, held to be in the way of European crops and cattle, were reduced to about 500. Yet buffalo, Coates reflects, were not detested or mutilated. Native Americans sometimes were; and pathological hatred was also visible in the ruthless campaigns against wolves, where complete eradication was the goal. In colonial New England, Coates writes, the killing of Native Americans and of wolves was believed to be divinely sanctioned. In the organised campaigns against wolves, which reached their zenith in the region west of the Mississippi between the 1860s and the 1920s and employed shooting, trapping, poisoning, habitat clearance, torture and setting on fire, wolves were vilified in terms of pejorative human qualities reaching back into classical Greek antiquity (handed down from Aesop's fables) and early Christianity (the Bible casting the devil as the wolf from hell and enemies of the faith are wolves), and by association with hated human groups such as Native Americans. Settlers considered predator animals and Native Americans to have no claim on the continent, since, as hunters, they ranged across the land rather than inhabiting it. The triad of wolves, Native Americans, and wilderness was perceived, Coates says, as a threat to the civilisation the colonists felt they were establishing in North America from the time of the Puritan colonies onwards, its developing agricultural and pastoral economy of cattle, sheep, and wheat, and its social, cultural and spiritual health; the United States, as destined utopia and cornucopia, required their perpetual destruction and replacement.[11]

Coates's argument concerning destruction of Indigenous humans and animals and their landscapes and habitats, and their replacement by coloniser populations and their habitats and animal species, recalls Raphaël Lemkin's

---

11   Coates 1999: 163–173.

originating definition of genocide.[12] It also brings to mind Jared Diamond and Hugh Brody's 'world history' theories concerning the relentless spread for the last 8000 years of agricultural-commercial society across the planet, ruthlessly attempting to destroy all Indigenous hunter gatherer societies and ecologies in its path. In their argument, agricultural-commercial society is inspired by a mythos that the world belonged only to those who cultivated its land and dug into it for resources.[13]

The Australian Light Horse: heroes, massacrists

In Australian military history, the Light Horse who during World War I were so effective in campaigns against the Turkish (and German and Austrian) forces in Sinai, Palestine, and Syria, have been characteristically praised as legendary heroes, their courage, daring, resourcefulness, horsemanship, and impatience with (especially British) military hierarchy, being lauded as the result of their predominantly rural upbringing. While in Palestine, the Light Horse were under the immediate command of the Australian and imperial career soldier, general Sir HG (Harry) Chauvel, who in 1919 wrote the preface to a celebratory war history, *Australia in Palestine*, its editors HS Gullett and Chas Barratt. Here Chauvel enthuses that the Australian Light Horseman is of a 'type peculiarly his own and has no counterpart that I know of except in his New Zealand brother'. Chauvel feels that his 'fearlessness, initiative and endurance' are owing to the 'adventurous life he leads in his own country' where he has been accustomed to 'facing danger of all sorts from his earliest youth'; perhaps, Chauvel suggests, these qualities are 'inherited from his pioneer parents'. Chauvel also admires the Light Horseman for his 'good-fellowship and camaraderie', 'invariable good humour', and 'chivalry': all such exist in the 'free and open life of the Australian Bush'.[14] In such praise, the Indigenous peoples of Australia are nowhere in sight, except perhaps in the curious perhaps coded reference to the horseman 'facing danger of all sorts from his earliest youth', with its reverse narrative of threat to his rightful or assured presence on the land.

How could such men, with their superior rural values derived from their pioneer parents who were so important in the colonisation of the continent, commit a massacre when the war was already over and the Anzac horsemen were waiting to return to the antipodes? In his biography, *Chauvel of the Light Horse*, AJ Hill tells us that the 'tragedy' of Surafend was a 'bitter blow to Chauvel'.[15]

In 1923, HS (Henry) Gullett, as part of Australia's official war history under the general editorship of Charles Bean, published *The Australian Imperial Force in*

---

12   Lemkin 1944: 79–80.
13   Diamond 1992; Waswo 1997; Brody 2002; Dorrian: 27–51; Docker 2008a: chs 1 and 7.
14   Gullett and Barrett 1919: xiii.
15   Hill 1978: 192–193.

Sinai and Palestine 1914–1918, where he constructs what we might call the ur-narrative of the Surafend massacre, inscribing the strange mix, part exculpatory, part condemnatory, that provides the motifs, images and tropes for almost all succeeding purported descriptions of what occurred. Post armistice, in their camps at Tripoli and on the Philistine plain, after a very successful campaign that secured the defeat of the Ottoman forces in Sinai, Palestine, and Syria, the light horsemen, Gullett writes, participated in an 'unfortunate incident' that was destined to throw a 'shadow' over their last days in Palestine. It has to be recognised, however, he adds, that they were intolerably provoked, by the Indigenous inhabitants in one way, and the British high command in another; indeed, they should be regarded as victims of both. Next to the camps of the Anzac Mounted Division of Australians and New Zealanders lay 'the native village of Surafend', which elicits the following racial typing from Gullett: 'All the Arabs of western Palestine were thieves by instinct'. The 'natives of Surafend', he continues, 'were notorious for their petty thieving'. At night, the Australians and New Zealanders, 'sleeping soundly, were a simple prey to the cunning, barefooted robbers, and night after night men lost property from their tents'. In this image, the Light Horsemen are 'prey' to shoeless Arabs perceived as stealthy predatory scavengers.[16]

Furthermore, the British policy was, says Gullett, not to punish 'these debased people'. The British high command regarded them as 'devout Moslems, kin not only to the Arabs of the Hijaz' – a reference to the Arab army from southwest Arabia who, famously accompanied by TE Lawrence as British liaison officer, had revolted against the Turks and were fighting their way towards Damascus[17] – but also to 'the Mohammedans of India'. Gullett is here putting in place a key element of the ur-narrative: the interests of dominion soldiers like the Australians and New Zealanders were being demeaningly subordinated to the wider imperial interests of the British empire whose forces included many Indian soldiers, and where the Hijaz Arabs were allies with the British against the Turks. Furthermore, Gullett complains, 'the Arabs, a crafty race, quick to discern British unwillingness to punish their misdeeds, exploited their licence to extreme limits'; also, the British were unfairly disposed to blame the Australians for 'any looting' that occurred 'against the natives': an interesting admission that Anzac forces *had* been looting the local Bedouin people.[18]

Gullett's official history provides the template description of how the Surafend massacre occurred.[19] As is often the case with massacres or scenes of violent retribution, a single individual of one's own group is injured or killed. In

---

16   Gullett 1923: 787–788.
17   Lawrence 1935[1926]; Lawrence 1927.
18   Gullett 1923: 787–788; Pappé 2004: 14–71; Doumani 1999: 11–40.
19   Perry 2009: 492–496.

this case, a New Zealand soldier is shot by a Bedouin, 'the native' who had been stealing in his tent. The New Zealanders, their whole camp immediately aroused, and 'working with ominous deliberation', then trace the 'footsteps of the Arab' to Surafend. The New Zealanders throw a 'strong cordon' around the village, no Arab being allowed to leave. All day, Gullett says, the New Zealanders 'quietly organized for their work in Surafend', and then, early in the night, marched out 'many hundreds strong' and surrounded the village. In his narrative, Gullett stresses that only the male Bedouin were harmed. When they entered the village, the 'New Zealanders grimly passed out all the women and children', and then, 'armed chiefly with heavy sticks, fell upon the men and at the same time fired the houses'. Many Arabs, Gullett tells us, were killed and few escaped injury; the village was demolished and set on fire, and the flames from the 'wretched houses lit up the countryside'. The Anzacs next 'raided and burned the neighbouring nomad camp' and then went 'quietly back to their lines'. General Allenby and his staff, however, were stationed nearby, and could not fail to see the 'conflagration and hear the shouts of the troops and the cries of their victims'.[20]

Gullett concedes that what happened 'cannot be justified', and affirms that Surafend 'should not be forgotten'. Nonetheless, he insists, 'in fairness to the New Zealanders, and to the Australians who gave them hearty support', we have to consider that the soldiers 'were the pioneers and the leaders in a long campaign'. They had just lost a 'veteran comrade' at the 'hands of a race they despised'; consequently, he feels, they became 'angry and bitter beyond sound reasoning'.[21]

In terms of massacre studies, we can observe recognisable elements. The actions of the massacrists combine rational planning and frenzied action: the New Zealanders and Australians deliberate and organise all day; however, they also exhibit irrationality, for, as Gullett phrases it, they 'were angry and bitter beyond sound reasoning', though deliberation returns afterwards when they go 'quietly' back to their lines. They simultaneously conceal as they act: they 'fell upon the men', Gullett relates, and 'at the same time fired the houses', then 'raided and burned the neighbouring nomad camp'. Did they burn both to terrorise the villagers and neighbouring camp people, in a way that might recall Foucault's evocation at the beginning of *Discipline and Punish* of punishment as exemplary spectacle and warning, *and* to conceal evidence of what they had done? Burning of bodies was characteristic of the massacres that the colonisers of Indigenous Australia had perpetrated – the history of genocide and massacre conducted by the white *pioneers* the Light Horse were heir to.[22]

---

20 Gullett 1923: 788–789.
21 Gullett 1923: 788–791.
22 Cf Moses 2004, 2008.

Gullett also reveals, while sharing in it, the racism of the Light Horse towards the Indigenous Palestinians, a feature of coloniser attitudes that was strongly part of nineteenth century and especially rural Australian history; when Gullett says that 'the shouts of the troops' could be heard, did such shouting include ugly racist imprecations?

Surafend has become a source of unease even agony for those who fervently wish to see the Light Horse as deserving of the same honour and recognition as Gallipoli in Australian military and national history. Egregiously, the Light Horse as they killed and burned had gone from how they wished to perceive themselves, as victims of the Bedouin and British, to being dishonourable victimisers. The consequences were immediate. In searing memory of the soldiers there, General Allenby, as the British commander-in-chief of the Egyptian Expeditionary Force, told the assembled Light Horse that he once had admired them but he admired them no more; they had revealed themselves to be cold-blooded murderers. The soldiers felt that because of his anger over Surafend, Allenby in future years unfairly denied the Light Horse the battle honours and rewards they deserved, and in doing so was enacting on the whole Light Horse a form of collective punishment given that only a portion were involved.[23] (The Anzacs themselves, we might note, had enacted collective punishment on a whole village and nearby camp for the actions of one man.) In the writing of military history, there was from the beginning attempts to censor or minimise mention of Surafend. Lachlan Coleman reports that Gullett wrote to Bean protesting at Chauvel's attempts to censor what he was writing about Surafend, with Bean writing back that Gullett should tell the story for, if not, 'you would be concealing from Australians a truth'; it is of interest that Coleman says that the Light Horse used bayonets as well as clubs and picks.[24] DM Wyatt, a retired soldier and military historian, notes that in 1919 Brigadier General Cox, later a prominent federal parliamentarian, addressed the members of the 3rd Light Horse Regiment, which had been directly involved in Surafend, with the advice, 'We will speak of this incident no more', though, Wyatt adds, Surafend had lingered in the minds of surviving members of the regiment for the rest of their lives. Wyatt reveals that it had been suggested to him that he should not discuss Surafend.[25]

Surafend has long been referred to as an incident, the usual term for it in Australian military history. I suggest, however, that for Australian history the significance of the massacre and burning of the Indigenous Palestinian village and camp is as a displaced allegory of the settler colonisation of Indigenous Australia. A potent reason, that is, why information, discussion, and memory

23   Gullett 1923: 787–791; Jones 2007: 198; Coleman 2007: 62.
24   Coleman 2007: 62–63.
25   Wyatt 2006: 96–101.

have been so repressed is that Surafend questions heroic narratives both of the Australian Light Horse in Palestine and of white settlement in Australia. In even more far-reaching terms, Surafend is an allegory of all settler colonialism which, in Raphaël Lemkin's view, as I have contended elsewhere, necessarily involves genocide and massacre as a technique of genocide.[26]

For the Palestinians, the massacre was a harbinger of more massacres to come, of a tragic history.

Surafend, Gallipoli and Israel

One text that does not share the relegation of the Surafend massacre to an 'unfortunate incident', as Gullett had referred to it, is Paul Daley's *Beersheba: A Journey through Australia's Forgotten War* (2009). It is an engagingly personal exploration of the Australian Light Horse in Sinai and Palestine. A senior journalist, Daley begins his journey as an outsider to Australian military history, and this gives his text a certain detachment. Doubts and uncertainties fissure *Beersheba* between a positive narrative of the Light Horse and a counter narrative of alternative perspectives that erode the author's initial confidence; the result is a kind of perturbed polyphonic text of unresolved attitudes, of anxiety towards histories the author had set out to admire. Daley explains early on that, in comparison to Gallipoli, he had barely heard of the Charge of Beersheba, but once he began his research into it he wanted to challenge the 'Gallipoli-centric Anzac story'. He also confesses that he had never heard of Surafend, until, as part of his research, he goes to interview (in 'benign Australian suburbia') Chanan Reich, an 'Israeli academic who specialises in relations between his country and Australia'. They talk about Beersheba for a while, and then the Israeli academic suddenly asks Daley, does he know about the massacre by the Australians. With that question, Daley says, his story was set on a different course.[27] Now he will wonder how the 'myth and legend' of the Australian Light Horse can be reconciled with a 'shameful' act of 'extreme cowardice and premeditated violence'?[28] He will ponder if it is because of this massacre that the Charge of Beersheba, once considered a famous military victory, the last great cavalry charge in history, barely features in popular Australian mythology, in contrast to Gallipoli, a military defeat.[29]

---

26 Cf Docker 2008b: 81–101.
27 Daley 2009: 1–7.
28 Daley 2009: 8.
29 Excerpts from *Beersheba* appeared in the *Sydney Morning Herald*, 25 July 2009, Good Weekend section, entitled 'One Bloody Secret'. In the Good Weekend's letters page of 15 August 2009, Caroline Graham, a keen student of the Australian Light Horse in the Middle East, wrote: 'My great-uncle was in the Australian Light Horse and I have much admiration for the troops' courage. But Paul Daley is right in "One Bloody Secret" (July 25): raising topics such as the Surafend massacre is "uncomfortable". I presented my own research on the Light Horse at a conference in 1987, mentioning Surafend and other misdeeds, such as the burning of villages

His research into Surafend presents Daley with disturbing questions about the massacre and the conduct of the Light Horse in Palestine, which he explores in the last third or so of the book, not least the 'premeditated nature of the crime' and the 'lingering cover-up' that ensued for decades afterwards. Daley is appalled by the way the Australians covered for each other after the massacre, denying to the military courts of enquiry that any of them were there, and 'comprehensively' blaming the New Zealanders in a 'breathtaking and farcical' way. The most remarkable and unsettling perspective about the behavior of the Light Horse comes when Daley listens to the tape of an interview between the army historian Doug Wyatt, referred to above, and trooper Harold 'Ted' O'Brien, of the 3rd Light Horse Regiment's C Squadron, which had comprised mainly men from Tasmania. Even though Wyatt had not asked him. O'Brien, now a very old man, suddenly begins very agitatedly to talk about Surafend.[30]

O'Brien admits to being there during the massacre, that he was a perpetrator, with tortured memories of the extreme brutality of war. After the New Zealand sergeant was killed by a Bedouin, the old soldier relates, the New Zealanders and Australians went out to the village and 'went through it with a bayonet'. Wyatt asks O'Brien if the Tasmanian Light Horse were involved: 'Oh yes. Our squadron was there. I was down there. I don't know what I did with it, I was cranky and that. But they had a good issue of rum and they did their blocks', O'Brien repeats, reminding us of Ray Evans' observations about massacre perpetrators in the colonisation of Australia, 'Yeah, I was there, but I don't know if I did anything like that'. Wyatt asks what did the Light Horse, who had drunk rum and where 'everyone did their block', actually do in Surafend? O'Brien tells him that there were cows, ducks, geese, and 'kids' there, but the Light Horse 'all went for the men with the bayonet and they got it'.[31]

At the very least, then, as often occurs in massacres, the children were forced to watch their fathers and male relatives being murdered. Were any women there, a question that interests Wyatt: 'The women then moved out, I suppose?' O'Brien replies, rather mystifyingly: 'There were some left. And they trekked out. They left their village and they went away. It was a bad thing. It was a real bad thing.'[32] If there were women there, as well as kids, did they too have to watch their husbands, brothers, uncles and sons over a certain age, being killed by the New Zealanders and Australians who had lost their blocks?

---

in post-war Egypt. My paper was attacked in the press back then; I hope Paul Daley gets a better reception. It's just that up till now we have avoided unpalatable truths.' Caroline Graham, 'One Bloody Secret', Good Weekend, *Sydney Morning Herald*, 15 August 2009.

30   Daley 2009: 252, 267, 270, 273.

31   Daley 2009: 274–276.

32   Daley 2009: 276.

O'Brien also tells Wyatt how much the Light Horse disliked the 'wicked' Bedouins. Because the Light Horse did not know what side the Bedouin were on, they were 'treated as enemies', and so, 'You'd shoot them on sight.'[33]

As well as Surafend, O'Brien reveals other horrific memories, of behaviour including his own that he now thinks was 'ungodly'. In particular he describes the time when he stabbed a dying Turkish soldier in the stomach so that he could rob him when dead: 'we used to go through them – you know. ... we was going to rob the dead sort of business'. O'Brien relates in detail how he and his mates looted coins from the dead and also used Turkish bodies for target practice: 'We used to pot-shot them and you would see them up like that and they'd bounce. Oh, dear, it was a bit of sport'.[34]

A final observation. In *Beersheba* the author travels back and forth between Australia and Israel, the Beersheba battle field being near the modern Israeli city of Be'er Sheva in the Negev. In Israel, Daley meets Israelis who celebrate the Light Horse charge at Beersheba in 1917 because in their view it paved the way for the British Mandate, which enabled mass Jewish immigration and Zionist political and military organisation, and then the 1948 War of Independence and the founding of the Jewish state. He also meets Christian fundamentalists like Kelvin Crombie, an Australian who believes that the Light Horse's victory has prepared the way for the return of the Messiah to the holy land, and who has for many years conducted guided tours of the Light Horse scene of heroism.[35]

What Daley's book does not explore is an idea suggested by his inquiries and experiences, that there is an affinity between Australia and Israel as two settler colonial societies with an inevitable history of massacre of their indigenous peoples. *Beersheba* reveals no awareness – here is a limit to its polyphony – of the work of Israeli New Historians such as Ilan Pappé, who in his groundbreaking *The Ethnic Cleansing of Palestine* (2006), evokes how much of the ethnic cleansing of 1948, that which the Palestinians refer to as the Nakba, the disaster, was done by massacre, including the massacre of a village, Dawaymeh, near Beersheba.[36]

---

33 Daley 2009: 275.
34 Daley 2009: 274–276.
35 Daley 2009: 192–193. Cf Crombie 1998: 368: 'Perhaps in fact those Jewish and Christian Bible-believing people have been right. Perhaps the return of the Jewish people to the Land of Israel, and more specifically to Jerusalem, may lead to the final conflict of the ages and be a prelude to the coming, or return of the Messiah.'
36 Pappé 2006: 195–197, also refers readers to 'The Dawaymeh Massacre', the report by the UN's Palestine Conciliation Commission of 14 June 1949, now accessible on the Internet, which observes that the massacre was, in many respects, 'more brutal than the Deir Yassin massacre'. In the *Sydney Morning Herald*, 14 November 2009, Good Weekend, p. 38, a Palestinian-Australian, Rihab Charida, refers to how, in 1948, when her father was nine, his Palestinian village, Safsaf, was assaulted by Zionist forces, her father witnessing 'a massacre where men from the village were lined up and shot.' Rihab Charida refers to the diaries of an Israeli officer, Yosef Nahmani, who wrote that 50–60 villagers were shot and several women raped. She also tells of a trip in 2004 where she hired a car and drove to the village; Rihab rang her father on her mobile phone, and when

When asked about the women at Surafend, Ted O'Brien had said, 'There were some left. And they trekked out. They left their village and they went away.' We can pause to wonder if any of the women who were survivors of the massacre at Surafend made their way to the village of Dawaymeh, thence to experience the horror of mass killing for a second time.

A surrogate massacre: *Wake in Fright*

'Hey, the Americans killed every buffalo in the country and almost wiped out every Indian tribe' ('*Wake in Fright*: An Interview with Ted Kotcheff', 27 May 2009)[37]

Let us glance at the now notorious kangaroo massacre scene in *Wake in Fright*, set in a fictional Australian outback town and its red earth surrounds. Its director a Canadian who has spent most of his working life in London, *Wake in Fright* is a coruscatingly brilliant film, a profoundly unsettling study of Australian male society of the late 1960s (it was shot in 1969, much of it in Broken Hill). The film explores the ironic possibilities of the *Bildungsroman*, a study of disintegration where the chief character, John Grant (Gary Bond), an emblematic figure of the intellectual as outsider, learns how desperately much he wants to be an insider, to become part of the embrace of homosociality. The unnerving intensity of *Wake in Fright* inheres in its unstable generic elements, in particular social realism mixing with the poetics of excess of baroque. Walter Benjamin, discussing in *The Origin of German Tragic Drama* the Baroque theatre, literature and art of the seventeenth century, suggests that baroque reveals an agonising violence of style, an eccentric mode that revels in its own visuality and theatricality, in extravagance and exaggeration; its spectacles create a characteristic feeling of vertigo. Benjamin likens baroque to early twentieth-century German Expressionism.[38]

Briefly, *Wake in Fright* creates a world where John Grant, middle-class, well spoken in an educated almost 'English' voice, bookish, chooses to gamble with all his pay, at an all male two-up game, hoping if he wins to return to the city and be released from his teaching bond with the Education Department. He loses almost all his money, and by the end of the film owns little but his city suit, now dusty and ragged, and a rifle. While Grant occasionally sarcastically protests against the pressures to conformity in the working class culture he is invited to join, it becomes clear that he also desires it. Once the men realise he wishes to

---

she began to evoke the surrounding hill and mountains, he interrupted his daughter and described the rest of the scene as he remembered it. 'At least', Rihab's father said, 'my voice has made it home.' Concerning the massacre of Safsaf, see Pappé 2006: 184–185.

37 Kotcheff 2009. In the interview, Kotcheff says: 'I'm Canadian and Canada has the same British colonial background as Australia'.

38 Benjamin 1996: 49–51, 54–56; Docker 2001: 191, 218.

be part of them, they are indeed friendly and welcoming. We see Grant at every step enjoying a masculinist desire to be drawn into exclusive company with other men, gambling and drinking beer, indeed drinking, drinking, drinking. The men drink beer in the all-male hotel bars, at parties, on trains, anywhere they can. Like his new mates, Grant now becomes completely indifferent to the women of the outback, including Janette, the young woman at a party who invites him to take a walk and make love, in a bizarrely passive and joyless way; but Grant, having imbibed for hours with the men at the party, is too drunk and vomits nearby. Women, we see, are to be ignored because they interrupt male sociality, they draw men away from the group, they might divide men. There is, however, no male violence towards women, indeed the men reveal no interest in them in any way, they are regarded as powerless and irrelevant, and the women, leading separate lives, like Janette or two young women in a hotel foyer, appear insuperably bored.

There is, nevertheless, a great deal of violence in *Wake in Fright*, either enacted or implied. As a kind of rite of passage into their world, a group of men he gets to know at the party where he fails Janette, invites Grant to drive with them into the bush for a kangaroo shoot. Interpreted through the settler-colonial focus of massacre studies, they wish to kill an Indigenous animal perceived by the settlers as vermin, a competitor for their introduced plant-eating animals. At this point, Grant's membership of male society is strengthened by his being given a gun by one of the kangaroo shooters. The group includes the miners Dick (Jack Thompson) and Joe (Peter Whittle) as well as Doc Tydon (Donald Pleasance), who has given up medicine for his ruling passion, beer. The graphic joyful slaughter, very hard to watch, culminates in Grant being set a final test of membership, to kill a kangaroo by hand with a knife; reluctant at first, because he sees it is very young and already injured, he launches into a frenzied stabbing and mutilation. After the kangaroo hunt, the men drive back to an old hotel, shoot it up with their rifles, drink beer till they are ecstatically awash with it, fight and embrace each other, while the ex-doctor stands on his head and pours beer into his mouth. Beer becomes like the fabled inland sea, an alternative to the coastal waters next to which city people exist. Grant in the film dreams for a moment of being at Bondi with his city girlfriend Robyn. In this dream-memory, Robyn is confident, strong, active, looking down on a prone John Grant lying on the beach, a powerful Aphrodite figure rising from the waves. The city is associated with water as a principle of female vitality. The outback is associated with beer as a kind of water surrogate, flowing over the men's faces, hair, clothes, bodies. It is also associated with guns, Grant keeping his rifle, to be treasured as iconic of his membership of the male group, in his suitcase. The Doctor is also an emblematic figure who, standing on his head drinking, inverts all his education and training, as might in the future happen with the

Teacher; they are drawn to each other as minds on the edge of nothingness. The kangaroo massacre culminates in what Kotcheff in interview refers to as Doc Tydon's sexual assault of Grant.

In *Wake in Fright* the kangaroo massacre is, in my view, a surrogate for the actual historical massacres of Australia's Indigenous peoples, leaving the hauntingly empty landscape that we see at the beginning and end of the film. I should make it clear that I am not arguing that killing kangaroos as such, for example for food, is wrong. What I am suggesting is that the white men's erotic delight in slaughtering the kangaroos recalls the genocide and massacre studies historian Dan Stone's theories of collective effervescence in mass killing, an enjoyment of violence and the theatre of violence, the perpetrators experiencing a heightened sense of belonging to their own group.[39] In general in the film, the male group works by a hierarchy of racial inequality. The group is not composed solely of Anglo men, there are European migrant men as well, that is, there is a kind of inclusive coloniser cosmopolitanism at work, where hospitality and group membership are extended to an Englishman like Doc Tydon or white males from Europe.[40] Clearly lower in the male hierarchy, however, is the Chinese cook called 'Chink' we glimpse for a moment in the café, preparing meals for the gamblers whose faces are studies in rapt concentration. We also do see Indigenous characters, a child in the school at the beginning, a man on a pub verandah, though they have no speaking parts. There is, however, a key scene on a train. Near Grant is an old Indigenous man, sitting alone, who looks out the window at the empty landscape and begins to sing a melancholy song. Here Grant, the educated outsider, could have kept the company of another outsider.[41] But then a festive group of white men also in the carriage throw Grant a beer, he catches it and joins them. He immediately gives in to their ressentiment, their desire to accept him only if he is like them and does what they do, because – he now knows of himself – his keenest desire is not to be perceived as an outsider or be an outsider. The solitary old Indigenous man sings quietly mournfully on, in a train passing by a landscape which once his ancestors had peopled as their cosmos.[42]

Wake in Fright appeared in 1971 during a late 1960s, early 1970s time when conventional viewpoints, and modes of masculinity and femininity, in Australian

---

39   Stone 2004: 45–65; Stone 2006: 211.

40   Concerning coloniser cosmopolitanism in relation to hospitality, see Waswo 1997: 138, 140–148; Docker 2008a: 170–171, 183, 218.

41   Kotcheff 2009 relates that 'the point of having the Aboriginal person is that he, too, is felt to be outside the community, and so there is identification between the two. That both are outsiders was the point I was trying to make.'

42   Ashenden recalls a similar moment in *The Overlanders* (1946), directed for Ealing Studios by the British director Harry Watt. An Aboriginal stockman is heard chanting; asked what he is singing about, the film's heroine Mary Parsons replies: 'About the time these people owned the land probably. When they were happy.' Ashenden 2008: 2–3.

society were being challenged with the rise of the New Left, the counter culture, Indigenous-led activism and critiques of racial discrimination. An intellectual culture and new histories arose that were sharply critical of received attitudes towards women, gender, sexuality, Indigenous dispossession, anti-Asian racism, and the sending by governments of Australian troops to support imperial wars like the American war in Vietnam.[43] John Grant, the intellectual in the outback, chose to succumb to conformity, while the alternative intellectual cultures gaining in analytic strength and theoretical sophistication chose to be like the cultural figure in Georg Simmel's famous essay 'The Stranger', outside and inside their society at the same time.[44]

A massacre averted: Baz Luhrmann's *Australia*

It is, I think, precisely the new intellectual culture of the 1960s and beyond, challenging Australian settler colonialism as a project of nationalism and racism, that influences Baz Luhrmann's *Australia*. The film is, as we would expect from Luhrmann, a kind of postmodern extravaganza. In its poetics of excess, it is always drawing attention to its own theatricality, of parody and self-parody. It is also highly allusive and intertextual, including, as a kind of choric refrain, references to scenes and a tune ('Somewhere over the Rainbow') from *The Wizard of Oz*, which came out in 1939, the year when the film's actions begin. As in *Wake in Fright*, characters are emblematic figures rather than psychological portraits. The film reveals almost a surplus of mixed generic elements. Its establishing phases draw on burlesque and vaudeville, visible especially in Nicole Kidman's mode of acting, when her character, Lady Ashley, owner of Faraway Downs a cattle station in central Australia, arrives in the outback. She is a female version of a New Chum, an upper class English person to be made fun of by hardened locals, including he whom she will engage in a conflictual romance with, the Drover (Hugh Jackman). Towards the end of the film, there is transformation and metamorphosis. The final sequence of scenes are set in Darwin and on a church-run island mission nearby, to which are sent abducted Indigenous children, including Nullah (Brandon Walters), the 12-year-old Indigenous boy who is a hero of the film. Now mock epic and mock romance move into epic with its war scenography, and melodrama where characters represent extremes and undergo extremes.[45]

Let us quickly create a conversation between *Wake in Fright* and *Australia*. Each presents itself as a kind of parable, a creation story, yet *Australia*, coming out nearly four decades later, questions and inverts many of the patterns and attitudes of the earlier film, especially in terms of 'race' and also gender.

---

43   Cf Docker 1988: 289–307.
44   Wolff 1950: 402–408; Docker 2001: 86–87, 125.
45   Cf Docker 1994: 252; Brooks 1976: 4, 35, 54.

Where in *Wake in Fright* the white male community is the centre of the film's actions and observations, and Indigenous people and non-Indigenous women are marginalised (I cannot recall any sighting of Indigenous women in *Wake in Fright*), in *Australia*, the reverse occurs. The film begins with Nullah as narrator explaining that the 'white fellas' say he is a 'half caste', and that if he is caught by the police he will be taken away to the mission island near Darwin, highlighting the plight of the Stolen Generations as central to Australian history. Nullah's father is the villainous Fletcher (David Wenham), who wishes to usurp Faraway Downs for himself, and refuses to acknowledge Nullah as his son: much later in the film, Lady Ashley, at an upper class ball held in Darwin to raise funds for the taking of children to the mission island, publicly draws attention to the refusal of white fathers to acknowledge their paternity, scandalising the upper class women there.[46] Never far away from Nullah is his grandfather, King George (David Gulpilil), a kind of choric commentator and spiritual guide whose Indigenous language is translated in sub-titles. In terms of gender, Lady Ashley as English aristocrat and owner of a huge cattle station is at the centre of the film, an elite woman with considerable power to widen the possibilities of what women can do. After Nullah's mother drowns while trying to keep him concealed from the police who have come to take him away, Lady Ashley becomes increasingly maternal in her regard for him. For quite a while in the movie, however, she insists, against the advice of the Drover, that Nullah cannot leave her and Faraway Downs and go with, as he wishes to, his grandfather into Arnhem Land to learn Indigenous cultural knowledge to do with country, ceremony and stories. 'You belong here', she says to Nullah, to the consternation of Drover, raising the general question of colonisation and belonging.

Lady Ashley's assimilationist desire here is an obstacle that strains her relationship with Drover. For his part, Drover has to overcome a legendary Australian male desire, that we glimpse in *Wake in Fright* in relation to the Teacher and Janette or the Teacher's apparent loss of interest in his city girlfriend, not to commit to relationships with women. We can recognise Drover as a cultural figure stepping intact out of the pages of Russel Ward's radical nationalist *The Australian Legend* (1958), which had famously contended that out on the western plains, far from Australia's coastal cities, a nomad tribe of (white) bush workers had developed a mystique formative for the nation as a whole, of egalitarianism, hospitality, mateship, independence, skepticism. Ward observed that the legendary Australian male was a rolling stone, without the impediment of family.[47] 'No man hires me, noone fires me', the Drover ritually insists, and he is only dissuaded from this legendary view by his Indigenous co-drover, brother

---

46 Cf Curthoys 2002: 109. Lady Ashley also scandalises the upper class women at the ball by wearing a red cheongsam, perhaps a reference to Tracey Moffatt's famous haunting image of a woman in a Chinese red dress.
47 Ward 1966[1958]: 1–2, 13, 254–255; Docker 1984: 15–16, 36, 119.

in law and friend, Magarri (David Ngoombujarra). The Drover has fought in World War I, but when he returns he learns his Indigenous wife, Magarri's sister, had died, since no white hospital (in a possible allusion for American audiences to what happened to Billie Holiday) had been willing to accept her as a patient. Magarri, perhaps upholding Indigenous values stressing kinship, family and relationships, upbraids the Drover for insisting on his independence when he clearly loves Lady Ashley. The Drover is alienated from his fellow white drovers because he mainly keeps the company of his Indigenous relatives and friends; as he says, the other white drovers see him as black, and he in turn detests their ugly racism and their support for discriminatory practices like Indigenous people being refused service in hotel bars. Here, in his anti-racism, is the Drover's difference from Russel Ward's legendary figure.

In this conversation between *Wake in Fright* and *Australia*, then, a major difference is clear: in *Wake in Fright*, the men in the outback town form a closed androcentric community which excludes white women and Indigenous people. In *Australia*, it is *les autres*, *les étrangers*, Indigenous and non-Indigenous, male and female – Nullah, King George, Drover, Magaree, Nullah's female relatives including Bandy, Lady Ashley – drawn together in their desire to save Nullah from being captured by the police, who form an alternative community to conventional white coloniser society. Also, the heroism we associate with epic is distributed across and amongst all of those in this alternative community, it certainly does not inhere only in the Drover. It is Nullah's supreme moment of heroism that I focus on here, reprising motifs of massacre studies. Recall that King Carney the cattle baron has ordered his employee Fletcher, a pure melodrama principle of evil, and some of his drovers, those who despise the Drover for being too friendly with Indigenous people, to prevent Faraway Down's cattle being delivered to Darwin. They attempt to do this by poisoning water holes and by fire, frightening the cattle into stampeding towards the edge of a precipice. Nullah, at the edge of the cliff, using Indigenous powers taught him by his grandfather, who is nearby, sings the cattle into quietness and submission, averting their mass death. Nullah's foot, however, nearly slips, for a frightening moment we think he might fall and die. It is difficult, watching these scenes, not to think that there is an allusion to a well-known and distressing feature of massacres of Indigenous groups in Australian history, often involving in memory and story their being driven over cliffs, with perhaps the only survivor a child, to be taken away by the coloniser massacrists. When Nullah averts the massacre of cattle and is embraced as a hero by those who admire and love him, including a Madonna and child scene with Lady Ashleigh, a kind of *pietà*, there is perhaps a surrogate wish fulfillment that the long history of massacres of Indigenous peoples, often at the edge of cliffs, did not (have to) happen. More generally, the suggestion in the film is that the history of extreme violence against the continent's Indigenous peoples would not have happened if the European colonisers had had the attitudes the good white characters in the film now possess.[48]

In *Wake in Fright*, the animals massacred had been kangaroos, an Indigenous herbivore and a competitor to animals such as cattle brought in by the colonisers in an act of ecological genocide. In *Australia*, Nullah saves cattle, in a kind of utopian vision where pro-Indigenous Australians and Indigenous Australians come together in a common effort that includes a settler-colonial pastoral economy that has replaced the Indigenous economy and its relationships to land. However, by film's end, Lady Ashley agrees that Nullah should go with his grandfather to Arnhem Land to learn vital cultural knowledge. The film, that is, does not try to reconcile a depressing contradiction between loss of economy and cultural continuity. While the genocidal loss of Indigenous economy, it would appear, has to be historically accepted, the continuance of Indigenous cultural knowledge is now valued as profoundly important. Yet, we might think, how can there be continuity when there is no economic basis sustaining it? (Here we might think of scenes of desolation and boredom in a remote town in Central Australia in Warwick Thornton's superb *Samson and Delilah*, released in 2009.)

However, when in *Australia* Darwin and the nearby mission island are attacked by invading Japanese, the stolen children and the largely white Australian society created in the film become common victims, with fires burning in the town as well as on the ships in the harbour. Sympathy that had ebbed away from the socially conventional white characters in relation to Indigenous people can now return as they share suffering and death.

In this aspect, the film ends on a note more in tune with the legend of Gallipoli, of Australians as a whole as victims, a perpetrator society that, mythologically, is not a perpetrator society.

References

Ashenden, Dean 2008, 'Luhrmann, us, and them', *Inside Story*, 18 December 2008: 1–5.

Benjamin, Walter 1996, *The Origin of German Tragic Drama*, John Osborne (trans), Verso, London.

---

48 Garry Maddox, 'Luhrmann's happy ending to an Australian story', *Sydney Morning Herald*, Weekend Edition, 8–9 August 2009, relates that before casting Walters as Nullah in the film, Luhrmann visited the family in their Kimberley homeland; he was invited back for the handover in June 2009 of native title to almost 40,000 square kilometres of land to the Nyangumarta community, which includes the family of Brandon Walters.

Brody, Hugh 2002, *The Other Side of Eden: Hunter-Gatherers, Farmers, and the Shaping of the World*, Faber and Faber, London.

Brooks, Peter 1976, *The Melodramatic Imagination: Balzac, Henry James, Melodrama, and the Mode of Excess*, Yale University Press, New Haven.

Coates, Peter 1999, '"Unusually cunning, vicious and treacherous": the extermination of the wolf in United States history', in *The Massacre in History*, Mark Levene and Penny Roberts (eds), Berghahn Books, New York: 163–183.

Coleman, Lachlan 2007, 'The Surafend Incident: not all of the ANZAC story is laudable', *Wartime: Official Magazine of the Australian War Memorial* 39: 62–63.

Crombie, Kelvin 1998, *Anzacs, Empires and Israel's Restoration 1798–1948*, Vocational Education and Training Publications, Perth.

Curthoys, Ann 1999, 'Expulsion, exodus, and exile in white Australian historical mythology', in *Imaginary Homelands: The Dubious Cartographies of Australian Identity*, Richard Nile and Michael Williams (eds), University of Queensland Press, Brisbane: 1–18.

— 2002, *Freedom Ride: A Freedom Rider Remembers*, Allen & Unwin, Sydney.

Daley, Paul 2009, *Beersheba: A Journey through Australia's Forgotten War*, Melbourne University Press, Melbourne.

Diamond, Jared 1992, *The Rise and Fall of the Third Chimpanzee*, Vintage, London.

Docker, John 1984, *In a Critical Condition*, Penguin Books, Melbourne.

— 1988, ' "Those halcyon days": the moment of the New Left', in *Intellectual Movements and Australian Society*, Brian Head and James Walter (eds), Oxford University Press, Melbourne: 289–307.

— 1994, *Postmodernism and Popular Culture: A Cultural History*, Cambridge University Press, Melbourne.

— 2001, *1492: The Poetics of Diaspora*, Continuum, London.

— 2008a, *The Origins of Violence: Religion, History and Genocide*, Pluto, London.

— 2008b, 'Are settler-colonies inherently genocidal? Re-reading Lemkin', in *Empire, Colony, Genocide: Conquest, Occupation, and Subaltern Resistance in World History*, A Dirk Moses (ed), Berghahn, New York: 81–101.

— 2010, 'The origins of massacres', in *Theatres of Violence: Massacre, Mass Killing, and Atrocity in History*, Philip Dwyer and Lyndall Ryan (eds), Berghahn Books, New York: in prep.

Dorrian, Mark 2001, 'On some spatial aspects of the colonial discourse on Ireland', *The Journal of Architecture* 6: 27–51.

Doumani, Beshara B 1999, 'Rediscovering Ottoman Palestine: writing Palestinians into history', in *The Israel/Palestine Question*, Ilan Pappé (ed), Routledge, London: 11–40.

Greengrass, Mark, 1999, 'Hidden transcripts: secret histories and personal testimonies of religious violence in the French wars of religion', in Mark Levene and Penny Roberts (eds), *The Massacre in History*, Berghahn Books, New York: 69–88.

Gullett, HS 1923, *The Australian Imperial Force in Sinai and Palestine 1914–1918*, Angus and Robertson, Sydney.

— and Chas Barrett (eds) 1919, *Australia in Palestine*, Angus and Robertson, Sydney.

Hill, AJ 1978, *Chauvel of the Light Horse: A Biography of General Sir Harry Chauvel, G.C.M.G., K.C.B.*, Melbourne University Press, Melbourne.

Jones, Ian 2007, *A Thousand Miles of Battles: The Saga of the Australian Light Horse in WWI*, ANZAC Day Commemoration Committee, Queensland.

Khan, Yasmin 2007, *The Great Partition: The Making of India and Pakistan*, Yale University Press, New Haven.

Kotcheff, Ted 2009, '*Wake in Fright*: An interview with Raffaele Caputo', *Senses of Cinema*, online journal, no 51, <www.sensesofcinema.com/2009/featur-articles/ted-kotcheff-interview/>

Lambert, David, and Alan Lester (eds) 2006, *Colonial Lives Across the British Empire: Imperial Careering in the Long Nineteenth Century*, Cambridge University Press, Cambridge.

Lawrence, TE 1927, *Revolt in the Desert*, Jonathan Cape, London.

— 1935[1926], *Seven Pillars of Wisdom*, Doubleday, Doran and Co, New York.

Lemkin, Raphaël 1944, *Axis Rule in Occupied Europe: Laws of Occupation, Analysis of Government, Proposals for Redress*, Columbia University Press, New York.

Levene, Mark 1999, 'Introduction', in *The Massacre in History*, Mark Levene and Penny Roberts (eds), Berghahn Books, New York: 1–38.

— and Penny Roberts (eds) 1999, *The Massacre in History*, Berghahn Books, New York.

McKenna, Mark 2002, *Looking for Blackfellas' Point: an Australian History of Place*, University of New South Wales Press, Sydney.

Moses, A Dirk (ed) 2004, *Genocide and Settler Society: Frontier Violence and Stolen Indigenous Children in Australian History*, Berghahn, New York.

— (ed) 2008, *Empire, Colony, Genocide: Conquest, Occupation, and Subaltern Resistance in World History*, Berghahn, New York.

Pandey, Gyanendra 2001, *Remembering Partition: Violence, Nationalism and History in India*, Cambridge University Press, Cambridge.

Pappé, Ilan (ed) 1999, *The Israel/Palestine Question*, Routledge, London.

— 2004, *A History of Modern Palestine: One Land, Two Peoples*, Cambridge University Press, Cambridge.

— 2006, *The Ethnic Cleansing of Palestine*, Oneworld, Oxford.

Perry, Roland 2009, *The Australian Light Horse*, Hachette Australia, Sydney.

Semelin, Jacques 2003, 'Towards a vocabulary of massacre and genocide', *Journal of Genocide Research* 5.

Shohat, Ella 1988, 'Sephardim in Israel: Zionism from the standpoint of its Jewish Victims', *Social Text* 19/20, Autumn: 1–35.

— 1992, 'Antinomies of exile: Said at the frontiers of national narrations', in *Edward Said: A Critical Reader*, Michael Sprinker (ed), Blackwell, Oxford: 121–143.

— 2006, *Taboo Memories, Diasporic Voices*, Duke University Press, Durham.

Stone, Dan 2004, 'Genocide as transgression', *European Journal of Social Theory* 7: 45–65.

— 2006, *History, Memory and Mass Atrocity: Essays on the Holocaust and Genocide*, Vallentine Mitchell, London.

Ward, Russel 1966[1958], *The Australian Legend*, Oxford University Press, Melbourne.

Waswo, Richard 1997, *The Founding Legend of Western Civilization: From Virgil to Vietnam*, Wesleyan University Press, Hanover.

Wolff, Kurt H (ed and trans) 1950, *The Sociology of Georg Simmel*, The Free Press, Glencoe, IL.

Wyatt, DM 2006, 'The Surafend Incident', in *Tasmania's A.I.F. Lighthorsemen*, Peter James Pickering (ed), Self-published, Hobart: 96–101.

Part two: myths

4. Remembering the referendum with compassion

FRANCES PETERS-LITTLE

History is a bit like water; eventually it will find its own level.

Paul Keating, former Prime Minister of Australia[1]

In May 1967, Australian voters were asked to vote in a referendum to determine whether two references in the Australian Constitution, which discriminated against Aboriginal people, should be removed.[2] The first reference was section 51, which stated that:

> The Parliament shall, have the power to make laws for the peace, order, and good government of the Commonwealth with respect to, clause xxvi, that the people of any race, other than the Aboriginal people in any State, for whom it is necessary to make special laws.

The second was section 127, which stated that:

> In reckoning the numbers of the people of the Commonwealth, or of a State or other part of the Commonwealth, Aboriginal natives should not be counted.

When the votes were counted, up to 90.7 per cent of Australians voted 'Yes' in favour of removing the words, *'other than the aboriginal people in any State'* in section 51(xxvi) and the whole of section 127.[3] It was the highest ever recorded in a federal referendum. Australians were obviously feeling compassionate.

It is now over 40 years since the Referendum, and it appears many historians remain undecided whether the amendments made to the Australian constitution

---

1   Hon Paul Keating interviewed by Frances Peters-Little for the *Vote Yes for Aborigines* documentary film, Sydney, 2006. The quote comes from the reply he gave me when I asked him 'Do politicians care about history?'

2   National Australian Archives, fact sheet, accessed 8 December 2009: <http://www.naa.gov.au/about-us/publications/fact-sheets/fs150.aspx>

3   89.43 per cent of Australian voters voted Yes, however the figure often quoted is 90.77 per cent, but this figure excludes the 1.58 per cent of votes that were informal, cited in Williams 2000: 28.

authorised by the Referendum were a complete waste of effort or indicated a stroke of genius by the campaigners. While some are convinced the Referendum brought about the necessary changes needed to liberate Aborigines from years of disenfranchisement and discrimination others insist the campaign did very little to change the political climate for Aborigines but instead left behind a trail of 'myths'.[4] The main purpose of this paper is to discuss 'myths' (if myths they be) that have long been associated with the Referendum. The other purpose is 'not' to argue how effective the 1967 Referendum was, but to demonstrate why I think those who have a compassionate view of the 1967 Referendum are no less accurate in their representation of Aboriginal history than those who do not. To illustrate this point I will be referring to *Vote yes for Aborigines*[5] a documentary film I wrote and directed in conjunction with SBS TV commemorating the 40th anniversary of the referendum as a part of the *Unsettling Histories* project.[6]

Unsettling histories

Having a compassionate and open mind for Indigenous storytelling was a key component in the *Unsettling Histories* project. As an Aboriginal historian, I have always been interested in collecting oral histories and sharing those stories in a number of ways, visually and aurally, that can be told and communicated by Aboriginal people. It was while working on the project with historian Ann McGrath from the Australian National University (ANU), and Margo Neale a senior curator from the National Museum of Australia (NMA), I came across a quote by American historian Peter Nabokov who wrote about Native American history that 'history was too important to be left to historians alone'.[7] Since beginning the project I have referred to the Nabokov expression several times but I am yet to cite the original quote which I suspect is deeply rooted somewhere in European history.[8] The suggestion that history was too important

---

4   Main proponents of the idea that the referendum brought about a monumental change to grant Aborigines new rights and freedoms are historians Jennifer Clark, Sue Taffe, Ann Curthoys, Gordon Briscoe and Jackie Huggins. Main opponents of the idea the referendum brought about a monumental change to grant Aborigines new rights and freedoms are Bain Attwood and Andrew Markus, Tim Rowse and John Gardiner-Garden.

5   *Vote Yes for Aborigines* is a 52-minute documentary film that revisits those involved with the 1967 Referendum and the social attitudes and influences that led to the event. *Vote Yes for Aborigines* went to air on SBS television on 27 May 2007.

6   The *Unsettling Histories* project was an Australian Research Council project that I had been a Chief Investigator with Ann McGrath and Margo Neale, from 2003 to 2007. Outcomes from the project were two films, a major photography exhibition and a publication.

7   Nabokov 2000: vi.

8   The term can also be cited in Jewish American Professor of Law and Legal Historian Eben Moglen's work on the *Making History: Israeli Law and Historical Reconstruction* who wrote 'just as war is too important to be left to the generals, history is too important to be left to the historians'. In this article, Moglen was paraphrasing a quote by former French Prime Minister George Clemenceau who said, 'war is too important to be left to the military'. Others who have used the term are Astronomer Donald Edward Osterbrock who titled his paper *The View from the Observatory: History is Too Important to be Left to the Historians*; and historians Sally Alexander, Raphael Samuels and Barbara Taylor in the 1970s.

to be left to historians alone struck a chord with me as an Aboriginal historian reminding me of just how much Aboriginal history, since colonisation, has gone unobserved, forgotten or perhaps distorted by historians.[9]

The *Unsettling Histories* project focused on the various modes of Aboriginal historical practice and explored other modes outside of the written text, from films, exhibitions, photography, Indigenous painting to map-making, song and poetry art forms to sporting events and so forth. Drawing from alternative sources to record our histories is something that Maori scholar Linda Smith, is very much in favour of and stresses, and rightly so, that 'very few indigenous people if any, would have a need to perceive, practice or teach history the same way as the coloniser'.[10] One of the outcomes of the *Unsettling Histories* project was the volume of essays called *Exchanging Histories*, which I co-edited with Ann McGrath and Ingereth Macfarlane. The *Exchanging Histories* volume commemorated the 30th edition of the journal *Aboriginal History*. Our intention was to bring together a collection that would 'investigate what the "history wars" was not, and that was to consider the ongoing practices of history-making and ideas about history by indigenous Australians'.[11] Other outcomes of the *Unsettling Histories* project were a series of public forums and university lecture series of the same name and three historical documentary films. One film was by McGrath called *A Frontier Conversation*[12] a 54-minute film that documents a unique collaboration between indigenous and white historians from Australia and North America, and I made the other two. The first of the films was called *Our Community*[13] a 30-minute documentary made in conjunction with a photographic exhibition[14] that shared the same title, and a one-hour documentary film called *Vote Yes for Aborigines*.

---

9   In his book *Doing Oral Histories* (2003) oral historian Donald Ritchie quoted Louis Gottschalk, in *Understanding History* who wrote 'The numbers of historical writings are staggering but only a small part of what happened in the past was observed; and only a part of what was observed was remembered by those who observed it. Only a part of what was remembered was recorded; only a part of what was recorded has survived; only a part of what has survived has come to historians' attention; only a part of what has come to their attention is credible; only a part of what is credible has been grasped and only a part of what has been grasped can be expounded or narrated by the historian.' Gottschalk 1950.

10   Smith 1999: 28–29.

11   Peters-Little et al 2006: v.

12   '*A Frontier Conversation* raises more questions than answers – from cultural appropriation and copyright, to land rights, the role of language and art, and what history means to Indigenous communities in the current climate of cultural reclamation and survival.' Synopsis by Ronin Films cited at Ronin Films website, accessed 8 December 2009: <http://www.roninfilms.com.au/feature/545.html>

13   '*Our Community* is a film that reveals that, despite the cultural diversity and the challenges before them, the people of the Walgett, Lightning Ridge and Sheepyard communities share a pride, passion, resilience and an inexorable spirit of 'belonging'. Throughout the film, past misconceptions about racial and economic divisions are clarified and benevolent bonds are celebrated.' Synopsis by Frances Peters-Little, cited at Ronin Films website, accessed 8 December 2009: <http://www.roninfilms.com.au/feature/516.html>

14   The *Our Community: A Great Place to Be* photographic exhibition was a joint project between The Australian National University's Australian Centre for Indigenous Histories, and the National Museum

At the time we were making our films, other ANU historians such as Donald Denoon, Brij Lal and Tessa Morris-Suzuki from the Research School of Pacific and Asian Studies shared the view with us that historians have much to learn from working with other mediums such as journalism and literature. Morris-Suzuki says much academic writing is 'essentially unreadable, which is a pity, because a lot of it has something interesting to say'.[15] Lal pointed out that 'People are interested in lives and in human stories, rather than in abstract theories, a notion that has been lost to academia in the past 20 or so years'[16] and both Denoon and Lal argue that while 'archival, documented history can be accurate it cannot always be *true* in the way that fiction can'.[17] Also suggesting that historians may need to find 'truth' using other mediums is American historian Hayden White. White says more historians may wish to 'engage in the language of film, for not only is it a legitimate discourse in its own right, but visual representations of history have their own genius in the realms of landscapes, scenes, atmosphere, and such representations are not just more verisimilar, but also more accurate'.[18]

Those involved with the *Unsettling Histories* project viewed the criticisms of our focus on filmmaking from some of our academic peers in the ANU as symptomatic of the prejudices that academics have against filmmakers in general. Historians often think that filmmakers are inclined to trivialise the past. Since making her film, which was her first, McGrath has challenged other historians on this issue, arguing that the fact they have been trained to deliver the results of their research only in text should not hinder them from recognising film as a genuine mode of historical practise and a major resource.[19]

Speaking as someone who has a documentary filmmaking background and became a historian later in life, I certainly object to the view that films are an inferior form of history making and believe films can be an extremely useful medium for historians to draw from and to engage with. One of the main reasons I enjoy making historical documentary films is because it is possible to interact directly with people on a one-to-one basis who can share their own stories, so that viewers get to hear another version of Aboriginal history and not just an

of Australia. It explores the concept of 'community' in multicultural rural Australia. Curated by Frances Peters-Little and Barbara Paulson, the exhibition toured regional New South Wales throughout 2005–2006. Photographers who participated in the exhibition were Sharon Aldrick, Ron Blake and Juno Gemes.

15   Morris-Suzuki 2004.

16   Lal 2004: 1–3.

17   Jan Borrie interview with Research School of Pacific and Asian Studies Professors Donald Denoon, Tessa Morris-Suzuki and Brij V Lal about their curious position as 'academics who write' – fiction, poetry and autobiography respectively, Canberra, March 2004, cited at: <http://rspas.anu.edu.au/qb/articleFile.php?searchterm=5-1-3>

18   White 1988 cited in Gunn 2006: 68.

19   McGrath 2009.

academic interpretation. Another reason I like making historical documentary films is that it allows for room for a personal, compassionate and emotional reading of the past.

As an Aboriginal filmmaker, I am optimistic about the future of Aboriginal filmmaking. Not only do I hope to see more Aboriginal filmmakers teaching Aboriginal history to a more visual and technologically savvy youth, I also look forward to seeing more Aboriginal filmmakers recordings of our history; a particularly important issue since there are still many more Aboriginal people who make films than there are Aboriginal historians. American anthropologists Faye Ginsburg and Fred Myers regard the effect Aboriginal artists and filmmakers have had on understandings of Australian history over the past two decades as immense. In their words, the impact

> Aboriginal filmmakers are making locally and overseas has already been significant and persistent, and that it is expanding despite the alarming political turn against gains made by indigenous Australians over the last decade, not only by right-wing politicians but intellectuals as well.[20]

Making *Vote Yes for Aborigines*

It was during the latter part of that particular decade (1997–2007) that Ginsburg and Myers refer to that I began writing the script for *Vote Yes for Aborigines*. John Howard, the then Prime Minister of Australia, was in the throes of putting together an Australian Citizenship Act, so it was a time I thought particularly fitting to be making a film about the history of Aboriginal citizenship.[21] The film revisits those involved with the 1967 Referendum and the social and political attitudes and influences that led to the event. While writing the script I envisaged bringing together the voices of historians and politicians with those of Aboriginal and non-Aboriginal people who were part of the referendum campaign. Bringing together such a diversity of voices is something that I feel is sadly lacking in too many history books.

The chosen participants included former Australian Prime Ministers, the Honourable Paul Keating from the Australian Labor Party and the Honourable Malcolm Fraser from the Liberal Party. Other politicians were the former Federal Minister for Aboriginal Affairs Fred Chaney from the coalition government and current Australian Labor Party member and descendant of the Bundjalung tribe, Warren Mundine. Historians interviewed were Gordon Briscoe, John Maynard

---

20   Ginsburg and Myers 2007.
21   The 'Act sets out how you become an Australian citizen, the circumstances in which you may cease to be a citizen and some other matters related to citizenship', quoted from Commonwealth Consolidated Acts. *Australian Citizenship Act 2007* – section 2a: <http://austlii.law.uts.edu.au/au/legis/cth/consol_act/aca2007254/s2a.html>

and Jackie Huggins, Bain Attwood, Ann Curthoys, Sue Taffe and Jennifer Clark. Others appearing in the film were those who had been involved with the 1967 Referendum campaign in one form or another such as Dulcie Flowers, Joyce Clague and Jimmy Little. Unfortunately, I had to edit out Jack Horner, Steve Larkin and Jon Altman because of technical problems and had to rely upon earlier footage of Faith Bandler whose husband Hans, was in serious ill health at the time we were shooting.[22]

The film opens with a voice-over of John Howard giving his speech on Australia Day in 2006. The words we hear from Howard are, 'Most nations experience some level of cultural diversity while also having a dominant cultural pattern running through them. In Australia's case, that dominant pattern comprises Judeo-Christian ethics, the progressive spirit of the Enlightenment and the institutions and values of British political culture. Its democratic and egalitarian temper also bears the imprint of distinct Irish and non-conformist traditions.' Howard's words set the tone of what to expect in the film. Then we cut to a number of vox-populis, asking people what they think it means to be an Australian citizen. The first response was from a group of Indian immigrants; one speaks and says, 'It must mean something, to be Australian; it must mean something.' An older white Australian male says, 'It's a lot of do with mateship.' A younger white male says, 'Yeah, it's good really. We are probably one of the luckiest countries in the world.' A 20ish couple, he is white and she is Asian, he says, 'I'm not really sure what it means to be an Australian.' She giggles. An older white woman says, 'I don't know.' A younger Aboriginal woman says, 'It's not really a question anybody really asks me, because we've been here for 40,000 years.' An older Aboriginal man says, 'Well I'm not an Australian citizen, I'm a citizen of the Wiradjuri nation.' And a very young Aboriginal boy with his face painted in ochre says 'I think about mostly the culture, and getting in and doing stuff.'

As difficult as it was for all my interviewees to find a definitive statement about what it meant to be an Australian citizen, they all agreed that a resoundingly high majority passed the 1967 Referendum. Where opinions begin to differ is on the question of whether the amendments made to the Constitution provided better outcomes for Aboriginal people. During the interviewing process it became clear that most of my interviewees were interested in discussing two main issues, Australian citizenship and the 'myths' of the referendum; in this chapter, I will focus on the latter.

---

22 Footage from Faith Bandler interview with Robyn Hughes, 1994 from the Australia Biography Series.

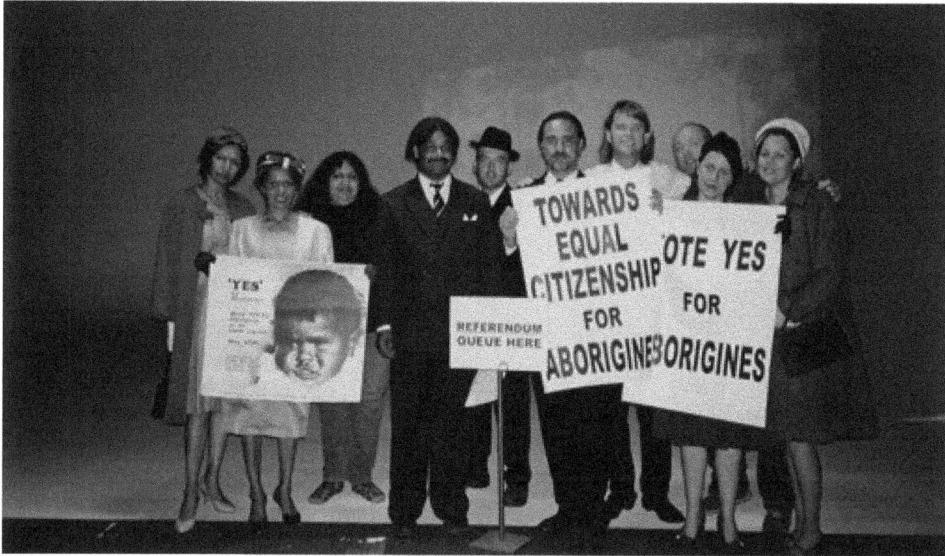

Fig 1. Cast and Crew for *Vote Yes for Aborigines*, Film Australia, September 2006 (From L-R Frances Williams, Esther Cohen, Frances Peters-Little, John Blair, Eman Ruggeri, Yani Demetriou, Sean Kennedy, Simeon Bryan, Cathy Payne, Suzy Ingram)

The 'myths'

While there are any number of hypotheses defining myths and/or mythologies, what I am referring to in this instance is the concept of 'myth' as an idea or a story that has been passed down from generation to generation that in time becomes thought of as fact or history.[23] Although the term 'myth' conjures up notions of speculation and fantasy to some extent, what I intend to do is state why I think some 'myths' are more truthful than others based on the lived-experiences and the knowledges of Aboriginal people. It is just one small step towards telling a more complete history about Aboriginal people and the 1967 Referendum. The most common 'myths' since 1967 that have been contested by scholars in recent years are as follows;

(1) that the referendum gave Aborigines the right to vote,
(2) that it allowed Aborigines to be counted in the census, and
(3) that it gave Aborigines citizenship.[24]

---

23   Roland Barthes is perhaps the most well known French literary theorist, philosopher and critic who has written extensively on the subject of mythologies in his works in his book *Mythologies*, published in 1957.
24   Other 'myths' associated with the 1967 Referendum include the idea that it brought about wage equality, social security and maternity allowance and that it gave the Commonwealth government the right to make laws for the benefit of Aborigines, however I will only be addressing points (1) to (3).

The right to vote

Proponents of the argument that the referendum did not give Aborigines the right to vote but that Aboriginal people already had that right are Bain Attwood and Andrew Markus. Attwood and Markus write 'Aboriginal people speak of the referendum in a way that scarcely has any historical verisimilitude', and have commented on a number of respected novelists, reputable historians and anthropologists who they say are mistaken.[25] Adding to their case is one of Australia's leading constitutional lawyers George Williams who makes the point that Aboriginal people were allowed to vote before the 1967 Referendum and says that although 'changes to the constitution have been popularly seen as granting indigenous people equal rights, and in particular the right to vote, this is not correct'.[26] Though Attwood, Markus and Williams are in theory accurate, I argue that the operative word here is the 'rights' to vote and that there were many factors preventing Aboriginal people from voting before 1967 that changed after the referendum.[27]

Overlooking crucial details affecting Aboriginal people's rights to vote in his research brief, author John Gardiner-Garden wrote 'technically male Aboriginals had the right to vote since colonial times and by 1895 Aboriginal women in South Australia shared the same right'.[28] He writes about polling booths stationed at Aboriginal reserves at Point McLeay and such, permitting Aboriginal men and women to vote in the first Commonwealth Parliament in 1901. Some of these rights were lost in the 1920s and 1930s, but by 1962, he argues, were returned when the Menzies-led Commonwealth government granted Aboriginal people the right to vote in Federal elections, which meant that all Aborigines living in Western Australia and Queensland could now vote. What is wrong with Gardiner-Garden's argument here is that he has assumed that because the Commonwealth government granted Aborigines voting rights, Aborigines thereby had complete liberty to vote at will, which of course is untrue. From Gardiner-Garden's perspective, one could easily be forgiven for thinking that Aborigines could freely make the choice to vote and that polling stations were accessible for Aborigines living in remote and rural regions, and that it was the responsibility of Aboriginal people to take full advantage of these rights.

In my interviews with several of the participants in my film, many offered clear accounts of how they and other Aboriginal people did not enjoy these 'rights' as

---

25   Attwood and Markus cite Tim Winton, Stuart McIntyre, Heather Goodall, Ann McGrath, Richard Broome and Barry Morris as some of the few who have misunderstood the results of the referendum.
26   Williams 2000: 28.
27   The changes are talked about by Joyce Clague and Jimmy Little who worked on a campaign to get Aborigines on the electoral roll after the 1967 Referendum.
28   Gardiner-Garden 2007.

such. Aboriginal historian John Maynard who had been writing the biography of his grandfather Fred Maynard, at the time I interviewed him, emphasised how difficult it was to get Aboriginal people to vote in New South Wales.[29] John Maynard said,

> Now we could vote in state elections, and most of us didn't know that, but my grandfather set out to inform Aboriginal people right throughout this state that they could vote. Now up on the north coast the Protection Board, certainly through the police, had hounded and harassed the Aboriginal activists of that particular period, they were under surveillance and threats were made against their own basically driving people like my grandfather and others who tried to encourage Aborigines to vote, to go underground.[30]

Aboriginal activist and member of the Federal Council for Australian Aborigines and Torres Strait Islanders (FCAATSI)[31] Joyce Clague stated that before she joined FCAATSI, encouraged by visiting activists like Jack Horner,[32] the perception that she and others might wonder into town and vote at their own free will is false. Labor Party member, Warren Mundine, from Baryugil Mission, whose family *did* vote, says;

> I don't think people understand what a different world we lived in; we tend to forget those days. The Aboriginal Protection Act in New South Wales was not abolished until two years after that referendum. So I suppose our equivalent were blacks in America you know, you go to the deep south and they were citizens of America, they had constitutional rights, they had voting rights but they could not exercise those rights, because if you turned up to vote you did so at considerable risk.[33]

The concept that Aboriginal people could exercise freedom of choice and had access to vote, as Gardiner-Garden implies, is also misleading considering that many Aboriginal people lived in remote areas and many, who spoke English as

---

29 Fred Maynard was born in 1879. A wharf labourer in Sydney Maynard established the Australian Aboriginal Progressive Association (AAPA) in 1925. The AAPA proposed for all Aboriginal families to receive inalienable grants of land and free entry to public schools. He was also strong opponent of the Aboriginal Protection Board.

30 John Maynard interviewed by Frances Peters-Little for the *Vote Yes for Aborigines* documentary film, Sydney, 2006.

31 Gordon Briscoe interviewed by Frances Peters-Little for the *Vote Yes for Aborigines* documentary film, Canberra, 2006. Briscoe's description of FCAATSI is that it 'developed out of a meeting of interested groups and began in Adelaide in 1958 as a private organisation of people from the churches, the trade unions, and a few articulate Aboriginal people who, some of whom were exempt, and some of whom were still wards of the State in which they lived'.

32 Joyce Clague interviewed by Frances Peters-Little for the *Vote Yes for Aborigines* documentary film, Sydney, 2006.

33 Warren Mundine interviewed by Frances Peters-Little for the *Vote Yes for Aborigines* documentary film, Sydney, 2006.

a second language, did not have the necessary literacy and numeracy skills. For those who did have the skills, they had been expected to vote for candidates who had little or no regard for them or their needs according to Aboriginal singer Jimmy Little, who had a high public profile in the Australian music industry at the time. Little stated in my interview with him;

> One of the glaring matters of voting was as I saw it back then, and still now today, is that a lot of our people thought, why should I vote for somebody I don't know, and somebody who doesn't know me and my needs, why should I put them in office? And so a good majority of Aboriginal people within the country as well as the city, had doubts about coming to the electorate roll and polling booths voting somebody in that they didn't know anything about.[34]

During the time of the referendum, Clague approached Little to use his status as a celebrity to appear on film to encourage the thousands of Aborigines who were yet to register on the Australian electoral roll. Following the referendum, Clague became instrumental in setting up polling booths in remote areas where Aborigines were yet to vote. She offers a brief scenario and says;

> Thankfully, I was able to set up an education program for our people up there in the territory and I did it in the language of the Pitjantjatjara, and Warlpiri. Now they didn't have polling booth out at some of those places, you know, and you're looking at you know, three, four hundred people at a time. But I was able to say to the minister at the time, instead of doing this they can do the postal voting. But some of them were rejected because all they did was put their thumbprints on them or cross and, and then, someone else would do the rest of the filling for them you know, which was wrong.[35]

The 1967 Referendum was clearly a starting point for many Aboriginal people on a national level, it was not ideal and had numerous awkward beginnings, just as Clague described in the previous scenario, but opened a number of avenues for Aboriginal people to progress. The 1967 Referendum provided people like Little and Clague a new sense of hope, opportunity and freedom to take charge of their own affairs as a 'people', a nation even, and allowed them and other Aborigines to vote in ways that became meaningful to them and the rest of the nation.

---

34 Jimmy Little interviewed by Frances Peters-Little for the *Vote Yes for Aborigines* documentary film, Sydney, 2006.
35 Joyce Clague interviewed by Frances Peters-Little for the *Vote Yes for Aborigines* documentary film, Canberra, 2006.

Being counted in the census

In their attempt to dispel the 'myth' that the 1967 Referendum allowed Aborigines to be counted in the census, historians Tim Rowse and Len Smith emphasise that the Commonwealth Bureau of Census and Statistics counted Aborigines since 1911[36] as they 'conceived them'.[37] They argue that the removal of section 127 which stated *'In reckoning the numbers of the people of the Commonwealth, or of a State or other part of the Commonwealth, aboriginal natives should not be counted'* had 'little if anything to do with the popular perception that the Australian Constitution was racially discriminatory'.[38] In my interview with him, Attwood does not say section 127 was discriminatory but said that,

> The federal government was under considerable pressure to amend the two most negative sounding references, sections 51 and 127, but did not necessarily accept those aspects of the constitution as racially discriminatory, but were concerned how they had been perceived both nationally and internationally.[39]

Arguing the case that Aboriginal people *were* essentially disregarded by the Australian constitution are John Chesterman and Brian Galligan who write,

> The constitutional treatment of Australia's Aboriginal people is cryptic and enigmatic. The commonwealth constitution that formally created the Australian nation and set up its federal system of government in 1901, mention Aboriginal people only twice, in its 128 sections. Moreover, both instances were by ways of exclusion.[40]

Joining Chesterman and Galligan in their criticism of the Australian constitution is Aboriginal human rights lawyer Larissa Behrendt who argues that to understand the Australian constitution at the time it was written is to realise some of the key assumptions of those who framed the constitution. She says that framers of the constitution held the belief, as white men, that they were superior to Aborigines who they mostly believed were fast on the way of become extinct.[41]

In regards to section 127 of the Constitution and the census collection on Aboriginal people, Rowse and Smith admit that they are mostly interested in how governments defined and collected data but were indifferent to lived-

---

36   Rowse and Smith 2008: 4.
37   What is meant by 'as the conceived them', is a matter of blood quantum, that is who was full-blood or half-caste, and so on. See Rowse 2002: 2.
38   Rowse and Smith 2008: 1.
39   Bain Attwood interviewed by Frances Peters-Little for the *Vote Yes for Aborigines* documentary film, Melbourne, 2006.
40   Chesterman and Galligan 1997: 58.
41   Behrendt 2000: 12.

experiences of Aboriginal people and our knowledge of ourselves. As they say in their unpublished paper, 'The survival of the Aboriginal population',[42] one of their main objectives were to identify a time during the 1960s when Australia may have ceased to have an Aboriginal population altogether and curious to why one still exists.[43] While on the surface, it looks as if it could be interesting it falls short. A remarkably dull paper it provides readers with a detailed but dry recording of events and governmental definitions and practices carried out by the Bureau between 1961–1971. Much of it harking back to a time when it was not unusual to hear references made to Chinese, 'Negroes', Afghans and Aborigines as $\frac{1}{2}$ castes, $\frac{1}{4}$ castes or $\frac{3}{4}$ castes, subjected to the 'finer grading of their fractional descent', regardless of the fact that most Australians, particularly Indigenous Australians find this language extremely inappropriate and highly insensitive.[44]

Despite the obvious problems attached, the subject of blood capacity, 'race' and descent has been a topic that has fascinated Rowse for some time, making him somewhat the expert for more than a decade, and he has written about the subject in at least ten other publications,[45] with which he writes with the same lack of insight[46] and compassion.[47] For me, the most redeeming feature of the Rowse and Smith paper is when they quote two well-known Aboriginal activists of the time. The first is poet Kath Walker[48] and the other is Chicka Dixon. They quote Walker as having said:

> Regarding the identification of an Aborigine surely the white man makes it very hard for himself in getting the census information by bringing in this caste business, quarter-caste and three-quarter-caste, etc. I notice

---

42   The paper is part of an ongoing project Rowse and Smith have been working on as part of their Australian Research Council Discovery Project since 2006 and part of a presentation given by Rowse and Smith for the History Program in the ANU seminar series, May 2007.

43   Rowse and Smith 2008: 2.

44   Rowse and Smith 2008: 3.

45   Rowse's interests in indigenous blood quantum can be found in the following books and papers; Rowse 1998, 2002, 2004, 2005, 2007, 2009a, 2009b. In addition, he is currently involved with working on another Australian Research Council Discovery Project with Smith called 'The Politics of Indigenous Enumeration in Australia Canada and New Zealand – a History, 2006–2009'.

46   Criticism of Rowse's lack of insight in the human element has been noted by Rick Rutjens who wrote, about Rowse's book, *Nugget Coombs: A Reforming Life*, 'It is a pity that Rowse does not capture the essence of this remarkable man in his 400-plus pages. Instead what he offers up is an amalgam of records, short snippets of facts trawled from the vast trove of Coombs's papers, departmental archives and other records. There is no sense of narrative, little exploration of the wider social and political environment in which Coombs lived, worked and thought.' Rutjens 2003.

47   Rowse has been accused of ignoring all the nastier parts of Australian history and for viewing Aborigines as a people who have come from a remarkably serene and pleasant landscape and have only themselves to blame for their disadvantages in Hal Wootten's speech at the launch of Tim Rowse's book *Indigenous Futures*, at the ANU Co-op Bookshop, 26 September 2002, Canberra, copy of speech cited at:

<http://www.anu.edu.au/caepr/system/files/Publications/topical/woottenonrowse.pdf>

48   Kath Walker changed her name to Oodgeroo Noonucul in 1989. Her traditional name refers to the paperbark tree on her traditional land Stradbroke Island.

he does not do this in the European world. Surely we can identify the Aborigine as one who identifies himself as an Aborigine – and we can well do without caste.[49]

Dixon was quoted in an article in the *Sydney Morning Herald* a few days before the 1967 Referendum as saying:

> A 'yes' vote would end a long-standing insult to the Aboriginal people in the census.... We don't exist officially – yet we pay taxes. We don't exist – yet we are subject to a net of restrictive laws. We don't exist – yet we have to serve in the Army and accept the other responsibilities of citizenship. We don't mind accepting our responsibilities, but in return we want white Australia to recognise officially that we exist. We want to be human like everyone else.[50]

Both are statements that reflect how important it was for Aboriginal people to feel included in the census, regardless of whether the government said they were or not, and both are statements, which I believe, are a key to understanding why the referendum had such a huge impact upon the way Aboriginal thought about themselves.

Arguing against the view the 1967 Referendum had little or no bearing on Aborigines being counted in the census, is economist Jon Altman. In my interview with him, Altman stated that the 1967 Referendum technically recognised Aborigines to be counted in the 1971 census undefined by the state in terms of blood quantum. He says that while the 1971 figures were low,[51] the census then allowed comparisons to be made between Aboriginal and non-Aboriginal people, and says 'social indicators, like the things we hear about today, employment, income, housing, health status, etc., it was the availability of statistics on indigenous people in the census that allowed us to make those sorts of comparisons'.[52] In spite of this, such comparisons are somewhat artificial and unhelpful according to Rowse, who has come up with another suggestion for focusing on the socio-economic differences between Aboriginal and non-Aboriginal people. He suggests that it is perhaps 'better to face up to indigenous

---

49 Kath Walker in Sharp and Tatz 1966: 13, quoted in Rowse and Smith 2008: 1.

50 Chicka Dixon statement cited in Attwood and Markus 1997: 116, cited in Rowse and Smith 2008: 10.

51 The figures were low compared to current figures because of many factors, for example, not everyone participated in the census. In addition, many Aboriginal people were yet to identify as Aboriginal because of the stigma attached or because they were prevented from doing so, or that many Aboriginal people were institutionalised or fostered out, or were not told they were Aboriginal.

52 Jon Altman interviewed by Frances Peters-Little for the *Vote Yes for Aborigines* documentary film, Canberra, 2006.

socio-economic diversity and to discuss what differences of indigenous outcome are consistent with social justice and what differences of indigenous outcome are an affront to indigenous standards of fairness'.[53]

Broaching the subject on an entirely different level from Rowse, Altman provides a historical background why he thinks the gap continues to exist. Altman says:

> Indigenous people today are disadvantaged for a complex set of reasons. The first and more obvious is that they were dispossessed of their land and even though we've had land rights and native title that's returned land to some indigenous people, the vast majority of the indigenous population today still remain dispossessed. We also need to recognise that, indigenous people have had a long overdue history of neglect and there's been enormous under expenditure on indigenous people, and as Australian citizens and I think that this has left an enormous legacy. A combination of all these factors, mixed in with fundamental cultural difference for many indigenous groups, means that indigenous people really find it very hard to compete, in mainstream Australians society.[54]

As an Aboriginal filmmaker and historian, I am more drawn towards a compassionate understanding as to why so many Aboriginal people and our services are still under-resourced and our communities are largely disadvantaged and continue to use the statistics in some of my films, because I think they provide a key indication of the unequal status between Aborigines and non-Aborigines in Australia today.[55]

Granting citizenship

Joining Rowse and Smith, Attwood and Markus, and Gardiner-Garden and other proponents in their quest to unravel the technicalities of the Australian constitution and reveal the 'myths' of the referendum is historian Melissa Nobles and political scientist James Jupp, who have recently argued that regardless of the misunderstandings surrounding the referendum, Aborigines were citizens before 1967. Nobles writes 'as a result of the 1948 Nationality and Citizenship Act, Aboriginal people, along with other Australians, became Australian citizens'.[56] Jupp says, prior to Australia Day 1949, the status of citizens of Australia did not exist and that most persons resident in Australia were British subjects but became Australian citizens, including Aborigines, on

---

53   Rowse 2008.
54   Jon Altman interviewed by Frances Peters-Little for the *Vote Yes for Aborigines* documentary film, Canberra, 2006.
55   I have included statistics between Aboriginal and non-Aboriginal people in two of my films, *Oceans Apart* (1991) and *Vote Yes for Aborigines*.
56   Nobles 2008: 48.

Australia Day 1949.[57] Irrespective of their 'correct' observations, the belief that the 1967 Referendum gave Aborigines citizenship remains strong in the minds of many people.

When I had asked Bain Attwood, in my interview with him, why he thought so many supposed the referendum gave Aboriginal people citizenship rights Attwood thought that the idea that the referendum gave Aborigines citizenship arose from out of the campaign slogans and strategies that were used at the time. He stated:

> Many people went to the polls on the 27th of May 1967 believing that by voting 'yes' you were going to bring about a national policy, federal control and citizenship rights for Aboriginal people. And if you look at the campaign material that is prepared, those matters are emphasised again and again. You look at posters and they say 'Right wrongs, vote yes', 'Vote yes for citizenship rights', many people, I think, voted in the referendum believing that they were granting Aboriginal people citizenship rights and that they were granting them the right to vote as part of a citizenship right.

Coming down strongly against the argument that the campaigners misled the Australian public is former member of the Federal Liberal Party (1972–1983) and Minister for Aboriginal Affairs Robert Ian Viner who says Attwood and Markus, and Gardiner-Garden were wrong to say the 1967 Referendum, or at least the post-1967 Referendum, was built on mythmaking. Viner is of the view that the realities of discrimination and disability that drove decades of Aboriginal activism were not myths but a result of successful politicking,[58] helped along by some of the parliamentary 'back-benchers' at the time and William Wentworth,[59] Gordon Bryant[60] and Kim Beazley Senior.[61] Viner also takes the compassionate view that the Australian people were persuaded to support a campaign that pushed for the rights for Aborigines to have 'equal citizenship' rights. Viner writes,

> Paucity of income, education, housing, health, employment, cultural identity and recognition was a reality; the denial of freedom of movement was a reality; the denial of access to social services by entitlement was a reality. The denial of rights to vote and to equal justice before the courts were realities; the forced removal of people from their traditional lands

57   Jupp 2001: 119.

58   Viner 2007: 17–19.

59   William Wentworth, a member of the Liberal Party, was Australia's first minster in the Office of Aboriginal Affairs between 1968 and 1971.

60   Gordon Bryant (3 August 1914 – 14 January 1991) was an Australian politician, a member of the Australian Labor Party, and was the Minister of Aboriginal Affairs between 1972 and 1973.

61   Kim Beazley Snr served in the Australian Labor Party for 32 years, from 1945 to 1977.

and homes and the taking and occupation of traditional lands without compensation and the denial of ownership of traditional lands were all realities. None were myths'.[62]

Others I have interviewed who have joined Viner in saying that the reason why the Australian people went to the polls that day believing they were helping to assist in giving Aborigines 'equal citizenship' rights are Sue Taffe, Jennifer Clark and Fred Chaney. According to Sue Taffe:

> The referendum was about two clauses in the constitution. One clause was to do with Aboriginal people not being counted in the census, so they got rid of that, and the other clause was about giving the commonwealth the power to make special laws for Aboriginal people as a people, as a group. Now of course the commonwealth already had the power to make laws for Aboriginal people just as part of the Australian community, but the campaigners wanted this special power because they believed it was a little bit like affirmative action. They believed that it was necessary for laws to be made to counteract the damage of dispossession and to help Aboriginal people to, become a part of Australian society. So it was about citizenship if you like.[63]

Historian Jennifer Clark very clearly explains in an interview why the Australian public was less concerned about the politics or the legalities of the Australian constitution.

> The government's role is to look at the constitution and legislation from a legal point of view. But the general public are not looking at the constitution from a legal point of view, they're looking at Aboriginal lives, they're looking at what Aborigines can do or can't do. They're looking at the fact that in some states of Australia at this time, some Aborigines could not marry without permission, could not move from place to place, in some places they were not in control of their own money. In some places, the mission or the employer would take the wages and the Aborigines were given rations instead so they did not have control over their own affairs. Some people began to argue that Aborigines were treated like children in this sense and were not able to determine their own lives; these were the issues that affected Aborigines in particular but seemed to be important to their supporters at the time.[64]

---

62 Viner 2007: 17–19.
63 Sue Taffe interviewed by Frances Peters-Little for the *Vote Yes for Aborigines* documentary film, Melbourne, 2006.
64 Jennifer Clark interviewed by Frances Peters-Little for the *Vote Yes for Aborigines* documentary film, Sydney, 2006.

In my interview with Fred Chaney, the former Federal Minister for Aboriginal Affairs (1978–1980) and co-chair of Reconciliation Australia (2000–2005), Chaney said that it was easy to understand why the Australians believed Aborigines were not citizens of Australia because Aborigines were not living as other Australians. He said:

> Well they were denied access often to education. They were denied access to social security, they were denied access to alcohol, which some might say in retrospect is probably, was now when we see the depredations of alcohol that's pretty sad. But the denial of basic civil liberties, the control over movement in many cases, the control over who you could marry, I mean the most amazing array of controls which in a sense destroyed the capacity of the Aboriginal community. I mean they were cut out of normal Australian life virtually.[65]

From the comments made by Taffe, Clark and Chaney, it becomes more understandable why Aboriginal people and the Australian public, and politicians even, went to the polls that day believing they were voting for the rights of Aborigines to become equal citizens, and were not just there because they were hoodwinked by the campaigners. That in effect people voted that day because they wanted to feel as though they were contributing towards a better future for Aboriginal people.

When I had posed the question 'What had they thought about their citizenship rights before and after the 1967 Referendum?' to a number of the Aboriginal interviewees for the film all had agreed on two things. They all said at some point that before the referendum that they did not think of themselves as Australian citizens as such, but as second-class citizens at the very most. However, after the referendum they thought they could at least have the choice to choose whether they wanted to think of themselves as Australian citizens. All the Indigenous interviewees, from Gordon Briscoe, Warren Mundine and Jimmy Little to the comments in the vox-pops in the first three minutes of the film, could now at least choose to think of themselves as Aboriginal or as Australians.

One of the first people I asked how he felt about being an Australian citizen before the referendum was historian Gordon Briscoe. In the interview, Briscoe

---

65 Fred Chaney interviewed by Frances Peters-Little for the *Vote Yes for Aborigines* documentary film, Sydney, 2006.

explained to me how he and Charles Perkins, as residents of the Northern Territory, were governed by the Northern Territory Aborigines Welfare Act[66] and became wards of the State.[67]

> Aborigines wanted to seek a life outside of government control needed to apply to government for a special exemption. And this then gave them citizenship. We didn't want exemption from the Act so much as we wanted clauses changed in the Act which gave us the right to do things but still be Aborigines. We didn't particularly want an exemption, but we wanted to do things, we wanted the right to associate with one another, we wanted the right to become union members. We wanted the right to own property outside, as Aborigines. These are the kinds of things that we wanted changed to allow us to do that.[68]

Aboriginal politician Warren Mundine also gave an account what life was like for him growing up prior to the 1967 Referendum.

> Aboriginal people of my generation and older tell you stories with the mission managers and the welfare officers just turning up and walking into your house, checking you out to see if you were clean; if you cleaned your teeth, your ears were clean, your hair, made sure your clothes were ironed, made sure you were dressed, your shoes were polished, the house was clean the washing and ironing was done the lawn was mowed and all that type of thing; people think they're an exaggeration, they can't believe that – that people were – you know, were treated like children, and that's not an exaggeration, that's a fact, that's how people were treated.[69]

Popular Aboriginal entertainer Jimmy Little, who was born near the Victorian border but reached the heights of his career in the 1960s, said that his chance to break free of a second-class citizenship, was to leave home and move to Sydney, but for his father, it meant he had to apply for an exemption certificate.

> People of my generation knew that for a long time we were second class citizens, but felt the need to move to the cities. So while we were

---

66 The Federal government passed the Northern Territory Aboriginals Ordinance in 1911. The Chief Protector is made the legal guardian of every Aboriginal and 'half-caste' child under 18 years old. Any Aboriginal person can be forced onto a mission or settlement and children can be removed by force.

67 In 1957, the Northern Territory Welfare Ordinance 1953 comes into operation thus making all Aborigines wards of the state, meaning that the state, or territory held authority over the legal rights of Aboriginal people on matters that white Australians could enjoy freely, that is the right to drink alcohol or enter into a hotel was one of the rights denied.

68 Gordon Briscoe interviewed by Frances Peters-Little for the *Vote Yes for Aborigines* documentary film, Canberra, 2006.

69 Warren Mundine interviewed by Frances Peters-Little for the *Vote Yes for Aborigines* documentary film, Sydney, 2006.

coming together as different tribes in a modern sense we had to deal with another tribe, urban tribes if you like. But for my poor old dad god-bless him, he had to have what we termed back then, a dog collar. He had to have a permit to go onto a mission and off the mission, and things of that nature.[70]

When I had asked them how did they feel about their status as Australian citizenship 40 years after the referendum, their answers varied. Briscoe said:

I'm an Australian citizen um, in some sense, in a partial way. I accept that the fact that there are governments that have platitudes about democracy. But those democratic values are not the kind of democratic values that I have which are an international type. I accept that I have some citizenship in Australia but I don't agree with the kind of treatment that white Australia and its governments and Britain have allowed the Australian governments to denude us from our real heritage. Our heritage is built on what white people think. Not what we think. And this is tantamount to the kind of contempt that Australian government, State and Federal have had for political organisations that deal with Aboriginal rights.

Mundine's response to the question did he feel like he was an Australian citizen was:

Well I- I um.. it's- it's beyond me, it's bigger than me um.. I've um.. I've received the benefits of that, you know, my lifestyle ah.. my achievements in life was- was done because of the sacrifices of people that come before me and the people who struggled for the last two hundred years ah.. the people that we know so well about like the Pearl Gibbs and the- and the ah.. William Ferguson's and many other people; the- the Tent Embassy, you know, the people in the 20s and 30s who rallied for citizenship rights'.[71]

Little says:

I'm Australian made, in every sense of the word. But before me, I was the first sunrise people, the same blood that runs through the veins of me today, ran through my first grandfather, my first grandmother. And that's centuries ago. So, how can I not be proud of being a warrior in modern times from the early times on this planet. It's just that in our time frame, all of us, we have to make a contribution, we have to take

---

70   Jimmy Little interviewed by Frances Peters-Little for the *Vote Yes for Aborigines* documentary film, Sydney, 2006.
71   Warren Mundine interviewed by Frances Peters-Little for the *Vote Yes for Aborigines* documentary film, Sydney, 2006.

our share of the pie, take our credits where credit is due. And those of us who take too much pie, we have to pay the consequences. So it's a matter of proportion, and it's a matter of trust, it's a matter of lacking greed, it's a matter of having passion.[72]

Conclusion

As an Aboriginal filmmaker and historian, I very often make films about the things I write about and vice-versa. For the *Unsettling histories* project, for example, I wrote a paper called *The community game: Aboriginal self-definition at the local level,* about the Aboriginal community of Walgett in 2000 and then made a film called *Our community* five years later. In the case of the 1967 Referendum, I made the film *Vote yes for Aborigines* first, and decided to write about the subject later. In terms of writing this chapter, what I set out to do was discuss the 'myths' associated with the referendum and to demonstrate why I think a compassionate view of history is vitally important to understanding Aboriginal history as a whole. In terms of myths, in this chapter I have argued that while in theory the referendum did not grant Aborigines the 'right' to vote, Aborigines did not enjoy the same rights and access, but that the referendum had made it easier for them to vote or at the very least, made the idea of voting more meaningful to them. What I have argued in the case of being counted in the census is that the 1967 Referendum made it possible for Aborigines to be counted in the census undetermined by government terms, and that this had made a major break through in the ways Aborigines began to identify their needs and socio-economic status. Finally, I have argued that while changes to the Australian constitution did not technically give Aborigines citizenship, what the referendum did achieve, was perhaps for the first time since colonisation, Aborigines on a national level, could now have a choice to consciously and publicly accept or reject what white Australia had offered them in terms of their status as Australians.

In terms of making the film, it was not, however, until my last interview for the *Vote yes for Aborigines* documentary, with the former Prime Minster of Australia, Paul Keating that I decided how I was going to pull the film together and, consequently, how I would write about it. The question I posed to Keating at the time was, 'did politicians care about history?' his reply was that *'history was a bit like water, that eventually it would find it own level'*, 'it' meaning, the truth, or at least, what people would end up believing to be the truth. It is with this view in mind that I have argued that one cannot truly understand the 1967 Referendum without understanding the 'myths' associated with it and

---

72   Jimmy Little interviewed by Frances Peters-Little for the *Vote Yes for Aborigines* documentary film, Sydney, 2006.

why they have lasted for so long. While it is understandable for historians to try to 'level the waters' that Keating talks about by writing about the referendum in terms of abstract theories, I believe that we have so much more to learn from the 'myths' associated with it, and how we might remember the 1967 referendum, with compassion, in the future.

References

Bain Attwood and Andrew Markus 1997, *The 1967 Referendum: or when Aborigines did not get the Vote*, Aboriginal Studies Press, Canberra.

Behrendt, Larissa 2000, *The 1967 Referendum: 40 Years on*, University of New South Wales Press, Sydney.

Chesterman, John and Brian Galligan 1997, *Citizens without Rights: Aborigines and Australian Citizenship,* Cambridge University Press, Melbourne.

Gardiner-Garden, John 2007, 'The 1967 Referendum—history and myths', Research Brief no. 11 2006–07, Parliamentary Library, Parliament of Australia, Canberra, accessed 10 May 2010: <http://www.aph.gov.au/library/pubs/rb/2006-07/07rb11.htm#myths>

Ginsburg, Faye and Fred Myers 2006, 'A history of indigenous futures: accounting for indigenous art and media', *Aboriginal History* 30: 95–110.

Goot, Murray and Tim Rowse 2007, *Divided Nation? Indigenous Affairs and the Imagined Public*, Melbourne University Press, Melbourne.

Gottschalk, Louis 1950, *Understanding History: a Primer of Historical Method*, Alfred A Knopf, New York.

Guynn, William H 2006, *Writing History in Film*, Routledge, New York.

Jupp, James 2001, *The Australian People: an Encyclopaedia of the Nation, its People and their Origins*, Cambridge University Press, Melbourne.

Lal, Brij 2004, 'Creative endeavours', *Quarterly Bulletin* 5(1), accessed 10 May 2010: <http://rspas.anu.edu.au/qb/articleFile.php?searchterm=5-1-3>

McGrath, Ann 2009, 'Must film be fiction?', *Griffith Review* 24, Griffith University, accessed 10 May 2010: <http://www.griffithreview.com/edition-24-participation-society/222-essay/659.html>

Morris-Suzuki, Tessa 2004, 'Creative endeavours', *Quarterly Bulletin* 5(1), accessed 10 May 2010: <http://rspas.anu.edu.au/qb/articleFile.php?searchterm=5-1-3>

Nabokov, Peter 2000, *A Forest of Time: American Indian Ways of History*, Cambridge University Press, Melbourne.

National Australian Archives, fact sheet, accessed 8 December 2009: <http://www.naa.gov.au/about-us/publications/fact-sheets/fs150.aspx>

Nobles, Melissa 2008, *The Politics of Official Apologies*, Cambridge University Press, Cambridge, USA.

Peters-Little, F, A McGrath and I Macfarlane (eds) 2006, *Exchanging Histories, Aboriginal History* 30.

Ritchie, Donald 2003, *Doing Oral History*, Oxford University Press, Oxford.

Rowse, Tim 1998, *White Flour, White Power: from Rations to Citizenship in Central Australia*, Cambridge University Press, Melbourne.

— 2002, 'Towards a history of Indigenous statistics in Australia', in *Assessing the Evidence on Indigenous Socioeconomic Outcomes: a Focus on the 2002 NATSISS*, Boyd Hunter (ed), ANU E Press, Canberra: 1–11.

— 2004, 'Indigenous autobiography in Australia and the United States', *Australian Humanities Review* 33: 1–12.

— (ed) 2005, *Contesting Assimilation*, API Network, Perth.

— 2008, 'The politics of "the gap" in Australia and New Zealand', a paper presented in the Centre for Aboriginal Economic Policy Research, Australian National University, 28 May 2008, accessed 10 May 2010: <http://www.anu.edu.au/caepr/system/files/Seminars/presentations/Rowse_Gaps.pdf>

Rowse, Tim and Len Smith 2008, 'The Survival of the Aboriginal Population', unpublished paper, Canberra.

— 2009, 'Official statistics and the contemporary politics of Indigeneity', *Australian Journal of Political Science* 44(2): 193–211.

— 2009, 'The ontological politics of "closing the gaps" and official statistics', *Journal of Cultural Economy* 2(1–2): 33–48.

Rutjens, Rick 2003, 'Tim Rowse, Nugget Coombs: a Reforming Life (book review)', *Journal of Australian Studies* 77: review of books.

Sharp, IG and CM Tatz (eds) 1966, *Aborigines in the Economy*, Jacaranda, Brisbane.

Smith, Linda Tuhiwai 1999, *Decolonizing Methodologies: Research and Indigenous Peoples*, University of Otago Press, Dunedin.

Viner, Hon Ian 2007, 'Are Aboriginal and Torres Strait Islanders on the road ahead or the road back?', *Australian Indigenous Law Review* 11, Special Edition: 17–19.

White, Hayden 1988, 'Historiography and historiophoty', *American Historical Review* 93(5): 193–199.

Williams, George 2000, *A Bill of Rights for Australia*, University of New South Wales Press, Sydney.

5. Idle men: the eighteenth-century roots of the Indigenous indolence myth

SHINO KONISHI

One of the most devastating and enduring myths about Indigenous people is that they are '"lazy", "indolent", "slothful", "erratic" and "roving"' and simply 'don't want to work'.[1] In their historiographic study of Indigenous labour history Ann Curthoys and Clive Moore urged historians to 'come to terms with the popular racist assumption that Aborigines and Torres Strait Islanders did not work'.[2] Many have challenged this myth by examining diverse aspects of Australia's colonial history. Some have claimed that Indigenous people were given little incentive to work, sometimes receiving pitiful rations or brutal treatment, while others have uncovered little-known histories of Indigenous workers.[3] It has also been argued that Western forms of labour were incommensurate with the Aboriginal ethos of communality, or that Indigenous employment was unwanted because the settler-colonial 'logic of elimination' sought to 'replace the natives on their land' rather than exploit their labour.[4] While these approaches all shed light on important facets of Indigenous labour history, they do not fully redress the Indigenous indolence myth. In order to do so, we need to explore the first European perceptions of Aboriginal people's industriousness and ingenuity.

William Dampier recorded his frustration at his failure to extract 'some service' from the Aboriginal people he discovered in the north-west coast of Australia in 1688, in what is the first detailed Western account of Aboriginal people. The English buccaneer hoped that these 'miserablest people in the world' would prove themselves useful as his 'new Servants' and carry his water barrels back to the boats. The Europeans gave the friendlier of the Aboriginal men 'ragged' old clothes in the hope that this 'finery would have brought them to work

---

1   Broome 1994: 216; Office of the Minister for Aboriginal and Torres Strait Islander Affairs 1994.
2   Curthoys and Moore 1995: 2.
3   Broome 1994: 217–218, 220.
4   Reynolds 1990: 87–95; Wolfe 2001: para 5.

heartily for us', and then placed six-gallon barrels on their shoulders, gesturing that they should be carried. Unfortunately the Aboriginal men just 'stood like statues … and grinned like so many Monkeys', leading Dampier to believe that the 'poor Creatures do not seem accustomed to carrying Burdens'. They not only appeared ignorant of the practice, but even seemed to reject the concept of work, for they 'put the clothes off again and laid them down, as if clothes were only to work in'.[5] Dampier's account of the Aborigines' 'unfitness for labour' provided the foundation for the elaborate and influential eighteenth-century discourses on Aboriginal idleness and ignorance which underpin the enduring myth that Indigenous people are unduly indolent.

Eighteenth-century explorers witnessed many different examples of Aboriginal people's labours, although these were almost exclusively limited to that concerning basic survival, such as obtaining food and seeking shelter. They described and illustrated various Aboriginal manufactures, such as weapons, tools, and assorted canoes and dwellings, as well as their methods for hunting and fishing. To the European eye these represented the full extent of the Aboriginal people's industriousness and ingenuity, and their evaluations of these were overwhelmingly derogatory. It was not uncommon for the Europeans to view them as a 'stupid and indolent set of people' or 'ignorant and wretched'.[6] However, the most damning appraisals were reserved for Aboriginal men, who were almost universally seen as oppressive tyrants who exploited their women's labour.

These perceptions were not solely determined by Aboriginal men's actual labours or lack thereof, but instead reflected eighteenth-century ideas about the nature of so-called savage societies' 'arts and industry'. Enlightenment thinkers had pondered the reasons why some societies seemed not to have progressed to the same civilised state as Europeans, and assumed that for the most part it was because, as the Comte de Buffon said of the North Americans, 'they were all equally stupid, ignorant, and destitute of arts and industry'.[7] Although this is a somewhat crude and idle conclusion in itself, eighteenth-century philosophers expended great energy explaining savage man's apparent indolence and ignorance, elaborating theological, physiological, and environmental causes. Their ideas on labour and land use were inevitably influenced by imperial and commercial interests, as slavery and colonisation shadowed their discussions of Indigenous industry.

The explorers' observations of the Aboriginal men's labour were unusually uniform compared to their accounts of other Indigenous practices, and belied

---

5   Dampier 1998: 221.
6   Bowes Smyth 1979: 57; Furneaux 1961: 735.
7   Buffon 1950: 4.

the complexity of eighteenth-century ideas about industry and intelligence. This chapter will examine the explorers' accounts of Aboriginal men's contribution to the procurement of food, their purported economic reliance on women, and the insights into their ingenuity revealed through their manufactures, and consider how these representations reflected the European myth of Indigenous indolence and ignorance.

Enlightenment discourses on savage indolence

By the eighteenth century, Western attitudes to labour especially that involved in food production regarded it not only as an activity necessary for survival, but also a sign of Christian piety. Late in the previous century, John Locke pronounced that 'God and his Reason commanded [man] to subdue the earth, … and therein lay out something upon it that was his own, his labour'.[8] This belief persisted, and at the close of the century was echoed by Thomas Robert Malthus, who held that 'The supreme Being has ordained, that the earth shall not produce food in great quantities, till much preparatory labour and ingenuity has been exercised upon its surface'.[9] He did not suggest that obtaining food was the sole aim, but instead proposed that to work was a virtue, claiming that 'Evil exists in the world, not to create despair, but activity', so in order to avoid it we must 'exert ourselves'.[10] Such efforts, according to Malthus, encouraged ingenuity and inaugurated the march towards civilisation, for he speculated that 'had population and food increased in the same ratio, it is probable that man might never have emerged from the savage state'.[11]

Piety was not considered the only reward for such physical exertions, however, for according to Stuart Banner, it was believed since antiquity that 'the invention of agriculture … gave rise to property rights in land'. To illustrate this point he draws on Virgil and Ovid: 'It was only when "Ceres first taught men to plough the land" … that land was first divided. When there were "[n]o ploughshares to break up the landscape"… there were "no surveyors [p]egging out the boundaries of estates"'.[12] As many historians have shown, notwithstanding some significant challenges regarding the rights of Nomadic peoples, this belief endured into the late eighteenth-century.[13] It is best exemplified by the Swiss jurist Emmerich de Vattel, who, according to Bruce Buchan and Mary Heath, maintained that 'agriculture was an "obligation imposed upon man by nature"'. Vattel argued that 'peoples who subsisted on the "fruits of the chase" without

---

8   Locke 1963: 321–341.
9   Malthus 1926: 360.
10   Malthus 1926: 395.
11   Malthus 1926: 364.
12   Banner 2005: para 16.
13   Reynolds 1987.

cultivating the soil "may not complain if more industrious Nations should come and occupy part of their lands'".[14] Thus savage peoples' failure to till the soil was not only construed as a sign of their indolence but also as evidence that they did not possess property rights.

Other European thinkers looked beyond the Bible and international law for explanation of Indigenous indolence, drawing instead on ancient ideas concerning the climate, environment and bodily humours. According to historian Roy Porter, 'humoral medicine', originating with Hippocrates in the fifth century BC, 'stressed analogies between the four elements of external nature … and the four humours … whose balance determined health'.[15] These bodily fluids also corresponded to four temperaments, which the Greeks had aligned to different national characters, perceiving themselves as superior to both the phlegmatic northern Europeans and choleric North Africans.[16] In his eighteenth-century taxonomy of mankind Carolus Linnaeus also attributed humours to particular 'races', but this time ascribed the phlegmatic humour to *Homo afer* instead. Thus, Africans became 'crafty, indolent, [and] negligent', while *Homo Europaeus* was now sanguine – 'gentle, acute, [and] inventive'.[17]

Historian of medicine Mark Harrison argues that the eighteenth- and nineteenth-century belief that climate determined constitution was a return to the Hippocratic theories which divided climates into healthy and unhealthy, with those which were hot and wet deemed to be debilitating.[18] This conception of the torrid zones, or tropical climates, as deleterious to one's constitution was also favoured in the eighteenth century, with Montesquieu being perhaps its greatest exponent. He explored the effects of climate on societies in *The Spirit of Laws* (1748), drawing inspiration from humoral theories, physiological studies, and anecdotes about newly discovered lands.[19] Such research allowed Montesquieu to claim authoritatively that people from colder climates were more industrious than those from hotter environments. He posited that 'Cold air contracts the extremities of the body's surface fibers', which then 'increases their spring', whereas 'Hot air' does the opposite, so 'decreases their strength and their spring'. 'Therefore', Montesquieu claimed, 'men are more vigorous in cold climates'.[20] This ostensibly physiological evidence also suggested that the indolent tropical body was inherently lacking in ingenuity and intelligence, for its physical debilitation was believed to enervate the body's 'spirit'.

---

14 Buchan and Heath 2006: 8–9.
15 Porter 1997: 9.
16 Porter 1997: 57.
17 Linne 1806[1735] I: 9.
18 Harrison 1999: 34.
19 Harrison 1999: 92–94.
20 Montesquieu 1989[1748]: 231.

Consequently, in the torrid zones, Montesquieu speculated, there would be 'no curiosity, no noble enterprise, no generous sentiment; inclinations will all be passive there; [and] laziness will be happiness'.[21]

Montesquieu also appeared to endorse the Atlantic slave trade by suggesting that 'servitude will be less intolerable than the strength of spirit necessary to guide one's own conduct'.[22] Immanuel Kant echoed this belief, stating that 'All inhabitants of the hottest zones are exceptionally lethargic', and, perhaps in a nod to slavery, claimed that for some 'this laziness is somewhat mitigated by rule and force'. His environmental thesis also addressed colonisation and conquest. In his praise of the 'inhabitants of the temperate parts of the world', he included that they 'work harder' and are 'more intelligent', and reciting various exemplars, claimed that 'they have all amazed the southern lands with their arts and weapons', which is 'why at all points in time these peoples have educated the others and controlled them'.[23] Not all of Kant's inquiries into Indigenous ingenuity were so ostensibly considered, however, for at other times he looked no further than skin colour for explanation, observing of a 'Negro' slave, 'this fellow was quite black from head to foot, a clear proof that what he said was stupid'.[24]

Another possible explanation for the savage man's indolence and lack of inventiveness was the European belief that he forced his women into lives of toil and hardship. Kant wondered 'In the lands of the black, what better can one expect than what is found prevailing, namely the feminine sex in the deepest slavery?'[25] Malthus similarly claimed that the 'North American Indians', like 'most other savage nations', exploited their women, and moreover, that this enslavement was worse than any produced in Western society. He claimed that here women were 'much more completely in a state of slavery to the men, than the poor are to the rich in civilised countries'.[26] These diverse Enlightenment discourses on savage indolence, particularly the notion that women were kept in a state of domestic slavery, captured the imagination of the Europeans who explored Australia in the late eighteenth-century and haunted their accounts of Aboriginal men's labours.

At the expense of the weaker sex

Over time, the explorers pieced together more of the Aborigines' daily routine through combining their occasional observations with speculations on what

---

21   Montesquieu 1989[1748]: 234.
22   Montesquieu 1989[1748]: 250.
23   Kant 1997[1900–1960]: 64.
24   Kant 1960[1764].
25   Kant 1960[1764].
26   Malthus 1926: 41–42.

remained unseen. Unaware of the secret and sacred nature of Aboriginal people's engagement with the arcane world, and ignorant about the basis of their laws and customs, the Europeans witnessed a life which they considered utterly bereft. The First Fleet officers thought that they merely eked out an existence; Judge-Advocate David Collins never saw them to 'make provisions for the morrow', and thought that they 'always eat as long as they have anything left to eat, and when satisfied stretch themselves out in the sun to sleep'. He 'observed a great degree of indolence in their dispositions' and suggested that they would continue to slumber 'until hunger or some other cause call[ed] them again into action'.[27]

Marine Lieutenant Captain Watkin Tench had the same opinion, believing that it was only 'the calls of hunger and the returning light' which roused the Aboriginal man 'from his beloved indolence'. He concluded that 'one day must be very much like another in the life of a savage', admitting that 'in their domestic detail there may be novelty', but asserted that 'variety is unattainable'.[28] Lieutenant-Commander Pierre Bernard Milius, second pilot on Baudin's *Naturaliste,* simply attested that the Port Jackson Aborigines' natural tendency was laziness.[29] The Aboriginal men's lassitude, the explorers decided, was 'at the expense of the weaker vessel the women' who were seen to fish for hours from their canoes in Port Jackson, or diving the cold and treacherous Tasmanian waters for shellfish.[30]

In both Tasmania and on the mainland the Europeans were struck by the seeming inequity in the distribution of labour. D'Entrecasteaux's sailors 'noticed that the men did nothing, and left everything for the women to do'.[31] Moreover, the explorers thought that the women would suffer at the brutal hands of the idle men if they did not feed them. In Port Jackson Collins alleged that if the women returned from their canoes 'without a sufficient quantity to make a meal for their tyrants, who were asleep at their ease, they would meet but a rude reception on their landing'.[32] It was this seeming injustice which marred the Tasmanian Aboriginal men in the eyes of d'Entrecasteaux's crew. In all other respects the Frenchmen considered the islanders' society to be an ideal exemplar of the state of nature, so they quickly sought to eradicate this blemish, and rectify the women's treatment.

On their third visit with a Tasmanian group at Port du Nord (North Port, Recherche Bay), d'Entrecasteaux's men finally saw how the women prepared

---

27   Collins 1975: 499.
28   Tench 1996[1789,1793]: 258.
29   'Leur penchant naturel qui est l'indolence'. Milius 1987: 48.
30   Collins 1975: 499. See also Banks 1998: 129; Péron 1975[1809]: 194–196.
31   Raoul 1993: 306.
32   Collins 1975: 499.

their meals. First they stoked a fire for cooking, as well as adjacent fires which they could use to dry and warm themselves after returning from the icy waters. The women then dived into the sea, picking 'crayfish, abalones, and other shell-fish' with a small stick, and carried them back to shore in a woven bag they had hung around their necks. After returning to the beach they cooked their catch, 'distribut[ing it] to their husbands and children', and then kept 'renew[ing] this exercise until the appetites of the whole family [had] been satisfied'.[33]

This was the first time that the Frenchmen had witnessed this 'most arduous domestic work', and they were absolutely horrified by it. Gunner Jean-Louis Féron sympathised with the 'extraordinarily thin' women, and considered that this 'tiring work' was too much for 'so delicate a sex'.[34] 'It gave us great pain', botanist Jacques de Labillardière passionately asserted, 'to see these poor women condemned to such severe toil'. He even worried that they might be 'devoured by sharks, or entangled among the weeds that rise from the bottom of the sea'.[35]

D'Entrecasteaux's naturalists used signs to 'communicate to the men that this pain should be spared' the women, but had great difficulty in comprehending the men's reply, although they assumed that the Aborigines had understood their interrogation. The Frenchmen at first misconstrued the Indigenous men, and believed that they had claimed that diving 'would kill them'. These ostensibly rational men of science would not accept that 'leaving the fishing to the women [was] the result of some superstitious ideas' so continued with their interview, and then deduced from their gestures that the men considered that their 'sole occupation consisted of walking about' or resting.[36] Although this was the first time they had witnessed the women's labours, and therefore they could not be sure that it exemplified their domestic routine, the Europeans completely accepted the men's apparent answer because it tallied with their notions of domestic slavery in savage societies.

While acknowledging the Enlightenment premise that 'among all savage peoples the work must devolve upon the women', the chivalrous explorers refused to allow this to continue in Tasmania, so 'often entreated their husbands to take a share of the labour at least, but always in vain'.[37] Trying another tactic, the Frenchmen thought a technological innovation might alleviate the women's burdensome toil. Labillardière deduced from his brief observations that 'they had no fish-hooks', so 'gave them some of [theirs], and taught them how to use them'. Unlike their later counterparts, d'Entrecasteaux's men did not realise that the Aboriginal Tasmanians, unlike the mainland Aboriginal people, refused to

---

33   D'Entrecasteaux 2001: 144.
34   Féron 1993: 287.
35   Labillardière 1800: 309–310.
36   D'Entrecasteaux 2001: 144; Féron 1993: 287.
37   Labillardière 1800: 309–310.

eat vertebrate fish, so naively 'congratulat[ed them]selves at having supplied them with the means of diminishing one of the most fatiguing employments of the women'.[38] Fortunately for their sense of chivalry, they did not stay in Tasmania long enough to realise that this ostensible improvement was also 'in vain'.

Despite the explorers' general consensus that the Aboriginal men were exceedingly indolent, and their explicit claims that the men did little more than lie around and sleep while their women toiled away as exploited drudges, their accounts are actually peppered with detailed descriptions of the men arduously fishing and hunting. The Europeans had mixed opinions as to the effectiveness of these practices: a small number appreciated the level of skill and patience the Indigenous methods demanded, while most were not above laughing at their seemingly rudimentary techniques, equipment, and scant rewards. None of the explorers, however, recognised these activities as work. Historian Alan Frost contends that Lockean thought had rendered European conceptions of labour (in the early stages of society at least), as exclusively defined by that involved in 'domesticating animals or … maintaining an agriculture'.[39] Since neither James Cook, nor any of the other explorers 'saw one Inch of Cultivated land in the whole Country', they had already decided *a priori* that the Indigenous men were indolent.[40] Consequently, we have to look past the explorers' editorial incursions which explicitly claim that the indigenes were lazy in order to excavate their varied impressions and evaluations of the Aboriginal men's labours.

Fishing was the activity that the explorers recorded in the most detail because it was an occupation which they could observe from the safety and comfort of their boats. Along coastal areas on the mainland it was noticed that 'fish [were] their chief support', and that 'Men, women, and children [were] employed in procuring them; but the means used [were] different according to the sex'.[41] Many of the First Fleet officers focused on the women's fishing tasks because they often did this alone in their canoes, so it was an opportunity for the European men to approach the women away from the purportedly jealous eyes of their husbands.[42] However, there are many descriptions of the men fishing, including an extraordinarily detailed account by Tench, which takes the form of an imagined narrative of a typical day in the life of a savage.

Tench begins his account with the Aboriginal every-man waking from his slumber and setting off towards the rocks where he could 'peep into unruffled

---

38   Labillardière 1800: 313. Aboriginal Tasmanians apparently stopped eating fish approximately 4000 years ago, although there is much conjecture over why. Davidson and Roberts 2009: 28–29.

39   Frost 1990: 72.

40   Cook 1955–1967 I: 396.

41   Collins 1975: 461.

42   Ann McGrath has explored some of these accounts in her analysis of the First Fleet officer's depictions of their own chivalry. McGrath 1990: 189–206.

water to look for fish'. Finding some, he would then 'chew a cockle and spit it into the water' as bait for any unwary prey, and then aim his fish-gig to strike when the opportunity finally arose. 'Transpierc[ing]' his fish with the spear's barbs he would then drop the weapon, allowing the fish to float to the surface buoyed by the wooden shaft, and then haul it towards him. 'But sometimes', Tench noted, 'the fish [had] either deserted the rocks, ... or [were] too shy', so the fisherman would have to employ other means to catch them.

On these occasions the man would launch his canoe, travelling into deeper waters where he could 'dart his gig at them to the distance of many yards' and was 'often successful' in catching mullets or other smaller fish. Tench advised his readers that 'these people suffer[ed] severely' when prevented from fishing, for they have

> no resource but to pick up shellfish, which may happen to cling to the rocks and be cast on the beach, to hunt particular reptiles and small animals, which are scarce, to dig fern roots in the swamps or gather a few berries, destitute of flavour and nutrition which the woods afford.[43]

Tench's meticulous and unusual ethnographic account provides fine details on the Aboriginal men's different methods for obtaining food, and reflected his appreciation of the degree of skill they possessed in catching fish. It also illustrated that, contrary to British claims, the men were not completely indolent and also contributed to the family economy in various ways.

Surgeon George Worgan's account goes even further, for he observed that after the men finished spearing fish from the rocks, having 'caught enough for a Meal, and [starting to] feel hungry', they would then 'call the Women on shore', and upon their return, the men would 'haul up the Canoes' for them. His account even suggests that the men contributed to the cooking, for after mentioning the men's courteous conduct he stated that '*They* then gather up a few dry Sticks, light a fire ... and broil their Fish'.[44] Collins described a similar incident in which Bennelong prepared the meal. He observed the man's sister and wife fishing from a 'new canoe which the husband had cut in his last excursion to Parramatta' for her, while Bennelong, who had been looking after his sister's child, met them to haul the canoe ashore. He then sat on a rock and 'prepar[ed] to dress and eat the fish he had just received', while his sister slept and his wife ate 'some rock-oysters'.[45]

---

43 Tench 1996[1789,1793]: 260. Collins also documented the range of food sources they ate to the Britons' 'wonder and disgust', such as 'large worms and grubs' which a European servant of his 'often joined them in eating' and assured the judge-advocate that 'it was sweeter than any marrow he had ever tasted', and eels which they caught in traps 'at a certain season of the year'. Collins 1975: 461–463.

44 My italics. Worgan 1978: 16–17.

45 Collins 1975: 492–493.

These accounts of the Aboriginal men's involvement in fishing and other daily labours should sit somewhat uncomfortably with the Europeans' explicit claims that the Indigenous men were indolent. Yet because they are mostly description their implication that Aboriginal men did not shy away from work and actually contributed to their family economies is only implicit and has unfortunately eluded many scholars. Norman Plomley simply asserts that 'the women were wholly concerned with food gathering' and that they were 'completely subservient to their men', and Colin Dyer uncritically recites the explorers' accounts of the men's laziness and 'ill-treatment of the women'. He even concludes that such treatment 'gave rise' to the nineteenth-century explorer Dumont D'Urville's claim that the Aboriginal women 'can only find pleasant the lives they lead with the Europeans who treat them far better'.[46] And finally, in examining Collins' aforementioned account of Bennelong and his family, Inga Clendinnen admits that it 'is indeed a charming scene', but warns against 'sentimentalis[ing] it', because it counters her thesis that the Aboriginal men possessed a 'contest culture', so were 'very' violent towards the women. While she unquestioningly accepts the explorers' descriptions of Aboriginal violence she is sceptical about this pacific episode, speculating that had 'Baneelon's women returned empty-handed, we have to assume that the scene would have been less pretty'.[47] Yet, it is not only modern scholars who have ignored these implicit accounts of the Aboriginal men's labours and contributions to the family economy. It seems the explorers themselves were also blind to the contradictions between their descriptions and appraisals, because they were so influenced by Enlightenment philosophies on savage indolence. This tendency is most apparent in their speculations on Aboriginal hunting practices.

Due to the brief nature of the majority of these expeditions' sojourns in any one place, very few of the explorers actually witnessed the Aboriginal men hunting during the period.[48] Perhaps because it was a strictly codified practice, as suggested by Collins' account of the *Yoo-long Erah-ba-diang* ceremony, or that the foreign observers were an impediment to a successful hunt, so the Aboriginal men only went out when the strangers were far away. Consequently, the Europeans had to rely on conjecture to understand how the Aboriginal men hunted the exotic and shy animals found in the Australian countryside. The kangaroo in particular interested the explorers because it was the largest animal they discovered, and they had found it to be especially fast and difficult to catch.

All of the explorers at various times noted the Aborigines' use of kangaroo skins in their manufactures, so their possession of these hides would suggest

---

46   Plomley 1983: 206; Dyer 2005: 153–156.
47   Clendinnen 2003: 159, 162–163.
48   For descriptions of hunting from a later period see Dyer 2005: 67–71.

that they must have been successful in hunting this elusive quarry. During his interviews with the Tasmanian Aborigines Labillardière had been shown an animal skin pierced with two holes 'which had been made apparently with the point of a spear'. On seeing one of the men demonstrate throwing this weapon, the botanist deduced that 'they launch it with sufficient force to pierce the animal through and through', so happily accepted that the men were competent huntsmen.[49] However, notwithstanding the drudgery of the women, these particular Frenchmen held the local Aboriginal society in high esteem, so easily accepted that the Aborigines had a high degree of proficiency in their long established customs and practices. Oddly, such logic was not employed by all of the explorers.

The First Fleet surgeon Arthur Bowes Smyth was highly critical of the Aboriginal men. While acknowledging that 'Sometimes they feast upon the Kangaroo' he claimed that they were 'too stupid & indolent a set of people to be able often to catch them'. This hypothesis could only be rationalised by his assumption that the British were by nature superior marksmen, so when they discovered that the animals were 'so extremely shy that 'tis no easy matter to get near enough even to shoot them', he concluded that the Aboriginal men must fare comparatively worse.[50] John Wilby, midshipman on the *Adventure*, Cook's companion ship on his second voyage, came to a similarly tenuous conclusion about the Aboriginal Tasmanians' hunting ability.

In February 1773 the *Resolution* and the *Adventure* were separated due to the bad weather experienced in Antarctic waters, so the latter set course for the rendezvous point in New Zealand and on the way landed briefly in Tasmania. During their stay at Adventure Bay the Britons saw signs that the place was inhabited, but failed to encounter a single person. However, this lack of contact did not prevent them from describing the Indigenous people. Just by observing the few material items discovered, Wilby immediately assumed that the Aborigines 'have nothing to Live on but Shellfish'. Like Bowes Smyth, his conjecture was based on his fellow Britons' limited success in shooting game, because he found that 'the Birds, what few there are, [were] so shy, that [it was] difficult to get a Shot at them'.[51]

The tenuousness of their claims is illuminated by examining an account by Worgan, who had observed the Europeans' same difficulty in shooting game, but came to the opposite conclusion. Not long after arriving in Port Jackson the surgeon listed the various 'Water Fowls' that the British had killed, but noted that only 'one Black Swan has likewise been shot'. Apparently there were

---

49   Labillardière 1800: 300.
50   Bowes Smyth 1979: 57–58.
51   Wilby 1961: 151 n.

'Many of these', but the shooters had 'sometimes go[ne] out for a whole Day, and not [been] able to get a shot at a single Bird'. Worgan decided that the swans were 'extremely shy, as indeed may be said of all the animals here' and, in contrast to Bowes Smyth and Wilby, surmised that this was because 'they [were] harassed by the Natives'.[52] These contradictory claims based on similar evidence illustrates the Europeans' limited understanding of the Aboriginal practices, and the extent to which some of the explorers had been swayed by the prevailing Enlightenment beliefs about savage societies. Their faith that such peoples must be completely divorced from the so-called civilised led some of the explorers to propose preposterous explanations about Aboriginal hunting methods.

Bowes Smyth, who had considered the Port Jackson men to be 'too stupid & indolent' to spear kangaroos, still had to explain how they managed to obtain the hides, so the imaginative surgeon proposed an alternative method. The First Fleet officers had noticed that many of the trees had 'regular steps chop'd at abt. 2 foot asunder in the Bark' and had pondered their purpose. From merely observing the trees, Bowes Smyth speculated that 'they mount these' carrying 'large stones', and then passively 'lie in ambush till some Kangaroos come under to graze' and then suddenly 'heave the stone upon [the animals] & kill them'.[53] His wild theory was undermined by later observations that the trees 'were notched' by the 'people of Port Jackson' so they could 'ascend [them] in pursuit of opossums'.[54]

The largely baseless assertions that the Aboriginal men were lazy and exploitative of their women were determined *a priori* by the contemporary philosophers' disquisitions on the indolent savage, and later historiography illustrates that such perceptions lingered long into the next centuries. While such appraisals were certainly disagreeable and unfair, it was the explorers' damning criticisms of the Aboriginal men's ingenuity and intelligence which had more serious implications.

Their general powers of mind

The explorers, having established in their minds that the Aboriginal men were indolent, then had to investigate the truth of theories such as Montesquieu's which suggested that savage people's sluggishness would enervate their minds. Some immediately assumed that this was the case. Milius posited that the Port Jackson Aborigines were immersed in the most profound ignorance, and William Anderson, surgeon on Cook's third voyage, claimed that:

---

52   Worgan 1978: 21.
53   Bowes Smyth 1979: 57–58.
54   Flinders 1814: 46.

With respect to personal activity or genius we can say but little of either. [The Aboriginal Tasmanians] do not seem to possess the first in any remarkable degree, and as for the last they have to appearance less than even the half animated inhabitants of Terra del Fuego.[55]

Yet, others, such as Tench, tried not to be so prejudiced, and instead adopted a more judicial approach. He noted that some of 'their manufactures display ingenuity, when the rude tools with which they work and their celerity of execution are considered'.[56] Consequently, most explorers decided that the Aboriginal men were completely ignorant and lacked ingenuity, or else conceded that their industry was tolerable when taken into appropriate consideration.

Given the difficulties in communicating without a common language, ascertaining Indigenous men's intellectual acuity was no easy task, and the explorers could only do so by examining either the ingenuity of their manufactures or how they reacted to European technology. De Gérando instructed the Baudin expedition to learn about the savages' industries by describing their methods used in 'the construction of huts, and the making of clothes', and ascertaining if 'they know metals' and the use of fire. He also recommended that 'some efforts [should] be made to make [the savages] set about [their manufactures] better', in order to gauge how quickly they could learn new techniques and therefore become civilised.[57] While these specific instructions were only given to one expedition, this method seems to have been intuitively used by all of the voyagers, irrespective of whether or not they actually encountered any Aboriginal people.

As stated earlier, the *Adventure* landed in Tasmania in 1773 after being separated from the *Resolution*. Tobias Furneaux, the captain of the ship, is described by the editor of Cook's journals, John Cawte Beaglehole, as possessing an 'incuriosity' which prevented him from being a great explorer, because he readily abandoned the question of whether or not Tasmania was geographically connected to the mainland.[58] Yet, his 'incuriosity' is more evident in his failure to try and meet any of the Aborigines, especially since the British considered that it was 'very remarkable that no European [had] ever seen an Inhabitant of Van Diemen's Land – & it [had been] more than 130 years since it was first discovered'.[59] Although Furneaux did not meet any Aboriginal people, he did not let this fact prevent him from appraising their industry and intelligence.

While the explorers described a range of tools, weapons, wares, watercrafts and fish and eel traps made by the Aboriginal people, it was their shelters

55   'Ce people est encore plongé dans la plus profonde ignorance'. Milius 1987: 48; Anderson 1967: 786–787.
56   Tench 1996[1789,1793]: 255.
57   De Gérando 1969[1800]: 96.
58   Beaglehole 1961: xxxv, lxviii–lxix.
59   Burney 1975: 39. In actual fact, unbeknownst to the English, the French explorer Marc-Joseph Marion-Dufresne had encountered Tasmanians a year before. Beaglehole 1961: lxix.

which captured their attention because the hut's seemingly makeshift nature suggested that the indigenes were nomadic. Further, for the likes of Furneaux and his crew, dwellings were almost the only Indigenous manufacture they witnessed, so the Europeans simply had to make the most of describing them. Consequently I will limit my discussion here to the explorers' discussions of the Aboriginal habitations.

In examining the huts Furneaux discovered that they were made from a tree bough which was 'either broke or split and tied together with grass in a circular form [with] the longest end stuck in the ground, and the smaller part meeting in a point at the top, and covered with Ferns and bark'. He thought that the huts was 'so poorly done that they will hardly keep out a showr [sic] of rain', so concluded that 'their houses seem'd to be built but for a few days' only, and that they 'wander about in small parties from place to place in search of Food and are activated by no other motive'. Further, he 'never saw the least signs of either Canoe or boat', so it was 'generally thought they have none', and that they were 'quite ignorant of every sort of Metal'.[60] Based on these brief observations of their material culture, Furneaux surmised that the Aboriginal Tasmanians were 'a very Ignorant and wretched set of people'.[61]

The captain was not alone in his disparaging assessments of their dwellings. His crewmate, James Burney, thought 'their Huts ... ill contrived'; when Cook set foot in Tasmania on his third voyage he referred to them as 'mean small hovels not much bigger than an oven'; and even Baudin who was often relatively measured in his evaluations, considered them 'the most miserable things imaginable'.[62] Similarly, at Port Jackson Collins claimed that their 'habitations [were] as rude as imagination can conceive ... affording shelter to only one miserable tenant', and Bowes Smyth labelled them 'miserable Wigwams'.[63] And on the west coast in Eendracht Land, north of Shark Bay, Péron found some semi-circular huts 'made of shrubby plants' which he considered 'crude', but 'none the less the most finished examples that [they] had occasion to observe in New Holland'.[64]

The explorers were somewhat surprised by the poverty of the Aborigines' buildings, because, according to Furneaux, they were 'natives of a country producing every necessity of life, and a climate the fairest in the world'.[65] Evidently, he had expected that such ignorance could only be found in the 'torrid zones', as hypothesised by many Enlightenment philosophers. Lieutenant

---

60   Baudin also noted that the Tasmanians appeared 'to have no knowledge of iron and its usefulness. They did not attach the slightest importance to the nails that [they] wanted to give them and returned them to [the French] as serving no purpose', but he refrained from judging them on it. Baudin 1974: 350.
61   Furneaux 1961: 735.
62   Burney 1975: 38; Cook 1955 I: 396; Baudin 1974: 345.
63   Collins 1975: 460; Bowes Smyth 1978: 57.
64   Péron and Freycinet 2003[1824]: 138.
65   Furneaux 1961: 735.

John Rickman of the *Discovery,* the companion ship on Cook's third voyage, was similarly perplexed by the Aborigines' ignorance and lack of industry despite Tasmania's hospitable climate. Noting that 'when Nature pours forth her luxuriant exuberance to cloath this country with every variety', it was very 'strange' to the Europeans that 'the few natives [they] saw were wholly insensible of those blessings'. Instead of taking advantage of their fertile environment, they 'seemed to live like those beasts of the forest in roving parties, without arts of any kind, sleeping in summer like dogs, under the hollow sides of the trees'.[66] The Britons' allusions to the natives' ostensible animality betrayed their utter contempt that the Aborigines could, in their eyes, waste such a bounteous land. Furneaux and Rickman were so confounded that they did not even speculate on any possible reasons for this, although, fortunately for the modern reader, others did.

In Port Jackson John Hunter noticed that the Aborigines' 'ignorance in building, [was] very amply compensated by the kindness of nature', so understood that they had little need for industry. To prove this he even went so far as to make the extraordinary claim that one of nature's gifts was the 'remarkable softness of the rocks, which encompass the sea coast, as well as those of the interior parts of the country', so they did not have to erect comfortable dwellings.[67] Perhaps these, and similar ethnographic accounts describing the ostensible absence of arts and industry amongst savage societies in temperate climates, led Malthus to counter the claim that it was only the torrid zones which induced ignorance and apathy. In 1798 he proposed that 'In those countries, where nature is the most redundant in spontaneous produce, the inhabitants will not be found the most remarkable for acuteness of intellect'. Consequently, Malthus affirmed, 'Necessity has been with great truth called the mother of invention'.[68] Believing that the 'savage would slumber forever under his tree unless he were roused from his torpor by the cravings of hunger, or the pinchings of cold', Malthus claimed that it was necessities such as 'procuring food, and building himself a covering' which forced the savage to 'form and keep in motion his faculties'.[69]

A similar thesis was embraced by Péron in his attempt to understand why the aforementioned huts of Eendracht Land were, in his esteem, uniquely superior to any others found in New Holland. He acknowledged that so 'much effort and care' in their construction 'would seem at first to indicate a more advanced state of civilisation' of these people, than those in other parts of the country. However, he claimed that such a position would be wrong, for he contended that the huts' superiority was instead 'the consequence of a deeper misery and

---

66   Anonymous 1781: 43–44. Cook similarly noted that they 'move from place to place like wild Beasts in search of food'. Cook 1955 I: 396.
67   Hunter 1968[1793]: 40–41.
68   Malthus 1926: 358.
69   Malthus 1926: 357.

more pressing need'. Péron elaborated that '[h]owever accustomed the native may be to the inclemencies of the atmosphere and the seasons, he can never be absolutely insensible to them', so to this end he would seek out ways to minimise his discomfort, even if he could not completely eradicate it. The Frenchman pronounced that the 'very efforts that he will make to achieve this end will always be in fairly exact proportion to the discomfort that he experiences'.[70]

The Shark Bay climate was very erratic, for Péron noticed that a 'fresh, very dry morning [gave] way to a burning day which ends, in turn, in an excessively damp, cold night'. So while he accepted that the Aboriginal Tasmanians lived 'in a colder climate', the 'vicissitudes' of Eendracht Land ensured that it was worse. He believed the native had to 'guard himself' by 'building shelters, disposed in such a way as to furnish salutary shade during the day and an essential refuge from the cold and damp at night'.[71] Although he does not explicitly say as much, Péron's thesis countered Montesquieu's proposal, because Péron believed that those natives 'so near the tropics' possessed more ingenuity than those in the more temperate climes.[72] Of course his thesis only encompassed Indigenous people, and did not compare all people who lived in temperate climates, such as Europeans.

The other method the explorers had for investigating the Aboriginal men's intellect was to gauge how they reacted to the ostensibly superior European manufactures and technology. They pompously displayed their weapons, musical instruments, bottles, clothes, and trifles, anticipating that the Aboriginal people would admire and covet them. Often they were disappointed by the lacklustre Indigenous reaction. However, by showing the Aboriginal men their tools they not only looked for acknowledgment of their ostensible superiority, but were keen to ascertain whether or not savage man could understand the tools' purpose, and adopt their use for themselves. The explorers ethnocentrically presumed that if the savages could recognise that the European wares were of course superior, and immediately eschew their own technology in their favour, that this would signal that the Aborigines were in fact intelligent.

Anderson, who like Labillardière also failed to realise that the Aboriginal Tasmanians did not eat vertebrate fish, was surprised that 'They were even ignorant of the use of fish hooks' because they did not seem to 'comprehend the use of some of [the Britons'] which [they] were shown'. Their 'indifference [and] general inattention' to this equipment (which would have enabled them to procure food they did not actually eat), was taken by Anderson as 'sufficient proofs of [their intellectual] deficiency'.[73] In the European mind, this level of

---

70   Péron and Freycinet 2003[1824]: 140.
71   Péron and Freycinet 2003[1824]: 141.
72   Péron and Freycinet 2003[1824]: 140.
73   Anderson 1967: 787.

unresponsiveness did not bode well for the Aborigines. On the same voyage Cook decided that this 'kind of indifferency is the true Character of [the Tahitian] Nation', for he was dismayed to realise on his third voyage there that 'Europeans have visited them at time for these ten years past, yet we find neither new arts nor improvements in the old'. With some indignation he exclaimed 'nor have they copied after us in any one thing'.[74]

Yet some of the explorers did find that the Aboriginal men would copy them, and demonstrate their comprehension of the Western tools. The very first time Alexandre d'Hesmivy d'Auribeau, captain of d'Entrecasteaux's *Recherche,* met with a group of Aboriginal men in Tasmania he showed some of them 'the use of the axes, saws, knives, nails, etc.' and he noticed that 'they understood very quickly'.[75] One man, who appeared to be the 'head of the household', and was greatly esteemed by the Frenchmen as 'a very intelligent man', quickly grasped the utility of the axe, and immediately 'cut down several trees with a dexterity which many Europeans would not equal'.[76] The men seemed 'so very eager in desiring the objects' especially the axe which, in his opinion would be the most beneficial to them, that d'Hesmivy d'Auribeau thought they exhibited 'surprising intelligence'.[77] While the French assessments of the Aboriginal Tasmanians' intellects were certainly more complementary than those of the British, they were no more ethnographically reliable, and still largely determined by European prejudices. In fact Tench railed against both kinds of viewpoints in his disquisition on the Aboriginal men's 'general powers of mind'.[78]

'Ignorance, prejudice, [and] the force of habit', said Tench, 'continually interfere to prevent dispassionate judgement'. To illustrate this he reported hearing 'men so unreasonable as to exclaim at the stupidity of [the Aboriginal] people for not comprehending what a small share of reflection would have taught [the officers] they ought not to have expected'. At the same time, Tench also lambasted those who 'extol for proofs of elevated genius what the commonest abilities were capable of executing'.[79] Had he been aware of the views of d'Entrecasteaux's men, he might have included chopping wood as an example of these 'commonest abilities'. He pronounced that the Aboriginal people as a nation 'would certainly rank very low, even in the scale of savages' if one was measuring 'general advancement and acquisitions', and that 'a less enlightened state … can hardly exist', when considering that they were 'strangers to clothing', felt the 'sharpness of hunger', and were 'ignorant of cultivating the earth'.[80] However,

---

74   Cook 1967 III Pt 1: 241.
75   D'Hesmivy d'Auribeau 1993: 280.
76   Raoul 1993: 305.
77   D'Hesmivy d'Auribeau 1993: 280.
78   Tench 1996[1789,1793]: 252–254.
79   Tench 1996[1789,1793]: 252.
80   Yet, he did admit he had met individuals in Port Jackson who 'possess a considerable portion of that acumen, or sharpness of intellect, which bespeaks genius'. Here he considered Arabanoo, Bennelong and

Tench argued, gauging Aboriginal reactions to European wares was a somewhat limited approach in understanding the indigenes' intelligence, for, by doing so most Europeans were not able to 'discriminate between ignorance and defect of understanding'.[81]

The fact that the Aboriginal people ran an 'indifferen[t] and unenquiring eye' over the European artworks and manufactures presented to them during tours of the British houses, should not, according to Tench, have been considered 'proofs of [their] stupidity and want of reflection', because such items were 'artifices and contrivances' not familiar to the Aborigines, so of no consequence to them. However, he claimed, when they saw objects which related to their world, such as 'a collection of weapons of war' or 'the skins of animals and birds', the Aborigines 'never failed to exclaim' or to 'confer' with one another, wondering if the 'master of that house' was a 'renowned warrior, or an expert hunter'. Thus Tench believed that such recognition on their part indicated that they did not have a 'defect of understanding', but were instead merely 'ignorant' about these foreign things.[82] To conclude his lengthy disquisition Tench tackled the thorny question of agriculture.

Evidently, some of the British could begrudgingly accept that savage societies did not cultivate the earth, but expected that upon being introduced to it, the indigenes would immediately recognise agriculture's superior benefits, and enthusiastically embrace it. Like Cook, the only explanation some Europeans could devise for Indigenous people's failure to adopt subsistence farming, was that they were too indifferent and intellectually deficient to do so. Tench addressed this view when he admitted that, 'it may be asked why the same intelligent spirit which led [the Aborigines] to contemplate and applaud the success of the sportsman and the skill of the surgeon did not equally excite them to meditate on the labours of the builder, and the ploughman'. Tench had already acknowledged the contemporary consensus that all 'savages hate toil and place happiness in inaction ... Hence they resist knowledge and the adoption of manners and customs differing from their own'. So, in response to the question of agriculture he pronounced that 'what we see in its remote cause is always more feebly felt than that which presents to our immediate grasp both its origin and effect'.[83] Tench rationalised that, like Europeans, the Aborigines were attracted to activities which produced immediate benefits, and agricultural harvests, which could not be reaped until the distant future, were hardly an enticing prospect.

Colby, whom, as we have already seen, Tench often engaged with intellectually, and had been both charmed and challenged by their different characters. Tench 1996[1789,1793]: 253.

81   Tench 1996[1789,1793]: 253.
82   Tench 1996[1789,1793]: 253–254.
83   Tench 1996[1789,1793]: 253–254.

Tench's lengthy examination of the Aborigines' 'powers of mind' and the nature of their industries incorporated European assumptions about savage indolence, but not in an exclusively uncritical way. Unlike most of his contemporaries he did not seek to quickly confirm Enlightenment theories on the inherent lassitude and intellectual deficiencies of savage peoples. Tench believed their daily lives and labours to be simple, but recognised the pragmatism of their indifference to the ostensibly superior European modes of subsistence and technology. While the contradictions in the explorers' editorial incursions and descriptions of the Aboriginal men's indolence, combined with the flimsily substantiated speculations on Aboriginal methods of procuring food and constructing their dwellings, reveal the extent to which the explorers were influenced by the Enlightenment philosophies on savage indolence and ignorance, disquisitions such as Tench's are even more illuminating. His thesis suggests that the explorers could engage with the theories rather than just parrot them, and, on occasion, see the intricacies of Indigenous societies and mount complex arguments to explain them. Unfortunately Tench's sophisticated interpretation of Indigenous industry was an isolated example then, and even today remains a remarkably nuanced and considered disquisition.

Conclusion

The European explorers recorded many examples of the Aboriginal men's labours including how they procured food and constructed their shelters and tools. Their depictions of the men's bodies employed in these diverse actions illustrate that the men were very energetic in their daily lives. The accounts display the Aboriginal men's agility, dexterity, perseverance, and strategy in hunting and fishing, their ingenuity and pragmatism in building their dwellings and making their wares. Yet, the explorers' prevailing opinion concerning this range of activities and qualities was that the men were simply indolent, ignorant, and brutal.

The consequence of these theories was that Indigenous people were constructed *a priori* as unduly indolent and ignorant. In an age of slavery and imperialism, savage peoples were perceived as undeserving of their bounteous land and freedom for they did not practice agriculture so could not make productive use of them. Such ideas must have been at the forefront of the explorers' minds when they recorded their impressions of the Aboriginal men's labour for it dominated their explicit evaluations. However, at times they presented alternative views, and even sophisticated and nuanced critiques of European civilisation and ways of thinking. So the explorers' journals are far richer textual sources on eighteenth-century European ideas and mores than much of the historiography reveals, and presents a more complex, multifaceted picture of Aboriginal industriousness that counters the enduring myth of Indigenous indolence.

References

Primary Sources

Anderson, William 1967, 'A Journal of a Voyage Made in His Majesty's Sloop Resolution', in *The Journals of Captain James Cook on his Voyage of Discovery*, JC Beaglehole (ed), Hakluyt Society, London, vol 3, part II: 721–986.

Anonymous, [attributed to Lieutenant John Rickman] 1781, *Journal of Captain Cook's last Voyage to the Pacific Ocean, on Discovery; Performed in the years 1776, 1777, 1778, 1779, illustrated with Cuts, a Chart, shewing the Tracts of the Ships employed in this Expedition, Faithfully narrated from the original MS, E Newberry*, London.

Banks, Joseph 1998, *The Endeavour Journal of Joseph Banks: The Australian Journey*, Paul Brunton (ed), Harper Collins Publishers in association with the State Library of New South Wales, Pymble.

Baudin, Nicolas 1974, *The Journal of Post-Captain Nicolas Baudin Commander-in-Chief of the Corvettes Géographe and Naturaliste*, Christine Cornell (trans), Libraries Board of South Australia, Adelaide.

Bowes Smyth, Arthur 1979, *The Journal of Arthur Bowes Smyth: Surgeon on* Lady Penryth *1787–89*, Paul G Fidlon and RJ Ryan (eds), Australian Document Library, Sydney.

Buffon, Georges Louis Leclerc Comte de 1950, 'A Natural History, General and Particular' [1749], in *This is Race: An Anthology Selected from International Literature on Races of Man*, Earl W Count (ed), Henry Schuman, New York: 3–15.

Burney, James 1975, *With Captain James Cook in the Antarctic and Pacific: the private journal of James Burney, second lieutenant of the Adventure on Cook's second voyage, 1772–1773*, Beverley Hooper (ed), National Library of Australia, Canberra.

Collins, David 1975, *An Account of the English Colony in New South Wales*, Brian Fletcher (ed), AH & AW Reed in association with the Royal Australian Historical Society, Sydney.

Cook, James 1955–1967, *The Journals of Captain James Cook on his Voyage of Discovery*, JC Beaglehole (ed), 3 vols in 4, Hakluyt Society, London.

Dampier, William 1998, *A New Voyage Round the World: The Journal of an English Buccaneer*, Mark Beken (ed), Hummingbird Press, London.

De Gérando, Joseph-Marie 1969[1800], *The Observation of Savage Peoples*, FCT Moore (trans), University of California Press, Berkeley.

D'Entrecasteaux, Bruny 2001, *Voyage to Australia and the Pacific 1791–1793*, Edward Duyker and Maryse Duyker (eds), Melbourne University Press, Carlton South.

D'Hesmivy d'Auribeau, Alexandre 1993, 'D'Hesmivy d'Auribeau's first meeting with the Natives, 1793', in *The General: the Visits of the Expedition Led by Bruny d'Entrecasteaux to Tasmanian Waters in 1792 and 1793*, Brian Plomley and Josiane Piard-Bernier (trans and eds), Queen Victoria Museum, Launceston: 279–284.

Féron, Jean-Louis 1993, 'Journal of Jean-Louis Féron, gunner', in *The General: the Visits of the Expedition Led by Bruny d'Entrecasteaux to Tasmanian Waters in 1792 and 1793*, Brian Plomley and Josiane Piard-Bernier (trans and eds), Queen Victoria Museum, Launceston: 286–288.

Flinders, Matthew 1814, *A Voyage to Terra Australis*, G&W Nicol, Pall Mall.

Furneaux, Tobias 1961, 'Furneaux's Narrative', in *The Journals of Captain James Cook on his Voyage of Discovery*, JC Beaglehole (ed), Hakluyt Society, London, vol 2: 729–745.

Hunter, John 1968[1793], *An Historical Journal of the Transactions at Port Jackson and Norfolk Island...*, Australiana Facsimile Editions No. 148, Libraries Board of South Australia, Adelaide.

Kant, Immanuel 1997[1900–1960], 'On countries that are known and unknown to Europeans', in *Physical Geography* [Physische Geographie], in *Gesammelte Schriften*, Reimer, Berlin, vol 2, KM Faull and EC Eze (trans) reprinted in Emmanuel Chukwudi Eze (ed) 1997, Race and the Enlightenment: A Reader, Blackwell Publishers Ltd, Cambridge, Mass: 58–64.

— 1960[1764], *Observations on the Feeling of the Beautiful and Sublime*, JT Goldthwait (trans), University of California Press, Berkeley.

Labillardière, Jacques de 1800, *Voyage in Search of La Pérouse, Performed by Order of the Constituent Assembly, During the Years 1791, 1792, 1793, and 1794*, John Stockdale, Piccadilly, London.

Linne, Charles 1806[1735], *A General System of Nature*, William Turton (trans and ed), 7 vols, Lackington, Allen and Co, London.

Locke, John 1963[1690], *Two Treatises of Government*, Peter Laslett (ed), Cambridge University Press, Cambridge.

Malthus, Thomas Robert 1926, *First Essay on Population* 1798, Royal Economic Society and Macmillan & Co Ltd, London.

Milius, Pierre Bernard 1987, *Recit du Voyage aux Terres Australes par Pierre Bernard Milius, Second sur le Naturaliste dans l'expedition Baudin (1800–1804)*, Jacqueline Bonnemains and Pascale Hauguel, (eds), Société havraise d'études diverses, Muséum d'histoire naturelle du Havre, Le Havre.

Montesquieu, Charles de Secondat 1989[1748], *The Spirit of Laws*, Anne M Cohler, Basia Carolyn Miller, and Harold Samuel Stone (trans and eds), Cambridge University Press, Cambridge.

Péron, François 1975[1809], *A Voyage of Discovery to the Southern Hemisphere, performed by order of the Emperor Napoleon, during the years 1801, 1802, 1803, and 1804*, [Richard Phillips, London], repr. by Mark Walsh Publishing, North Melbourne.

— and Louis de Freycinet 2003[1824], *Voyage of the Discovery to the Southern Lands: Book IV, Comprising Chapters XXII to XXXIV*, 2nd ed, Christine Cornell (trans), The Friends of the State Library of South Australia, Adelaide.

Raoul, Joseph 1993, 'Extracts from the journal of Joseph Raoul, Second pilot on the Recherche, for 1793', in *The General: the Visits of the Expedition Led by Bruny d'Entrecasteaux to Tasmanian Waters in 1792 and 1793*, Brian Plomley and Josiane Piard-Bernier (trans and eds), Queen Victoria Museum, Launceston: 304–307.

Tench, Watkin 1996[1789, 1793], *1788: Comprising 'A Narrative of the Expedition to Botany Bay' and 'A Complete Account of the Settlement at Port Jackson'*, Tim Flannery (ed), The Text Publishing Company, Melbourne.

Wilby, John 1961, Journal, AB Adventure, PRO Adm 51/4522/14 Entry for Monday 15th March 1773, in *The Journals of Captain James Cook on his Voyage of Discovery*, JC Beaglehole (ed), Hakluyt Society, London, vol 2: 151.

Worgan, George 1978, *Journal of a First Fleet Surgeon*, Library Council of New South Wales in association with the Library of Australian History, Sydney.

Secondary sources

Banner, Stuart 2005, 'Why Terra nullius? Anthropology and Property law in early Australia', *Law and History Review* 23(1): 76 paras. Available online, accessed 17 November 2008: <http://www.historycooperative.org/journals/lhr/23.1/banner.html>

Beaglehole, JC 1961, 'Introduction', in his edition of James Cook, *The Journals of Captain James Cook on his Voyage of Discovery*, Hakluyt Society, London, vol 2: xix–cxiii.

Broome, Richard 1994, 'Aboriginal workers on south-eastern frontiers', *Australian Historical Studies* 103: 202–220.

Buchan, Bruce and Mary Heath 2006, 'Savagery and Civilization: From Terra Nullius to the "Tide of History"', *Ethnicities* 6(1): 5–26.

Clendinnen, Inga 2003, *Dancing with Strangers,* Text Publishing, Melbourne.

Curthoys, Ann and Clive Moore 1995, 'Working for the white people: an historiographic essay on Aboriginal and Torres Strait Islander labour', *Labour History* 69: 1–29.

Davidson, Iain and David Andrew Roberts 2009, '14000BP: being alone: the isolation of the Tasmanians', in *Turning Points in Australian history,* Martin Crotty and David Andrew Roberts (eds), University of New South Wales Press, Sydney: 18–31.

Dyer, Colin 2005, *The French Explorers and the Aboriginal Australians, 1772–1839*, University of Queensland Press, St Lucia.

Eze, Emmanuel Chukwudi (ed) 1997, *Race and the Enlightenment: A Reader*, Blackwell Publishers Ltd, Cambridge (Mass).

Frost, Alan 1990, 'New South Wales as *terra nullius*: the British denial of Aboriginal land rights', in *Through White Eyes,* Susan Janson and Stuart Macintyre (eds), Allen & Unwin, Sydney: 65–76.

Harrison, Mark 1999, *Climates and Constitutions: Health, Race, Environment and British Imperialism in India 1600–1850*, Oxford University Press, New Delhi.

McGrath, Ann 1990, 'The white man's looking glass: Aboriginal-colonial gender relations at Port Jackson', *Australian Historical Studies* 24(99): 189–206.

Office of the Minister for Aboriginal and Torres Strait Islander Affairs 1994, *Rebutting the myths: some Facts about Aboriginal and Torres Strait Islander Affairs*, AGPS, Canberra. Available online, accessed 14 June 2009: <http://www.austlii.edu.au/au/other/IndigLRes/1994/1/index.html>

Plomley, NJB 1983, *The Baudin Expedition and the Tasmanian Aborigine 1802,* Blubber Head Press, Hobart.

— and Josiane Piard-Bernier (trans and eds) 1993, *The General: the Visits of the Expedition Led by Bruny d'Entrecasteaux to Tasmanian Waters in 1792 and 1793*, Queen Victoria Museum, Launceston.

Porter, Roy 1997, *The Greatest Benefit to Mankind: A Medical History of Humanity from Antiquity to the Present*, Harper Collins Publishers, London.

Reynolds, Henry 1990, *With the White People*, Penguin Books, Ringwood.

— 1987, *The Law of the Land*, Penguin Books, Ringwood.

Wolfe, Patrick 2001, 'Land, labor, and difference: elementary structures of race', *The American Historical Review* 106(3). Available online, accessed 21 July 2009: <http://www.historycooperative.org/journals/ahr/106.3/ah000866.html>

6. 'These unoffending people': myth, history and the idea of Aboriginal resistance in David Collins' *Account of the English Colony in New South Wales*

RACHEL STANDFIELD

Until the development of the discipline of Aboriginal history in the 1970s, the accepted conclusion of most Australian historians in the twentieth century was that the country was settled peacefully with little resistance from Aboriginal people. The scholarship of Aboriginal history has analysed and complicated this notion of peaceful settlement right across the country and throughout the history of colonisation. In the recent historiography of the very beginning of white settlement, however, the first five years of British settlement around Port Jackson are largely depicted as 'peaceful', in contrast to later periods of settler violence on the frontier. Alan Atkinson has written of the 'spirit of reciprocity which existed between Black and White at the very beginning'.[1] Inga Clendinnen depicted the first five years of white settlement as the time 'before cynicism set in'.[2] Her conclusions have led Robert Manne to view the first years of settlement as 'perhaps the only time in colonial Australia when the British and the Aborigines lived together not on the basis of subordination but equality'.[3] This time is seen not only as characterised by equality, but also as lacking conflict over land. Clendinnen believed that early administrators 'as yet had no awareness of possible conflict over land'.[4] Josephine Flood's recent monograph stated that the expansion of British settlement to the Hawkesbury region in the 1790s was 'Australia's first conflict over land'.[5] Deirdre Coleman has described this as an 'increasing orthodoxy' where the first years of settlement

---

1 Atkinson 1991: 154.
2 Clendinnen 2003: 5. For analyses of Clendinnen's perspectives on Aboriginal sexuality and sovereignty, see also Konishi 2008; Morrissey 2007.
3 Coleman 2004: 206.
4 Clendinnen 2003: 5.
5 Flood 2006: 52.

are seen as without conflict over land. The absence of land conflict fits with a more general theme in the historiography that the initial period of settlement was 'more innocent, more enlightened, less racist' than later colonial times.[6]

There are perhaps a number of reasons for this tendency to see early British settlement as without conflict. Some of these recent histories may be the product of their particular time in contemporary politics. Clendinnen, for example, expressed her hope that by examining British attempts to understand a different culture she was furthering 'social justice' between Indigenous and non-Indigenous Australians.[7] This depiction of first settlement also, I would suggest, rests on insufficient analysis of the journals of the British officers, and in particular their discourses of class and race. One exception is Thomas Keneally's *The Commonwealth of Thieves*, whose analysis of the representations of convicts and Aboriginal people in the First Fleet journals is more nuanced than some other recent readings.[8] This chapter also seeks to analyse the portrayal of convicts, to demonstrate how discourses of class impacted on the portrayal of relations between the British and Aboriginal people, shaping the representation of Aboriginal people as peaceful and unoffending.

This essay offers a detailed analysis of one publication by an officer of the First Fleet, that written by the first Judge-Advocate of the New South Wales colony, and secretary to Governor Phillip, David Collins. Collins published his *Account of the English Colony in New South Wales* in two volumes in 1798 and 1802.[9] The author's central roles in the administration mean, as Alan Atkinson has pointed out, that his work 'echoed the original spirit of the state' and he was 'Australia's original historian'.[10] The Eora occupied a position of particular importance in Collins' *Account*, with several chapters discussing ongoing relations between the locals and the newcomers, and a separate ethnology being included in the publication. Interrogating British representation of Indigenous resistance in a text such as this is important because it is closely linked to the colonial history of the country and the denial of Aboriginal sovereignty and land rights.

Collins and Aboriginal resistance

In the *Account*'s first mention of encounter with Aboriginal people, Collins initiated a complex discourse combining a record of Aboriginal displeasure, a suggestion that the people were peaceful, and also an expression of concern

---

6   Coleman 2004: 206, 201. Evans 1999 outlines the potential role of conflict studies in Australian history writing and Broome 2005 provides a more nuanced and complex reading of violence in the first settlement of Victoria.

7   Clendinnen 2003: 5.

8   Keneally 2005.

9   Collins 1798, 1802. For details of Collins' colonial career, see Currey 2000.

10   Atkinson 1991: 172, 91.

about the impact of colonisation on the Indigenous population. Collins first mentioned Aboriginal people while describing an exploration party, headed by Phillip and including Collins, travelling north along the coast from Botany Bay searching for a site for permanent settlement:

> Their little fleet attracted the attention of several parties of the natives, who all greeted them in the same words, and in the same tone of vociferation, shouting every where 'Warra, warra, warra', words which, by the gestures which accompanied them, could not be interpreted into invitations to land, or expressions of welcome.[11]

Collins thus acknowledged Aboriginal resistance to the British but by combining it with description of the British party as a 'little fleet' downplayed any sense of threat to the locals. Aboriginal people in turn were characterised as peaceful and accommodating, Collins stating that in a previous encounter with the Botany Bay people they did not view the British 'as enemies or invaders of the country and their tranquillity'.[12] He did, however, add in a crucial footnote to his conclusion that the British were not seen as invaders: 'How grateful to every feeling of humanity, would it be that we could conclude this narrative without being compelled to say, that these unoffending people had found reasons to change both their opinions and their conduct'.[13] This footnote appeared to question whether the Port Jackson settlement was as peaceful as the British had hoped and to reflect on the disturbance it had caused the Eora.[14] Crucially, however, in its use of the term 'unoffending' Collins also characterised Aboriginal people as of no threat to the colony. Nicholas Thomas has stated that Collins saw the Indigenous population as 'both essentially benevolent and fatally unknowing' even while he writes about their 'belligerence', concluding that Collins 'never makes resistance a theme'.[15]

Thomas is right; Collins did not make resistance a theme. In this tendency he was following those British travellers who had been before him. In fact, one of the reasons Australia was chosen as the site for convict settlement was because resistance from Aboriginal people was not expected. Certainly in evidence to the Committee of Transportation meeting to consider a convict settlement in 1779 and 1785, Joseph Banks, the most influential British person to have encountered Aboriginal people, highlighted their supposed lack of resistance. While encounters with Aboriginal people had been fleeting and marked by a lack of common language, Banks did not hesitate to use his impressions as

---

11   Collins 1798: 3.
12   Collins 1798: 3.
13   Collins 1798: 3.
14   Deirdre Coleman has identified moments where the 'dispossessing intruders register both triumph and uneasiness' as a theme of discourses of 'romantic colonization'. Coleman 2005: 14.
15   Thomas 1999: 35.

evidence to the Committee. On both of the occasions he testified before the Committee Banks advocated Botany Bay as his preferred site for settlement. In 1779 he stated that based on his experience of New South Wales in 1770 there was 'little probability of any opposition' from the Indigenous population. He had seen very few people at Botany Bay and assumed the country was 'thinly peopled'. Central to his evidence was an imagined colonial scenario marked by a lack of Aboriginal resistance; he thought the people armed and 'treacherous' but cowardly because they avoided confronting the voyagers.[16] When Banks testified again in 1785, the Committee asked about Aboriginal defensive capacity and weaponry as well as whether land could be ceded or sold. Banks believed land could not be sold, because while the *Endeavour* had been in Australia 'there was nothing we could offer that they would take' except food.[17] Banks repeated his comments from six years before, that there were few Aboriginal inhabitants, who looked 'inclined to Hostilities' but 'did not appear at all to be feared'.[18] When the Committee asked whether the Indigenous inhabitants would obstruct a party of colonists and prevent their settlement, Banks answered emphatically 'Certainly not'; his experience led him to believe 'they would speedily abandon the Country to the New Comers'.[19]

Assumptions of a sparsely populated and undefended country, developed out of the *Endeavour* voyage and reiterated by Banks, had major consequences. They meant that Phillip's instructions did not compel him to negotiate for settlement. His instructions did, however, direct him to collect further information about Aboriginal people, to

> endeavour to procure an account of the number inhabiting the neighbourhood of the intended settlement, and report your opinion to one of our Secretaries of State in what manner our intercourse with these people may be turned to the advantage of this colony.[20]

Merete Borch has argued that these instructions allowed scope for a policy change towards Aboriginal people once settlement had started. She concluded that if colonial officials had recommended a treaty, the metropolitan government would have negotiated with Aboriginal people. Borch remained puzzled, however, by the continued lack of negotiation as knowledge increased about Aboriginal people and 'their hostility towards settlement on their land was being clearly displayed'.[21] The issue here, then, becomes one of whether British observers really did think Aboriginal people were hostile to the British settlement.

---

16   Quoted in Borch 2004: 86.
17   King 1985: 55–56.
18   King 1985: 54–55.
19   King 1985: 60–61.
20   Quoted in Borch 2004: 79.
21   Quoted in Borch 2004: 104.

Governor Phillip's thoughts about resistance were implicit in his plans for the new colony, set out in his 'Conduct of the Expedition and the Treatment of Convicts' in 1787.[22] While Phillip believed the Aboriginal population might be larger than the numbers that Cook had seen, he saw need only for 'throwing up a slight work as a defence' against them. Endeavouring to establish the colony without any disputes with Aboriginal people, Phillip planned to completely separate the convicts and ships' crews from interacting with Aboriginal people, fearing that convicts and crew would come to possess Aboriginal weapons, that Aboriginal women would be mistreated and 'the natives disgusted'.[23] Phillip may not have seen Aboriginal people as a threat, but he thought Māori the best deterrent for the crimes of murder and sodomy. He planned to send offenders to 'the natives of New Zealand, and let them eat him'.[24] As Raymond Evans and Bill Thorpe have explained, the convict system rested on the construction of convicts as a 'criminal class' creating a presumption that convicts were always at fault.[25] Penny Russell has stated that convicts and other undesirable groups were used as 'scapegoats' within the colonising project, and so they would come to be in the *Account*.[26]

In understanding British perceptions of Aboriginal responses to the British settlement, David Collins's *Account* takes on a very important role in the production of knowledge about Aboriginal resistance and in the shaping of British policies towards the Indigenous population. From the very beginning of his description of encounters between the British and the Eora, there were Eora attacks he *could* have described as resistance, but the presence of the convict population meant that he did not have to contemplate them as such. Collins would consistently blame convicts for Aboriginal attack, and in doing so he maintained his representation of Aboriginal people as unoffending, without the agency necessary to resist the colonisation of their country.

In March 1788, convicts began to be speared as they left the confines of the settlement; one was 'dangerously wounded with a spear, the others very much beaten and bruised by the natives'.[27] The explanation Collins provided for the initial attack would be repeated on numerous occasions over the coming months – while the convicts denied provoking Aboriginal people the Judge-Advocate did not believe them.[28] In May 1788 one convict was wounded and another killed when they 'strayed' beyond the settlement, and two other convicts were killed when cutting rushes, having been 'pierced through in many places

---

22   Phillip 1892[1787]: 50–54.
23   Phillip 1892[1787]: 52.
24   Phillip 1892[1787]: 53.
25   Evans and Thorpe 1998: 17.
26   Russell 2005: 36.
27   Collins 1798: 23.
28   Collins 1798: 24.

with spears, and the head of one beaten to a jelly'.[29] Collins' reporting of such incidents began to form a pattern whereby convicts were said to be 'offending' Aboriginal people and 'straggling', with violent encounters being repeatedly conceptualised as isolated occurrences rather than being seen as reflective of ongoing hostility towards the settlement. Even as violence escalated Collins did not perceive that Aboriginal people may have been retaliating against the British presence on their land or attacking the colony itself. In response to the death of the rush-cutters Phillip sent out an armed party to find the offenders. This initiated Phillip's strategy of reprisals if those hurt were working for the support of the colony, and especially if they were gathering food. The Governor, attempting to find and 'secure' those who killed the men, sent out 'a strong party well armed'.[30] Phillip could not find the offenders – although how he would have known them if he met with them is unclear – but instead encountered a group of two to three hundred Aboriginal people. They had a 'friendly' meeting, perhaps due to the overwhelming weight of Aboriginal numbers, and exchanged spears for hatchets.

With dwindling fishing stocks in the winter of 1788 Collins reported that the Eora 'appeared to be in great want'.[31] They confronted a British fishing party and took half the catch in an attack described as showing strategy and marking a change from the previous Eora approach of waiting to be given fish.[32] It was impossible for the British to tell if the Aborigines were 'driven by hunger, or motivated by some other cause', but they sent an armed officer on subsequent fishing trips.[33] During June and July there were more violent incidents but also more friendly interaction between convicts and Aborigines. Some groups were hostile but others were friendly:

> In one of the adjoining coves resided a family of them, who were visited by large parties of the convicts of both sexes on those days in which they were not wanted for labour, where they danced and sung with apparent good humour, and received such presents as they could afford to make them; but none of them would venture back with their visitors.[34]

Thus, in the initial months a complex relationship was developing between the colonists and the Indigenous people of the Sydney region. While Collins always blamed the convicts for provoking Aboriginal people, we cannot discount the possibility that convicts were deliberately targeted as they moved about alone

---

29   Collins 1798: 30.
30   Collins 1798: 31.
31   Collins 1798: 31.
32   Collins 1798: 31.
33   Collins 1798: 31. Raymond Evans has written about similar Aboriginal reactions to another large British settlement (that of the Moreton Bay convict settlement from 1824) and he has argued that the Nunukul people's forcible seizure of crops can be seen from the perspective of extracting 'land rents'. Evans 1999: 60.
34   Collins 1798: 37.

and unarmed, and travelled with difficulty in an alien landscape. In another respect the Aboriginal strategy of targeting convicts away from the settlement suited the British officers as it helped to control the population of prisoners. In effect the Eora became a police force, patrolling the boundaries of the open-air prison that was the new colony, and making it easier for the administration to keep the prisoners physically confined. Along with the violent confrontation, however, there was at least one friendly meeting, an unusual description that alerts us to silences within the text. Collins was concerned to record the administrative detail of the colony and to document breaches of the law in his role as Judge-Advocate, and as such the *Account* does not generally document the daily life of the convicts outside of the interest of the colonial administrators; it could not document the daily lives of the Eora.[35]

In October Collins reported the death of another convict 'who had been looked upon as a good man'. He had accompanied an armed party to gather food but was killed when he left the group: 'his head beat to a jelly, a spear driven through it, another through his body, and one arm broken'.[36] The concept that Aboriginal people were unoffending, however, framed Collins' discourse such that episodes of resistance did not change his ideas. His refusal to consider that the Eora might defend what had been, less than a year earlier, their home, resulted in a simplistic narrative that split the colonists between officers displaying goodwill and convicts filled with vice. Despite this discourse, however, the colonial approach to relations with the Eora was changing in significant ways. Phillip shifted his approach from management of the convicts, by government order and threat, to trying to directly manage the Eora. His strategies reflect the normalisation of violence within administrative practices in penal and colonial situations. With the next Aboriginal attack, an attempted spearing of another convict, Phillip sent out the military to retaliate, to force Aboriginal people away from the white settlement.[37] The strategy had shifted from original encouragement of friendly relations with the Eora, to making an armed show of strength to keep the Indigenous population from the edge of the settlement.

By December 1788 the colonial authorities had settled on kidnapping to manage the Eora, as they 'were becoming every day more troublesome and hostile'. Kidnapping would allow the British to learn the local language so that the Indigenous population 'might learn to distinguish friends from enemies', and in December 1788 Arabanoo, a Cammeraygal man, was captured.[38] Arabanoo's

---

35 Laugeson 2002. Laugeson has described how commentators noted the English spoken by Aboriginal people reflected convict slang. This sort of evidence demonstrates that even though Phillip had wanted complete separation between convicts and Aborigines, and the Collins *Account* was often silent on interaction between convicts and Aborigines, complete separation was outside of the control of the administration.

36 Collins 1798: 43.

37 Collins 1798: 44–45.

38 Collins 1798: 49.

kidnapping did not stop the strikes at the periphery of the colony. Collins' report of another Eora attack on a party of rush cutters early in 1789 provides us with an insight into the other reasons that may have been behind Arabanoo's capture. Collins wrote that the Aboriginal people had attacked the British

> notwithstanding they must have known at that time we had one of their people in our possession, on whom the injury might have been retaliated. He, poor fellow, did not seem to expect any such treatment from us, and began to seem reconciled to his situation. He was taken down the harbour once or twice, to let his friends see that he was alive, and had some intercourse with them which appeared to give him much satisfaction.[39]

As well as the desire to learn language and prove the colonisers' 'friendly' intentions, the British tactic of kidnapping can also be seen from the perspective of hostage taking to prevent attacks against the settlement. To view kidnapping in this light is to take seriously British concern about Eora resistance, and belies the simplistic conclusion that Aboriginal people were unoffending.

Collins was belatedly realising that Phillip's original plan to keep the convicts segregated from the Indigenous population would not work, as the 'impracticability' of the scheme, he wrote, 'became every day more evident'.[40] Collins stressed that government orders to avoid leaving the settlement had been devised for the good of convicts, but they ignored them, as they were not 'thinking beings'.[41] When a convict was killed collecting vegetables at Botany Bay, 16 men from his brick-making work gang went in search of revenge, armed with wooden stakes.[42] They met with and were repelled by a group of about 50 Eora, who killed another man and wounded six more. The Governor's response was to attempt to regulate the Aboriginal and convict violence by using state-sanctioned punishment and military power in response. Lawrence Stone has concluded that the role of the British military state during this period was 'monopolizing as much as possible of legitimate violence', and Phillip's actions in this instance display this imperative for state control of violent acts.[43] He sent an armed party to Botany Bay to collect the bodies. He ordered all of the convict revenge party to receive 150 lashes and wear a leg iron for a year. In addition he launched a military patrol around the settlement to warn the Eora, with two groups of soldiers sent, 'one toward Botany Bay, and the other in

---

39   Collins 1798: 53.
40   Collins 1798: 57.
41   Collins 1798: 57.
42   Collins 1798: 57.
43   Stone 1994: 7.

a different direction, that the natives might see that their late act of violence would neither intimidate nor prevent us from moving beyond the settlement whenever occasion required'.[44]

Arabanoo's death in the smallpox epidemic that ravaged his people in May 1789 gave Phillip a 'determination to procure another [captive] at the first favourable opportunity' and two men were captured in November 1789.[45] Colebe, a Cadagal man, only stayed a few days before escaping, but Bennelong, a Wahngal man, was thwarted in his attempt to escape with Colebe, and lived in the Port Jackson settlement until his eventual escape in May 1790. In the edited collection of Phillip's despatches, the first British publication on the New South Wales colony, the kidnapping was characterised as 'the kindest piece of violence that could be used'.[46] Coleman has read this phrase as epitomising the 'chivalric discourse' which masks 'dominion as kindness, gallantry and good intentions whilst bolstering the intruders' sense of their own superiority'.[47] This chivalric discourse is, she has suggested, 'seductive', as it allows the characterisation of Australian colonial beginnings as 'somehow pristine, a period of genuine curiosity and friendly overtures, untainted by the frontier racial violence which was to follow in the nineteenth century'.[48] Perhaps also seduced by this chivalric discourse, Clendinnen uncritically reproduced Lieutenant William Bradley's description of the kidnapping which he was ordered to carry out. Describing it as 'by far the most unpleasant service I was ever ordered to execute', Bradley recounted the way he lured Bennelong and Colebe with gifts of fish before hauling them into the boat.[49] Rather than focus on the British use of kidnapping, Clendinnen has wondered 'what possessed' the Indigenous men 'to wade out to a British boat'? She did not consider the Eora's distress for want of food, their previous shows of resistance at British refusals to share fish, or their attempts to extend their ideas of obligation and reciprocity to the Europeans who were living on their land. Instead, Clendinnen speculated that they came towards the boat to allow Bradley to kidnap them because the two men were playing a 'game of dare'. While Clendinnen stressed that she was not suggesting 'they wanted to be captured', she nevertheless characterised the kidnapping as a case of 'competitive daring that went wrong' for the Indigenous men.[50] Theatricality and gamesmanship have replaced coercion in this reading, which has been divorced from the operation of state power and the serious business of colonial management of Indigenous peoples in order to undertake the colonisation of their lands.

---

44   Collins 1798: 58.
45   Collins 1798: 86.
46   Phillip 1789: 79, quoted in Coleman 2005: 165.
47   Phillip 1789: 79, quoted in Coleman 2005: 165.
48   Phillip 1789: 79, quoted in Coleman 2005: 165–166.
49   Quoted in Clendinnen 2003: 105.
50   Quoted in Clendinnen 2003: 106.

Neither the kidnapping of Bennelong, however, nor his eventual return to his people and ongoing relationship with the British, stopped conflict. Perhaps the most serious of the attacks, for both the Aboriginal population and for the British, was the spearing of the convict gamekeeper McIntyre in December 1790.[51] McIntyre was suspected of cruelty towards Aborigines, and he was speared at a time when the colony was on the brink of starvation. Phillip mounted another armed party in retaliation, and charged the military to return to the settlement with the heads of ten Aboriginal men.[52] When the first reprisal raid was unsuccessful, with the soldiers unable to find any trace of Indigenous people, Phillip sent them out again. It seems clear that the failure of the soldiers to take revenge was more to do with their own lack of knowledge of Eora country than for want of trying. Clendinnen has claimed that the expedition was Phillip's attempt to 'protect' Aboriginal people from the 'racist terror' of other British settlers, which would 'come soon enough'.[53]

The attack on McIntyre was of such seriousness that Collins admitted for the first time in his *Account* that Aboriginal attacks might be about land, stating that:

> we had not yet been able to reconcile the natives to the deprivation of those parts of this harbour which we occupied. While they entertained the idea of our having dispossessed them of their residences, they must always consider us as enemies, and upon this principle they made a point of attacking the white people whenever opportunity and safety concurred.[54]

This is a crucial admission, but it is one that is not seriously considered within the synthetic ethnological assessment of Aboriginal society that Collins included in his *Account*. In one key part of this ethnology, the section dealing with property, we can see Bennelong's attempts to explain his relationship to country to the British, and view the way the British reacted to such information. Collins devoted only one paragraph to Bennelong's explanation of Aboriginal property ownership. This is the passage in full:

> Their spears and shields, their clubs and lines, &c. are their own property, they are manufactured by themselves, and are the whole of their personal estate. But, strange as it may appear, they have also their real estates. Ben-nil-long, both before he went to England and since his return, often assured me, that the island Me-mel (called by us Goat

51 Collins 1798: 143.
52 Collins 1798: 143–144.
53 Clendinnen 2003: 181. Coleman has dismissed this conclusion as 'nothing less than wishful thinking, an implausible distortion of the record', Coleman 2004: 208.
54 Collins 1798: 147.

Island) close by the Sydney Cove was his own property; that it was his fathers', and that he should give it to By-gone, his particular friend and companion. To this little spot he appeared much attached, and we have often found him and his wife Bar-rang-a-roo feasting and enjoying themselves on it. He told us of other people who possessed this kind of hereditary property, which they retained undisturbed.[55]

While Collins was prepared to admit a sense of personal ownership of goods, he had more trouble explaining, or admitting to, Aboriginal ownership of land. He stated that Aboriginal people believed they owned land, 'strange as it may appear', given the British assumption that there was no concept of land ownership in Aboriginal society, and that Aboriginal people lived in a 'state of nature'. Giving authority to Bennelong's assertion of his own, as well as other people's, attachment to and ownership of particular areas of land was a move which could threaten to undermine a tenet of European thought on the basis of which the colony of New South Wales had been founded.[56] Bennelong's assertion of his continued connection to country and maintenance of his relationship to land attest to the other forms of resistance utilised by Aboriginal people and their maintenance of culture in the face of the colonisation of their land. As Frances Peters-Little has described: 'Aboriginal people were constantly resisting and maintaining "Aboriginality" even though the dominant view of resistance was generally limited to understanding "resistance" only in terms of violence on the frontier'.[57]

Thus, no matter what Bennelong told the British about his peoples' relationship to country, and no matter how the Eora retaliated against the British, Collins did not attempt to assimilate this new information into his assumptions about the level of advancement of Aboriginal society. Collins described Aboriginal people as having only the most rudimentary form of social development; the preface to the *Account* spoke of the rare occurrence of establishing a colony 'in the most remote part of the habitable globe; it is seldom that men are found living in a state of nature'.[58] The idea that the Eora lived in a state of nature was reiterated at the beginning of the ethnological section of the *Account*:

> We found the natives about Botany Bay, Port Jackson, and Broken Bay, living in that state of nature which must have been common to all

---

55   Collins 1798: 598–599.

56   For a description of individual relations to particular areas of country in Aboriginal culture, see Goodall 1996: 9.

57   Peters-Little 2005.

58   Collins 1798: ix.

men previous to their uniting in society, and acknowledging but one
authority. These people are distributed into families, the head or senior
of which exacts compliance from the rest.[59]

Robert Dixson has concluded that Collins' work owed a large debt to Lord
Monboddo's *Of the Origin and Progress of Language*.[60] In particular, Dixson
concluded that, while Collins did not place Aboriginal people in the very
lowest state of humanity, believing them above a 'Brutish State' by virtue of
their organisation into families, 'apparently in deference to Lord Monboddo, he
continued to describe them as living in a "state of nature"'.[61] This assessment of
Indigenous society was also useful from the perspective of colonial endeavour,
however, as it placed Aboriginal society at a level which did not have a
conception of property ownership. In effect, it ignored Aboriginal peoples' own
articulation of their property rights to reiterate the conclusions that Aboriginal
people had no property rights which Cook had expressed, and which had
formed the basis of the decision to settle without negotiation.

Merete Borch has suggested that the British government was open to new
information about Aboriginal society, realising that the initial colonisation
had been based on partial knowledge developed out of fleeting encounters.
While it was difficult for Collins to admit, he eventually came to recognise that
Aboriginal people had a sense of property rights in land, and that they resisted
white settlement. Ten years after settlement was initiated, Collins' *Account*,
with its reluctant story of Aboriginal resistance and one solitary paragraph
on Indigenous property ownership, was published in England. By this time,
however, British settlement was expanding apace, and the sceptical explanation
of property rights was too little and came too late to change the form of the
colonial project.

In addition, Collins' publication came to hold an influential place in the
development of racial thought about Aboriginal people, thus ensuring that
his views on both race and resistance became enshrined in dominant British
understandings of Australian Indigenous people. The *Account* was used by
natural scientists hungry to assimilate knowledge of newly discovered peoples
into their theories of human difference. A report on Collins' work was published
in the *Edinburgh Review* in 1803, attributed to Sydney Smith, which praised
Collins as an author, stating that the 'book is written with great plainness and
candour'. The reviewer felt the most important contribution of the *Account*
was the discussion of Aboriginal people, their physical features and cultural
characteristics. They supposedly had only a rudimentary knowledge of politics

---

59   Collins 1798: 544.
60   Burnet 1773–1792.
61   Dixson 1986: 24.

and seemed 'to have scarcely advanced beyond family-government'. Their small population was caused by Aboriginal 'ferocity of manners' combined with the 'sterility of their country'. Smith concluded that Aboriginal people were 'extremely low, in point of civilization, when compared with many other savages, with whom the discoveries of Captain Cook have made us acquainted'.[62] The *Account* was also integral to the assessment of Aboriginal people offered by James Cowles Pritchard in 1813 in his highly influential *Researches into the Physical History of Man*,[63] which became a 'landmark in British racial science'.[64] While Pritchard also used the accounts of European voyagers such as Dampier and Cook, he relied heavily on the work of Collins.[65] Pritchard described Aboriginal people as the 'squalid companions of kangaroos', who 'may be seen crawling in imitation of quadrupeds', an unflattering description which he used in contrast to the spectacle of a European coronation ceremony and which was closely based on Collins' description of a 1795 corroboree which had included dances imitating kangaroos and dingoes.[66]

Thus, far from providing new knowledge which could form the basis of negotiation between Aboriginal people and the British, Collins' work reiterated ideas that Aboriginal people did not resist, and was used by metropolitan thinkers to argue that Aboriginal people were low on the hierarchy of humanity.

Resistance in histories of the region

The *Account*'s descriptions of Māori, whom British colonists were also contacting at this time, demonstrate how an expectation of resistance could impact on British behaviour. Collins included as an appendix to the first volume of the *Account* a report from Phillip Gidley King, Lieutenant Governor of Norfolk Island, on his interaction with two North Island Māori men. King had ordered the men, Tuki and Huru from the Muriwhenua region in the north of the North Island, kidnapped and brought to the island to teach the convicts how to weave flax. He detained them on Norfolk Island from April to October 1793. New Zealand histories agree that kidnapping Tuki and Huru was an affront to Māori.[67] Judith Binney has stated that 'the chiefs were insulted by the manner of their removal'.[68] Anne Salmond described the kidnapping 'as a strange way to create

---

62   Smith 1803: 34.
63   Pritchard 1973[1813]: 261–272.
64   Stepan 1982: 2.
65   Pritchard 1973[1813]: 265.
66   Quoted in Wheeler 2000: 293, and see Collins 1798: 566, 570.
67   Binney 2004; Salmond 1997.
68   Binney 2004: 15.

an alliance', but she also implied that kidnapping was a prudent British policy, and that Māori naturally displayed caution towards the visitors, because of the history of violent contact between Māori and Europeans in the region.[69]

While Tuki and Huru's kidnapping led to the collection of ethnographic information, as did the kidnapping of Arabanoo, Bennelong and Colebe, the information provided by the Māori captives was received and reproduced in a very different manner. Firstly, Tuki and Huru were understood to occupy important places in a hierarchical Māori society. Huru was described as a warrior and Tuki a priest, with the men proving to have no knowledge of making flax, as women undertook this task.[70] Huru's status as a warrior confirmed for the British their understandings of Māori as a 'warrior race', formed on Cook's Pacific voyages.[71] Tuki further entrenched this idea when he drew for the British a map, reproduced in the *Account*, which demarcated tribal regions governed by their respective chiefs and included details of the number of warriors belonging to each place. North Island people were said to be in a 'constant state of warfare with other tribes', but during times of peace traded for flax and greenstone.[72] The map also included the 'immense pine trees' growing near the Hokianga River, which became the basis of a later trade in timber by New South Wales merchants.[73] The map not only sparked interest in a trading relationship with Māori, but it also entrenched ideas that Māori had property rights, and that chiefs owned land which they defended with warriors.[74] The British imagined an imperial relationship, but did not consider colonisation. The authority accorded to Tuki's map in the *Account* legitimised Māori perspectives of their own society within European ethnology, and differed markedly from the one sceptical paragraph Collins devoted to Aboriginal ideas of their land ownership.

Māori resistance, be it actual physical resistance or the threat of it, is taken for granted in New Zealand historiography, for example in the works of Judith Binney and Anne Salmond, and is seen as shaping British actions in their encounters with Māori. New Zealand historians assume what Australian historians at times do not, that the Indigenous population resisted the imperial power that intervened in their country. In doing so they also reiterate the perspectives of early British observers who, representing Māori as a warrior race, always expected Indigenous peoples in New Zealand to resist them. As Michael King concluded:

---

69   Salmond 1997: 209.
70   Collins 1798: 521.
71   Standfield 2008.
72   Collins 1798: 522.
73   Salmond 1997: 16.
74   Salmond 1997: 524–525.

Australian Aboriginal people were assumed to be less martial than Maori, less organised and vigorous, and therefore easier to control in the operation of a colonial enterprise. This decision protected Maori from a concerted attempt at foreign colonisation of New Zealand for a further 50 years and gave them time to better adjust to the implications...[75]

Dialogue with New Zealand histories can encourage Australian historians to question British assumptions about Aboriginal people, especially one so intertwined with racial thought and the lack of recognition of sovereignty as the notion that Aboriginal people did not resist the settlement at Port Jackson. This idea was so powerful at the time that it continued to be expressed no matter how the Eora reacted to the British, and it has proved so enduring since as to resurface in our current reflections on early white settlement. Engaging with these regional histories can serve to remind Australian historians that British travellers and colonists made their early observations of indigenous peoples in the light of prevailing discourses of race and class, as well as that of British imperial ambition.

References

Atkinson, Alan 1991, *The Europeans in Australia: A History, vol 1, The Beginning*, Oxford University Press, Oxford.

Binney, Judith 2004, 'Tuki's universe', *New Zealand Journal of History* 38(2): 215–232.

Borch, Merete Falck 2004, *Conciliation – Compulsion – Conversion: British Attitudes Towards Indigenous Peoples, 1763–1814*, Rodopi, Amsterdam and New York.

Broome, Richard 2005, *Aboriginal Victorians: A History since 1800*, Allen & Unwin, Crows Nest, New South Wales.

Burnet, James, Lord Monboddo 1773–1792, *Of the Origin and Progress of Language*, 6 vols, A Kincaid and W Creech, T Cadell, Edinburgh and London.

Clendinnen, Inga 2003, *Dancing with Strangers*, Text Publishing, Melbourne.

Coleman, Deirdre 2004, 'Inscrutable history or incurable romanticism? Review of Inga Clendinnen's *Dancing with Strangers*', *Heat* 8: 201–213.

— 2005, *Romantic Colonization and British Anti-Slavery*, Cambridge University Press, Cambridge.

75   King 2003: 114.

Collins, David, 1798 and 1802, *An Account of the English Colony in New South Wales, with remarks on the dispositions, customs, manners, &c., of the native inhabitants of that country. To which are added some particulars of New Zealand. Compiled by permission, from the MSS of Lieutenant-Governor King, by David Collins Esquire, Late Judge-Advocate and Secretary of the Colony, Illustrated by Engravings*, T Cadell, jun and W Davies, London.

Currey, John 2000, *David Collins: A Colonial Life*, Miegunyah Press and Melbourne University Press, Carlton South.

Dixson, Robert 1986, *The Course of Empire: Neo-Classical Culture in New South Wales, 1788, 1860*, Oxford University Press, Melbourne.

Evans, Raymond 1995, 'Blood dries quickly: conflict study and Australian historiography', *Australian Journal of Politics and History* 41(special issue): 80–102.

— 1999, 'The Mogwi take Mi-an-jin: race relations and the Moreton Bay penal settlement, 1824–1842', in *Fighting Words: Writing about Race*, Raymond Evans (ed), University of Queensland Press, St Lucia: 48–79.

— and Bill Thorpe 1988, 'Commanding men: masculinities and the convict system', *Journal of Australian Studies* 56: 17–34.

Flood, Josephine 2006, *The Original Australians: Story of the Aboriginal People*, Allen & Unwin, Crows Nest, New South Wales.

Goodall, Heather 1996, *Invasion to Embassy: Land in Aboriginal Politics in New South Wales*, 1770–1972, Allen & Unwin in association with Black Books, St Leonards, New South Wales.

Keneally, Thomas 2005, *The Commonwealth of Thieves*, Random House, Milsons Point, New South Wales.

King, Jonathan 1985, *'In the Beginning...': The Story of the Creation of Australia from the Original Writings*, MacMillan, South Melbourne and Crows Nest.

King, Michael 2003, *The Penguin History of New Zealand*, Penguin, Auckland.

Konishi, Shino 2008, 'Wanton with plenty: questioning ethno-historical constructions of sexual savagery in Aboriginal societies, 1788–1803', *Australian Historical Studies* 39(3): 356–372.

Laugeson, Amanda 2002, 'The politics of language in colonial Australia, 1788–1850', *Journal of Colonial History* 4(1): 18–40.

Morrissey, Phillip, 2007, 'Dancing with shadows: erasing Aboriginal self and sovereignty', in *Sovereign Subjects: Indigenous Sovereignty Matters*, Aileen Moreton-Robinson (ed), Allen & Unwin, Crows Nest, New South Wales: 69–70.

Peters-Little, Frances 2005, 'An Aboriginal session on Gandhi's Indian Home Rule interview about history and passive resistance, 1909', *Borderlands e-journal* 4(3), accessed 15 May 2010: <http://www.borderlands.net.au/vol4no3_2005/peters_session.htm>

Phillip, Arthur, 1892[1787], 'Phillip's views on the conduct of the Expedition and the Treatment of Convicts', reprinted in *Historical Records of New South Wales*, vol 1, part II, Charles Potter Government Printer, Sydney: 50–54.

—1789, *The Voyage of Governor Phillip to Botany Bay; with an Account of the Establishment of the Colonies of Port Jackson and Norfolk Island*, John Stockdale, London.

Pritchard, James Cowles 1973[1813], *Researches into the Physical History of Man*, reprinted with an introductory essay by George W Stocking Jnr, University of Chicago Press, Chicago and London.

Russell, Penny 2005, 'Unsettling settler society', in *Australia's History: Themes and Debates*, Martin Lyon and Penny Russell (ed), University of New South Wales Press, Sydney: 22–40.

Salmond, Anne 1997, *Between Worlds: Early Exchanges between Maori and Europeans, 1773–1815*, Viking Press, Auckland.

Smith, Sydney (attributed) 1803, 'Review of David Collins, *An Account of the English Colony in New South Wales*', *Edinburgh Review* 11: 3.

Standfield, Rachel 2008, 'Violence and the intimacy of imperial ethnography: the *Endeavour* in the Pacific' in *Moving Subjects: Mobility, Intimacy and Gender in a Global Age of Empire*, Antoinette Burton and Tony Ballantyne (eds), University of Illinois Press, Urbana and Chicago: 31–48.

Stepan, Nancy 1982, *The Idea of Race in Science, 1800–1960*, Macmillan Press, London and Basingstoke.

Stone, Lawrence 1994, *An Imperial State at War: Britain from 1689 to 1815*, Routledge, London and New York.

Thomas, Nicholas 1999, *Possessions: Indigenous Art, Colonial Culture*, Thames and Hudson, London.

Wheeler, Roxann 2000, *The Complexion of Race: Categories of Difference in Eighteenth-Century British Culture*, University of Pennsylvania Press, Philadelphia.

7. Demythologising Flynn, with Love: contesting missionaries in Central Australia in the twentieth century

DAVID TRUDINGER

Central Australia was (and is) both a mythical and a contested landscape. The historical contest there was not always confined to whites and Indigenous people, or to land-hungry settlers and distant administrators. Nor were its myths only ancient, indigenous ones. One of the better known Australian 'myths' is that of John Flynn (1880–1951), the founder of the Australian Inland Mission (AIM) and the man who through the innovative Royal Flying Doctor Service (RFDS) brought medical assistance to people isolated in the Australian outback. The canonisation of Flynn commenced in 1932 with Ion Idriess's book, *Flynn of the Inland*, which represented him as a paragon of all the virtues, as a saint of the Inland.[1] Even Flynn saw the book with some irony as creating 'my mythical self'.[2] This construction of Flynn as a kind of universal, ministering spirit of the Outback has been developed subsequently in newspapers, books, films and television, reaching its apotheosis with Flynn's portrait on the 20-dollar note. Fulsome encomiums continue to be presented to a humanitarian 'on the highest level' and, along with Parkes, Monash and Bullwinkle, 'one of the founders of the national spirit of Australia'.[3]

However, the reorientation of Australian historiography in relation to Indigenous people in the last two or three decades has forced some preliminary scrutiny of the Flynn myth, particularly in relation to his attitudes towards Aboriginal people.[4] This essay enters this contested territory, by looking afresh at Flynn in the context of internal debates between Presbyterian missionaries in the 1930s and 1940s. The key players in these debates, apart from Flynn himself, were Dr Charles Duguid (1884–1986), the sponsor of Ernabella, a significant twentieth century missionary venture to Aboriginal people in the Centre, and missionary,

---

1   Idriess 1932.
2   Cited in Hains 2002: 3.
3   Godfrey and Ramsland 2004: 28; Fischer 2009: 141.
4   See, for example, Griffiths 1993; Nelson 2001; Hains 2002, 2003, 2004.

linguist and teacher, JRB Love (1889–1947). I suggest that Flynn's long career, famously and single-mindedly dedicated to throwing a 'mantle of safety' over the Inland through the provision of communication and medical services, may also have been notable for a culpable indifference towards Indigenous people and an exclusion of them from his vision for the Inland. I also argue that Flynn's attitudes towards Aborigines, and those of the AIM, were strenuously contested by important denominational colleagues at the time.

Memory, as well as myth, plays a part in this story. Some of the memories are mine. I remember the opening of the John Flynn Memorial Church in Alice Springs in 1956; I am six and I am there with my missionary mother and father.[5] The Governor-General, Sir William Slim, dedicated the Church. I am unaware of Slim's earlier pronouncement that Flynn's hands were stretched out like a benediction over the Inland but I do have an inchoate sense that Flynn, only five years dead, is already being constructed as a sort of 'national saint'.[6] About this time I am also being educated through the School of the Air, courtesy, I am told by my parents, of Flynn and Alfred Traeger.[7] I am impressed, and remain so, with reservations. Flynn's stewardship, through the medium of the AIM, of the white settlers of the Inland was superb, and has ever since been generously acknowledged by a grateful (white) nation.

On the other hand, the 'stewardship' of Indigenous people was a task that Flynn left to others. Justifications for this omission, where it has been recognised, have been varied. The principal 'defence' used by the AIM itself was that other arms of the Presbyterian Church, its Board of Missions and missions for Aborigines, dealt with Aborigines, not the AIM. Another rationale was that Flynn could not have achieved what he did without a single-minded devotion to the cause of the white settler.[8] An explanation sometimes attached to this argument but often merely implied was that any accommodation with the 'blacks' would have resulted in the disaffection of the whites and the consequent loss of effectiveness of the AIM.[9] The respected Lutheran missionary FW Albrecht of Hermannsburg believed that the medical assistance given to Aborigines, admittedly as out(side) patients at AIM hospitals and through the RFDS, was ultimately more beneficial for Aborigines than almost anything else done for them by Europeans.[10] Dr

---

5   My parents were missionaries at Ernabella.

6   See Hains 2002: 168.

7   Traeger worked with and for Flynn in developing a communication network for the Royal Flying Doctor Service (RFDS) and the School of the Air, and famously invented the pedal wireless: see Behr 1990.

8   A 'defence' used often by some experienced Centralian hands: Winifred Hilliard, a long-term missionary at Ernabella and author of the pioneering *The People in Between* (see Hilliard 1976), argued this in recent discussions with the present author.

9   JRB Love understood this justification instinctively, with his experience in the Outback, although he thought the AIM should have stood up against the 'bush' discourse (see below).

10   Albrecht in later years wrote to Duguid: 'If Flynn had intended the Aerial Medical Service in the first place for white settlers, God had had His plans for the Aborigines, so that in real fact very many more Aborigines than white people, old and young, benefited from this service': Albrecht to Duguid, 28 March

George Simpson of the AIM in an exchange of letters with Charles Duguid in 1935 also argued perceptively that by casting his 'mantle of safety' over the Inland, Flynn made it possible for white women to migrate there and thus 'ease the pressure' on abused Aboriginal women.[11] Later commentators suggested, more broadly, that Flynn prepared the Outback for 'the new age for the Aboriginal people'.[12]

These are, in the main, substantive defences of varying degrees of merit, which in a larger work would need to be taken into account in a balanced consideration of Flynn's significant contribution to his country. Taken together they suggest that at least the indirect influence of Flynn's work on the Indigenous population of the Outback may well have had some positive elements. But hitherto, the case against Flynn, if there is one, has essentially relied on sins of omission. I am suggesting here that at least a provisional argument exists for sins of commission on Flynn's part as well, some thinking and behaviour actually antithetical to Indigenous interests. To unravel that story, we need first to look at the relationships between our protagonists, Flynn, Duguid and Love, whose paths, like tracks in the desert, crossed, separated, aligned or collided over the first half of the twentieth century in Central Australia.

JRB Love and John Flynn

In 1912, the Presbyterian Church of Australia commissioned John Flynn to conduct a survey of 'religious conditions' in the Northern Territory. According to Flynn's first biographer, his preparations for the journey related both to the subjects of 'aborigines as well as whites': '[Flynn] had many discussions with his friend Robert Love, a young schoolteacher at Leigh Creek.'[13] Indigenous people, however, did not figure prominently in Flynn's Report or his plans for an Australian Inland Mission (AIM), which was to be a mission to the white settlers of the Inland. The Presbyterian Church speedily approved and established the AIM within the year. Later in 1912, Love set out from Leigh Creek in South Australia to report on 'the present condition' of the Aborigines 'in the North' for the same Presbyterian Church. Perhaps he had divined that Aborigines were not part of Flynn's vision. Perhaps they had agreed on some sort of division of labour. We do not know. In his Report, Love recommended that the Church establish missions 'to the blacks' in this large area, but this advice was not carried out. By the time his report was received in December 1914, and published in 1915, the Great War was under way. The question of establishing new missions to the Aborigines, if it had been seriously considered

1971, Papers of FW Albrecht, Burns-Albrecht Collection, South Australian Museum Archives, AA662.
11   See Trudinger 2004: 122–123.
12   For example, see Griffiths 1993: 168.
13   McPheat 1963: 60.

at all, was deferred indefinitely. The Church instead proceeded to fall in behind the powerful and popular force the AIM was becoming, with Flynn at its head. For his part, however, Love had been ready. As he wrote to Flynn in 1914:

> shall the Church be prepared to act at once [on his Report], and make a proposition to me as a layman, I shall at least seriously consider it. Failing either of these alternatives, my intention is to come back to bush-whacking till I fall off a horse or bump into a spear. I could go back to a respectable sort of life in the South with the approval of my friends, but for myself I do not think I shall ever do so.[14]

In fact Love's Church was not 'prepared to act' in establishing a mission for Aborigines anywhere in Australia for another 23 years, until Duguid's Ernabella in 1937.

After their 'reporting on the North', the careers of Love and Flynn took divergent courses. By the end of the 1920s, Love had been to war in Palestine, won the Military Cross and the Distinguished Conduct Medal, acquired a divinity degree and ordination, and had been working as a Presbyterian missionary to Aborigines, in Mapoon, Queensland and in Western Australia, at Kunmunya in the Kimberley. John Flynn was continuing to construct the increasingly influential AIM and fashioning his 'mantle of safety' over the Inland.[15] Love and Flynn continued to correspond occasionally, keeping in touch, with intermittent discussions about Aboriginal matters. They both appear to be in the mainstream of contemporary racial discourse in Australia that saw European civilisation as the apogee of societal development, and Europeans as certainly superior to 'native' races. Both believed as did significant members of the scientific and intellectual communities in the creation, despite some residual anxieties, of a preeminent white Australian race or type.[16] Yet there were differences between them.

JRB Love

Love's attitudes towards Aboriginal people were often ambivalent. The discourses of European conquest, development and racial triumphalism both clash and merge in Love's thought with those of reparation, responsibility, and redemption. In his 1914 Report, the young schoolteacher had stridently

---

14   Love to Flynn, 9 February 1914, John Flynn Papers, National Library of Australia [hereafter NLA], MS3288, Box 3, Folder 2.

15   This familiar story is told in McPheat 1963; Griffiths 1993; Rudolph 2000. I do not want to give the impression through brevity that the 'rise' of the AIM was inevitable or easy, or to under-estimate Flynn's achievement. That his organisation was becoming a significant and important actor, as he himself was, is I think indisputable.

16   Anderson 2002.

advised the Church that 'it would be foolish to argue that all men are equal. The blackfellow is inferior and must necessarily remain so'.[17] Despite this inequality, he had told Flynn earlier that the destinies of the two 'races' were inextricably entwined: 'The question of white and black are wholly bound up in each other. We cannot deal with one apart from the other.'[18] This view was partly generated by Love's concerns about sexual relationships between white and black in the Inland. He commented to Flynn on the consequences of these unions in language that is objectionable to us now but was relatively standard usage at the time: 'The half-caste is a nigger, and can only (but for some exceptions) marry a black or a half-caste. The quadroon is a white, and should be brought up as such.'[19] With his distaste for hybridity, shared by Flynn, complicating his arguments for a unity of approach, Love did not convince the older man, whose long career appears to have been characterised by a determination, soon after the commencement of his work with the AIM, to deal only with the one and not with the other.

On one seminal matter, the dispossession of the Indigenous peoples of Australia and its consequences, Love's views were unusual for his time. In 1922, while at Mapoon, he published a small 36-page booklet called *Our Australian Blacks* in which he proposed a paternalistic but powerful theory of colonial duty towards Aborigines.[20] The duty arose 'because we are living on their land … we have taken it from the people who first owned it, without paying for it'. Love argued that the dispossession was justified: '[we] had the right to take the land, which was not being developed, and to put it to better use', which did reflect thinking among many white colonial Australians.[21] He was careful, however, to explain that 'the Blacks did not cultivate the soil [because] there is no native plant in Australia that can be cultivated to produce large food crops … so the blackfellow had no chance to develop the country'.[22] Love's acknowledgement of the environmental deficits that Aborigines had been faced by Aborigines on this continent was one that was not commonly made. He went on to present a further and crucial corollary to the justified dispossession: the right to dispossess creates an obligation to care for the dispossessed, as a gesture of recompense and reparation. This duty became, for Love, paramount: 'no honest or Christian person would say that we have a right to live in a land without taking proper care of the aborigines'.[23]

---

17 Love 1915: 29.
18 Love to Flynn, 9 February 1914, John Flynn Papers, NLA, MS3288, Box 3, Folder 2.
19 Love to Flynn, 9 February 1914, John Flynn Papers, NLA, MS3288, Box 3, Folder 2.
20 Love 1922. Despite the fact that this booklet's audience is children, or perhaps because of it, Love's exposition of a complex colonial duty is succinct and lucid.
21 Love 1922: 35.
22 Love 1922: 8.
23 Love 1922: 35.

In 1926, Love was dryly deprecatory to Flynn about his own work at Mapoon: 'the ordinary routine work about smothers one and there is little time to raise one's head and look around. I suppose the case of some 350 niggers and half-castes is a fairly useful job, though a good deal different from earlier visions.'[24] In the same year, Love accepted an appointment as superintendent of Kunmunya Mission in Western Australia where he was to remain for 14 years. By the late 1930s, he had built a large reputation within church circles as a linguist, anthropologist, and scholar.[25] He has been described by the Presbyterian historian Robert Scrimgeour as 'one of the greatest sons' of the South Australian Church, a 'friend of the Aborigines', and by John Harris in his magisterial survey of the Aboriginal encounter with Christianity as an exemplary and progressive missionary.[26] Yet Love could still write in 1936, after 15 years of missionary enterprise, that a mistake of the 'young enthusiast' might be to treat 'the Aborigine as an equal, which can only lead to friction and heartbreak'.[27] Earlier, in 1930, he had cited his pride in the Lamarckian 'type' that had evolved in the Antipodes, the 'white Australian', but had emphasised also the need for 'honour' in national conduct towards the Aborigines.[28] Love grasped the fundamental and moral nature of the obligations conferred on Europeans by the original sin of dispossession. For a man enmeshed as he was in the discourses of empire, of race and white civilisation, JRB Love *was* making an effort, as he had put it, 'to deal honourably and wisely with the Aboriginal'.[29] But was John Flynn doing so?

Charles Duguid and John Flynn

In the first issue of the AIM newspaper, the *Inlander*, in 1913, Flynn acknowledged that 'the condition of these blacks is not what one would like to see, but one must not fly to hasty conclusions about causes and remedies'.[30] White residents of the Inland were generally kind, pitying and generous towards Indigenous people,

---

24 Love to Flynn, 25 April 1926, John Flynn Papers, NLA, MS3288, Box 4, Folder 7.
25 Love had translated part of the Bible into the Worora language of the Kimberley area, completed a MA in linguistics at Adelaide University, corresponded with AP Elkin and written for *Oceania* about matters anthropological, and had produced a book which outlined, for its time, a new and progressive missiology: see Love 1936. Love's missiology emphasised the *grafting* of Christianity onto Indigenous culture and spirituality in contrast to the orthodox exclusivist view that Christianity had to *replace* Indigenous pagan beliefs. To later historians such as John Harris, Peter Biskup, and Richard Broome, JRB Love was an exemplary progressive missionary, practicing a moderate, tolerant and patient policy of 'enlightened gradualism' (Biskup), an example of a 'liberal humanitarian missionary' (Broome): see Harris 1990: 543–544; Biskup 1973: 127; Broome 1994: 109–110.
26 Scrimgeour 1986: 215–216; Harris 1990: 543–544, 836–838.
27 Minutes of Proceedings of the General Assembly of the Presbyterian Church of Australia 1936, Presbyterian Church of Australia [hereafter PCA]: 96. Love is cited, however, in the same year (1936) as writing: 'I yield to none in recognizing the real intellectual ability of the Australian Aborigines' (cited in McKenzie 1969: 245). This statement and the one in the text, while not necessarily contradictory, give some indication of Love's ambivalence regarding Aborigines.
28 Love, cited in McKenzie 1969: 260.
29 Love, cited in McKenzie 1969: 260.
30 Flynn 1913: 10.

according to Flynn's optimistic view, but he conceded that these attitudes were ones 'in which domestic animals share'. Whites were struggling to survive, or prosper, themselves and could do little to help. While the Church needed to do 'something for the blacks, especially for the half-castes', said Flynn, 'we cannot enter into this difficult problem now'.[31] This statement is a succinct representation of Flynn's attitude to Aborigines, an apparent synecdoche of a broader abandonment. While John Flynn did make some sympathetic statements about Aborigines in the first years of the AIM's existence, particularly in the first few issues of the *Inlander*, these 'sympathetic noises' appear to trail away into an awkward and revealing silence as his public career blossomed.[32] By 1937, he could write to an AIM operative that 'I believe the idea is emerging that the AIM's job is to care for the souls of the dispersed whites and to assist to establish and maintain appropriate organizations to care for the bodies of whites and blacks alike and the nearest approach to souls which may be lingering in the dusky hides of the latter'.[33] Flynn's early sympathy seemed to be dissipating into something like indifference.

There was, and still is, a debate about the extent to which Aboriginal people were excluded from Flynn's imagining of the Australian community.[34] Certainly, from about 1934 on, Dr Charles Duguid was convinced that Flynn's attitude, and that of his organisation, towards Aborigines was 'not human let alone Christian'.[35] Duguid loomed large in the small universe of the South Australian Presbyterian Church of the early to middle twentieth century. Born in Scotland in 1884 and migrating to Australia in 1912, Duguid had become one of Adelaide's leading surgeons by the 1920s. His first visit to Central Australia took place in 1934 and led to a fierce commitment to the Aboriginal cause.[36] Duguid was adamant that Flynn denigrated Aboriginal people. Central to Duguid's charge was the allegation that Flynn had warned him in 1934 that he was 'wasting his time among so many damned dirty niggers'.[37] In return, Flynn was said to have told the Secretary of the Board of Missions in 1936 that Duguid 'should have had his head chopped off years ago'.[38] Such were the polemics of Presbyterians.

---

31   Flynn 1913: 11.
32   An example of Flynn's early sympathy with the plight of the Aborigines: 'It should be quite unnecessary at this late day for us to point out that the black man as a member of the human race has a right to increasing opportunities of self-development ... surely we must ... do something for those whom we clean-handed people have dispossessed in the interests of superior culture': Flynn 1915: 27.
33   Flynn to Frank Pierce, 11 September 1937, Papers of John Flynn, NLA, MS 3288, Box 4, Folder 11.
34   See Hains 2002, 2003, 2004.
35   Duguid to Minister Perkins (copy), 2 October 1934, Duguid Papers, NLA, MS 5068, Series 1: general correspondence, 1918–1974 [hereafter Series 1].
36   See Duguid 1972: chapter 10.
37   Duguid 1972: 100. See also Tim Rowse's account of Duguid's first visit to Central Australia and his subsequent breach with the AIM and Flynn: Rowse 1998: 76.
38   Duguid to MacKenzie (copy), 11 February 1937, Duguid Papers, NLA, MS 5068, Series 1.

It was not only the use of the term 'nigger' that was offensive to Duguid, although it is obvious that he disapproved of it.[39] As we have seen, Love used it frequently as well. Flynn's major offence, to Duguid, was his implied indifference to and dismissal of Aborigines as a waste of time. Did Flynn say the offending words? Duguid was prone to hyperbole, and could be vituperative, but he was not, I think, a liar. Brigid Hains in her recent book on Flynn downplays Duguid's allegation as being 'nearly forty years after the event'.[40] But Duguid's charge was well known at the time within his Church.[41] And there is little doubt that John Flynn at least privately spoke disparagingly of Aborigines. We have two impeccable witnesses to this 'fact': Howard Zelling, prominent lawyer and judge and elder in the Presbyterian Church of South Australia, and Pastor FW Albrecht. In the context of a furore in 1972 over the charge that John Flynn was a racist, Zelling wrote in the *Advertiser*: 'Whatever Flynn might have said on public platforms, he left no one in doubt in private conversations that his views were: (a) that the Aborigines were dying out and (b) they were lazy, shiftless good-for-nothings'.[42] Albrecht, the missionary at Hermannsburg, had observed in a letter to Duguid the previous year that 'I knew only too well that Flynn had little time for Aborigines; in our talks he often told me that their outlook in life personally and as future citizens was hopeless.'[43] But was there more to Flynn's thinking than indifference and an assumption of racial and cultural superiority?

The Smith of Dunesk Gift

When Charles Duguid was elected as the first lay Moderator of the South Australian Presbyterian Church in 1935, he immediately proposed a scheme to establish a mission among the Pitjantjatjara in the far north-west of the state. He charged his Church with a 'special moral responsibility' to the Aborigines of South Australia because of the misuse of a substantial 'gift' made in the nineteenth century by a Scottish woman, Mrs Henrietta Smith, of the estate of Dunesk. The gift had been donated for 'the aborigines of South Australia' but had been used instead to start John Flynn's AIM, a mission solely for the white pioneer population. An obligation, Duguid argued, now rested on the Church to divert the money, still being utilised by the AIM, back to its original purpose.[44]

---

39   Duguid to MacKenzie (copy), 11 February 1937, Duguid Papers, NLA, MS 5068, Series 1.

40   Hains 2002: 125–126.

41   He even relayed the story in a letter to the head of that church in 1939: Duguid to MacKenzie (copy), 25 February 1939, Duguid Papers, NLA, MS 5068, Series 1.

42   *The Advertiser* (South Australia), 6 September 1972: 5.

43   Albrecht to Duguid (copy), 28 March 1971, Papers of FW Albrecht, Burns-Albrecht Collection, South Australian Museum Archives, AA662.

44   *Presbyterian Banner: the Organ of the Presbyterian Church in South Australia* 40(4): 10, in Papers of the Presbyterian Church of South Australia [hereafter PCSA Papers], Mortlock Collection [hereafter MC], State Library of South Australia [hereafter SLSA].

With resources scarce in the later 1930s, during the Depression and later in the context of war, the Smith of Dunesk funds now became a point of conflict for the local Church. In a sober assessment in 1986, historian Robert Scrimgeour commented: 'The Smith of Dunesk story is one that does not reflect credit on the Free Church of Scotland nor on the Presbyterian Church in South Australia. Throughout its history the bequest has been accompanied by frustration, discontent, and controversy.'[45] I would add: intrigue, deception, and cupidity. It is a long and complex narrative which I have examined at length elsewhere.[46] However, it is integral to the 'contest' involving Duguid, Love and Flynn, and a brief account of it weaves through the remainder of this text.

When Mrs Smith arranged for land to be purchased on her behalf in South Australia, she was dissuaded, almost certainly by someone associated with the Church in South Australia, from directing the proceeds 'to the evangelization and education of the Aborigines of South Australia', as she had wished.[47] The deed of gift in 1853 only committed the annual rental income of the property to be applied 'to promoting the cause of the Gospel in South Australia'. But accompanying and later letters of Mrs Smith made it clear that her intention remained that her money, when possible, ought to be directed towards the Aborigines.[48] However, the South Australian Church, after a period of quiet but lucrative accumulation, was determined in 1893 to put the money to 'other pious purposes', relying on the fact that the deed did not mention Aborigines while solemnly promising not to forget 'the interests of the aborigines'.[49] Their interests, having been largely ignored by the Church since 1853, were forgotten for another 40 years.

The Smith of Dunesk Mission, on the strength of the regular funding from Mrs Smith's properties, was established in 1895 in Beltana on the western fringe of the Flinders Ranges in South Australia, where a succession of padres, travelling by horse and buggy from station to station, operated a lonely ministry of worship (with a portable organ) and distribution of literature and good works to white settlers. A nursing sister was employed at Oodnadatta in the mission area from 1907. A travelling missionary and a nursing sister, bringing spiritual and physical health to the white Inland: this was a model that interested the Smith of Dunesk 'missioner' appointed in 1911, John Flynn.[50] In Beltana, before catching the train and boat to Darwin for his survey of the Territory, he built a medical

---

45   Scrimgeour 1986: 106.
46   Trudinger 2004: chapters 4–6.
47   Scrimgeour 1986: 107–108. Six parcels of land of 80 acres each were purchased in 1851–1852.
48   At one point, Mrs Smith put her case in these terms: 'again I say not whites and no other colony has any right to a farthing of it': cited in Scrimgeour 1986: 108.
49   1893 Minutes, 8, Minutes of Proceedings of the South Australian State Assembly of the Presbyterian Church of Australia (hereafter Blue Books), PCSA Papers, MC, SLSA.
50   Flynn had previously become interested in 'the Bush' in Victoria, conducting two Shearers' Missions and producing a popular booklet *The Bushman's Companion*: see Flynn 1910.

hostel, inaugurated a quarterly paper *The Outback Battler*, conducted services at Farina, Marree and at Leigh Creek where he met 'the young schoolteacher, Robert Love'. His vision, with his discourse, was already moving vigorously out from himself to take in panoramic vistas:

> We are running well. Let nothing hinder us. The best and the brightest, the purest and most beauteous will ever be found clustered round the Cross of Christ. Let our devotion be complete in ourselves, and let us take no rest until our privileges and blessings are shared by all our nation, and by the child nation displaced by us, yet still within our gates.[51]

Flynn's language is revealing here. The inexorability of 'let nothing hinder us' is striking. 'Displaced' normalises and naturalises the original dispossession of the 'child race': children, also, move aside for adults, a natural social gesture. And while they too should share in our beneficence and 'privileges', the twist is in the phrase 'within our gates', which carries a connotation of 'the enemy within', some impurity within the 'pure and beauteous' body politic. As he laid his plans before his Church for a transformative project for the white people of the Inland, Flynn's ambivalence towards its Indigenous inhabitants is apparent.

The Smith of Dunesk Gift and the AIM

From 1912, the Smith of Dunesk Mission was progressively taken over by the AIM. Within 20 years, all the proceeds of the Smith of Dunesk fund were now to be devoted to the work of the AIM.[52] By 1935, the AIM, which had been developed on the model of the Smith of Dunesk Mission, had swallowed up the parent organisation. The Smith of Dunesk Mission had been founded and funded on deception, misappropriation and a deliberate refusal to follow the express wishes of the benefactor for the benefit of the Aborigines of South Australia. Duguid was now inexorable in pursuing the re-appropriation of the money. The State Assembly of the Presbyterian Church conceded that at least part of the revenue from the Gift should be put to the use of the proposed mission, but failed in March 1936 to nominate how much.[53] Better news for Duguid came in May when the Board of Missions decided to approve the formation of the mission Duguid was sponsoring, Ernabella, and to recommend it to the General

51 *The Outback Battler*, no 2 (1 July 1911), SRG 123/334, Smith of Dunesk Mission Committee. 7 Printed Items, PCSA Papers, MC, SLSA.
52 Presbyterian Church of SA, Blue Books, 1931, Report of Smith of Dunesk Committee, PCSA Papers, MC, SASL. See also Scrimgeour 1986: 115.
53 Presbyterian Church of SA, Blue Books, 1936, Report of the Smith of Dunesk Committee, PCSA Papers, MC, SASL.

Assembly of the Church when it met in September later that year.[54] Crucial support for Duguid's mission also came from Love, who from Kunmunya added his comments on the Smith of Dunesk matter:

> I have been sore about this taking of blacks' money to help the whites, who were never in so dire need, ever since I was interested in the blacks; but my small voice went nowhere with effect. I am very glad that you have taken steps to right this wrong. Mind, the AIM is, I think, one of the greatest forces for good in our branch of the Church.[55]

Love's point as to the relative needs of the 'blacks and whites' of the Inland was one rarely made at that time. Love is I think also implying that the journey to the Centre by whites was generally voluntary, thus the moral case for priority in assistance was weakened.

The issue of the mission and the Smith monies remained divisive. Even the decision of the 1936 General Assembly of the Church to approve the Duguid Mission was distracted by controversy as Duguid now charged Flynn with obstruction: '[he] did everything in his power to stop the Mission I am sponsoring'. Duguid accused Flynn of posing as a friend to the native while working subtly to forestall the mission.[56] How much truth was there to this allegation? There may have been some organised attempt at the 1936 General Assembly to obstruct the establishment of the Mission, by the use of delaying tactics.[57] While the evidence is persuasive but not conclusive, it is interesting to note that Brigid Hains, generally supportive of Flynn, cites an unnamed Duguid supporter as describing Flynn as 'the devil incarnate' for his ability to argue for increased Aboriginal missions while at the same time undermining Duguid's work at Ernabella.[58] Flynn's derogatory remark about Duguid cited earlier probably reflects an irritation with Duguid's attacks on the AIM as an organisation uncaring of Aboriginals, and similar comments about Flynn himself, which are littered about his writings, letters and, doubtless, his conversations, as well as Duguid's activism regarding Aborigines. His personal manner, abrasive and judgmental, was also not likely to endear him to Flynn.

---

54   Matthews to Duguid, 22 May 1936, Duguid Papers, NLA, MS 5068, Series 1.
55   Love to Duguid, 20 April 1936, Duguid Papers, NLA, MS 5068, Series 1.
56   Duguid to MacKenzie (copy), 11 February 1937, Duguid Papers, NLA, MS 5068, Series 1.
57   The Minutes of the 1936 Assembly show that after the motion to inaugurate Ernabella, an amendment was moved requiring the consent of the majority of the State Assemblies to the mission, which if successful would have resulted in at least delaying, if not defeating, the venture. According to Duguid, Flynn spoke in support of the amendment but 'a senior Presbyterian minister from Queensland' who said he was 'puzzled' by the opposition to the venture, and called on the withdrawal of the amendment apparently turned the tide. It was withdrawn: see Minutes of Proceedings of the General Assembly of the Presbyterian Church of Australia: September 1936, PCA: 63–64; also Duguid 1972: 120–121.
58   Hains 2003: 33.

During this period, Duguid retained Love's full support.[59] The Kunmunya missionary was forthright on the Smith funds and the AIM: he was 'disappointed' that John Flynn was hostile to the Mission. He understood, he said, the chief reason: 'dislike of losing the "Smith of Dunesk" money'. Love was also critical of the modus operandi of the AIM regarding Aborigines, suggesting that the AIM tended 'to follow the lead of the station people in this [hostile] attitude to the blacks, rather than give the lead.' Love called for 'justice for the blacks'.[60] He also offered to help in the establishment of Ernabella, making two visits to the mission site in 1937 in preparation for the mission. Love's Report to the Board recommended that the mission proceed as planned. The publicly circulated versions of this Report excised a section that had trenchantly criticised the attitude of the AIM towards Aborigines.[61] Perhaps not surprisingly, the Board of Missions had decided that it was neither politic nor sensible to fan the flames of division within the Church, or to upset the powerful figure of Flynn.

Love attempted unsuccessfully to persuade the 1938 Assembly of the South Australian Church to divide the annual Smith of Dunesk funds equally between the AIM and Ernabella Mission. The Church did, however, grudgingly and gradually, allocate more to Duguid's venture than it had the previous year,[62] and concern grew within the AIM as to the ultimate trajectory of the distribution.[63] In 1939 the Church in Scotland, as trustees of the gift, suddenly sold the Smith of Dunesk properties on the grounds that Mrs Smith's original intentions regarding the 'education and evangelisation' of the Aborigines of South Australia had to be given weight now that, with the establishment of Ernabella, there was 'an activity among them' (the Aborigines).[64] The Scottish Church directed that the

---

59   Pastor Albrecht also continued to offer Duguid positive support for his mission. He told the Adelaide doctor that he, too, had had his differences with Church colleagues who thought 'it was a foolish thing to do to waste time and money on Aboriginals': Albrecht to Duguid (copy), 29 November 1935, Burns-Albrecht Collection, South Australian Museum Archives, AA662.

60   Love to Duguid, nd, probably late November 1936, Duguid Papers, NLA, MS 5068, Series 1.

61   The unexpurgated version was originally appended to a letter written by Love to the Board of Missions: Love to Matthews, 16 July 1937, Papers of JRB Love, MC, SLSA, PRG 214, Series 1, general correspondence: item 82. The edited version of the Report was published in the Minutes of Proceedings of the 1939 General Assembly of Australia. A characteristic example of Love's (excised) criticism of the AIM: 'I am shocked and distressed at the attitude of the Presbyterian Church towards the Aborigines, as evidenced by the AIM hostel at Oodnadatta. No one with long experience of life in the bush would advocate that Aborigines and whites should be cared for in the same ward; but the care of the Aborigines at this hostel is far from satisfactory.'

62   Presbyterian Church of SA, Blue Books, 1937, Report of Smith of Dunesk Committee, Financial Statement, PCSA Papers, MC, SASL; also see Minutes 9 and 37.

63   Presbyterian Church of SA, Minutes of AIM Executive 19 April 1938 (Minute 38/152), PCSA Papers, MC, SASL, SRG 123/360.

64   Webster to Martin, 4 September 1939, Presbyterian Church, PCSA Papers, MC, SASL, SRG123/331. It is hard to avoid the conclusion, however, that the 'home' church had finally lost patience with squabbling colonials in the 'paradise of dissent' and washed its hands of the matter. Future negotiations regarding the dispersal of the funds, now capitalised, were left entirely in the jurisdiction of the South Australian Church.

interest from the proceeds of the sale be divided equally between the AIM and Ernabella.[65] The pro-AIM forces in South Australia fought a rearguard action to retain their preponderant share of the income but the game was up.

The intervention of the overseas Church had finally tipped the balance in the Smith of Dunesk matter firmly in the direction of the pro-Ernabella forces. The 1940 Assembly voted to provide half of the available Smith of Dunesk funds to Ernabella. Duguid had wanted three-quarters. His frustration at this outcome was countered by his optimism over the announcement of the appointment of JRB Love as Superintendent of Ernabella, to take effect from March 1941. Duguid thought this appointment 'the greatest stroke of fortune for Ernabella'.[66] With its hand finally forced, the South Australian Assembly in 1942 determined that three-quarters of the Smith Funds were to be allocated to Ernabella, and one-quarter to the AIM. It was to remain at this allocation into the future.[67] It was a full seven years since Duguid had forced the issue and a century since the donor had made clear her intention to assist the Aborigines of South Australia, 'with not a farthing to the whites'. The AIM had been wounded slightly in the skirmish over the Scottish monies but in the larger scheme of things it moved on irresistibly, simultaneously creating and attaching itself to powerful national narratives of development, progress and nation-building.

Re-evaluating Flynn

At the end of this small but significant episode in parochial Presbyterianism, what do we now make of the myth of 'John Flynn', national saint? Successive commentators have had increasingly to consider Flynn's relationship with Indigenous Australians. In Ion Idriess's hagiography in 1932, which spectacularly constructed the icon of Flynn of the Inland, Aborigines are almost completely absent except as exotic, dangerous savages, speaking (but not heard) in 'guttural' tones, and spearing cattle and white men in 'bad-nigger' country.[68] The first 'official' biography in 1963, by Scott McPheat, treats the Flynn narrative as solely having reference to white people.[69] 'Aborigines' are not mentioned in the index, and rarely in the text. Little is revealed in McPheat's book of Flynn's attitudes to the Aborigines, unless one can infer something from the silence. A recent biography on Flynn by Max Griffiths, in 1993, provides

---

65   The proceeds from the sale of the properties were ⊠5792, a not inconsiderable sum at the time.
66   Duguid to Webster (copy), 30 September 1940, Duguid Papers, NLA, MS 5068, Series 1.
67   How far into the future is unclear, although Reverend Bill Edwards, the last missionary superintendent at Ernabella before it was given back, with the Pitjantjatjara Lands, to the Pitjantjatjara (Anangu) people in the early 1980s, thought it was possible that monies from the 'Smith Fund' were still being distributed to Ernabella in the late 1970s: Reverend Bill Edwards, pers comm, 2002.
68   Idriess 1932.
69   McPheat was a padre in the AIM and was commissioned by the organisation to write Flynn's biography nine years after his death in 1951.

a more comprehensive and balanced assessment of Flynn's attitudes towards Aboriginal people.[70] Although writing of Flynn from a position of sympathy and admiration, Griffiths acknowledges a racial element present in Flynn's thinking, but sees it as a reflection of the attitude of most of the Australian community. Flynn shared with that community the idea that Aborigines were a poor and primitive people who were likely to remain so, and were thus, in a sense by definition, excluded from the 'imagined community' of the Inland and the rest of the nation. Yet, somewhat incongruously, a smiling Aboriginal stockman adorns the frontispiece of Griffith's book.

Brigid Hains's 2002 book, *The Ice and the Inland: Mawson, Flynn and the Myth of the Frontier*, confronts Flynn's alleged racism even more directly.[71] Hains argues the frontier has become embedded in the modern Australian imagination as a permanent fixture, a potent myth, as she says, of a nation tempered by the struggle to live in an extreme natural environment. She sees Flynn, along with Douglas Mawson, as central to the creation of the frontier myth. These two 'heroes', she concludes, were essentially nation-builders, shaping and enhancing the 'symbiotic relationship' between the metropolis and the frontier.[72] Hains, like Griffiths, accepts Flynn's 'blind spot' in relation to the Aborigines and the racial problems of the frontier but places him somewhere in the middle of the spectrum of the racial attitudes of his day. In a subsequent article, examining Duguid's charges against Flynn, Hains has again provided a nuanced and sympathetic picture of a man who, while occasionally denouncing the treatment of Aboriginal people, was 'slow to do anything about it in his own institutions'. As Love suggested at the time, Hains concurs that Flynn and the AIM formed an alliance with a deeply racist white settler culture that left them on one side of a great divide. Nevertheless, she cautions against 'moralistic historical judgment' on Flynn's 'incomplete humanitarian vision'.[73] The whole matter is also complicated, Hains suggests, by Duguid's apparently complacent acceptance of the need for removal of mixed-blood Aboriginal children from missions in the name of uplift and improvement.[74] It is true that most actors in Central Australia were enmeshed, to a greater or lesser extent, in the implicating discourses of the time. Very few came, or left, with clean hands. It is perhaps ironic that Flynn himself saw this clearly: Australians, he wrote once, who 'have been reading to Aborigines the "move aside" clause, will surely be called up to render an account of our stewardship – God only know how soon'.[75]

---

70   Griffith 1993.
71   Hains 2002.
72   Hains 2002: 171–176.
73   Hains 2003: 34.
74   Hains 2003: 32.
75   Hains 2003: 35.

I have argued that by apparently aiding and abetting attempts to resist Duguid's efforts to attach resources clearly misappropriated to European uses to an Aboriginal cause and to establish a Mission for Aborigines John Flynn was pursuing policies *directly* inimical to Indigenous welfare and interests. It is highly unlikely that Flynn did not know the details behind the Smith of Dunesk controversy or believed that since the Deed of Gift did not specify Aboriginals as recipients that that was the end of the argument. Duguid raised all these matters in his Moderator's Address, and afterwards in a number of public statements, as well as private correspondence to authorities within the Presbyterian Church, in which he pointedly referred to the AIM's (mis)appropriation of the money. At the very least, as JRB Love said, it would have been a 'fine thing' for the AIM to have released the money willingly. As well, Howard Zelling, an eminent jurist, noted during the Flynn 'furore' in 1972 that John Flynn was Moderator-General of the national Presbyterian Church of Australia during the Smith of Dunesk controversy and that 'he certainly did not use the weight of his high office to help Dr. Duguid's struggle to get justice for Aborigines'.[76] The early history of the Smith Fund may have been clouded by misinformation, but from 1935 at least, when Duguid shone a coruscating light on the matter of 'taking of blacks' money to help the whites', as Love had put it, it was incumbent on Flynn to react. That he reacted the way he did suggests a strategy of subtle resistance to Ernabella, possibly confirmed by his behaviour at the 1936 General Assembly.

Love's arguments against his Flynn on behalf of the Aborigines, had two underlying premises. The first was the simple but profound point that their need was greater than that of the whites. The second was that if Flynn, as a respected voice in the Centre, had made more positive interventions in favour of Aborigines, he might have shifted white settler opinion to a more sympathetic stance. Yet Love also understood, from his experience of the bush, the power of the resistance to that shift, that indeed respect was granted to the AIM by white settlers precisely *because* Flynn, while a 'religious man', was seen as 'one of us', a white man, advocating white colonisation of the Inland, with an implied exclusion of the blacks.[77] Love appears to have accepted that this was an understandable, if regrettable, constraint on Flynn's freedom of action. However, these matters continue to leave a stain on his reputation as a 'national saint'. Indeed, it was the 'straight-out' Albrecht, on whose mission Flynn had first tested Traeger's famous wireless sets, who once said of the AIM founder

---

76   *The Advertiser* (South Australia), 6 September 1972: 5.
77   That this is not the whole story is evident in that missionaries, such as Winifred Hilliard and FW Albrecht, people sympathetic to Aborigines, and who devoted their lives in service with them, continued to respect Flynn, despite recognising some lack of fervour on his part regarding Aborigines.

that 'it is wrong to surround Flynn with a sort of a halo of a saint' and that acts of discrimination by the AIM against Aboriginal people 'cast a dark shadow over Flynn and his work'.[78]

Conclusion

John Flynn saw the Inland as a vast palimpsest over the inexorable erasure of whose original, Indigenous inscriptions he wished to write the nation-building, domesticated, racially homogenous script of modernity.[79] Duguid and Love were also inexorable in their opposition to this erasure, although Love may have accepted its inevitability. While Flynn and Duguid, ironically, shared similar beliefs, in a Protestant Gospel of Social Justice, with a humanitarian rather than an evangelical vision and the necessity for the development of the Inland as a necessary ingredient in nation building, they parted ways on the matter of the Aborigines. We can hardly accuse Duguid of indifference to the fate of the Aboriginal people of the continent. One senses with Flynn something akin to the process which occurred with Arthur Phillip at the beginning of the European encounter with the Aborigines of this continent, memorably described by WEH Stanner in the first issue of *Aboriginal History* as 'the history of indifference thus begins'.[80] In fact, at some point, Flynn's indifference appears to have developed into a sort of stubborn intractability on the matter of the Aborigines, whether through frustration, money concerns for the AIM, empathy for settler sentiment, personality clashes, or ideology, or perhaps a hardening amalgam of all these factors. JRB Love, on the other hand, had steered a middle course between these two restless engines of energy and ambition, Flynn and Duguid. In the end, Love's sense of his 'bad conscience', of the inexorability of the duty owed to the 'blacks', an obligation born out of the original dispossession, held sway for him, as it had not for John Flynn. Love, although often caught in racialist discourses, diverged, when it mattered and to his credit, towards the cause of the peoples whose mythic worlds Flynn's inexorable white men had usurped.

---

78   Letter from Pastor FW Albrecht re Dr John Flynn, nd, Albrecht Material 1926–1978, Lutheran Archives. The 'straight-out' reference is to the title of Albrecht's biography: Henson 1994.

79   I wish to use the concepts from the title of one of Emmanuel Levinas' essays, 'Bad Conscience and the Inexorable', as a sort of unifying theme for this conclusion: see Levinas 1986. It seems to me that the notion of a 'bad conscience', or more precisely the sensitivity or lack of sensitivity to a 'bad conscience' summarises the distinction I am trying to draw here between Love and Duguid on the one hand and Flynn on the other. The inexorability of the careers and personalities of Flynn and Duguid especially, on many layers, requires little comment. Duguid died in his 103rd year, still apparently fuming at Flynn until the end.

80   Stanner 1977.

References

Primary sources

Papers of FW Albrecht, Burns-Albrecht Collection, AA662, South Australian Museum Archives, Adelaide.

Albrecht, FW, Albrecht Material 1926–1978, Lutheran Archives, Adelaide.

Papers of Charles Duguid, MS 5068, Series 1: general correspondence: 1918–1974, National Library of Australia (NLA), Canberra.

Duguid, Charles 1946, *The Aborigines of Australia: Broadcasts and an Address*, Australian Broadcast Corporation, Adelaide.

Papers of John Flynn, MS 3288, NLA, Canberra.

Flynn, John 1910, *The Bushman's Companion: A Handful of Hints for Outbackers*, Brown, Prior & Co, Melbourne.

— 1913, 1915, issues of the *Inlander*, 1(1) 1913; 2(1) 1915.

Papers of JRB Love, Mortlock Collection, PRG 214, State Library of South Australia, Adelaide.

Love, JRB 1915, *The Aborigines: Their Present Condition as seen in Northern South Australia, the Northern Territory, North-West Australia and Western Queensland*, Arbuckle, Waddell and Fawckner, Melbourne.

— 1922, *Our Australian Blacks*, Brown, Prior Co Pty Ltd, Melbourne.

— 1936, *Stone-Age Bushmen of Today: Life and Adventure among a Tribe of Savages in North-Western Australia*, Blackie and Son Ltd, London and Glasgow.

Papers of the Presbyterian Church of Australia, ML MSS 1893, Mitchell Library, Sydney.

— 1936 Minutes of Proceedings of the 1936 General Assembly of the Presbyterian Church of Australia, Sydney.

Papers of the Presbyterian Church of South Australia, Mortlock Collection, State Library of South Australia, Adelaide.

Presbyterian Church of South Australia, 'Minutes of Proceedings of the South Australian State Assembly of the Presbyterian Church of Australia (Blue Books)', Mortlock Library, Adelaide.

Secondary sources

Anderson, Warwick 2002, *The Cultivation of Whiteness: Science, Health and Racial Destiny in Australia,* Melbourne University Press, Melbourne.

Behr, John 1990, 'Traeger, Alfred Hermann (1895–1980)', Australian Dictionary of Biography, vol 12, Melbourne University Press, Melbourne: 251–252.

Biskup, Peter 1973, *Not Slaves not Citizens: The Aboriginal Problem in Western Australia, 1898–1954,* University of Queensland Press, St Lucia.

Broome, Richard 1994, *Aboriginal Australians: Black Responses to White Dominance 1788–1994,* 2nd edn, Allen & Unwin, St Leonards, New South Wales.

Duguid, Charles 1972, *Doctor and the Aborigines,* Rigby, Adelaide.

— 1978, 'Tribal Nomadic People', *Australasian Nurses Journal* 7(12): 27.

Fischer, Tim 2009, 'An overdue salute: John Monash of Jerilderie and Melbourne', *Sydney Papers* 20(4): 134–141.

Godfrey, John R and John Ramsland 2004, 'David, Stanley and Norman Drummond: a "fair deal" for the New South Wales country child in schooling and welfare, 1924–1983', in *Journal of the Royal Australian Historical Society* 90(1), June: 22–35.

Griffiths, Max 1993, *The Silent Heart: Flynn of the Inland,* Kangaroo Press, Kenthurst, New South Wales.

Hains, Brigid 2002, *The Ice and the Inland: Mawson, Flynn, and the Myth of the Frontier,* Melbourne University Press, Melbourne.

— 2003, 'Inland Flynn: Pioneer? Racist? Or Product of His Time?', *Eureka Street,* May: 31–34.

— 2004, 'Antipodean Alchemist', *Meanjin* 63(1): 27–33.

Harris, John 1990, *One Blood: 200 Years of Aboriginal Encounter with Christianity: A Story of Hope,* Albatross, Sydney.

Henson, Barbara 1994, *A Straight-out Man: FW Albrecht and Central Australian Aborigines,* Melbourne University Press, Melbourne.

Hilliard, Winifred 1976, *The People in Between,* Seal Books, Rigby, Adelaide.

Idriess, Ion 1973[1932], *Flynn of the Inland,* Angus & Robertson, Sydney, [A&R Classics].

Levinas, Emmanuel 1986, 'Bad conscience and the inexorable', in *Face to Face with Levinas*, Richard A Cohen (ed), State University of New York Press, Albany: 35–40.

McKenzie, Maisie 1969, *The Road to Mowanjum*, Angus and Robertson, Sydney.

McPheat, W Scott 1963, *John Flynn: Apostle to the Inland*, Hodder and Stoughton, London.

Nelson, Penelope 2001, 'National vision, John Flynn and the blind spots of leadership', *Sydney Papers* 13(2): 20–32.

Rowse, Tim 1998, *White Flour, White Power: From Rations to Citizenship in Central Australia*, Cambridge University Press, Melbourne.

Rudolph, Ivan 2000, *John Flynn: of Flying Doctors and Frontier Faith*, 2nd edn, Central Queensland University Press, Rockhampton, Queensland.

Scrimgeour, Robert J 1986, *Some Scots Were Here: A History of the Presbyterian Church in South Australia 1839–1977*, Lutheran Publishing House, Adelaide.

Stanner, WEH 1977, 'The history of indifference thus begins', *Aboriginal History* 1(1): 3–26.

Trudinger, David 2004, 'Converting Salvation: Protestant Missionaries in Central Australia, 1930s–1940s', unpublished PhD thesis, Australian National University, Canberra.

Part three: memory and oral history

8. Paul Robeson's visit to Australia and Aboriginal activism, 1960

ANN CURTHOYS

Paul Robeson, a famous African American singer with a deep bass voice who brought a dramatic opera singing style to popular songs and was best known for his rendition of the timeless 'Ol' Man River', visited Australia in October and November 1960. The Australian Peace Council had invited him in 1950; soon afterwards, the United States government had confiscated his passport because of his communist sympathies and loyalty to the Soviet Union.[1] When his passport was returned in 1958, Paul Robeson and his wife Eslanda went on many singing tours, in an effort to earn some of the money lost during the hard unfriendly years of the 1950s, and to advocate a number of political causes – international peace, workers' rights, and gender and racial equality. The last of those tours was to Australia and New Zealand. This chapter is an account of that tour, especially as it related to Indigenous people and political activism around Indigenous rights.

Paul Robeson had always led an international life, as a performer and political figure, in a spirit of internationalism that characterised his generation of radical African Americans. It is a spirit that I also recognise in my own communist family upbringing; as in many communist households in the middle decades of the twentieth century, my mother had a particular fondness for Paul Robeson and often played his records. I especially remember that she had a record of the infamous Peekskill concert of September 1949, which was violently broken up by anti-communists after Robeson had sung to 20,000 sympathisers. Living in Newcastle, which Robeson did not visit, I did not hear or see Paul Robeson myself, but I was keenly aware in a more general sense of his importance in Left-wing circles. I first thought of studying his Australian tour in detail when researching for my book, *Freedom Ride: a Freedom Rider Remembers* (2002),

---

1   See mention of an invitation from the Australian Peace Council for its conference in April 1950, in the *Argus*, 22 June 1950, copy held in 'Paul Robeson and Madam Sun Yat Sen – Proposed visit', National Australian Archives [hereafter NAA], Series A33, Control Symbol 1950/2/2697. See also letter on Council on African Affairs, Inc letterhead from Paul Robeson to Nance Macmillan, Australian Peace Conference, 330 Little Flinders Street, Melbourne, on 27 June 1950, regretfully declining an invitation to the Melbourne Conference that year: 'Paul Robeson', Connie Healy collection, Fryer Library, UQFL 191.

which traced the history of the Australian Freedom Ride of 1965. In the course of that research, a number of the freedom riders mentioned that they had been influenced by hearing Robeson sing in 1960.[2] I was intrigued, and eventually decided to explore the visit in detail. My larger concern in researching and writing this essay is to understand how a politics of racial equality emerged in the context of, and ultimately helped change, the politics of the Cold War.

One of the best-remembered episodes of the tour occurred in Sydney. At a private screening in the function room of his hotel in Sydney, Robeson saw a film featuring Indigenous Aboriginal people.[3] One of those present was Faith Bandler, an Australian of Pacific Islander descent who is now well known as a key figure in the campaign for Indigenous rights and especially for the Yes vote in the referendum of 1967 to change the Australian constitution. She recalled the event over 30 years later:

> I had an occasion to meet him, after meeting him at the airport, and to show him a film that was made on the Warburton Ranges. And I shall never forget his reaction to that film, never. It was a film taken on a mission station where the people were ragged and unhealthy and sick, very sick. And we took this film and we showed it to him. He was staying in the Hotel Australia and we showed him the film and Paul then was wearing a black cap on his head, to keep his head warm. He was no chicken then, of course, and Islanda [sic] always insisted that before a concert he should rest that day, but she allowed him to come down and have a look at the film, in the Starlight Room, as they called it, in the Hotel Australia and as he watched the film the tears came to his eyes and when the film finished he stood up and he pulled his cap off and he threw it in his rage on the floor and trod on it and he asked for a cigarette from someone. Well a lot of people smoked in those days so there was no shortage of cigarettes and Islanda said to me, 'Well it's many years since I've seen him do that'. He was so angry and he said to me, 'I'll go away now, but when I come back I'll give you a hand'. He was beautiful, but he died and he didn't come back.[4]

This account is becoming legendary, perhaps partly because it is readily available on the internet. In July 2009, journalist Shane Maloney evoked it in a short piece with the title 'Faith Bandler and Paul Robeson' in *The Monthly* magazine.[5] Moving and informative as it is, Bandler's account is necessarily partial; indeed,

---

2 Curthoys 2002: 37, 66.
3 Holmes 1999: 99.
4 Bandler 1993.
5 Maloney 2009; see also Lake 2002: 86.

it is a small part of a larger story. Here, using documentary, visual, aural, and oral history sources, I explore this larger story, asking what Paul Robeson's visit meant, both at the time and since, for Indigenous people.[6]

Paul Robeson, performer and political activist

African-American connections with Indigenous people in Australia have a long history. These interactions have been both political and cultural. John Maynard has drawn attention to the political influence of the Marcus Garvey movement on Aboriginal waterside workers in the early twentieth century.[7] Culturally, there have been influences through dance, but one of the main sites of connection has been music, more specifically through singing. Gospel and hymn singing was much encouraged on many evangelical missions, and visits by entertainers, including African American entertainers, were quite common.[8] These visits go back to the nineteenth century; for example, the Fisk Jubilee singers, an *a cappella* ensemble of Fisk University students known especially for their singing of spirituals, visited the Maloga Mission in 1886.[9] These connections persisted into the twentieth century, and from the 1950s especially, a series of African American entertainers visiting Australia met with and performed for Aboriginal people. Pastor Doug Nicholls encouraged a number to come to his Gore Street Church of Christ in Melbourne, including Mattiwilda Dobbs, an African American opera singer, Harry Belafonte, and pianist Winifred Atwell.[10] Harry Belafonte completed a major tour of Australia just two months before Robeson, in August 1960,[11] and Marian Anderson came soon after, in 1962.[12] Odetta, an American singer best known for her rendition of 'O Freedom' at the March on Washington in 1963, visited in 1965.[13] Such visiting singers seem to have sought out Aboriginal people; Margaret Valadian, one of the Indigenous people who met Paul Robeson in 1960, remembers that she 'also met with

---

6   The most detailed account of the Robeson tour of Australia and New Zealand so far is in Duberman 2005[1988]. His four-page account relied on newspaper sources, Mrs Robeson's letters back to her family, and some material sent to him by an Aboriginal rights lawyer, Lloyd Davies, based in Perth. He was unable to visit Australia, however, and he wrote to me recently saying he was delighted I was doing this project, as he was conscious the Australian and New Zealand part of the story deserved further research: 'I never got around to travelling to Australia; by then, I guess, I was plain worn out!'
7   Maynard 2007: ch 3, 'Inspiration and Influences'.
8   Dunbar-Hall 2004: 41–42.
9   Abbott and Seroff 2002: 3–27.
10   Australian Broadcasting Commission 1955. See also Broome 2005: 290–291; Costa 2006: 77.
11   Belafonte was featured on the cover of Woman's Day on 15 August 1960. For an account of his Brisbane concert on 24 August 1960, see *Courier Mail*, 25 August 1960: 3.
12   Keiler 2002: 302–304.
13   Roadknight 2001.

Marian Anderson and Odetta when they came to Brisbane'. The 'Go Tell it on the Mountain Singers', who were touring in early 1965, farewelled the Freedom Riders when they left the University of Sydney on 12 February 1965.[14]

While a number of these visitors were involved in the Civil Rights movement and had strong political convictions, no visit was more political than Paul Robeson's. Robeson was throughout his life a deeply political and often controversial figure. Born in 1898, his father was a former slave who had become a Presbyterian minister, while his mother came from a prominent African American Philadelphia family. After studying at Rutgers University, where he became a well-known college footballer, and Columbia University, where he studied law, he turned to acting. He became famous for his lead roles in several Eugene O'Neill plays, and then Shakespeare, his Othello the first acted by an African American for over a century. From there he moved to singing, with huge record sales internationally in the 1930s and 1940s, including in Australia. He also acted in a number of films, and through records and film became popular in Europe as well as the United States. Despite his pro-Communist politics, he remained popular in the United States during World War II, when the Soviet Union and the United States were allies. His Broadway Othello in 1942–1943 was an enormous success, and in its wake came a number of major honours and awards, such as the Abraham Lincoln Medal for 'notable services in human relations'.[15]

After the war, however, with the tensions between the United States and the Soviet Union growing, Robeson faced a quite different political environment. He stubbornly insisted on his support for the Soviet Union, often saying that it was the first country to treat him simply as a human being. Like many Communists, he refused to believe the negative reports of the Soviet Union were true, seeing them as disinformation spread by the Soviet Union's enemies. In 1949, he attended a World Peace Congress in Paris, and was reported to have said that African Americans would not support the United States if war broke out between the United States and the Soviet Union. This comment, which Duberman argues was misquoted (he had actually said, 'We shall not make war on anyone. We shall not make war on the Soviet Union'), was a major source of his subsequent ostracism.[16] In 1950, his Communist and Soviet sympathies led to the United States government depriving him of his passport. Trapped within the United States in a hostile atmosphere, he found his performance opportunities drying up, with concerts cancelled and recordings withdrawn from sale.

---

14   *Tribune*, 24 February 1965: 1.
15   Duberman 2005[1988]: 281.
16   Duberman 2005[1988]: 341–342; Beeching 2002: 339–354, esp 341.

The restrictions on Robeson's travels abroad during the 1950s have an interesting context. As Mary Dudziak writes in her book, *Cold War, Civil Rights*, African Americans were important to the United States attempt in the context of the Cold War to counter Soviet and other accusations of racial repression and subordination. 'African Americans travelling abroad could bear witness to the character of American equality'.[17] Those who could be trusted to say the right thing from the government's perspective found their way eased; those, like Robeson, who could not, were blocked in various ways. Other African American political leaders who found their ability to travel overseas curtailed in the 1950s included the veteran WEB du Bois, and others like Louis Armstrong were closely monitored.[18]

His performance opportunities now limited, Robeson became a political activist within the United States. He continued to work closely with Communist organisations and allied peace organisations. He was prominent in the Civil Rights Congress, a controversial and vigorous Communist-led organisation that fought for African American rights in the Cold War period.[19] He was a leading figure in the Civil Rights Congress's 'We Charge Genocide' petition of December 1951, submitting it to the UN Secretariat in New York at the same time as William L Patterson, the petition's main author, submitted it to the UN General Assembly in Paris.[20] Presented only 11 months after the UN Genocide Convention went into effect, the petition argued that the lynching and other forms of assault on the lives and livelihood of African Americans from 1945 to 1951, especially the frenzied attacks on returning Black American veterans, amounted to genocide.[21] In addition to skilled legal challenges, the Civil Rights Congress engaged in picketing, demonstrations and petitioning, for example in the cases of Willie McGee, Rosa Lee Ingram, the Trenton Six, and the Martinsville Seven.[22] The Civil Rights Congress strongly believed that a focus on Jim Crow laws and deprivation of Blacks' rights would be an embarrassment for the United States abroad and might hasten overdue reform. It was to be proved right in this judgment; and the American Civil Rights movement a decade later successfully adopted these CRC tactics.[23] The Civil Rights Congress itself, however, collapsed in 1956, its close association with Communism too disabling for a role in the new Civil Rights movement, which was anxious to

---

17   Dudziak 2000: 61.
18   Dudziak 2000: 61–62, 66.
19   Horne 1988: 13–21, 48, 69.
20   Patterson 1971: 184; Horne 1986.
21   Civil Rights Congress 1951: 8. See also Curthoys and Docker 2008.
22   Horne 1988: 13–21, 48, 69.
23   Dudziak 2000; Von Eschen 1997.

distinguish itself from the Communist-influenced African-American politics of a decade earlier.[24] Earlier leaders were set aside and a new generation emerged. Robeson, with his Communist associations, was seen as a liability.[25]

For Robeson personally, however, the worst was over by 1958 when his passport was returned; in that year, he returned to prominence triumphantly with a concert at Carnegie Hall.[26] He based himself in London and travelled widely in Europe and Africa. In 1960, he agreed to undertake a commercial tour of Australia and New Zealand, in a bid to make money after the years of effective blacklisting in the United States. The offer of more than $100,000 for 20 concerts, with opportunities to earn more through television appearances, was too good to refuse.

The Australian tour, October – December 1960

Over an eight week period from early October to early December there were 12 Australian concerts – four in Sydney, three in Melbourne, two each in Adelaide and Perth, and one in Brisbane, plus several in New Zealand. The tour was organised commercially through a Sydney-based music entrepreneur, DD O'Connor Productions Ltd, of Sydney, in association with RJ Kerridge. In each city, the concerts were sold out or largely so, and attracted extremely enthusiastic audiences. There were at least two different programmes, possibly more. In each, there were three sets of songs, divided by Janetta McStay's piano solos. In the first programme, the first set included opera and classical songs such as Handel's 'Art Thou Troubled?', 'The Ode to Joy' from Beethoven's Ninth Symphony, and Schubert's 'Cradle Song' and the second set consisted of Negro spirituals including 'Joshua Fit De Battle ob Jericho' and 'Swing Low, Sweet Chariot'. The last set consisted of songs from around the world – the 'Volga Boatman's Song', 'Water Boy', and the Scottish 'Eriskay Love Lilt'. The second programme had a similar structure, and its best-known songs included 'Didn't My Lord Deliver Daniel', 'Steal Away', and 'Goin' Home'.

The opening concert in Brisbane's Festival Hall on 15 October attracted an almost capacity audience of 5000 people, and the audience loved it. The Robesons then went to New Zealand for almost three weeks, where Paul met Maori on several occasions and expressed concern at their mistreatment and suppression of their culture. They returned to Sydney on 3 November; Paul Robeson performed four concerts there, on 7, 8, 12 and 14 November. There were three concerts in Melbourne – on 16, 18 and 22 November, two in Adelaide on 24 and 27 November, with the final two concerts in Perth on 1 and 3 December. There were

---

24   D'Emilio 2003: 178–179.
25   See Beeching 2002: 353.
26   *Tribune*, 12 October 1960: 7.

several television appearances, including one on a Sunday night programme called 'Spotlight' on ABC television, recorded on 5 November.[27] Robeson also appeared on the Christmas show of 'Hal Lashwood's Minstrels', broadcast on 15 December, where he sang 'Silent Night' and other songs to a group of children.

In his biography, Martin Duberman emphasises the testy confrontation between Robeson and reporters at his first Sydney press conference.[28] Overall, though, press coverage of his tour was largely sympathetic. Newspapers that would usually have been savage in their denunciation of anyone who defended the Soviet Union the way Robeson did treated him with respect and even in some cases liking and admiration. This was evident even before his arrival. The *Sydney Morning Herald* carried a story from its London Correspondent that spoke of his 'easy charm', and his eminence as a singer. When he lost his passport in the 1950s, the correspondent wrote, his friends deserted him: 'They forgot the highness of his heart, the generosity of his mind, his incomparable talents, and remembered only his political naiveté'.[29] The *Daily Telegraph* was also reasonably sympathetic, saying few questioned Robeson's sincerity, though they might disagree with his politics, and concluded the story by saying 'Robeson is at his best singing melancholy songs', perhaps because he was, as the story's headline had it, the 'loneliest man in show business'.[30]

Once the tour was under way, the positive reception continued. The concerts themselves were favourably reviewed. The *Courier Mail* reported that the Brisbane concert was 'greatly to the taste' of its audience. The reviewer liked his 'organ-like richness of tone, and the tremendous resonance in the lowest register'.[31] The *Sunday Mail* reviewer reported, 'We heard spirituals sung with a properly religious fervour; and heard and saw an audience give a demonstration of something like hero worship.'[32] The *Sydney Morning Herald* reviewer, RC (Roger Covell), said of the first of the four Sydney concerts that 'its extra-musical qualities were every bit as important to the total experience of the evening as the sounds produced by Robeson the singer'. Covell noted 'the enormous aura of benevolence and goodwill generated by his presence; an aura in which large and resounding concepts like freedom and amity, whether expressed in song

---

27 The evidence for his television appearances is very sketchy. 'Paul Robeson', FBI Report, NY 100-25857: 2351, refers to television interviews in Adelaide. The next page summarises some of the responses to Robeson in Adelaide, including one in the *Adelaide News*, 16 November 1960, 'What a fine man Paul Robeson looked and sounded in Sunday's "Spotlight", on Channel 2', viewed 5 October 2009:

<http://news.lp.findlaw.com/legalnews/entertainment/fbi/robes/robes02352.html>

28 Duberman 2005[1988]: 487–488.

29 *Sydney Morning Herald*, 9 October 1960: 106.

30 *Daily Telegraph*, 9 October 1960: 10.

31 *Courier Mail*, 17 October 1960: 10.

32 *Sunday Mail*, 16 October 1960.

or speech, seemed to tingle with new relevance'. He gives us an inkling of why responses were so positive when he went on to say that while the voice was familiar from films and recordings, hearing it in person was still a shock.

> It is as if the ground were to quake in musical terms, as if a sudden fissure had opened to reveal some subterranean reservoir of resonant darkness. This cosmic belch of a voice still has the power to astonish by sheer carpeted magnificence.[33]

Music reviewers made these kinds of comments throughout the tour. The *Adelaide Advertiser* reviewer, John Horner, was delighted with the tremendous success of the evening; he described the concert as a 'fine celebrity concert' behind which was the theme of universal brotherhood. Robeson, he wrote, 'is simplicity itself on the stage ... confining himself in every song to the simplest of the eternal verities'.[34]

The concerts were only part of the visit. Characteristically, Robeson had a political agenda as well – to meet with and give support to causes of peace and trade unionism. The arrangement of the more political aspect of the visit seems to have begun when Bill Morrow, of the Australian Peace Council and a former senator from Tasmania, met Robeson at a World Peace Council Bureau meeting in Moscow in 1959, and they discussed plans for the visit.[35] Once Robeson arrived, the Peace Council and state-based Peace Committees, Waterside Workers Union, Building Workers' Industrial Union, and the Australia Soviet Friendship societies all played a role in organising welcomes, social functions, and political meetings.[36] The Union of Australian Women organised in each city very well attended, successful, and well-reported events for Robeson's wife, Eslanda. An anthropologist, who had undertaken fieldwork in Africa, and the author of *African Journey*,[37] Eslanda was a major figure. Throughout the tour, she gave separate press interviews and emphasised the role of women in struggles for racial equality and peace.[38] Her talk to the Union of Australian Women branch in Perth was typical; the topics there were, in the words of the ASIO Agent's report, 'The Negro problem throughout the world; Peace; Africa and the Congo; The United Nations; Equal rights and power to vote for American Negroes; and The rights of the Australian aboriginal'.[39]

---

33   *Sydney Morning Herald*, 8 November 1960: 6.

34   Horner 1960: 11.

35   Johnson 1986: 275, 277.

36   See Anon 1961, 'Paul Robeson', Australian Security Intelligence Organisation (ASIO) Report, 9 March 1961, NAA, A6122/44 (1450).

37   *Courier Mail*, 15 October 1960: 13; Robeson 1945.

38   Her talk to the Melbourne audience of 400 women is reported in the Melbourne Communist newspaper, *The Guardian*, 24 November 1960: 8.

39   Australian Security Intelligence Organisation, Union of Australian Women, ASIO Report No 60/779: 62, series number A6119 (2006/00328495), Control Symbol 3873, ASIO, NAA.

There were innumerable meetings, receptions, impromptu concerts, garden parties, and luncheons, all of which had some kind of political or social purpose. At these events, Robeson sang, but because of the conditions of his commercial contract, this was always without musical accompaniment. The best remembered occasion on which this happened was Robeson's visit to the Sydney Opera House building site on 9 November. At the invitation of the Building Workers' Industrial Union, Bill Morrow of the Australian Peace Council took him there. As the *Daily Telegraph* reported, he talked to more than 250 workmen in their lunch hour, telling them they were working on a project they would be proud of one day. The workers sat on 'tiles, pipes, timber and scaffolding', and later mobbed Robeson for autographs. He also sang.[40] Wearing a large coat, he cupped his ear and sang solo to the building workers on site. Robeson himself said the day after his visit,

> Yesterday, I went down by the Opera House, standing around singing to the workers ... I could see, you know, we had some differences here and there. But we hummed some songs together, and they all came up afterwards and just wanted to shake my hand and they had me sign gloves. These were tough guys and it was a very moving experience.[41]

Many people have recalled this event since. One was John Aquilina, a Minister in the NSW Labor Government, who informed parliament on 20 October 1998 that his father had been a carpenter working on the Opera House site, and had been there that day. 'Dad told us that all the workers – carpenters, concreters and labourers – sang along and that the huge, burly men on the working site were reduced to tears by his presence and his inspiration'.[42] One reason the event is so well remembered is that it was recorded on film by Howard Rubie, a cinematographer with Cinesound, with both vision and sound of exceptional quality. ABC television has screened the film many times since.

Robeson sang to large meetings of waterside workers in Sydney, Melbourne, and Adelaide. On 10 November, he sang to a stop work meeting of thousands of workers at the Sydney Town Hall, called by the Waterside Workers' Federation to protest against the Crimes Bill, then before Parliament. The union's newspaper later commented, 'He made it the best stop work meeting ever'.[43] In Melbourne, the union held a stop work meeting on the seventh day of what became a ten-day stoppage, initially over the right to load ship stores, and then a protest against suspension threats and the cancelling of leave credits. As in Sydney, Robeson received a tumultuous reception. The *Maritime Worker* reported that

40 *Daily Telegraph*,10 November 1960: 15; *Tribune*, 16 November 1960: 10.
41 Transcript made by Sari Braithwaite from recording made of Robeson's speech at Paddington Town Hall, 10 November 1960.
42 NSW Legislative Assembly, *Hansard* 1998.
43 *Maritime Worker*, 1 Dec 1960: 4; *Sydney Morning Herald*, 11 November 1960: 6.

'Paul sang to the members the songs for which he is famous, Joe Hill, Water Boy, Ol' Man River, and then led the 4000 present in John Brown's body, explaining that John Brown had died that his father, a slave, should be free'. There were unprecedented scenes when Robeson left the stadium, 'Members climbing over seats to grasp his hand and the whole gathering was on its feet, stamping, shouting, and clapping. It had to be seen to be believed'.[44] When he entered the Wharfies' hall in Port Adelaide for a lunchtime address and recital, the workers gave him a standing ovation. The *Maritime Worker*'s Adelaide reporter, Jim Mitchell, wrote that he was greeted by '1,100 wharfies, tally clerks, seamen and their families who had gathered at lunch time to hear his address and impromptu recital'. The audience loved his songs and speeches, and 'the final "three cheers" at the end of the performance lifted the roof'.[45] Arthur Shertock wrote to me about this occasion.

> On that day it was jam packed with not only wharfies and seamen but also with shop workers and people from offices and banks. ... The lunch hour was long gone; I guess it was after three o'clock when finally he concluded his magnificent performance, with no musical accompanists. [As] far as I could see no one had left the hall.

At these Waterside Workers' Federation events, Robeson was typically given an Aboriginal object of some kind, to signify the wharfies' support for Aboriginal rights. The Sydney branch of the Waterside Workers' Federation gave him a print of an Albert Namatjira painting.[46] In Adelaide, the Waterside Workers' Federation gave him 'an authentic woomera throwing stick', which would 'remind him of his desire to learn more about the problems of the old Australians in our midst'.[47]

The Robesons and Indigenous people

Paul and Eslanda Robeson seem to have sought out Indigenous people wherever they went. In Brisbane, even before the first concert of the tour, Robeson met with Margaret Valadian, then 24, an Aboriginal student who was intending to do a social studies course at the University of Queensland, and then do welfare work amongst Aboriginal people (all of which she later did). She was quoted in the *Courier Mail* as saying, 'I have always been greatly inspired by Mr Robeson's work in the cultural field, and I wanted to meet him'.[48] She later attended his Brisbane concert, and went backstage afterwards to meet him.[49] 'He autographed

---

44   *Maritime Worker*, 1 December 1960: 4.
45   *Maritime Worker*, 15 December 1960: 7.
46   *Sydney Morning Herald*, 11 November 1960: 6.
47   *Maritime Worker*, 15 December 1960: 7
48   *Courier Mail*, 15 October 1960: 1.
49   *Truth* (Queensland edition), 16 October 1960: 1.

a copy of a 45rpm record for me', she recalled in 2008.[50] Robert Anderson, now an Aboriginal elder in Brisbane, remembers attending the Brisbane concert at Festival Hall, and being on security duty to help make sure the Nazi Party did not interfere.[51]

In Sydney, Robeson met people through the Aboriginal Australian Fellowship, which had started four years earlier and involved both Aboriginal and non-Aboriginal activists, with Faith Bandler probably its best-known representative.[52] Bandler reported to its December meeting that Eslanda Robeson had met Aboriginal people at La Perouse, an Aboriginal settlement in Sydney.[53] The Fellowship also co-sponsored one of the major events of the tour. With the NSW Peace Committee, it organised a reception on Thursday 10 November for the Robesons at Paddington Town Hall. Fifteen hundred people were present, including about 30 Aboriginal people, whom the Aboriginal Australian Fellowship had helped to attend.[54] Both Paul and Eslanda spoke, and Paul Robeson sang. Tom McDonald, the BWIU organiser responsible for getting Robeson to the Opera House, later recalled that

> the place was crowded and he performed solo for a couple of hours without any musical instruments and it was one of the most remarkable performances by an individual I can recall. What he did was, you know, he talked about some of the struggles he'd been involved in. He'd then recite a bit of poetry. He'd then say a bit about his philosophies.[55]

Earlier that day, Robeson had attended the informal film screening recalled by Faith Bandler. The screening was organised by Helen Hambly, one of the non-Aboriginal members of the Aboriginal Australian Fellowship, and Faith Bandler; also present was Alec Robertson, reporting for the Communist Party newspaper, *Tribune*.[56] The film Bandler describes upsetting Robeson so much, known as *Manslaughter* when shown on television in 1957 but more commonly referred to simply as 'the Warburton Ranges film', was made by Bill Grayden, a Western Australian Member of Parliament. Grayden had in 1956 successfully pressed for an inquiry by the Western Australian parliament into 'Native Welfare Conditions in the Laverton-Warburton Range Area', an area affected by the British government's atomic bomb testing at Maralinga. The Inquiry's Report was extremely critical of the condition of the Yarnangu (the Aboriginal people

---

50   Letter Margaret Valadian to Ann Curthoys, 9 August 2008.
51   Robert Anderson to Sari Braithwaite, 2008.
52   Goodall 1996: 276–277.
53   I have, however, been unable to find any corroboration of this meeting at La Perouse, despite searching Aborigines Protection Board and other records. See the 'Minutes of Monthly General Meetings', Minute for 7 December 1960, AAF Papers, ML MSS 4057.
54   'Robeson will "fight for our Aborigines"', *Sydney Morning Herald*, 13 November 1960.
55   McDonald 1994. See also McDonald and McDonald 1998: 100–101.
56   Holmes 1999: 99–100.

in that area) and received wide publicity; shocking many with its description of starvation and extreme deprivation. It was strongly criticised in the press, however, for giving a misleading and exaggerated account, and in response to his critics, Grayden returned to the area with a movie camera, accompanied by Pastor Doug Nicholls and other Western Australian parliamentarians.[57] The resulting silent film, which lasts for just over 20 minutes, contained confronting images of Aboriginal poverty, starvation, injury, and disease in the Warburton and Rawlinson Ranges in the Central Aborigines Reserve, now known as the Ngaanyatjarra Lands. Doug Nicholls later told journalists: 'I wish I had not gone to the Warburton Ranges. I wish I hadn't seen the pitiable squalor, the sights of my people starving – the most shocking sights I have ever seen. Never, never can I forget.'[58]

As Sue Taffe points out, activists used the ensuing film effectively for several years to alert other Australians to the injustices experienced by Aboriginal people and to press governments to take greater responsibility.[59] By late 1960, when Hambly and Bandler showed the film to Robeson, the Fellowship had screened it many times, including at a Town Hall meeting in 1957 inaugurating the campaign for a referendum to change the Australian constitution. These screenings were usually to shocked non-Aboriginal audiences, but Fellowship members had also screened it to a meeting in the small New South Wales town of Walgett, which about 40 Aboriginal people attended, when making contact with local activists there. Over half those present signed the Fellowship petitions requesting a change to the constitution.[60] It had also been shown on television in Sydney and Melbourne in May 1957. While many saw the film as proving Aboriginal poverty and suffering existed, others thought it was highly selective and misleading. Importantly, it did not present the views of the Yarnangu people about their own lives or about their being filmed in this way. Pam McGrath and David Brooks point out that Yarnangu both then and since have sought to stress their own agency and choices rather than the film's portrayal of them as victims of government neglect; many Yarnangu also see the film as a gross invasion of privacy.[61] Nevertheless, the film was significant

---

57 Taffe 2008.

58 Victorian Aborigines Advancement League 1957, Analysis of Mr Rupert Murdoch's article [...], Melbourne: 2–3, as quoted in Attwood 2003: 150.

59 Taffe 2008.

60 Garland and McIlwraith 1957. Note that this report was the subject of much dispute within the AAF, mainly because it was feared that it contained defamatory material; Irene McIlwraith was expelled from the organisation for distributing the report without checking with the rest of the executive first. See also Fox and Bandler 1983: 65; McIlwraith, Irene to the Editor, *Walgett Spectator*, 18 September 1957, Walgett file, AAF Papers, ML MSS 4057/16.

61 McGrath and Brooks (forthcoming). Many thanks to Pam McGrath and David Brooks for allowing me to read this essay before its publication.

in mobilising support for demands for Aboriginal rights, and played a role the formation of the Victorian Aborigines Advancement League and, indirectly, in the formation a year later of the Federal Council for Aboriginal Advancement.[62]

Though Bandler does not mention it, there was a second film screened in Robeson's hotel that day. This was a short film, *People of Pindan*, made earlier that year by Cecil Holmes, a pioneering Australian documentary filmmaker. *People of Pindan* was in fact the pilot for a much more ambitious project. On the suggestion of British documentary film-maker Paul Rotha, Holmes planned to make a feature-length film, *The Flung Spear*. While in Perth at the end of 1959, he met established Left wing Australian author, Gavin Casey, who had written a novel, *Snowball* (1958) and a play on Aboriginal themes. Casey alerted him to the cooperative movement that was becoming popular amongst Aboriginal people in Western Australia, Queensland, South Australia and New South Wales, and especially to the mining cooperative at Port Hedland, as evoked in Donald Stuart's novel, *Yandy* (1959).[63] This was the Pindan cooperative, formed in the aftermath of the Pilbara pastoral workers' strike of 1946–9, led by tribal elders Clancy McKenna and Dooley Bin Bin along with white man Don McLeod.[64] Intrigued by Casey's story, Holmes went to Port Hedland, stayed at Aboriginal camps, listened to songs, watched ceremonies by the campfire, and made a short film about the cooperative. It became the pilot for the larger project.

On Holmes' return to Sydney, plans for *The Flung Spear* advanced quickly.[65] It was to be one hour in length, in colour, and would have three parts: the first would focus on Aboriginal workers in the pastoral industry, the second on Aboriginal fringe settlements, and the third on the co-operative movement.[66] Gavin Casey and another successful Left wing author, Kylie Tennant, were to work with Holmes on the script, and a group of supporters formed a public company, Marngoo Films, expressly to raise the necessary finance.[67] Helen Hambly, who had organised the screening for the Robeson's of the pilot film, *People of Pindan*, and her husband were closely involved in Marngoo Films, and perhaps one purpose of this screening was to gain Robesons of the pilot film, *The Flung Spear* project. (In fact, *The Flung Spear* was never made, but Holmes later sold the pilot to the ABC.[68])

---

62   Taffe 2008. See also Attwood 2003: 149–151; Taffe 2005: 34–36.
63   For information on the cooperative movement in New South Wales, see Goodall 1996: 299–307.
64   Hess 1994: 65–83.
65   Holmes 1960; Holmes 1999: 98–100. See also Williams 1999: 215, 1994: 36–39.
66   'News of the Day', *The Age*, 14 March 1960: 2.
67   Marngoo Films 1960. The secretary of the limited company was Sidney Lloyd Hambly, and Sidney and Helen Hambly were two of the listed eight subscribers.
68   Holmes 1999: 86–99; Holmes 1986: 57.

Tribune reporter Alec Robertson reported Robeson's reaction to these two films:

> When he saw two films – one showing the misery of tribal aborigines in a WA desert reserve, and the other showing confident and healthy tribal aborigines running their own mining cooperative at Pindan – Robeson was beside himself with anger, compassion and determination to arouse more international action to assist the emancipation struggle of those he calls 'the indigenous people of Australia'. 'Why are you Australians tolerating that?' Robeson demanded. 'This is unbelievable. There is nothing primitive about these people's ability. There are no backward people anywhere – only people held back or forced back, by "overlords"'.

'Australia', Robertson continued, will hear more of Paul Robeson on this issue'.[69]

It was at the press conference after the Paddington Town Hall event that Robeson first spoke strongly about Aboriginal conditions and demands, and it seems very likely that his passionate comments were influenced by seeing the two films. He said he would return to Australia within six months to campaign for greater help for Aborigines and coloured people. 'If necessary, I will stomp up and down the country to help them', *Truth* quoted him as saying.

> You have a serious problem here in Australia. I hope, and I feel certain, that Australia will do the right thing by the colored people. I have nothing but admiration for Australia. I feel at home here. It is my kind of country and I am sure you are my kind of people.[70]

Newspapers picked up the story, with headlines such as 'Australia has a colour problem says Paul Robeson' and 'Robeson will "fight for our Aborigines"'.[71]

By the time they reached Perth, both Robesons were increasingly voluble about Aboriginal rights, though it is unclear how much additional contact they had with Aboriginal people after the Paddington concert. In Melbourne, they met opera singer Harold Blair, and may have met other Aboriginal people as well, though I have found no evidence of formal events organised by Aboriginal rights organisations.[72] When they arrived in Perth on 30 November, they were met by 200 cheering 'admirers from all walks of life', including a group of Aboriginal people, to whom Robeson said, 'I hope that soon they will treat you as well as they treat me'.[73] Non-Aboriginal supporters of Aboriginal rights were there

---

69   *Tribune*, 23 November 1960: 6. See also footnote 2 re accounts by Bandler.

70   *Truth* (Queensland edition), 13 November 1960: 11

71   *Truth* (Queensland edition), 13 November 1960: 11; *Sunday Mirror* (Sydney), 13 November 1960: 9. The *Northern Territory News* story was headlined '"I'll fight for the Aborigines" – Paul Robeson'; *Northern Territory News*, 15 November 1960: 3.

72   A search of the Council for Aboriginal Rights papers in the State Library of Victoria yielded nothing.

73   *Tribune*, 7 December 1960: 10.

too; Lloyd Davies, a non-Indigenous lawyer and activist for Indigenous rights was there[74] and noted Communist writer and public figure, Katharine Susannah Pritchard, author of *Coonardoo,* one of the first novels to depict Aboriginal characters sympathetically, gave a speech of welcome.[75] At a press conference in Perth that evening, Robeson rejected the idea that Aboriginal people might not be ready for equal rights. 'The fact that these people are not given citizenship is indefensible and inexcusable. They are human beings, they have a right to live.'[76] He repeated the promise made in Sydney that he would return. At his huge concert at the Capitol Theatre the next day, he said from the stage, 'I am coming back to Australia as soon as I can and the first place I want to go is amongst my black brothers, the indigenous people of Australia'.[77]

One of those at the concert was Colin Hollett, a railway union official. He approached Eslanda Robeson and through her invited Paul to sing the following day at the large railway workshops at Midland Junction. Paul agreed, but because of his Communist allegiance the works manager refused permission for the hastily organised concert to be held at the Workshops flagpole, the traditional site venue. Undaunted, and indeed welcomed by the Mayor of Midland Junction, Robeson sang at an open-air lunch hour concert on 2 December from the back of a truck at the entrance to the workshops. As the *West Australian* reported,

> [m]ore than 2000 people jammed an entrance to the railway workshops to hear the Negro singer. Children climbed trees to get a better view ... Robeson sang Water Boy, Joe Hill, Ol' Man River and other American folk songs intermingled with classical themes, Chinese tunes and Shakespearian extracts.[78]

The *Tribune* reported the whole audience joining in the singing of 'John Brown's Body', just as they had done in Melbourne.[79]

Later that same day, at a Peace Council reception at the Palace Hotel, Robeson made, according to one ASIO report, 'a strong point of the Aboriginal problem and made many references to this theme throughout his address'. He is quoted as saying, 'the day will come and it will not be long when they WILL have equal rights'.[80] Another ASIO report (this event seems to have had at least three ASIO agents present) quotes Robeson: 'when I look at my darker brothers and

74   Anon, 'Lloyd Davies': <http://www.austlit.edu.au.ezproxy2.library.usyd.edu.au/run?ex=ShowAgent&agentId=A%2bO4>

75   See Docker 1984: 30–33.

76   *Tribune*, 7 December 1960: 10.

77   *Tribune*, 7 December 1960: 10.

78   *West Australian*, 3 December 1960.

79   *Tribune*, 7 December 1960: 10.

80   'Paul Robeson – Welcomed at Afternoon Tea Party Organised by the Australian Peace Council (W.A. Division)', C/15/10, No 60/766, in file labelled Harold Godric Clements, ASIO, NAA, Series Number A6119.

sisters in Australia and see them look just like my sister and my cousins and I say folks, well, oh, I'll have to come back here and start something here – try to get somebody interested'.[81]

The Robesons left Australia, after another concert, on 4 December 1960. Several months later, Paul Robeson talked about his Australian visit to a German reporter in Moscow. He spoke enthusiastically, but then said:

> One thing has embittered me. On the fifth continent I encountered a phenomenon which I have experienced in Africa and America: racial discrimination in the most loathsome form … Here open extermination is effected. Here the public opinion in the world must go to work and say a serious word. I intend to return to Australia. I shall make films and give concerts. The proceeds shall benefit the aboriginal population languishing in poverty. I already did that in Africa, and now I want to repeat it once more in Australia.[82]

This reference to extermination reminds us of Robeson's role in the 1951 Civil Rights Congress's petition to the UN charging genocide against African Americans. In both cases, he saw people as confronting, but so far surviving, major threats to their existence as a people.

Paul Robeson never did come back, and in fact, this tour was to prove his last. By the time this interview was published, in April 1961, he was in a Soviet sanatorium suffering from severe depression, and he returned to the United States permanently in 1963. He gave a few low-key performances and then disappeared from public life until his death in 1976.

Influence and memory

The political influence of Robeson's tour on the movement for Indigenous rights is a little hard to estimate. It was, after all, part of a series of significant contemporary events and changes – the growth of political activism for Aboriginal rights, the thawing of the Cold War, and the increased influence of the American Civil Rights movement and of wider processes of decolonisation in Asia and Africa on Australian understandings of racial issues. African American freedom songs were important in influencing the consciousness of Australian Left wing students becoming interested in Aboriginal issues, especially the students involved in Abschol, Student Action for Aborigines, and the Freedom Ride of 1965. Former Freedomrider, Louise Higham, for example, told me that in her first year at the University of Sydney she had learned the powerful 'Jim Crow

---

81   'Australian Peace Council (WA Division), Visit of Paul and Eslanda Robeson', C/15/10, No 60/814, in file labelled Harold Godric Clements, ASIO, NAA, Series Number A6119.
82   *Neue Zeit*, 27 April 1961, as quoted in O'Reilly 1994: 378.

must go' message from many of the songs she heard in the concerts organised by the Folk Music club. Oral history interviews indicate that those who heard or met Paul Robeson in 1960 were often deeply affected. Faith Bandler, already an activist, was strongly encouraged by his emphasis on the human rights of Black people around the world, and his quick understanding of the importance of the Aboriginal cause.[83] Sue Johnston, another Freedomrider, told me that she had become interested in Aboriginal issues through hearing Paul Robeson sing in Sydney, as well as through her university study of race relations in American history.

The Robeson tour, now almost half a century ago, is surprisingly well remembered. For many people, their knowledge of the visit comes from a regularly repeated five minute short film on the ABC, which featured Robeson singing at the Opera House. For others, it comes from *Deep Bells Ring*, a play written by Nancy Wills in 1987, which told the story of Robeson's life and career, including his Australian tour. Sponsored by the BWIU as an Art and Working Life project through the Theatre Board of the Australia Council, it toured Brisbane, Sydney, Canberra and Melbourne to enthusiastic audiences. Some Aboriginal people have been in these audiences, sometimes leading figures; when the production came to Sydney, Chicka Dixon and Gary Foley were listed among those present.[84] In oral history interviews, it can be this play, as much as the original visit, that is now remembered. In Perth, in 2004, Robeson's singing to the workers from the back of a truck at the Midland Railway Workshops was commemorated with a free concert at the same site, featuring Perth baritone Andrew Foote singing many of the same songs that Robeson sang that day. On the centenary anniversary of Robeson's birth, in 1998, articles, radio programmes, and websites appeared commemorating Robeson and his visit. When giving papers on this project, those in the audience have often afterwards offered me many mementos such as programmes, and people have wanted to tell me they remember meeting or hearing Paul Robeson, perhaps shaking his hand. The emails sent to me and oral history interviews conducted by my research assistant, Sari Braithwaite, are often highly emotional, even after a space of almost 50 years. Nearly all of them have an intensely physical aspect, as people recall Robeson's voice, presence, size, colour, and handshake. They tend to stress Robeson's support for peace, and the trade unions, and some mention him in relation to Aboriginal rights.

These extremely positive memories, especially by people on the Left and in the performing arts, reinforce my sense that the visit of Paul and Eslanda Robeson was a huge success in its time. A few months after it was over, Jessie Street, a leading Aboriginal rights campaigner, wrote to Eslanda that '[t]hey are still talking about the visit of you and Paul out here', and the buzz and excitement

---

83   Lake 2002: 86–87.
84   The director Errol O'Neill supplied the author with a copy of his handwritten list of those attending.

lasted a long time after that.[85] Martin Duberman, relying on limited newspaper sources and especially on Eslanda's frank letters to her family detailing Paul's physical ailments, irritability, and periods of depression, tends to see it as a negative experience, indeed a 'grueling ordeal', and he seems to me to emphasise unduly the rare hostile press comments.[86] While this was indeed still the Cold War, and there was, unsurprisingly, public questioning of Robeson's staunch support for the Soviet Union, overall this was a reaffirming cultural event for a wide range of groups on the Left and those of Left sympathy generally. Robeson's undeniable stature as a singer and performer to some degree took him out of the specific Cold War context of the time, as some newspaper reviewers recognised, making him a complex figure that could admired despite, as well as because of, his politics. Eslanda Robeson was an impressive speaker, who attracted positive responses wherever she went. This broader acceptance meant that the Robesons' support for the Aboriginal cause was a powerful encouragement for growing activism by Aboriginal people and their supporters over the next decade.

Acknowledgements

I acknowledge the help of my wonderful research assistant Sari Braithwaite, who has shown true detective skills in finding a range of printed sources including major daily and trade union newspapers, archival sources, and concert programmes, and who has conducted oral history interviews in Melbourne and Brisbane. I also wish to thank Brian Aarons, John Docker, and Frances Peters-Little for their assistance.

References

Primary sources

Anon 1950, 'Paul Robeson and Madam Sun Yat Sen – Proposed visit', Series A433, Control Symbol 1950/2/2697, National Australian Archives (NAA), Canberra.

Anon 1961, 'Paul Robeson', Australian Security Intelligence Organisation (ASIO) Report, 9 March 1961, A6122/44 (1450), NAA, viewed 5 October 2009: <http://naa12.naa.gov.au/scripts/Imagine.asp>

'Australian Peace Council (WA Division), Visit of Paul and Eslanda Robeson', C/15/10, No. 60/814, in file labelled 'Harold Godric Clements', Series Number A6119, ASIO, NAA, Canberra.

---

85   Street 1961.
86   Duberman 2005: 487.

Australian Security Intelligence Organisation, 'Union of Australian Women', ASIO report no 60/779: 62, series number A6119 (2006/00328495), Control Symbol 3873, ASIO, NAA, Canberra.

Garland, W and McIlwraith 1957, 'Special Report and conclusions on interviews with the people of Walgett, NSW, and Impressions gained during the visit 6th to 10th September, 1957', Hannah Middleton Papers, ML MSS 5866/10, Mitchell Library, Sydney.

McIlwraith, Irene to the Editor, *Walgett Spectator*, 18 September 1957, Walgett file, AAF Papers, ML MSS 4057/16, Mitchell Library, Sydney.

Marngoo Films, Prospectus Marngoo Films Limited, Pearl Gibbs Collection, ML MSS 6922, Box 4, Mitchell Library, Sydney.

'Minutes of Monthly General Meetings', Minute for 7 December 1960, AAF Papers, ML MSS 4057, Mitchell Library, Sydney.

'Paul Robeson', Connie Healy collection, UQFL 191, Fryer Library, Brisbane.

'Paul Robeson', FBI Report, NY 100-25857: 2351, accessed 15 May 2010: <http://news.lp.findlaw.com/legalnews/entertainment/fbi/robes/robes02352.html>

'Paul Robeson – Welcomed at Afternoon Tea Party Organised by the Australian Peace Council (W.A. Division)', C/15/10, No. 60/766, in file labelled Harold Godric Clements, Series Number A6119, ASIO, NAA, Canberra.

Robeson, Eslanda Goode 1945, *African Journey*, The John Day Company, New York.

Street, Jessie 1961, letter to Eslanda Robeson, 16 April 1961, carbon copy in 2.10 Correspondence 2300-2397, February–August 1961, in Series I, Correspondence 1951–1975, Council for Aboriginal Rights, MS 12913, State Library of Victoria, Melbourne.

Secondary sources

Abbott, Lynn and Doug Seroff 2002, *Out of Sight: The Rise of African American Popular Music, 1889 – 1895*, University Press of Mississippi, Jackson, Miss.

Anon, 'Lloyd Davies', *Austlit* (the Australian Literature Resources), accessed 5 October 2009: <http://www.austlit.edu.au.ezproxy2.library.usyd.edu.au/run?ex=ShowAgent&agentId=A%2bO4>

Attwood, Bain 2003, *Rights for Aborigines*, Allen & Unwin, Sydney.

Australian Broadcasting Commission 1955, *Australian Broadcasting Commission Presents Mattiwilda Dobbs*, Town Hall, Sydney, Saturday, 23 July 1955, 18 pp, annotated programme, accessed 2 October 2009: <http://www.dacapo.com.au/ausprog.html>

Bandler, Faith 1993, interview for ABC Television series, *Australian Biography*, 25 March 1993, transcript accessed 30 September 2009: <http://www.australianbiography.gov.au/subjects/bandler/interview6.html>

Beeching, Barbara 2002, 'Paul Robeson and the Black Press: The 1950 Passport Controversy', *The Journal of African American History* 87: 339–354.

Broome, Richard 2005, *Aboriginal Victorians: A History since 1800*, Allen & Unwin, Sydney.

Casey, Gavin 1958, *Snowball*, Angus and Robertson, Sydney.

Civil Rights Congress 1951, *We Charge Genocide: The Historic Petition to the United Nations for Relief from a Crime of the United States Government Against the Negro People*, Civil Rights Congress, New York.

Costa, Ravi de 2006, *A Higher Authority: Indigenous Transnationalism and Australia*, University of New South Wales Press, Sydney.

Curthoys, Ann 2002, *Freedom Ride: A Freedom Rider Remembers*, Allen & Unwin, Sydney.

— and John Docker 2008, 'Defining genocide', in *The Historiography of Genocide*, Dan Stone (ed), Palgrave, Houndmills, United Kingdom.

D'Emilio, John 2003, *Lost Prophet: The Life and Times of Bayard Rustin*, Free Press, New York.

Docker, John 1984, *In a Critical Condition*, Penguin Books, Ringwood.

Duberman, Martin 2005[1988], *Paul Robeson: A Biography*, The New Press, New York.

Dudziak, Mary L 2000, *Cold War Civil Rights: Race and the Image of American Democracy*, Princeton University Press, Princeton.

Dunbar-Hall, Peter 2004, *Deadly Sounds, Deadly Places: Contemporary Aboriginal Music inAustralia*, University of New South Wales Press, Sydney.

Fox, Len and Faith Bandler 1983, *The Time was Ripe*, Alternative Publishing Cooperative, Chippendale, New South Wales.

Goodall, Heather 1996, *Invasion to Embassy: Land in Aboriginal Politics in New South Wales, 1770 – 1972*, Allen & Unwin, Sydney.

Hess, Michael 1994, 'Black and red: the Pilbara pastoral workers' strike, 1946', *Aboriginal History* 18(1): 65–83.

Holmes, Cecil 1960, 'An Aboriginal film in colour is born', *The Age* Melbourne, 12 November 1960.

Holmes, Cecil 1986, *One Man's Way*, Penguin, Ringwood.

Holmes, Sandra Le Brun 1999, *Faces in the Sun: Outback Journeys*, Viking, Ringwood, Victoria.

Horne, Gerald 1986, *Black and Red: W.E.B. Du Bois and the Afro-American Response to the Cold War 1944–1963*, State University of New York Press, Albany.

— 1988, *Communist Front? The Civil Rights Congress, 1946–1956*, Associated University Presses, London and Toronto.

Horner, John 1960, 'Paul Robeson is Everyman', *Adelaide Advertiser*, 25 November 1960: 11.

Johnson, Audrey 1986, *Fly a Rebel Flag: Bill Morrow, 1888–1980*, Penguin, Ringwood.

Keiler, Allan 2002, *Marian Anderson: a Singer's Journey*, University of Illinois Press, Illinois.

Lake, Marilyn 2002, *Faith: Faith Bandler, Gentle Activist*, Allen & Unwin, Sydney.

Maloney, Shane 2009, 'Faith Bandler and Paul Robeson', *The Monthly*, July 2009, accessed 30 September 2009: <http://www.themonthly.com.au/encounters-shane-maloney-faith-bandler-paul-robeson--1769>

Maynard, John 2007, *Fight for Liberty and Freedom: The Origins of Australian Aboriginal Activism*, Aboriginal Studies Press, Canberra.

McDonald, Tom 1994, interview with Richard Raxworthy, 23 August 1994, Labour Council of NSW Oral History Collection, National Library of Australia, Canberra.

McDonald, Tom and Audrey 1998, *Intimate Union: Sharing a Revolutionary Life*, Pluto Press, Sydney.

McGrath, Pam and David Brooks forthcoming, 'Hard looking: the historical entanglements of the documentary film *Manslaughter* (1957)', *Aboriginal History*.

NSW Legislative Assembly, *Hansard*, 20 October 1998, accessed 3 January 2008: <www.parliament.nsw.gov.au/prod/parlment/HansArt.nsf/V3Key/LA19981020036>

O'Reilly, Kenneth 1994, *Black Americans: the FBI Files*, Carroll and Graf, New York.

Patterson, William L 1971, *The Man Who Cried Genocide: An Autobiography*, International Publishers, New York.

Roadknight, Margret 2001, *From the Folk Rag* no 55, July 2001, accessed 2 October 2009: <http://users.tpg.com.au/folkrag/profiles/margrk.htm>

Stuart, Donald 1959, *Yandy*, Georgian House, Melbourne.

Taffe, Sue 2005, *Black and White Together FCAATSI: The Federal Council for the Advancement of Aborigines and Torres Strait Islanders, 1958–1973*, University of Queensland Press, St Lucia.

Taffe, Sue 2008, 'William Grayden', *Collaborating for Indigenous Rights*, NMA website, accessed 5 October 2009: <http://indigenousrights.net.au/person.asp?pID=967>

Von Eschen, Penny M 1997, *Race against Empire: Black Americans and Anticolonialism 1937–1957*, Cornell University Press, Ithaca and London.

Williams, Deane 1994, 'All that is left: the early life and work of Cecil Holmes', *Metro* 100: 36–39.

— 1999, 'Cecil Holmes', *The Oxford Companion to Australian Film*, Oxford University Press, Melbourne.

9. Using poetry to capture the Aboriginal voice in oral history transcripts

LORINA BARKER

This paper is a part of an ongoing research project I have been involved with since commencing my PhD at the University of New England. My interest in the documentation of oral histories, in particular my own community of Weilmoringle,[1] has been the main focus of my concerns since becoming an early career academic in 2004. Although I left my community several years ago, I continue to hold a strong (and in some ways complex) connection to my traditional country and the people who come from there. Most of the participants I refer to in this paper are Aboriginal members of the community, although I hope to involve non-Aboriginal people from Weilmoringle in the future.

I began recording the stories of members of my community in Weilmoringle in 2005. For the purposes of this paper, the community is both the research participant and the main intended audience for my research, and the core research method and source is oral history. My reason for conducting oral histories is that I believe Aboriginal histories and oral histories are intrinsically linked and for the most part have been largely ignored, misinterpreted or deemed as 'mythical' unreliable sources of knowledge by more traditionally text-based historians.

In using oral histories, I am tapping into the millennia long tradition of oral storytelling as the way that Aboriginal people's history and cultural knowledge has and continues to be conveyed. My dilemma is that I intend to convert these oral and aural experiences into print as a key way to communicate with wider audiences the memories and stories shared with me. Embedded in this conversion is the need to get the text versions of my recordings right. My research participants are speakers of Aboriginal English and it is crucial that the written versions of the oral narratives read and sound like how the participants speak. It is also crucial that the orality of the interviews and the importance of

---

1 Weilmoringle is an Aboriginal community and sheep station about one hour's drive north-east of Bourke.

oral history both as a form of memory and as a form of history are conveyed through the words on pages. Finally, it is important that the processes involved in consulting, interviewing, recording, transcribing and presenting are ethical and transparent.

I have written elsewhere about some of the challenges confronting Aboriginal researchers who choose to conduct fieldwork/research in their own community and with members of their family: the experience can be a frustrating, enjoyable and burdensome undertaking that requires the juggling of multiple, complex, overlapping and at times conflicting roles and responsibilities.[2] Here I focus on the challenges involved in converting the layered richness, sounds, silences and interactions of the memories recorded through an oral history interview into text. At one level, it is about transcription and editing; at another level, it is about capturing and conveying individuals' memories and stories and the ways in which those shared experiences – including my part in the sharing – become a powerful means to present Indigenous histories in ways that resonate with, and are accessible to, the owners of those histories.

Transcription is often described in the literature as a tedious and time-consuming process, one that is plagued with technical questions of what to include and exclude, as well as the problem of transforming the aural into written text. This paper considers these issues in relation to the accessibility of a transcript to the intended audience, in this case the research participants. I begin by reflecting on my personal experiences of the transcription process and some of the problems I encountered with both the recorded and transcribed versions. Concerned about my initial reactions, I began analysing my own responses and contemplated the effects and implications for the participants in my research. How would they react to a verbatim transcript? Would they feel threatened, embarrassed or upset? If so, how would they want their stories conveyed? How do I make the written word non-threatening and at the same time produce an accurate account of the recorded conversations? What are the alternatives? With these questions in mind, I looked at scholarly arguments that both support and oppose transcription. I sought alternative strategies used by other scholars to convert the voice into printed form. In my search for alternative styles, I discovered free verse poetry. This style is used for the purpose of re-creating in written form the emotion and movement of words as they are spoken and received in conversation, as well as to re-capture the imagery of the interview, and what took place: the interaction between interviewer and participant. Free verse poetry is also used to preserve the traditional practice of oral history storytelling and to create a text version that conveys participant's lived experiences and history.

---

2   Huggins 1995: 1.

The words of a transcript

Before embarking on my own research project, I had experienced interviews and transcripts as an interviewee. As a result, I had become more aware of the sound of my own voice and how my words looked in print. I had mixed reactions to the recorded and transcribed versions. As a result of these experiences, I am now endeavouring to make my research transcripts less intimidating and more accessible for my research participants. The personal accounts that follow are filled with mixed reactions – surprise, anxiety and amusement, and explain my approach to transcription.

As an undergraduate student I was a participant in and subject of a number of research projects. I was first introduced to the recorded narrative by linguist Diana Eades, who recorded a conversation between my cousin Karen Johnson and myself. The purpose of this recording was to demonstrate our use of English, what is known as Aboriginal English. My memory of this experience is a combination of nerves and excitement at being recorded, coupled with the cold sterile environment of a recording studio. A few months after the recording I received a letter from Eades explaining the accompanying audiotape and booklet entitled, 'The English Language: Past, Present and Future Study Guide 3'.[3] I skimmed through the booklet to the section containing my conversation with Karen, and was shocked at what I read and heard: strange and silly words on paper and the voice on tape were not like how I thought I spoke. Embarrassed, I packed the tape and booklet away.

A few years later, as a postgraduate student I was approached by a PhD student interested in documenting the experiences of Aboriginal postgraduate students. I agreed to participate in the research, which included several interviews. Some months later, I received the first of many verbatim transcripts. After reading the covering letter, I would scan two or three pages, before becoming bored with the material and I would pack it away. This was how I reacted to each and every transcript, and to be honest I was relieved when they finally ceased. In hindsight, I had willingly given my story, but providing feedback was another issue. The sheer volume made the task seem too time-consuming, especially when I had my own research to contend with. I was uninterested, and oblivious to how important my feedback may have been to the student's research. I had trusted the student researcher enough to share my educational experiences and to portray my story in an ethical and responsible manner, 'to do the right thing by [me] and not make [me] look ignorant' or silly.[4] But I did not want to read, let alone comment on, the transcripts of our interviews.

---

3   Eades 1996: 31–32.
4   Brehaut 1999: 29.

More recently, I read a copy of a transcript that Margaret Somerville (my PhD Co-supervisor) had transcribed from the recorded interview she had conducted with me. Scanning the transcript I soon realised how foreign the verbatim transcript seemed. Given that I found it difficult to read and understand, I also considered the effect and implications for the participants in my research. As I read through the transcript, my initial reaction was one of surprised shock and I was somewhat unsettled at my reaction. The written word seemed so strange. It did not look or read like how I think I speak, instead it looked and read like a foreign language. I thought to myself, 'do I speak like this; gosh I use a lot of ums', 'my words look silly and a little funny'. I was also a little concerned and curious about how I may have been perceived by the transcribers: What did they think of my words? Do they think I made sense? Did they think I knew what I was talking about? Horrified, I packed the transcript away. In retrospect, I had read through the transcript trying to feel the words, to hear the conversation, but what I received in return was merely black ink on white paper, words devoid of emotion and foreign to the eye. These were not my stories and my memories.

Listening to the recordings

My reservations about the verbatim transcript resurfaced when I began listening to my Weilmoringle recordings in preparation for transcription. Despite my earlier experiences I was not prepared for the shock and amusement of hearing my own voice being thrown back at me through the audio-speakers. I thought, 'My voice doesn't sound like me, it sounds like how my cousin Pattie speaks'. I began to laugh at my voice and immediately stopped the tape and told myself, 'I can't do this. It sounds too weird'. After regaining some composure, I pressed play and re-listened to the recording. 'Why does my voice sound so weird? Why am I laughing? This is serious stuff!' I wondered and chastised myself. I am not laughing at Uncle William's voice, he sounds the same. I'm not laughing at the stories he's telling me. I'm laughing at myself, because it doesn't sound like me, it sounds like my cousin Pattie! Was it Pattie or I who had conducted the interview, I asked myself, smiling as the thought entered my mind. Maybe I should record both our voices, to see how similar they really are. 'Yeah maybe I will' I said to myself as I ejected the tape and put it back in the filing cabinet. 'I can't handle my voice today, so I'll try again another day', I said in an attempt to convince myself.

Writing my voice back into the transcript

The result of my discomfort at the sound of my own voice was that, initially, when I did start transcribing I found myself writing my voice out of the transcript. I typed the words the way I write and not the way I speak. For example, 'there' instead of 'dere', 'you' instead of 'yah', 'used to' instead of 'use-tah'. After realising what I was doing, I quickly rewound the tape and listened more carefully to my pronunciations, until I was convinced that I had understood my own speech mannerism and changed each word accordingly. I discussed the problem with Margaret Somerville and she identified some possible reasons: it highlights the multiple, interrelated and overlapping nature of the roles that I have chosen to undertake as a community person, family member and researcher. More importantly, as a child I learnt how to speak and write in standard Australian English, and if and when I spoke or wrote in Aboriginal English, I was immediately corrected. While I try to incorporate and stay 'true' to each participant's voice, speech mannerism and idiosyncrasies, at the same time I face the problem of how to incorporate my own voice. It is through the process of transcribing that I am relearning how to listen to and write my voice back into the transcript.

All of these experiences both recorded and transcribed versions, were of much concern, and forced me to analyse my own reactions and to contemplate the effects and implications for participants. As a consequence, I searched the literature for arguments that both supported and opposed verbatim transcription, as well as to find alternative strategies used by scholars to convert the voice and the memories conveyed into printed form.

Getting the voice off tape onto page

I naïvely made the decision to fully transcribe each recording, long before I ventured out into the field, well before I considered or fully understood the enormity of the task I had set myself. Returning from the first field trip, I was determined to follow through with my earlier decision to fully transcribe. As I began transcribing I made the decision to transcribe each recording myself and to include every utterance, pause and background noise. The aim was to transport myself as interviewer and researcher back to the place and time of the interview in order to analyse and to deduce meaning. As Elizabeth Wright argues, 'the best person to prepare the transcript is the interviewer because he/ she was present at the interview'. She adds, '[d]oing your own transcribing is beneficial because you can edit in your own style as you go along and it gives you the opportunity to review the complete interview'.[5]

I was seeking my 'style' of transcribing and, in order to develop it, I became interested in how other scholars were transcribing and what methods they were using to convert verbatim transcripts into other forms of text. Rebecca Jones

5   Wright 2005: 57.

explained, '[t]here is no definitive formula for creating a written [transcript] from oral interviews'.[6] Rather, there are many different approaches and styles of transcribing and presenting speech into written form. The employment of a particular style may depend on a number of contributing factors: the project, the researcher's disciplinary background and the intended audience. Jones further adds that 'different project[s] may require different decisions to be made'.[7] Wendy Lowenstein was a firm believer that 'Oral history in print should be a "good read"'. At the same time she adds that the interviewer needs to keep in mind and avoid 'doing violence to the informant's story and content'.[8] Elizabeth Wright agrees that producing a 'readable written/printed document from spoken material' is important and should be done by 'using as closely as possible the narrator's words, [and] most importantly [reflect] the intent and meaning of the narrator'.[9] By contrast, Kate Moore is not interested in making the transcript readable. Instead she advocates vehemently for the inclusion of every utterance, which she believes to be 'valuable communicative evidence' that can be analysed and dissected for meaning.[10] Rosemary Block disagrees, saying that the inclusion of every word and sound does not 'add materially to the text', but instead creates unnecessary interruptions that should be omitted.[11] Francis Good reminds us that the printed version 'cannot adequately capture the music of speech', what Barry York calls its 'special charm'.[12] Good explains that as oral history researchers 'we must learn to live with the fact that transcription of the spoken word is more of an art than an exact science'.[13]

Poetically speaking: *free verse poetry*

Free verse is a poetic form and an alternative strategy, used by a number of scholars as a tool to convert voice into print. I have followed Rosemary Block, Daphne Patai, Krista Woodley, Loreen Brehaut and Katharine Elise Perry's suggestions on the use of this method. I have also tried to transcribe the recorded interview as accurately as possible in an attempt to capture both the participants' and interviewer's voices and their idiosyncratic ways of communicating. The main purpose for using free verse is to ensure that the written versions of the interviews are more accessible to the participants and that they capture the rhythm and tone of their shared memories.

---

6   Jones 2004: 25.

7   Jones 2004: 25.

8   Lowenstein 1992: 40.

9   Wright 2005: 60.

10   Moore 1997: 14, 15.

11   Block 1997: 33.

12   Good 2000: 104.

13   Good 2000: 104.

In seeking a form in which to present the interviews, I was inspired to experiment with free verse after reading Rosemary Block's article 'Voiceprint: From Tape to Page: Keeping Faith with the Voice', in which she experimented with free verse in an attempt to 'translate [the] liveliness to the page', and the 'colour, tone and emotion of the voice'.[14] Daphne Patai also wanted to maintain the essence of the informant's spoken words and used free verse to 'retain the meaning, tone, style and flavor of the original'.[15] Krista Woodley explained that her use of the poetic form to transcribe oral history interviews was to assist her in the 'analysis of the recording' as well as to 'help [her] data to sing'.[16] In contrast, Loreen Brehaut admits to using free verse as a direct result of her own anxiety over the presentation of an authentic and 'honest' narrative,[17] and Katharine Elise Perry utilised the poetic form to preserve her mother 'Ethel's voice' and for its 'musical qualities'.[18] I, on the other hand, have employed free verse in my research primarily for the benefit of the core audience, the participants and like Perry I too intend to preserve the participants' voices so that other 'family members [are able to see and] hear [the person] as they read them'.[19]

The nature of free verse

After submitting my first draft of this paper for comment to my supervisor, Janis Wilton and receiving her pencilled remarks, I realised I had not adequately defined free verse. Janis was particularly concerned 'as to why some of the interview materials transformed into poetry and others into free verse or indeed what distinguished the two'.[20] Admittedly, I was unsure about the difference. Now I was more confused, though pleased that Janis suggested I leave it for now and focus my attention elsewhere.

With the transcription models before me I experimented intuitively with some of my own interviews, but on being questioned about what I meant by free verse, I sought advice from a friend and colleague, Jane O'Sullivan, a Senior Lecturer in the School of Arts at the University of New England. A few weeks later I bumped into Jane and I briefly explained how I was experimenting with the verbatim transcripts and converting them into poetic form. Jane was very interested in my approach and offered to look at my work. A few days later we met for coffee and I took a few of my converted poems for Jane to give me her professional opinion. Jane also explained the functions of free verse poetry: 'it does not have regular metre (metrical structure) and does not have rhyming

---

14   Block 1995: 65.

15   Patai 1988: 17.

16   Woodley 2004: 49.

17   Brehaut 1999: 30.

18   Perry 2005: 1.

19   Perry 2005: 1.

20   Janis Wilton, pers comm, October 2006.

lines. So it is "free" from the conventions of particular poetical forms such as ballads and sonnets'.[21] Jane also directed me to the work of Dennis Tedlock and Gerard Manley Hopkins. In my search for a simplified explanation of free verse I also turned to the literature. Tom Furniss and Michael Bath explain, free verse 'does not conform to any metrical pattern'.[22] They also assert that the exclusion of rhyme does not necessarily deem it to be free verse.[23] Nevertheless, they do acknowledge that 'it … uses line divisions which shape the rhythms of the language for specific ends'.[24] They add that free verse or *vers libre*[25] 'allow[s] poets to take … radical liberties' in their writings.[26] This explains the unconventional characteristics that are common in free verse poetry: 'there is no punctuation, the shape is how it is punctuated; the image is echoed; there is music to a line'.[27] What I realised was particularly appealing about the use of free verse for my purpose was that it breaks with grammar and it does not force oral speech patterns into written prose. More importantly, it does not make the research participants' words look 'inferior', ungrammatical and unpunctuated.

From voice to free verse: one, two, three steps

At first glance, a transcript written in Standard Australian English might seem to be clearer and easier to understand, and it is certainly considered the most acceptable form for an archival document.[28] But, for the Aboriginal participants in my research, the verbatim transcript is not the only, or the most appropriate, form of converting the recorded interview to print form. Free verse is used as an alternative in an attempt to retain the speech mannerisms: the 'rhythm and rhetorical style', tone and accents of the speaker.[29] Also, within the context of this research the utilisation of free verse is intended to be less intimidating than a verbatim transcript.

My style of converting voice into free verse is a three-step process. Firstly, I fully transcribe each recording into a verbatim transcript and at the same time, make separate transcription notes about the interview. Secondly, I copy the completed verbatim transcript into another document and begin conversion, by taking out all of my questions and responses. I then arrange the narrator's words on the page by using lines and space to convey the narrator's speech mannerisms: when they have paused, have gone silent or have changed topics.

---

21   Jane O'Sullivan, pers comm, 6 November 2006.
22   Furniss and Bath 1996: 45.
23   Furniss and Bath 1996: 45.
24   Furniss and Bath 1996: 45.
25   Furniss and Bath 1996: 46.
26   Furniss and Bath 1996: 48.
27   Jane O'Sullivan, pers comm, 6 November 2006.
28   Brehaut 1999: 28.
29   Brehaut 1999: 28.

This step is what I call the unedited free verse. It is important to mention that while I do not edit the narrator's voice I do however, edit my voice so as not to interfere with the flow of the narrator's story. Nevertheless, my questions will appear in the text as background information to the free verse extracts. In the final step, the edited free verse, I make some minor editorial changes by omitting the narrator's false starts and repetition.

As mentioned before, I have chosen to fully transcribe, in the style suggested by Kate Moore to include the pauses, false-starts, hesitations (um, arh), repetitions (I mean to say, after all, and the) and the interviewer's verbal encouragements known as back-channelling (yeah, Mhm, uh-huh).[30] Also included are the 'natural speech patterns'[31] and 'dialect words [and] phrases'[32] as well as the 'phonetic spellings to suggest the sound of the dialect'[33] such as 'dere' and 'use-tah' and alongside them and enclosed in brackets are the meanings and English spellings 'there', 'used to'. Raphael Samuel suggested that this allows the reader to obtain a 'sense of the personal and individual' and it makes the story come alive.[34] I have also identified background noises by naming the sound in brackets placed at the end of the sentence. At times, when a word is not clear in the recording, I have added a word or a question mark to indicate my uncertainty. Rosemary Block points out that while the 'Transcript may not ... be essential for access [by participants], ... it is necessary for publication and perhaps for preservation purposes'.[35] While the participant will receive a copy of their verbatim transcript along with a copy of the audio recording and free verse poetry, the main purpose of the transcript is for archival deposit, which can then be accessed by other researchers who can infer their own interpretations of the recording.

As a guide, I have used Block, Patai, Brehaut, Woodley and O'Sullivan's suggestions for converting the voice into print. The following narratives are extracts from the original verbatim transcript that have been converted into free verse to demonstrate the utilisation of this method as a possible solution for ensuring the transcript and its contents are accessible to my research participants. Example one illustrates the process of converting the verbatim transcript into an edited free verse. Example two captures the rhythm of speech, and example three is an annotated free verse that aids my analysis of the recording.

---

30   Moore 1997: 17.
31   Block 1997: 33.
32   Samuel 1998: 390.
33   Samuel 1998: 391.
34   Samuel 1998: 390.
35   Block 1997: 33.

Example one: verbatim transcript to edited free verse

The following example is my initial attempt at converting voice into print. The aim was to convey to the reader a sense of the narrator's voice telling their story through the movement of words on the page. In the three-step process, I provide first a verbatim extract.

Verbatim extract (Growing up)

L: Yeah, ok, um so can you tell me a little about your um life experience, your childhood, about grow, things about growing-up at Weilmoringle, some things you might've [might have] done an' [and]

E: Yeah um the most um wonderful childhood I've [I have] known out there its jist [Just] so free

L: Mm

E: That there was no not like what's goin' [going] on today there was no alcohol or drugs an' stuff like that

L: Mm

E: We had arh go an' make our own fun

L: Mm

E: Yeah see um go for walks all day in arh or on the weekends we use-tah [used to] go lookin' [looking] for gum go walkin' [walking] lookin' [looking] for gum an' other times we'd [we would] go swimmin' [swimming] down at the bighole an-an' other times we'd-we'd make um instruments up um like guitars with um have a-have a bottle an' arh break the top off it

L: Do …

E: Take off a??? (unsure of words) an' stick yah [your] thumb in it

L: Yeah

E: An' knock it onto the other bottle for a guitar

L: Yeah

E: An' so we use-tah have some tins an-an' sticks an' for drums an' we'd have a concert each individual um person ad-tah [had to] get up an' sing their own song and do actions

L: Yeah

E: An' yeah it was a wonderful time out there at Weilmoringle …[36]

The second step is the unedited free verse created from the verbatim transcript. In this example I have not added or rearranged any words. That is, all the 'ums' and 'arhs' are included. Punctuation is only used here when sentences are otherwise difficult to understand, but all effort is made to 'preserve the texture of the speech'.[37]

Unedited free verse (Growing up)

Yeah um the most wonderful childhood I've known
     out there
          its jist so free
There was no
     not like what's goin' on today
          there was no alcohol or drugs an' stuff like that
We had-arh go an' make our own fun
     Yeah see um
          go for walks all day in arh
Or on the weekends we use-tah go lookin' for gum
     go walkin'
          lookin' for gum
An other times we'd go swimmin'
     down at the bighole
An-an' other times we'd-we'd make um
     instruments up um like guitars
          with um have a
               have a bottle
               an' arh break the top off it
Take off a…
     an' stick yah thumb in it
An' knock it on to the other bottle for a guitar
     An' so we use-tah have some tins an-an' sticks an' for drums
          An' we'd have a concert
Each individual um person 'ad-tah get up
     an' sing their own song an' do actions
An' yeah it was a wonderful time out there
     at Weilmoringle …

In the final step, the edited free verse, I have made some minor editorial changes and omitted the false starts and repetitive words, the 'yeah', 'um' and 'arh'.

---

36   Elva Barker interviewed by Lorina Barker, 27 October 2005.
37   Samuel 1998: 391.

With the participant's permission, this version would be included in the thesis, and if necessary their poem or story may undergo further editing: 'cutting, reorganizing and reshaping' to convey information during the presentation stage.[38]

Edited free verse (Growing up)

The most wonderful childhood I've known out there
    Its jist so free
There was no…
Not like what's goin' on today
    there was no alcohol or drugs
        an' stuff like that
We had-arh go an' make our own fun
    go for walks all day
On the weekends we use-tah go lookin' for gum
    we'd go swimmin'
        down at the bighole
Other times we'd make instruments up like guitars
    with a bottle
Break the top off it
    an' stick yah thumb in it
        knock it on to the other bottle for a guitar
We use-tah have tins an' sticks for drums
    an' we'd have a concert
        each individual 'ad-tah get up
            an' sing their own song an' do actions
It was a wonderful time out there
    at Weilmoringle …

Example two: capturing the rhythm of speech

Daphne Patai explains the structure of a poem: 'the shape of it and the breaks define our attitude and govern our reading. We have a different attitude to it than we would have if it was a newspaper article'.[39] Furniss and Bath also agree that the visual stimulus of a poem's layout 'alter[s] the way we read [it]'.[40] Patai further explains that the 'ordinary spoken words, like written words, can be arranged so as to call attention to their poetic and expressive dimensions'.[41]

---

38 Patai 1988: 17.
39 Quoted in Block 1995: 66.
40 Furniss and Bath 1996: 27.
41 Patai 1988: 20.

Patai uses Dennis Tedlock's technique of 'following the pauses and inflections in the speaker's speech' when re-transcribing her informant's interviews.[42] It is in the second example of free verse, that I have utilised both Patai's and Tedlock's suggestions to convey information, as I would do in prose. For example, personal background information: birth, marriages, the number of children; location of amenities: including houses, shower blocks; as well as details of events, dates and times. But unlike prose, I have chosen to include the participant's speech mannerisms to ensure that the reader hears the participant and not just a summary of their story. In the free verse I use line breaks, which indicate pauses or a change of topic and I use indentation to draw attention to the musical and poetical tone of the speaker's voice. The first step is the verbatim transcript followed by the unedited free verse and the third step is the edited free verse. What I have done in the extract 'Communal showers' is take what might be considered the everyday mundane details of a social environment and have presented them in a way that conveys the narrator's rhythm and tone of voice telling the story.

Edited free verse (Communal showers)

There was two parts of Weilmoringle
    I don't know why?
        But they called one en' top en'
           An' the other en' was the bottom en'
               We use-tah live at the bottom en'
An' the showers was situated
    Um
        Behin' me Arnie Maggie's place
There was two showers one for the boys
    An' one for the girls
        An' in the middle they had wash-basins
           Where yah wash clothes an' stuff
The first lotta runnin' water that we got on there
    Clean water ...

Example three: annotated free verse

As mentioned earlier, my utilisation of free verse is to ensure that the research participants are able to easily understand and interpret their stories. However, in the process I also discovered, like Krista Woodley, that it was a 'process to aid my analysis of the recording',[43] particularly when identifying some of the common

---

42 Patai 1988: 19.
43 Woodley 2004: 49.

themes of discussion and the participant's emphasis or avoidance of a topic. In the following example, I have incorporated Jane O'Sullivan's suggestions to show the pace of a person's speech by using the line breaks, indentation and the space on the page. As well as providing a code/key to indicate when a participant and the interviewer have laughed, by adding 'laugh' in brackets throughout the text. When a participant has raised his or her voice, **BOLD CAPITAL** letters are used to emphasise his or her boisterous response. The line breaks and indentation also signal when a person wanders off or changes topics and/or thought patterns. Step one is the verbatim transcript that is converted into the unedited free verse and the final step is the edited free verse as shown in the extract below.

Edited free verse (First day of school)

Yeah
      Very
            Very first day
I think
      We 'adda bit of scene
Because at that time
      I had my ole Arnie
          Goin' tah school
      Arnie Gwennie West
An' my first day [Drifting off, pulling herself back to the question]
      See
          Arnie Gwen took me tah school
Up at Weil we only had two
      Two lines where yah git in-tah
          Or four lines
              Two for the senior kids
                'an two for the junior kids
I was standin' [change of thought pattern]
      Got in line real good
          I lined up real great
              But I didn't realise that my Arnie would go off
                Because Weilmoringle school was jist
                    Two-roomed school
My Arnie went tah go one way
      I had-tah go the other way
          Outa the corner my eye
              I caught 'er goin' the other way
              So I took off runnin'
                Grabbed hold to 'er arms

Tah go with 'er

I was goin' like that
An' my teacher run tah git me see
'e draggin' me
Not draggin' me
'e was tryin' git me tah come back
tah all the rest the little kids
I was coo-ee-in' sayin'
"I WANNA GO WITH MY ARNIE"
An' 'e said
"No yah 'ave-tah come this other way"
I dunno, who was it
But someone walked past the school
An' seen it
They went home an' told Mum
The teacher was draggin' me
draggin' me aroun' [trail of thought
wandering off]
Mum come up there
For this young teacher
'cause 'e only was a young fulla
Chased him up one stairs
Down the other
Up the stairs an'
Down the other (laugh)
Then 'e
In the end
'e found the old principal
'e run behind
was hidin' behin' 'im
Mum was there coo-ee-in' at 'im
"YOU'D OR-TAH HIT MY BABY, LET ME HIT YOU" (laugh)
THAT WAS MY VERY FIRST DAY AT SCHOOL (laugh).[44]

How will participants respond?

Now that I have experimented with three different styles of free verse in an attempt to find my own unique approach it will be interesting to discover in follow-up sessions with participants their reactions to this method. How conducive was the use of free verse to each participant's understanding of their converted story? Was the text easier on the eye? To what extent do the methods

---

44   'Lois' (pseudonym) interviewed by Lorina Barker, 24 January 2006, transcript: 1–2.

used reflect the voice and the individual? Do they echo their memories and history? It will also be interesting to find out the preferred method, as Brehaut discovered from her reviewers, a group of school children from the Hammersley Range, Western Australia who were uninterested in the 'polished and precise' version in prose and English, what Brehaut refers to as the 'tidy whitefella version'.[45] I acknowledge GS Fraser's point about some of the problems common to free verse, especially how the research participants may read or interpret their stories. He explains, 'free verse runs more risks than other kinds of English verse, in that it cannot give always such clear and definite clues as regular verse about how the poet would like one to read it aloud (or hear it... in one's head)'.[46] Nevertheless, as Francis Good explained in his quotation of Barry York's argument for the utilisation of free verse poetry, 'sensitivity to the lyric aspects of speech can be a basis for presenting phrases or sentences in the manner of "verse libre ... poetry" which may bring us closer to aspects of the oral source'.[47]

In conclusion, while the transcript is an essential component of oral history research it is secondary to the recorded interview. The transcript's value lies in its accessibility to the intended audience. Although a verbatim transcript may be accessible to researchers and some participants who are familiar with the format and are able to analyse, interpret and deduce meaning from the material, it is not the only form. Rather there are several different methods that can be employed to make the transcript more accessible to Aboriginal people, such as free verse. However, how successful this approach is, in making the transcript accessible, will be determined by the research participants. Will they understand and obtain meaning from the transcript? More importantly, are they of the opinion that it reflects their stories and speech mannerisms?

The written record as poetry, like art, music and dance, is yet another way of capturing and transmitting cultural knowledge and people's lived experiences. But before we can record myth, memories and Indigenous histories, as researchers it is crucial that we consider how this can be culturally, sensitively and ethically achieved. As demonstrated in this paper, it can be accomplished through the consultation and interviewing processes and the recording, transcribing and presentation stages. Thus, as a transcription and translation technique, free poetic verse not only makes the research material readily available, it also provides our families and communities with a degree of ownership of their cultural knowledge and history.

---

45   Brehaut 1999: 28.
46   Fraser 1970: 78.
47   Good 2000: 103.

References

Brehaut, Loreen 1999, 'A terrible responsibility: editing the spoken word for print', *Oral History Association of Australia Journal* 21: 27–31.

Block, Rosemary 1995, 'Voiceprint: from tape to page: keeping faith with the voice', *Oral History Association of Australia Journal* 17: 65–73.

—— 1997, 'Comments on Kate Moore's "Perversion of the word: the role of transcripts in oral history"', *Words of Silence, Bulletin of the International Oral History Association* 1(1): 32–35.

Eades, Diana 1996, 'Audiocassette 3, Band 2 Aboriginal English and Band 4 Aboriginal Data', in *The English Language: Past, Present and Future Study Guide 3*, The Open University, Rochester: 28–33.

Fraser, George Sutherland 1970, *Metre,Rhyme and Free Verse*, JD Jump (gen ed), Methuen & Co Ltd, London.

Furniss, Tom and Michael Bath 1996, *Reading Poetry: An Introduction*, Pearson Education Limited, Harlow.

Good, Francis 2000, 'Voice, ear and text: words and meaning', *Oral History Association of Australia Journal* 22: 102–109.

Huggins, Jackie 1995, 'The theory, the practice and the frustrations', *Women Writing: Views and Prospects 1975–1995 Seminar*, National Library of Australia, Canberra, accessed 25 September 2009: <http://www.nla.gov.au/events/huggins.html>

Jones, Rebecca 2004, 'Blended voices: crafting a narrative from oral history interviews', *The Oral History Review* 31(1): 23 42.

Lowenstein, Wendy 1992, 'You just don't ask questions like that!', *Oral History Association of Australia Journal* 14: 40–43.

Moore, Kate 1997, 'Perversion of the word: the role of transcripts in oral history', *Words of Silence Bulletin of the International Oral History Association* 1(1): 14–25.

Patai, Daphne 1988, *Brazilian Women Speak: Contemporary Life Stories*, Rutgers University Press, New Brunswick.

Perry, Katharine Elise 2005, 'Tales full of music and strong and resourceful women: one woman's memories of a childhood spent in rural Queensland during the Depression', *Oral History Association of Australia Journal* 27: 1–7.

Samuel, Raphael 1998, 'Perils of the transcript', in *The Oral History Reader*, R Perks and A Thomson (eds), Routledge, London: 389–392.

Woodley, Krista 2004, 'Let the data sing: representing discourse in poetic form', *The Journal of the Oral History Society* 32(1): 49–58.

Wright, Elizabeth A 2005, 'Tales from the "scripts"', *Oral History Association of Australia Journal* 27: 56–62.

Part four: identity, myth and memory

10. Making a debut: myths, memories and mimesis

ANNA COLE

The 'first' Aboriginal debutante ball, held in 1968 in Sydney's Town Hall, like a lot of other 'firsts' in history, had a number of historical precedents. Since the early 1960s, smaller-scale local Aboriginal debutante balls had been held in country towns and on Aboriginal reserves around Australia, from Dubbo in New South Wales to Cherbourg in Queensland.[1] While significant locally and to those who participated these events were largely ignored outside the communities in which they took place. But in 1968, a year after the 'landslide' referendum when 90.77 per cent of Australians voted 'Yes to Aboriginal Rights', a Sydney-based organisation, the Foundation for Aboriginal Affairs (FAA), managed by a young Charles Perkins, held a large-scale Aboriginal debutante ball in the centre of town.[2]

The Foundation which ran the ball was established in 1964 in what Charles Perkins remembered was 'an old funeral parlour believe it or not' on George Street, Sydney, near Central railway station.[3] With some renovations, the building became known as 'The Centre', a 'solid three storey building in the heart of the city' close to transport links from all parts of the metropolitan area and rural New South Wales.[4] The organisation focused on civic welfare for the increasing Indigenous population moving into the city at that time. Perkins, while still a young activist and undergraduate was part of the initial fund-raising committee and became the first manager of the Foundation immediately after graduation. He remembered the involvement of Candy Williams, Ted Noffs, Col Hardy and Jimmy Little in the early days of the Foundation.[5] In its fundraising efforts the Foundation drew on the support of various members of

---

1 Cole 2000: 194–227.
2 See Attwood and Marcus 2007; Cole 2000.
3 Charles Perkins, full interview transcript, <www.australianbiography.gov.au>, p. 5.
4 Report of the First Annual General Meeting of the Foundation for Aboriginal Affairs [hereafter FAA], 12 August 1965, Mitchell Library [hereafter ML], MSS A463/63.
5 Charles Perkins, full interview transcript, <www.australianbiography.gov.au>, p. 5.

the establishment, including the Lord Mayor of Sydney, who became the first president of the organisation and Professor RW Geddes, senior anthropologist from the University of Sydney, the first chairman.[6]

The Foundation played a recognised role in Sydney's Aboriginal community during the 1960s and early 1970s. It had made a decision at its outset to 'regard as Aborigine any person who identifies as, or is identified by others to be Aboriginal'.[7] Unlike its government counterparts, such as the Aborigines Welfare Board, the Foundation recognised that its task was to assist in solving the social problems experienced by a group of people, rather than seek to control and define Aboriginal people or engage in precise arguments about the degree of ancestry of particular persons. Of the early days of the Foundation, Perkins remembers:

> I used to go and find employment for Aboriginal people around Sydney in the firms, and then I used to meet Aboriginal people coming in from the country, and I used to take them to the hospitals, and I'd ... help them to go out to the prisons ... And we used to run concerts there, oh they used to come in their hundreds from all over the place ... concerts and dances. And they were legendary.[8]

As it got more established the Foundation set up a number of active committees including 'Social Welfare', 'Education', 'Fundraising', 'Health', a 'Women's Auxiliary and a 'Dancing Group'. The dancing committee ran the first Sydney-based National Aborigines Day Observance Committee's Aboriginal debutante ball in July 1966 at the Paddington Town Hall as a fund-raiser. It was this dancing committee that ran the 1968 ball, described by journalist David Jaggar as 'the symbolic coming out of all Aboriginal people, following the referendum of the year before'.[9]

Esther Carroll ran the dance classes leading up to the event. In the crowd on the night were soon-to-be-activists such as Gary Foley dancing alongside the likes of Australian fashion icon Maggie Tabberer. Popular Indigenous musician, Jimmy Little, led the band. The young Indigenous debutantes and their partners were presented to then Prime Minister John Gorton. Photographs and footage of these beautiful young debutantes circulated in national newspapers, on national television via the Australian Broadcasting Commission, and a Japanese film crew filmed the event to show images of the ball back in Japan.[10]

---

6   Report of the First Annual General Meeting of FAA, 12 August 1965, ML MSS A463/63: 3
7   Report of Annual General Meeting of FAA, 12 August 1968, ML MSS A463/63.
8   Charles Perkins, full interview transcript, <www.australianbiography.gov.au>, p. 5
9   Jaggar, 'Call me old fashioned', *HQ magazine*, Summer 1992/3: 109–113.
10   Report of Annual General Meeting of FAA, 12 August 1968, ML MSS A463/63; *Sydney Morning Herald*, 16 July 1968.

Held on an unseasonably warm evening in July, 25 Indigenous women aged between 17 and 21 made their debut in 1968 in front of a 300 plus crowd. Author Ruby Langford-Ginibi who attended the ball with her daughter remembers seeing 'a grey-haired man walk up to her daughter, click his heels in salute, take her hand and lead her to the middle of the dance floor'.[11] The band struck up and away they waltzed.

> I couldn't see very well from my seat so I asked someone, 'who's that man dancing with my Pearlie?' Next day it was all the newspapers. Pearl had made history being the first Aboriginal ever to dance with the Prime Minister. I was so proud. For your daughter to get up there and dance with the man that ran this bloody country was a great high. I just felt real pleased that this had happened to my daughter, in her little handmade dress that I'd got from the Smithos.[12]

On the 40th anniversary of the historic 1968 ball, I was part of an Indigenous and non-Indigenous team who made a short preview for a documentary film about that night.[13] We wondered what those young women who had debuted in front of the Prime Minister, and the family and friends who had supported them, felt about the ball and the promise of the referendum 40 years on. As we began to talk about the event with former debutantes, their families and friends, it was immediately clear that the night had not become a source of cultural cringe, but triggered memories of good times, of pride and shared joy against a background of much tougher times.

Interviewed on the night by the ABC, Charles Perkins told the reporter, 'the idea behind it is to stimulate a sense of pride and dignity', and to help Aboriginal people 'become part of the community in a way that *we* think is acceptable'. Just prior to the ball, the Foundation had been fighting a Sydney Council ban on the use of halls for Aboriginal dances in Redfern and Darlington. Perkins, giving evidence at an earlier Parliamentary Inquiry into the Aborigines Welfare Board in 1966, catalogued the mundane and demoralising racial discrimination directed at urban Aborigines:

> I would say it [the ban] was based on racial discrimination … They have never said that to the Greek community or any cultural group … that has more or less been concerned with incidents near the hall … a fair judgement has not been made against us … as far as damage to the hall is concerned one boy playing in the band left his cigarette on the piano and it burned into the piano so we agreed that we would have to pay

11   Langford-Ginibi 1989: 141.
12   Langford-Ginibi 1989: 141.
13   November Films 2008.

for that and we paid it readily, without any hesitation at all. But there were half a dozen other burns on the piano and we had to pay for those as well.[14]

In this context, the 1968 ball with the Prime Minister attending in the Sydney Town Hall was a coup riding on the optimism of the referendum the year before. In their pretty shoes and carefully applied make-up the young women were not pretending to be white debutantes but self-consciously, proudly, if a little nervously, being Aboriginal debutantes symbolically coming of age as citizens of Australia. In the night, the debutantes interviewed by the ABC spoke to the camera with a mixture of nervousness and pride. Joyce Davison remembers 'I was eighteen, going on nineteen when I made my debut ... I felt like a princess walking down ... A little black princess'.[15]

Joyce, who holds a senior position within the Aboriginal Medical Service in Mt Druitt, was working in a factory in Chippendale in 1968. Her parents had moved from rural New South Wales to the city in the early 1960s in an attempt to avoid having any more of their children removed by the authorities. She explained that two of Joyce's sisters, for example, had been taken one morning from her Aunt's place while their parents attended a family funeral, on the grounds that they had been 'abandoned' Joyce recalled:

> I was brought up a sheltered sort of life because Mum had already lost seven of her kids taken away from her first marriage and I think that she was frightened that we would get involved in it ... we might get taken away. You know, don't speak out and say these things, which is, I don't know, right or wrong.[16]

On the night of the ball Joyce 'was a bit disappointed that Mum never came, or Dad. But they had their reasons. They never got into politics or anything but she had that much fear in her, they were frightened that us three youngest kids would be taken'. 'My dress cost six pounds ten', she also recounted with impressive detail. 'I got my beehive hairstyle done at the only Alexandria hairdresser that would serve "blacks"'.[17] She remembers her boyfriend of the time, now her husband of nearly 40 years, being too shy or ashamed to attend the ball, 'he dropped me off and waited 'round the back of the Town Hall and I went with my cousin's boyfriend of that time'.[18]

Raylene Smith also remembers the 1968 ball vividly and with pride. From the north coast of New South Wales, she was based in Sydney with extended family

14   Perkins 1966 Evidence: 283.
15   Davison 2007.
16   Davison 2007.
17   Davison 2007.
18   Davison 2007.

in 1968 because of work opportunities in the city: 'Everyone in Sydney was talking about this ball that was coming up, and would I like to be part of that … To me at the time I was just getting dolled up to go to this big ball'. Raylene and her husband have been married for over 30 years but she told us she has never met her in-laws who 'refuse to socialise with an Aboriginal woman'.[19]

Alice Hinton-Bateup recalled how the ball had made her feel: 'we were part of this big group of Aboriginal people together and it made you feel strong'.[20] Her father had given the tiara she wore on the night to her and she told us the story of how he got it for her:

> I didn't have any money left for the tiara and my Dad had a bet at the races on a Saturday morning and the first bet he had he won the daily double or something like that. And Dad came in with the tiara, just as I was getting my hair done. I mean where did he find the tiara for god's sake![21]

Remembering the ball 40 years later, Ruby Langford-Ginibi whose daughter Pearl was chosen by the Prime Minister to dance with remarked:

> there were a lot of questions asked about whether Aboriginal girls should be making their debs ball which was, you know, coming out of the white man's culture. It was something to show everybody that we were as good as anybody else and that we could dress up and be nice and pretty too.[22]

She remembered taking apart a dress she bought from a charity shop and sewing it back together to fit her daughter.

Shortly after the ball, Pearl was killed in a hit and run car accident and Ruby, mother of 'the first Aborigine in history to dance with the Prime Minister', remembers the intense financial and emotional difficulty of that time.[23] Not long after the night of the dance, Pearl's 14-year-old brother was arrested while playing with cricket equipment he had taken with friends from a shed at Newtown High School, and charged with petty theft. It was from the Daruk Training Home, where he was sent for six months for his 'first offence', that he came to his favourite sister's funeral on Christmas Eve, 1968. Langford-Ginibi recalled with pain, how her son, nicknamed Nobby, was kept handcuffed and supervised through the church service:

---

19 Smith 2007.
20 Hinton-Bateup 2007.
21 Hinton-Bateup 2007.
22 Langford-Ginibi 2007.
23 Langford-Ginibi, pers comm, 2007.

(Pearlie) had a large funeral ... I buried her with my father because I couldn't afford a plot of my own. Nobby was brought back from the boy's home. A fourteen-year-old boy handcuffed for his sister's funeral. The officer sat with him in the mourning car and later they took him straight back to the home. He wouldn't let anyone mention her name. He locked Pearl away in the back of his mind.[24]

The memories of the former debutantes and their friends and family complicate the image of the success of 'assimilation' or middle class respectability that the ball seemed to confer. While the image of the Aboriginal debutante was being publicised in government media and national papers in the 1960s as 'proof' of the 'success of assimilation', the women involved have memories that disturb this myth.[25] The pandemic of early deaths among Aboriginal communities, the Stolen Generations, and other stories of every-day racism in country towns around Australia existed simultaneously for the debutantes along with the pictures of white silk and satin dresses, the beehive hairdos and the curtsey to the Prime Minister.

Listening to the women talk, we realised with some enjoyment how little impact the presence of the Prime Minister had on them. In the archival footage of the night, the debutantes appear excited to be 'coming out' to Prime Minister Gorton, but 40 years down the track it was not his presence that had left a lasting impression. More important was the memory of a cousin who had partnered a debutante but since died, or the police presence around the Town Hall on the night, and the difficulty to be had hailing a cab home after the event. If assimilation was failing the Aboriginal women when they debuted in 1968, it was mutual. Attending the ball and curtseying to the Prime Minister was not about assimilation for the women or the organisers. By standing up and being counted as *Aboriginal* debutantes they gracefully transformed the reality of the genocidal fantasy dressed up as 'assimilation' that wanted to eliminate the category 'Aboriginal' from white Australia.

The national policy of assimilating Indigenous girls through the violence of removal policies and later through the policies of cultural assimilation played a part in the organisers' choice of a debutante ball. The campaign to close down Indigenous community dances in central Sydney and surrounding suburbs also played a part. As with the Freedom Rides led by Perkins a few years before the ball, the event can be seen to make visible longstanding concerns, such as the right of Aboriginal women and men to act in positions of authority, to socialise with whom you chose and perhaps eventually marry, and simply to access and enjoy central town buildings. Significantly, the debutante ball

---

24   Langford-Ginibi 1989: 141.
25   Cole 2000.

opened up a public space in the Sydney Town Hall where Indigenous sexual 'coming of age' could be performed. As debutantes, for example, they were not the victim: the statistics of the time that said Indigenous women were twice as likely to be the subject of violent sexual abuse as non-Indigenous. Such a performance could be seen to challenge the intention of the draconian policy and administration of Aboriginal people's personal lives under both 'Protection' and later 'Assimilation' policies that had sought to disperse and eradicate a proud self-identifying Indigenous community.[26]

Reflecting on the ball today upsets the still persistent myth of Indigenous people as the passive victims or on-lookers to modernisation in Australia. As the debutante ball illustrates, Indigenous people were the makers and co-producers of 1960s Australia. The image of the Aboriginal debutante eludes a desire for pure and simple definitions of what it means to be 'Aboriginal in Australia'. This desire to define 'Aboriginal' is challenged by the debutantes who are self-defining, complicated and fully human with all the contradictions that inevitably involves.

At the risk of oversimplifying, I would argue that currently all Indigenous Australians in remote Australia are being stereotyped, largely as degenerate and dangerous, in particular to their own children. This contemporary context contrasts with the words of Ruby Langford-Ginibi who said reflecting on the 1968 ball 'there was hope that we could be presented in a better way ... and that things would get better for our people'.[27] Amidst what Noel Pearson describes as 'a crisis in remote Aboriginal communities which the nation has so far failed to deal with',[28] it is a historically familiar scenario when the army and government representatives are sent in to Indigenous communities, ostensibly to 'save the children'.[29] This highly controversial, complex and unresolved territory is part of the wider context in which the debutantes' positive and striking representation of Indigenous women can be placed.

Mimesis

In engaging in the kind of intersubjective dialogue necessary to make the short preview of the film about the 1968 ball, we were called upon to understand the debutante balls and the women who had participated in them on their own terms rather than as mimicking 'white society' or as an assimilationist success

---

26   See Read 1982; Goodall 1995: 75–101; Ellinghaus 2003: 183–207.
27   Langford-Ginibi 2007.
28   Pearson 2007.
29   See Haebich 1988; Link-Up (NSW) and Wilson 1997.

story. During this collaborative project we were influenced by a conceptual framework from postcolonial studies that sees how the 'self' and 'other' are always 'solicited' by each other.[30] As Vincent Crapanzano wrote in 1985,

> One's sense of self is always mediated by the image one has of the other. (I have asked myself at times whether a superficial knowledge of the other, in terms of some stereotype, is not a way of preserving a superficial image of oneself).[31]

This kind of postcolonial approach sees the coloniser/colonised dialectic, for example, as a process that changes the identity of both the colonised and the coloniser. Such ideas work against static notions of identity that say, for example, you can only be a 'real' Aborigine if you conform to a stereotypical set of conditions, such as you come from a remote, traditional community, or can claim urban Indigenous status if you identify as a black activist in a fairly limited stereotypical way. This model of identity denies the realities and complexities of both Indigenous and non-Indigenous lives. In my case, I continue to learn about how my interest in Indigenous cultural politics in the era of the 1960s is revealing of my own identity and personal history along the axis of class, gender and culture.

I presented some of the content of this chapter at the conference in Barcelona from whence this collection originally stems.[32] At that conference, I talked with my friend Vanessa Castejon about her Spanish family's persecution and exile during the civil war there. This was a conversation we had begun in Geneva some years before when we were volunteering with an NGO providing technical support for the Working Group on Indigenous Peoples at the United Nations.[33] Vanessa's parent's experiences as exiles from the Spanish civil war, had, she felt influenced her interest and research into Indigenous Australian culture – a daughter of exiles seeking to research and advocate for those exiled within their own country.

At that conference in Barcelona this desire to understand more about the personal stories that motivate our research began to me to feel pressing. Gathering with academics from across Europe and Australia I found myself lost by paragraph two of the carefully argued, bullet-pointed, power-pointed papers wondering, how all of us, some with relatively little lived experience of 'Australia' had

---

30 Derrida 1981; JanMohamed 1985; Trinh T 1991.
31 Crapanzano 1985 cited in Trinh T 1991.
32 Universitat de Barcelona, 28–31 July 2008.
33 I volunteered with DoCip: Indigenous People's Centre for Documentation, Research and Information in 2003.

become interested in our research topics. If, as postcolonial studies argue, our sense of self is always mediated by our sense of the other what did this interest, especially in Indigenous Australia, say about us?

I had first begun to research Aboriginal debutante balls when writing a PhD about gender and the cultural politics of assimilation in Australia.[34] Photos of the Indigenous debutantes smiled graciously out from the social pages of local and national newspapers and the New South Wales state-sponsored magazine *Dawn: A Magazine for the Aboriginal People of NSW*, published from the late 1950s to the early 1970s. Indigenous critiques of white feminism had initially led to my interest in what the balls meant to those involved and to the wider politics of assimilation at the time. Indigenous theoreticians and activists challenged the assumptions of white feminists about an easily defined 'shared sisterhood', arguing that Indigenous and non-Indigenous women's interests differed in significant ways. In particular, differences existed around issues of family, sexuality and domestic violence.[35] For example, when white women called for abortion rights and liberation from being defined only by their maternal role, Indigenous women were fighting enforced sterilisation in some parts of Australia and the violent denigration and refusal of their maternal role through the widespread removal of Indigenous children from their families. When white women fought for the right for sexual freedom, for example, Aboriginal women fought derogatory stereotypes of 'black velvet'.[36] What might I learn about Aboriginal history and cultural politics if I listened to the women and men involved in these balls instead of reacting from my own feminist prejudices about them?

In the first version of this paper, I had a section a couple of pages long attempting to use the idea of mimesis as explicated by Taussig on colonial exchange to understand the Indigenous debutantes' motivations for being part of the ball. An anonymous reader of the first draft of this essay and Frances Peters-Little my section editor suggested there was less cross-cultural mimetic transformation going on than I might like to think. The ball, as Frances wrote, 'was more a "political strategy" designed by white politicians and black/white political activists' during the 1960s than it was 'a need for individual Aboriginal debutantes and their families to mime whites, for whatever reasons'. The ball in 1968 was a highly political strategised event, but the motivations of the women involved were about the sorts of things they were telling us: a chance to be together as proud young women, a chance to dress up and have some fun.

---

34   Cole 2000.
35   See Flick 1990: 63; Williams 1987: 66–73; Huggins 1987: 77–83.
36   See Goodall and Huggins 1992: 402.

Despite my best intentions to learn from what the women involved were saying, I listened but had not really heard them telling me what fun it had been. I puzzled over what I unwittingly thought of as 'western hegemonic' models of femininity, respectability and beauty. I read studies on gender and nationalism that argued, for example, that identities available to women from minority groups are constructed within power relations that provide what they call 'the framework for choice'.[37] In their analysis, identities which seem disempowering in some circumstances may be empowering in others. I thought this made sense for the debutante balls in their historical context.

In Britain, debutante balls were a way of ensuring 'suitable matches' among the elite classes. Traditionally, debutantes came out in front of the Queen, and once 'out' were publicly sanctioned as ready for marriage and procreation. In Australia, a policy of removing Indigenous children, specifically female children, from families and communities could make a public ceremony where Indigenous women publicly announced their 'coming of age' in the presence of their own community and elders a potent ritual of renewal of community and 'right matches' among Indigenous families.

However, as the women kept telling me, they did not see themselves at the time as fighters for equality or civil rights but as women on a big night out. As Christine Anu put it, the women were 'steppin' out in their deadly red shoes. Standin' up cause I'm, wearing something new'.[38] Within the broader historical context in which I was steeping myself, it was also true that Aboriginal debutante balls were, and are today, quite often 'just social events where girls can be involved outside of sporting events which are still largely dominated by the boys'.[39] The debutantes' real freedom from the historical processes all around them was not to be resisting assimilation or fighting it that night, but just to be themselves – young, stylish, 'groovy' women having fun.

The taxis that would not stop for them at the end of the night because they were 'Aboriginal', which some of the debutantes remembered 40 years on, or the police presence outside because of a large gathering of 'Aboriginals' in central Sydney, are another part of the same story. But having a ball, neither fighting nor 'resisting' but being proud of whom you are, dancing and enjoying a night out, was the greatest freedom of all in that moment. As the former debutantes told me it was about being with a big group of people, dressing up, looking great, feeling proud, knowing about the taxis and the police presence but knowing that we are more than the sum of our oppressions.

37   See Yuval-Davis and Anthias 1989: i–iv.
38   Anu 1995: track 10.
39   Frances Peters-Little, editorial comments, 2009.

I think my over-working the concept of mimesis was, in part, a bit to do with looking too long and too hard at one thing – an occupational hazard of the academic researcher. Your subject starts to swim in front of your eyes. However, as I thought more about this chapter, it dawned on me that the process of mimesis was mine. The 'mimetic faculty' as Taussig defines it is 'the faculty to copy, imitate, make models, explore difference, yield into and become other'.[40] He notes that 'writing itself is a mimetic exchange with the world ... it involves the relatively unexplored but everyday capacity to imagine, if not become the other'. In an 'older language', writes Taussig, this is 'sympathetic magic' and is as necessary to the very process of knowing as it is to 'the construction and subsequent naturalisation of identities'.[41]

> Mimesis plays this trick of dancing between the same and the very different. An impossible but necessary, indeed an everyday affair. Mimesis registers both sameness and difference, of being like and being other. Creating stability from this instability is no small task, yet all identity formation is engaged in this habitually bracing activity.[42]

If mimesis is the process of copying or imitating something in order to change yourself as well as the thing you imitate, isn't that what all of us who write about *Aboriginal History* are doing, at least in part? As well as helping me decipher more about the academic culture of which I am part, I felt I knew something more about this process of mimesis from my personal history. My mother's movement from working-class Londoner, with the 'wrong' South London accent that she modified to more 'BBC' English and later to professional middle class British-Australian was, in part, a process of imitation and assimilation. I knew something about the processes of assimilation from my own life as a British immigrant to Australia. The hiding involved, the invisible differences, and the re-invention as well as the freedom to be, to some extent, who you want to be. To identify with whom you choose from a range of new possibilities. To wear the finest clothes you save for one day, for example, and the bargain clothes from the Good Samaritans another.

It is about ten years ago that I attended my first Indigenous debutante ball, at Sydney's La Perouse with my friend Maria Nugent, and began listening and talking to those involved in the balls and thinking about the questions they raise about feminism, assimilation, identity and later, mimesis. It occurs to me now as I write this that I often feel like I am making my debut. As a 'new Australian' emigrating with my family from England to Western Australia, age seven. Being told to 'bring a plate' to my first Australian school sports carnival

---

40   Taussig 1993: ii.
41   Taussig 1993: xix.
42   Taussig 1993: 129.

and turning up with just that – an empty plate, feeling like an idiot as I did many times navigating the unchartered colloquialisms and invisible differences of the 'new Australian'. I married a man from London and live back here now, making my debut again, navigating a new world of English universities and now, as my kids get older, schools. I am a historian working in an Anthropology department. An Australian in London, a bit of a pom in Australia. A mother with young kids stumbling between motherhood and research. As I learn about how to keep a rhythm between my various roles alive, my desire to listen and learn, to share with and understand others who have juggled the demands of many roles and identities, takes on a new urgency and meaning. 'A fragmented identity is a strange thing' writes John Docker,

> [y]ou always feel other people are more secure and assured in their identity, which they're most certainly not. And you always have a feeling of not fully knowing yourself, or why strange desires, passions, and identifications erupt and endure.[43]

Acknowledgements

Many thanks to Lara Cole, Rani Chaleyer, Anne Delaney, Janine Matthews, and the former debutantes and their family who appear in the documentary preview: Joyce Davison, Ruby Langford-Ginibi, Rayleen Clarke and Alice Hinton-Bateup. Thanks also to Carole Cole and Frances Peters-Little for comments on the draft, and to Ann Curthoys, John Docker, Vanessa Castejon, Peter Read, Terri-Ann White, and Sue Ballyn for the Barcelona conference. Some material in this paper was first published in *Studies in Australasian Cinema* (2008, vol 2(1): 5–13).

References

Primary sources

Report of the First Annual General Meeting of the Foundation for Aboriginal Affairs [hereafter FAA], 12 August 1965, MSS A463/63, Mitchell Library, Sydney.

Report of Annual General Meeting of Foundation for Aboriginal Affairs [hereafter FAA], 12 August 1968, MSS A463/63, Mitchell Library, Sydney.

Secondary sources

Anu, Christine 1995, *Stylin' Up*, Mushroom Records.

---

43   Docker 2001: ix.

Attwood, Bain and Andrew Markus 2007, *The 1967 Referendum: Race, Power and the Australian Constitution*, Aboriginal Studies Press, Canberra.

Cole, Anna 2000, 'The Glorified Flower. Race, Gender and Assimilation in Australia', unpublished PhD thesis, University of Technology, Sydney.

Crapanzano, Vincent 1985, 'A reporter at large', *New Yorker*, 18 March 1985: 8–10.

Davison, Joyce 2007, Interview in *Dancing with the Prime Minister*, Lara Cole (dir), November Films.

Derrida, Jacques 1981, *Dissemination*, B Johnson (trans), University of Chicago Press, Chicago.

Docker, John 2001, *1492. The Poetics of Diaspora*, Continuum, London and New York.

Ellinghaus, Katherine 2003, 'Absorbing the "Aboriginal Problem": controlling interracial marriage in Australia in the late 19th and early 20th centuries', *Aboriginal History* 27: 183–207.

Flick, Barbara 1990, 'Colonization and decolonization: an Aboriginal experience', in *Playing the State: Australian Feminist Interventions*, Sophie Watson (ed), Verso, London and New York: 63–67.

Goodall, Heather 1995, '"Assimilation begins in the Home". The state and Aboriginal women's work as mothers in New South Wales, 1900 to 1960s', in *Labour History: Aboriginal Workers*, Ann McGrath and Kay Saunders (eds), Australian Society for Study of Labour History, Sydney: 75–101.

— and J Huggins 1992, 'Aboriginal women are everywhere. Contemporary struggles', in *Gender Relations in Australia: Domination and Negotiation*, K Saunders and R Evans (eds), University of Queensland Press, Queensland: 398–424.

Haebich, Anna 1988, *For Their Own Good: Aborigines and Government in the Southwest of Western Australia, 1900–1940*, University of Western Australia Press, Perth.

Huggins, Jackie 1987, 'Black women and women's liberation', *Hecate* 13(1): 77–83.

JanMohamed, Abdul 1985, 'The Economy of Manichean Allegory: the function of racial difference in colonialist literature', *Critical Inquiry* 12(1): 59–87.

Langford-Ginibi, Ruby 1989, *Don't Take your Love to Town*, Penguin Books, Australia.

— 2007, Interview in *Dancing with the Prime Minister*, Lara Cole (dir), November Films.

Link-Up (NSW) and Tikka Wilson 1997, *In the Best Interest of the Child? Stolen Children: Aboriginal Pain/White Shame*, Aboriginal History Monograph 4, Link-Up NSW Aboriginal Corporation and Aboriginal History Inc, Canberra.

November Films 2008, *Dancing with the Prime Minister*, Lara Cole (dir), DVD.

Pearson, Noel 2007, 'No more victims', *The New Statesman*, 16 August 2007, accessed 10 May 2008: <www.thenewstatesman.com/200708160023>

Perkins, Charles 1966, Part 1, 'Report and Minutes of Proceedings', in *Report from the Joint Committee of the Legislative Council and Legislative Assembly upon Aborigines Welfare*, Parliamentary Papers, 2 June 1966: 283.

Read, Peter 1982, 'A double-headed coin: protection and assimilation in Yass, 1900–1960', in *All that Dirt. Aborigines 1938*, History Project Inc, Canberra.

Smith, Raylene 2007, Interview in *Dancing with the Prime Minister*, (preview), November Films.

Taussig, Michael 1993, *Mimesis and Alterity: A Particular History of the Senses*, Routledge, London and New York.

Trinh T, Minh-ha 1991, *When the Moon Waxes Red: Representation, Gender and Cultural Politics*, Routledge, New York and London.

Williams, Elaine 1987, 'Aboriginal first, women second', in *Different Lives: Reflections on the Women's movement and Visions of the Future,* Jocelyn Scutt (ed), Penguin, Ringwood: 66–73.

Yuval-Davis, Nira and Floya Anthias (eds) 1989, *Woman-Nation-State*, Palgrave Macmillan, London.

11. Identity and identification: Aboriginality from the Spanish Civil War to the French Ghettos

VANESSA CASTEJON

Postcolonial studies, Indigenous politics, Aboriginal self-determination, Aboriginal claims in the United Nations, the image of Aboriginal people in France: these are the topics I have studied in the last 12 years. I have come to realise that I have also been researching my own history. I am not saying my story is part of Indigenous history – I am very far from indigenous: I am a product of exile. I am from nowhere, my parents even had Nansen passports for apatrids and refugees (they have always said they had apatrid passports only, as if their country had completely disappeared for them). I am from various places with different identities fighting all the time to define me. Without my knowing it, this conflict has led me to researching Aboriginal identity.

In this chapter, I want to ask whether those of us who are non-Indigenous academics looking at Indigenous issues, are using our research as part of our own unconscious quest for identity. I seek to explore the subjectivity of my work as an historian, my lie in wanting to tell 'the truth'. As the French sociologist Romain Pudal writes, 'Not many (academics) are ready to admit, and even less analyze, the intimate relationship they have with their subject of research or with the writing of their colleagues.'[1] Here, I want to take up his challenge in an attempt at ego-history,[2] and consider my intimate relations with the subject of my research – Aboriginal politics and identity. Because of who I am, this chapter is a meditation on the cultural transfers between Aboriginal Australia, the Spanish Civil War and the French ghettos.

---

1 Pudal 2004: 186.
2 Pierre Nora created this genre in the 1980s; he asked historians to apply the methods of history to their own story.

Being French and Spanish in Australia

My first identity was, I thought, French. I was born in France and I never wondered about my identity, I was French and that was it. I grew up in what is called in France a 'red suburb' (red because most of the cities there were and still are communist), the '9-3', a ghetto for immigrants and poor French people. I grew up in one of those cities where French rap was born, where riots took place in 2005. I was the 'French' girl in the class.

In the mid 1990s, on the day I asked for a birth certificate to apply for a grant to study Feminism in Australia for my PhD, I discovered I was born Spanish and my parents had changed my nationality to French only when I was 12. It was an identity shock. I was reading Sally Morgan's *My Place* (1987) at the time and this identification is the reason why I switched to Aboriginal politics.

I realised, at that time, that I had not always been French but I *really* discovered I was French in Australia a few years later, during a long stay there. In France nobody asks where you are from, it is a sort of taboo question as it implies that you might not be French. It is even ruder in the area where I was born, in that 'red suburb', that ghetto. If political correctness existed in France, it definitely would be politically incorrect to ask this question. In Australia, it is quite different. I have travelled extensively since I was 12 and nowhere else have people asked me so many times where I was from. Everybody asked me that question in Australia: I used to begin by saying that I was born and have always lived in France and my mother tongue was French. People would say: 'so you are French'. Then I used to say: 'both my parents are Spanish', and they would say: 'then you are Spanish'. I did not have the choice, people wanted to define my identity because I was not doing it. I had to think about it, find a way to define myself against imposed definitions at a time I was also studying Aboriginal politics at Monash University's Centre for Australian Indigenous Studies, working on how Aboriginal people had to define themselves against imposed definitions.

Years later, in July 2008, I attended a conference entitled 'Myth, Memory and History' at the Centre for Australian Studies in Barcelona. On a sunny morning there, as I was speaking to a very good friend who was also researching Aboriginal identity, I told her about my family. I told her that my anarchist uncle's father was part of the Republican government in Exile — he was, I said, part of the Aboriginal Provisional Government. I suddenly saw the link between my family history and why I was studying Aboriginal politics.

I realised I had always known about this link. 'Retroactive clues' began to appear. I had dedicated my PhD thesis on Aboriginal political claims and identity 'to my parents and family who have always wanted to believe in another future'. I was inventing a link between Aboriginal self-determination and sovereignty and my family's anarchism, its fight against Franco's regime. Even in Aboriginal politics, I wanted to find links with the extreme left. The Aboriginal Provisional Government fascinated me. I have always idealised Gary Foley and his revolutionary attitude – I remember a picture of him with a Keffieh – and I also admired the Black Panthers. I remember Isabel Coe calling young activists 'warriors' at the tent embassy in Sydney in 2000. After my PhD, I began to be interested in the Working Group on Indigenous Peoples at the UN, the creation of a global identity to contain all the indigenous identities. Indigeneity made in Geneva. Perhaps in my quest for Aboriginality I wanted to see if something could bring together all my own identities.

Aboriginal politics and the Spanish civil war

Is it possible to compare the road towards post-colonialism in Australia as embodied in Aboriginal 'liberation movements' with the civil war in Spain? Ella Shohat sees forced exile as a part of post-colonialism, in that it is a 'breaking-off with the imperial centre'.[3] I need to explore this idea. In the late 1930s, my grandfather initiated an anarchist community in Aragon. They were trying to establish something free of domination, a fair society with no chief. During the years of the conflict (1936–1939) my grandmother committed suicide, apparently because of threats from the communists (it is difficult to know more about it as my dad was four at that time and I never met my grandparents). She first tried to kill herself with her two children but a neighbour saved the three of them from gas. My grandfather was at the front. My great-grandmother also committed suicide. My father and his sister were taken away. My aunt, who was eight, had to work as a maid and my dad was sent from one member of the family to the other and then to a Jesuit orphanage until he managed, when he was 15, to come illegally to France to 'meet' his dad who was in exile.

My mum was forced into exile with her parents and sister in February 1939, along with 500,000 other Republicans during what is known as 'La Retirada'. My mother's family left everything behind and crossed the border with one suitcase. They were put in what were called 'concentration camps' in France. My grandfather, as he arrived there first, used to sleep in a hole in the sand and eat only a sardine a day.

---

3   Shohat 1992: 84.

Fig 1. The suitcase my mother's family arrived with on the beach of Argeles where the refugee camp was located

Until the 1950s, my mother says her family believed that they would ultimately go back to Spain. She remembers the time when they suddenly realised they would be 'displaced' forever; they would 'have to become French', dig new roots.

They ultimately did become French. Not on paper though, they are still Spanish today and they had remained refugees/ apatrids with Nansen passports until Franco's death in 1975. They became so French that they did not want their children to be Spanish. I had to learn Spanish at university because my family did not teach me Spanish or Catalan at home.

In 2004, in desperate need to 'link-up' with my Spanish self, with my roots, I wrote a letter to the Spanish consulate to explain that I was the daughter of two persons who were forced into exile after the Spanish civil war. I was given Spanish nationality in less than one month. It was about recognition and re-appropriation. My family, who actually dispossessed me from my Spanish identity to protect me, was puzzled by this choice. My mother ended up being proud of it but my dad still does not understand why I should want to be anything other than French. Two years later, my son was born and he was born French and Spanish. My son's name is Paco partly because it is the short name for François in Spanish (François means 'French' in old French).

Fig 2. My son playing in a replica refugee 'house', Argeles beach, February 2009

I can see so many connections between my family history and my interest in Australian Aboriginal politics and identity. Both my parents were force into exile. I guess this is the origin of my interest in the power of the government on children, my interest in the Stolen Generations, and in assimilation and racism as well. Perhaps I unconsciously assimilated what I thought were Aboriginal communities with my family history, my grandfather's desire for a stateless society. Maybe I also assimilated Franco's coup and the reactions to it with the power stolen from Aboriginal people and their sovereignty claims.[4] My interest in displaced populations and the power of the government in shaping identity relates closely to my family's history. My family did not tell me of my Spanish origins. They hid the truth; they lied to protect us, just as Sally Morgan's parents did in her classic autobiographical novel, *My Place*.[5] The experience of

---

4   Reynolds 1996: 136–154.
5   Morgan 1987.

assimilation was all around me, and I pursued it in my interest in Aboriginal identity. In a more general context, I see links between the two histories, both in oppression and in reconciliation. Since December 2008, the Spanish government has been giving Spanish nationality to all the descendants of refugees who ask for it[6] and there has been a kind of apology in France as well, in the region where some of the concentration camps were (the president of the region thanked the Republicans during the celebrations of the 70th anniversary, in February 2009).[7]

Fig 3. The 70th anniversary of 'La Retirada' and my father with the republican flag

Denial and pride in a French ghetto

If part of my identity is rooted in anarchism and exile, the other part is rooted in the suburb, the ghetto, the '9-3', where I grew up. I learnt the importance of this identity again in Australia, when I taught a class at Monash University entitled 'the ethnography of French Hip Hop culture'. The '9-3' used to be the French department No 93, the Seine-Saint-Denis, but a new clear identity arose a few years ago and it is now called '9-3' by the generation who wants to 'belong'.

---

6   Historical Memory Law, 28 December 2008, available at: <http://leymemoria.mjusticia.es> for the descendants of Spanish Nationals involved in the Civil War and International Brigade Volunteers.

7   Frêche 2009: 3.

Children of displaced people often build a new identity where they grow up, something they can relate to, keeping a bit of the idealised loss of identity but creating a new mix.

Even though, like many second-generation immigrants in the '9-3', I claim my Spanishness, I am unable to say more than one correct sentence in Spanish. But I can speak 'Verlan', the French suburban dialect. The 9-3 is very diverse but it has a language (also used in other Parisian suburbs), its music, its dance and, in general, its art (graffiti, djing, slam, rap) as the French hip-hop culture was born there. A mix of cultures gave birth to a new one. I always thought that I had to hide this part of my identity because in France it is not glorious to be from that ghetto. I denied my suburbanity. I worked on having no accent (young people from the suburbs often have this typical, not to stay stereotypical accent). I refrained from using 'verlan'. I did not wear the expected clothes; I wanted to look Parisian. I was in a strong denial of that place where people were exploited, dominated because of assimilationist, still colonial, policies. These people called 'second-zone citizens'. These people called by high profile politicians 'sauvageons'[8] (a mix of 'wild child' and 'savage'), or 'racaille'[9] ('scum') who had to be given the Karcher treatment,[10] a 'smelly', 'noisy' people 'living out from social security benefits'.[11]

It was not easy for me to be from there. I realise now that my interest in exclusion in Australia definitely comes from there. The 9-3 is the place in France where the link between the indigenous and the immigrant is the clearest. It is the place where the social but also the colonial 'split' is evident. Racism is apparent; the 9-3 is one of the places where the National Front (the French One Nation party) is very strong. The 'Far Right' and the extreme right have demonised the people from there by 'otherising' them. The Wikipedia definition for the word racaille, used by Nicolas Sarkozy in 2005, makes a link between 'race' and racaille, stating that the expression was purely racist. Le Pen, the head of the National Front, and extreme right websites call the people from the ghetto 'la racaille allogène', the 'non-Indigenous scum'. Here again, a vocabulary linked with my research.

A movement was born a few years ago, claiming recognition of the people from the 'ghetto' and it is called 'Les Indigènes de la République' (The Indigenous people of the Republic). It is in favour of a fight by the postcolonial peoples to build an autonomous political power.[12] In the name of the movement, the Republic might be a reference to the common reproach of communautarism,

---

8   Jean-Pierre Chevenement, 9 March 1998.
9   Nicolas Sarkozy, Minister of the Interior, 25 October 2005.
10   Nicolas Sarkozy, 20 June 2005.
11   Jacques Chirac, 19 June 1991.
12   Khiari 2006: 100.

people fencing themselves in their community, which would supposedly put the values of the French Republic in danger ... the solution being Integration. 'Les Indigènes de la République' is clearly fighting Integration as a policy.[13] Some journalists and politicians see the movement as a danger. It is trying to create 'an anti-colonial identity' in reaction to the conflict[14], just like the Aboriginal Provisional Government editing Aboriginal Passports and Birth Certificates and claiming the right to an Aboriginal State.

Just like the Aboriginal Provisional Government again, and like the Aboriginal Black Power in the late 1960s to early 1970s, les Indigènes de la République is not a real threat, it is only trying to make the problems visible. They are fighting invisibility outside the ghetto.

The forced invisibility is comparable to the situation of Aboriginal people: a few years ago, non Aboriginal Australians or even tourists could still say that had never met an Indigenous person. In France, people from small villages are afraid of the people from the ghettos, people they have never met or wanted to meet.

In France as well, racism is demonstrated by the absence of people from 'the ghetto', the 'cités', in the media. When they do appear on television or in the main newspapers the image of the descendants of immigrants in the suburbs is always full of stereotypes. They are seen as savages ('sauvageons' as they were called by minister Jean-Pierre Chevenement), burning cars, stealing, dealing drugs, destroying everything after demonstrations in Paris. The media and the 'non-suburbans', in general, do not see the people from the ghettos as victims but as oppressors, just like 'white Australians who see themselves as victims, struggling heroically against adversity, and those that place them as aggressors, forcing adversity onto others'.[15]

Sometimes anthropologists or journalists enter the ghetto and the situation is the same as in the Aboriginal communities: people are often afraid to be treated like animals in a zoo, and it is often actually the case.[16]

Historians Pascal Blanchard and Nicolas Bancel say that 'the suburb' has become a terra incognita for the media, the films and the political speeches, where none would dare enter.[17]

It is my Terra (Australis?) incognita that I want people to know about through my work.

---

13   On anti-integrationism see Hajjat 2005: 46–53.
14   Khiari 2006: 103.
15   Curthoys 2003: 187.
16   A famous scene of the film *La Haine*, by Mathieu Kassovitz, one of the first films on the suburbs, shows the reaction of young people to the intrusion of journalists filming them from their car.
17   Blanchard and Bancel 1998: 187.

The Great French Silence also applies to the 'suburbs'. The taboo history of the war in Algeria, for example, makes it difficult to link the problems of the suburbs with the colonial wars. Even the new Museum of Immigration in Paris does not stress these links. In February 2005, the French government passed a law to force teachers to stress the good aspects of colonisation (the President invalidated it a few months after). It is not only a white blindfold view of History; it is almost revisionist. The possibility of a collective memory is denied to the people from the ghetto. The 'suburbs' are not considered as a part of colonial history. It is not only a lack of recognition of their suffering but a rejection again, the denial of a possible common history. My denial of my 'suburbanity' ended in Australia. Partly because of my teaching on the French Hip-Hop culture, and partly because of my research, I discovered that I was very proud of being from there. If my blood and my innate feelings were Spanish, my soul was from the 9-3. I was not only French; I belonged to the 9-3. I became proud of being part of the excluded, of the Other, proud of this town, Bobigny, where I was born, where none would go for pleasure.[18] This pride is something common to the people who feel they 'belong' to the '9-3', according to 'Grand Corps Malade', one of the best and well-known slammers, in a song on the suburbs entitled 'Je viens de là' (I come from there).[19] This new identity was created as a reaction to discrimination and domination, just like Aboriginality, created out of many identities as a reaction to domination.

I also work by choice in the 9-3, in a university full of students who 'belong' (they say they 'represent'). I am now a spectator of the evolution of identity there. I have seen recently, for example, the appearance of a new word, used in some cases to define the people outside the suburbs: 'Babtou', the Verlan of 'Toubab' which used to mean 'the Whites' in French colonial Africa.

I am proud of being from this lively, bubbling, hybrid suburb, this post-colonial effervescence. I am very grateful to my research for this new awareness of who I am and my pride in being who I am. I became proud of being me thanks to Aboriginal politics, through an unconscious mix of discriminations, of displaced peoples who have survived, survived colonial policies and imposed definitions and it is now clear to me that the subject of research is never far from the researcher.

---

18   Desplechin and Darzacq 2006.
19   Video accessible on Dailymotion or YouTube, showing images and faces of the '9-3'.

References

Blanchard, Pascal, Nicolas Bancel and Sandrine Lemaire 2005, *La Fracture Coloniale*, Editions La découverte, Paris.

Blanchard, Pascal and Nicolas Bancel 1998, *De l'indigène à l'immigré*, Gallimard, Paris.

Curthoys, Ann 2003, 'Constructing national histories', in *Frontier Conflict, The Australian Experience*, Bain Attwood and SG Foster (eds), National Museum of Australia, Canberra: 185–200.

Desplechin, Marie and Denis Darzacq, 2006, *Bobigny Centre Ville*, Actes Sud, Paris.

Frêche, Georges 2009, 'Merci aux républicains espagnols', special edition on La Retirada, *L'Indépendant*, 20 February 2009: 1–24.

Hajjat, Abdellali 2005, *Immigration postcoloniale et mémoire*, L'Harmattan, Paris.

Khiari, Sadri 2006, *Pour une Politique de la Racaille, Immigrés, Indigènes et Jeunes de Banlieue*, Les Editions Textuel, Paris.

Morgan, Sally 1987, *My Place*, Fremantle Arts Centre Place, Fremantle.

Noiriel, Gérard 2003, *Penser avec, penser contre. Itinéraire d'un Historien*, Belin, Paris.

Nora, Pierre 1987, *Essais d'ego-histoire*, NRF Gallimard, Paris.

Perraud, Antoine 2002, 'Du mépris du peuple à la menace populiste, entretien avec Emmanuel Todd', *Télérama*, 27 April 2002.

Pudal, Romain 2004, Review of 'Noiriel (Gérard)-Penser avec, penser contre. Itinéraire d'un historien', in 'Les Sciences sociales en situation coloniale', *Revue d'Histoire des Sciences Humaines* 10: Sciences Humaines Editions, 183–186.

Reynolds, Henry 1996, *Aboriginal Sovereignty*, Allen & Unwin, Sydney.

Shohat, Ella 2007, 'Notes sur le "post-colonial" (1992)'. *Mouvements* 51, September-October, accessed 10 May 2010: <http://www.mouvements.info/Notes-sur-le-post-colonial-1992.html>

12. Urban Aboriginal ceremony: when seeing is *not* believing

KRISTINA EVERETT

I am an anthropologist. Like all anthropologists my research methodology is entrenched in participant observation fieldwork and like many anthropologists, my writing practice is primarily ethnographic. Following Ortner, ethnography encompasses many things, but minimally means 'the attempt to understand another life world using the self – as much of it as possible – as the instrument of knowing'.[1] That is, through long-term embodied engagement in relationships with research participants and their life worlds the researcher learns. By analysing one's own experience of learning about an 'other' life world the classical ethnographer is committed to writing what Geertz called a 'thick description'.[2] Ortner argues that such classical ethnographies produce understanding through richness, texture and detail. The 'thick, descriptive' ethnography that I write is inseparable from the participant observation fieldwork that I conduct. The writing occurs synchronously with the fieldwork. Texts including field notes, journal entries, letters, emails, photos and videos, which are not raw data, but necessarily a form of analysis and interpretation, and are later refined into articles like this one. Of course, the practice of immersion in others' worlds is problematic, partial and constrained, but, as Ortner makes explicit, an ethnographic approach is as much 'an intellectual positionality, a constructive and interpretive mode, as it is a bodily process in space and time'.[3]

The story that I tell here is my story of learning about the connection that a group of urban Aboriginal people make between a post-contact Aboriginal creation myth and their own version of a funeral ceremony. It is an ethnographic account of a ceremony that is not a 'traditional' Aboriginal ceremony, but one which is claimed by those who perform it as an expression of their still emerging identity. These people claim traditional Aboriginal ownership of a large part of what is now a modern Australian metropolis and are struggling to produce representations of this identity after a long period of dispossession and

---

1   Ortner 1995: 173.
2   Geertz 1993: 3.
3   Ortner 1995: 173.

marginalisation. They struggle because their claim is a big one, and there are many competing claims from other Aboriginal groups as well as the Australian state. They also struggle because they have been dispossessed of both their land, and of their traditional cultural practices. All they have to represent their Aboriginality now are practices that they have 'borrowed' from other Aboriginal groups, those that have been passed down through families as partial memories, those they have seen in films and advertisements, and those they develop from the dreams and imaginations of senior people. I use the pseudonym, 'Gwalan' to refer to them here because of fraught politics that I will describe below.

Gwalan have emerged in the last 30 years or so as 'a people'. Prior to their emergence as a named group, some of the people who now call themselves Gwalan lived as groups of disparate people living on the fringes of Australian society and identifying themselves as Aboriginal. They named themselves according to their attachment to specific suburbs, roads or creeks calling themselves 'Bridge Road Mob', or 'Platypus Creek Tribe' for example. Some people who now identify as Gwalan did not, however, know that they possessed Aboriginal heritage until academics including linguists, archaeologists, biologists, historians and anthropologists began researching Gwalan history and compiling genealogies.

Three to four hundred people now identify and are identified as Gwalan and continue to develop various ideas, values and philosophies about and expressions of their identity. Some are engaged in the various expressions of cultural renaissance and revival of Aboriginal traditions that characterise some aspects of Gwalan (re)emergence. These include singing, dancing, painting and various kinds of ceremony. Others, however, expressly do not engage in these kinds of cultural expressions and instead choose to represent themselves using different kinds of political methods including academic research, formal political speeches, protests and petitions. Not only, in fact, do these more formally politically represented Gwalan not engage in singing, dancing, painting and ceremony, but they actively and vocally dispute the authenticity of such representations claiming that they do not represent 'true' Gwalan heritage. The ceremony that I describe later and its effects are the cultural products of a group of about 150 Gwalan who are faced with the hostility and denigration of other Gwalan. Regardless of this, the ceremony has been performed regularly for at least 25 years and those who perform it now claim it as Gwalan tradition.

The very identity 'Gwalan' has been queried by outsiders, both Aboriginal and non-Aboriginal. In part, this is because this recent Indigenous identification has occurred in the era of land rights and native title. According to the *Native Title Act 1994* (Clth), claimants must prove that they are still 'attached' to a 'body of traditions, observances, customs and beliefs of Aboriginal people or a community or group of Aboriginal people, including those traditions, observances, customs and beliefs as applied to particular persons, sites, areas of land, things or relationships'. Because Native Title claims are arguably the ultimate recognition of Indigenous 'authenticity' by the Australian state, many Indigenous Australians struggle to conform to its demands. These demands, as Povinelli argues, are difficult enough for any Indigenous group to prove, but are virtually impossible for people who live in long colonised areas as Gwalan do.[4] There have been a number of (unsuccessful) Gwalan native title claims, generating considerable historical research.

Because Gwalan 'ethnogenesis' coincided with land rights, native title, and other state policies concerning recognition of Indigenous Australians' rights, it might be argued that it was an identity created to take advantage of those policies. This may indeed have been the reason at the time, or at least part of the reason. However, my experience of participating in and observing the practices that Gwalan today call their culture – ceremonies, dance, painting and language revival – leads me to take the view that whatever the earlier reasons for their development, these things have become such values in themselves that Gwalan cannot and will not relinquish them. These practices sustain group and individual dignity and self respect. One young Gwalan man told me that 'Without my culture I'm nothin''.[5]

Before I go any further, it is important that I explain what I mean by 'tradition' as it is practiced in the Gwalan context. Manning Nash insists that although tradition is mostly concerned with the past and is hence fundamentally backward-focused, it does have a future dimension.[6] This dimension involves the commitment of its carriers to preserve and continue traditional practices into the future. However, because of radical, long term disruption of cultural practices and because they have inter-married with many different groups of Aboriginal and non-Aboriginal peoples, Gwalan do not have one, common cultural tradition on which to draw. They consequently 'shelve' or 'sideline' all traditions other than their new Gwalan tradition. Everyone in the community is encouraged to be part of the project of producing this 'new tradition' and many are committed to preserving and continuing what are now claimed as traditional Gwalan cultural practices. As well as public spectacles including dancing, 'welcome to country' speeches and art exhibitions, Gwalan conduct private ceremonies meant for the benefit of their own members.

Not only have traditions changed to the point of being unrecognisable from the early records of colonists, but they also have become 'mixed up' with the traditions of other Indigenous and non-Indigenous peoples. Many currently practiced Gwalan traditions bear strong resemblance to practices described

---

4   Povinelli 2002: 39.
5   Everett, Fieldnotes, Euroka Clearing, September 2003.
6   Nash 1989: 14.

in the traditional Aboriginal anthropological literature and belong to people
other than Gwalan. One example of these practices is the painting of 'dot'
paintings that are more usually associated with paintings from the Central
Desert. Another is traditional Aboriginal dancing dressed in loin cloths with
symbols painted in white ochre marked on the dancer's skin. Some are based
on the memories, imaginings and dreams of older Gwalan descendants. Other
Gwalan traditions might have their origins in indigenous cultures from other
countries, reflecting a kind of 'global indigeneity'. Cultural exchange, support
and collaboration between Indigenous groups around the world have grown
in recent times, enabled and supported by new technologies including the
internet, more accessible travel, and increased participation in global markets
(especially art markets).[7] The trouble is that because these traditions do not
originate, or cannot be proved to have originated, with Gwalan ancestors who
lived in Gwalan country before 1788 they do not conform to the demands of
native title and consequently do not conform to dominant ideas concerning
Aboriginal 'authenticity'.

All Gwalan descendants are dislocated in significant ways from their heritage.
Gwalan language is no longer spoken, although a version has been revived from
the records of early British colonists and is used ceremonially in 'Welcome to
Country' ceremonies.[8] Detailed knowledge of traditional kinship relations is
no longer transmitted, and many Gwalan stories relating to specific places in
Gwalan country cannot be remembered. They are not, however, displaced from
their traditional country and although they have been forcibly separated from
religious systems that gave particular meanings to their connection to land, they
claim today that some knowledge, rituals and stories have survived and are now
being implemented in their contemporary quest to experiment with new ideas
about spirituality and land. These ideas, as I will describe, are adaptations of
past and present beliefs, histories, relationships and politics.

According to Gwalan, their Dreaming revolves around stories, beliefs and
rituals concerning a Gwalan ancestor figure, Baiame. The name Baiame is not
arbitrary. The belief in an 'All-Father' inhabiting the heavens by Aboriginal
peoples in south-eastern Australia was first documented in 1875 as occurring at
Wellington Valley Mission.[9] Here, Ridley quotes the Reverend James Gunther
as saying:

> There is no doubt in my mind that the name Baia-mai ...
> Refers to the Supreme Being; and the ideas concerning
> Him by some of the more thoughtful Aborigines are a

---

7   Cf Sissons 2005: 7–34.
8   See Everett 2009: 53.
9   Ridley 1875: 135 in Swain 1993: 154.

Remnant of original traditions prevalent among the ancients of the Deity.[10]

Baiame and his cult as it was practised late in the nineteenth and around the turn of the twentieth century is referred to in Manning, Cameron, Howitt, Mathews, and Lang with later authors including Elkin, Lane, Kolig, Maddock, and Swain also making reference to the cult.[11] Apart from using the name Baiame there is only one current practice performed by Gwalan that has any resemblance to those described in the literature. This practice is the carving of dendroglyphs: images or designs in the trunks of living trees. Although the group carve images in trees, the form of the carvings and the rituals associated with them bear no resemblance to the cult of Baiame as it is documented in the literature.

Dendroglyphs seem to have been carved exclusively in the south-east of the continent and are described by Lane as highly abstract geometric designs although some depicted European things such as trains, ships, horses, cattle, pigs and effigies of Europeans themselves.[12] Lane suggests that these carved trees may have served to represent Baiame's camp and gifts. Regardless of conjecture about the form and significance of dendroglyphs in the past, those made by Gwalan are an emblem for the group. All these dendroglyphs are images of turtles. Turtles are a modern Gwalan symbol of survival, longevity and, as land and water dwelling animals, adaptability.

The carving of the turtle image into the tree is part of a ceremony that is believed, community members tell me, to facilitate the transport of the spirit of a recently deceased community member from this earthly realm into the spiritual realm in the sky that is presided over by Baiame. Everyone I asked claimed that Baiame and his cult belong to Gwalan and that *Baiame* ceremony is their Dreaming.

Yet, when asked, many community members say that they are Roman Catholic. There is a strong connection between the community and a Catholic Centre in an outer suburb of the city. This link is an extension of long term associations many people have through family histories involving Catholic missionisation. Of those who do not have a history of missionisation, many do have a history of intermarriage with English and Irish Catholic convicts and free settlers. However, I do not think that this history is all that makes many Gwalan claim to be Catholic now. The Catholic Centre has become very much a community focus because some important community ceremonies such as weddings, funerals and Christenings are performed there. Many Gwalan are recipients of Catholic welfare through the Centre. The Centre also provides transport, a venue and

---

10   Ridley in Swain 1993: 127.
11   Manning 1882: 170; Cameron 1885: 364–365; Howitt 1904: 440–504; Mathews 1905; Lang 1899: 53; Berndt 1947: 334; Elkin 1975: 143; Lane 1978: 233; Kolig 1989: 255–256; Maddock 1982: 127; Swain 1997.
12   Lane 1978: 233.

programs which allow community members to engage in social interaction with each other and other local Indigenous peoples. In other words, the Centre and Catholicism provide Gwalan with much valued resources. Arguably, the most valuable of these resources are potential new members of the community. The Centre is an important source of new membership because it facilitates contact between Gwalan and other Indigenous people who now live on what is claimed as Gwalan land. These Indigenous people from other places may be searching for culturally appropriate ways to make more meaningful connections with that land.

It may seem that being Catholic and having Dreaming might be an impossible contradiction. Clearly Gwalan do not recognise a contradiction. The group routinely includes reference to Baiame in their Catholic rites. One example was a Christening I attended at the Centre, which, although presided over by a Catholic priest, included ceremonies and prayers associated with Baiame. It seems that the political and social value of having Dreaming is equal to the political and social value of being Catholic. Both are indispensible to the survival of the community. Having Dreaming authenticates Aboriginality and Gwalan claims. It also provides important symbolism relating to Gwalan identity. Being Catholic provides valuable material resources, and arguably even more importantly, precious new members without whom the community would have a hard time reproducing itself over time due to its small numbers.

The Burial Tree Ceremony

It had been six weeks since Uncle Sam passed away and the community had done their crying. Because Uncle Sam had been a Vietnam veteran and a high ranking police officer, a state funeral had been performed in the days after his death. The funeral had been attended by some community members, but their attempts to have input into 'Indigenising' the event had been thwarted by officialdom. The only signifiers of the deceased's Aboriginal identity were the little ribbons of red, yellow and black that his sisters wore pinned to their jackets. There had been considerable disgruntlement in the community since that day; many people told me that they thought it was disrespectful that the deceased was not honoured with an 'Aboriginal funeral'. When I asked what constituted an Aboriginal funeral people were quite confused, but the sentiment was perhaps most eloquently expressed by an old man when he said, 'Well, we get to do it our own way'.[13]

Uncle Sam's funeral was taken over by state symbolism because of his status in the broader Australian society. In most cases however, Gwalan can arrange their

---

13   Everett, Fieldnotes, April 2005.

own 'Aboriginal funeral' for deceased community members, within the limits of the law concerning the disposal of the body. Burial Tree Ceremonies, because they do not involve disposal of the body, are autonomous affairs performed in addition to other ceremonies. In Uncle Sam's case, the performance of a Burial Tree Ceremony six weeks after the state funeral gave Gwalan the opportunity to redress what some considered to be state intervention in community business. It also had the effect of affirming group identity by articulating the Aboriginal identity of the deceased and of the community.

It was explained to me that Uncle's spirit had used the time between death and ceremony to revisit all of its favourite people and places in the earthly realm. The ceremony would put an end to the spirit's wandering this world and facilitate its movement into another realm. On a cold winter's morning, I was invited to a site in a National Park west of the city to participate in the Burial Tree Ceremony. This ceremony, it was said, would send Uncle's spirit to the 'sky people'. Sky people, Gwalan tell me, are the spirits of ancestors who, before white people came to Australia, would have inhabited sacred places in Gwalan land. Now that these sites have been colonised by white Australia the spirits of Gwalan ancestors have been forced to relocate to the sky.

It is not possible to drive vehicles close to the site where a number of Burial Trees are situated. These trees have been scarred with designs during earlier Burial Tree Ceremonies. During the ceremony I describe below, a new tree is added to those at the site. When I arrived at the site and crossed a small dry creek bed from the site I had a clear view, however, of the six trees that, at that time, had already been scarred (sadly there are five more scarred trees there now). I also saw an open space (clearing) for camping, and an already burning fire in the middle of the clearing. There were 30 or so Gwalan adults and about 15 children. Adults were engaged in making and drinking tea, preparing food, chatting with each other and generally milling around. Many of the children were busy chasing the numerous Eastern Grey kangaroos which have been introduced to the park, and which constantly haunt the clearing in the hope of finding food.

As I approached the site, I was warmly greeted with the usual jokes and teases that I habitually trade with appropriate people and the more respectful greetings that are reserved for senior people. The general ambience was far from the sombre mood that might be expected of a funeral rite. There was a general air of anticipation if not excitement – something was going to happen.

Gwalan themselves refer to all of their more formal gatherings as ceremony including social gatherings and they also claim that the Burial Tree Ceremony involves ritual acts. These acts include the carving and grouting of the tree trunk. The performance of these acts is considered essential so that the spirits of the recently dead can pass from the earthly realm into the spiritual realm of the 'sky people'. Ritual must surely be understood in essence to be a specifically communicative action – an action that affirms culturally binding meaning and emotion. These acts, as I recount below, are also said, by Gwalan, to achieve other transformations, transitions and confirmations such as the transformation of the tree into an emblem of Gwalan identity as dendroglyph.

The first 'ritual act' constituting the Burial Tree Ceremony for Uncle Sam was the choosing of a tree which would serve as an appropriate focus for the ceremony by a group of elders, both men and women. Burial Trees are always estimated to be older than 200 years and are species known for their longevity. The tree for this particular ceremony was chosen within a grove of trees which exhibit the re-worked scars of earlier Burial Tree Ceremonies. The first Gwalan engraving ceremony occurred 30 years ago. This ritual, some people told me, should be repeated twice a year, but has occurred less frequently in my experience. This may be because there has been at least one death every year in recent years and 'renewal' rituals have been incorporated into 'full blown' ceremonies for new trees. Nevertheless the designs are re-grooved and re-grouted with white ochre paste often enough that the designs in the trees always look reasonably 'fresh'.

Gwalan men were busy removing a large, oval shaped piece of bark from the chosen tree so that the turtle design, which would be carved into the 'flesh' of the tree, would have a 'new', 'clean' space. When I asked a senior man whether the bark's removal would damage the tree, he replied:

> We never hurt trees ... Jest look at them other fellas [trees]
>
> What we done before. They's all lookin' good. I told ya before
>
> We choose these trees 'cause they older'n two hundred years.
>
> More'n whitefellas been 'ere. They been missin' us them oldfella [trees]. They been cryin' for us. Ceremonies.
>
> I tell ya what really hurts these oldfella trees. They been taken away from us – from their own real people. Now we're back an' these oldfellas [trees] need to get that whitefulla stuff off them [bark grown since colonisation].
>
> We gotta clear a space for the old ways again. Got to take off the whitefella bark. It don't hurt 'em.[14]

---

14   Everett, Video, Euroka Clearing, July 2003.

It seems that by removing the bark that 'belongs' to whitefellas, Gwalan 'open up' the tree to make a space for their own stories to be told. They make a symbolic 'clearing' on the tree, in time, in space in which to put their own story.

The National Park where Gwalan perform the Burial Tree Ceremony is regularly visited by groups of international tourists and their local guides who can be confident of sighting wildlife including many bird species, goannas and kangaroos. The Burial Tree Ceremony was in progress when a group of about 20 tourists accompanied by a tour guide unexpectedly encroached on the proceedings. These unwanted and unexpected on-lookers crowded about the tree as the men were carving. Yet, no matter how unwelcome such intrusion on Gwalan practices may be, the tourists were 'entitled' to be there. As part of a National Park, the ceremonial site is 'public place', not Gwalan place. The tour guide, employee of a private tour company and unknown to Gwalan, proceeded to present an authoritative commentary to the tourists explaining (wrongly) that the carved trees delineated a prehistoric space for dance and claimed that Aboriginal ceremony is no longer performed there. In other words, the tour guide denied the existence of Gwalan ceremony at the very moment of its expression.

The dismissive utterances of the tour guide, however, provided the opportunity for a senior Gwalan descendant woman and sister of the deceased to exhibit the ways in which Gwalan performance and Gwalan identity exists as that which is negotiated between Gwalan and non-Gwalan as well as between Gwalan. The Gwalan woman literally took the high ground by standing above the tourists on the high side of a slope. Below is a transcript, taken from a video, of what she said:

> Excuse me. This is not a dance ground. This is a ceremonial ground and you mob are standing in it and watching a Burial Tree Ceremony. This is the place where our people are taken by Baiame to be with the sky people. This is my brother. Over there is my mother. That one up there is me. We are [Gwalan] and we have always had ceremony here. It's jest that yous don't know about it.[15]

The Gwalan woman's words are a political claim to country and to relationships with country and other Gwalan past and present. It was an explanation of the proceedings that included an explanation of beliefs associated with the cult of Baiame, which Gwalan call their Dreaming. The use of Baiame stories in this context provided political linkages to a tradition that claims authentic Aboriginal identity in relations with non-Gwalan. They are, of course, more than that; the link to the cult of Baiame is inextricable from Gwalan ritual practice and from

---

15 Everett, Video, Euroka Clearing, July 2003.

their emergent and emerging group identity. Links between Dreaming, land and authentic identity are made explicit. As the woman's final words reiterate: 'we have always told our stories and performed our ceremonies. 'Yous fellas jes' don't know about them'. The Gwalan woman's claims were a demonstration of how emergent Gwalan identity must, necessarily take shape against and within the very terms of denial that 'outsiders' assert. Gwalan take opportunities to mitigate negative judgments by affirming their identity in response to those negative terms. This was done in this case by asserting the difference between Aboriginal knowledge as Dreaming and western knowledge as denial.

When I asked a number of Gwalan what they thought about the tourists and their intrusion their responses were mainly ambivalent. Most people saw the political necessity of explaining their presence and practices to whites, but no-one I asked was happy about what was considered a rude intrusion. One old lady's poignant response was:

> Whitefellas never see what's in front o' their nose. They's jes' gotta be told. Nothin' else for it. Jes' gotta be told. But it's exhaustin'. Git tired o' tellin' 'em. Why can't they jest leave us be?[16]

Authenticity, tradition, and Dreaming stories

It can be seen from my ethnographic description of the Burial Tree Ceremony that Gwalan have a significant 'authenticity' problem. The main reason for general reluctance to accept the authenticity of Gwalan cultural practices is because it has been widely documented, represented and subsequently believed, in various discourses, that urban Aboriginal traditions, especially urban religious traditions are, today, defunct. Tench and Collins began the depressing tale of the social and religious obliteration of south-eastern Australian Aboriginal societies.[17] It is story that has been picked up more recently by historians including Reynolds, Aplin and Goodall; by sociologists and political scientists such as Broome, Rowley and Jacubowicz; by linguists including Eades, Troy, and Walsh and Yallop; and by economists like Altman and Niewenhuysen.[18] Anthropologists making a similar point have included Stanner, Berndt, Barwick, Reay, Gale, Williams, Rumsey and Sutton, to name a few.[19]

Most accounts of urban Aboriginal practices in every discipline associated with Aboriginal Studies discount the possibility of surviving Aboriginal religious

---

16 Everett, Fieldnotes, Euroka Clearing, July 2003.
17 Tench 1788; Collins 1788.
18 Reynolds 1998, 1989; Aplin 1988; Goodall 1995; Broome 1996; Rowley 1972; Jacubowicz 1994; Eades 1976; Troy 1990, 1993; Walsh and Yallop 1993; Altman and Niewenhuysen 1979.
19 Stanner 1968; Berndt 1962; Barwick 1962: 88; Reay 1964; Gale 1977: 45; Williams 1988; Rumsey 1994; Sutton 2001: 125.

practices in cities. Cowlishaw, for example, argues that to attribute any kind of traditional knowledge to suburban Aboriginal elders is a form of racial essentialism – a false assumption that Aboriginality is somehow 'naturally' imbued with knowledge of ancient traditions.[20] This may indeed be true in some, or even most cases, but is not necessarily always the case and depends very much on what precisely 'counts' when we are talking about tradition and custom.

Owing largely to the crucial importance of being able to demonstrate 'tradition' and 'on-going connections to customs' in land rights and native title claims, some anthropologists and other academics have been testing the waters to see exactly what counts as tradition and on-going connections when they prepare reports for court cases. They have demonstrated that the legislation can be interpreted in different ways. Recent anthropological work in this area argues for recognising specific kinds of continuity in various urban and rural Aboriginal cultural forms that may have been previously discounted because they have changed over time. Among these new approaches are those of Taylor, the more recent work of Beckett, Merlan, and Macdonald, as well as my own work.[21] These newer ethnographies are set against discourses that have allowed Aboriginal tradition to be placed only in past practices which may only be continuous in areas remote from the polluting effects of western civilisation and which are said not to exist in the modernity of western towns and cities.

Do Gwalan have 'Dreaming'? I use the term 'Dreaming' here in a broad political way reflecting a generalised acknowledgement of Aboriginal spirituality, not in any specific sense. I acknowledge that there are many different 'Dreamings', as indeed, there are many different words in Aboriginal languages pertaining to concepts related to 'Dreaming'. I also acknowledge that the term 'Dreaming' is an extremely imprecise translation of immensely complex systems of meaning. Yet, what is important in this context is that Gwalan themselves say they 'have' Dreaming, and that they perform ceremonies and tell stories which are connected with a spiritual world-view that draws from Aboriginal heritage. 'Having Dreaming' also produces particular effects for Gwalan. Ceremonies associated with Dreaming effect particular transformations, transitions and confirmations, and support culturally binding beliefs.

Perhaps as importantly as effecting ritual transformations and affirming identity within the group, 'having Dreaming' is also a primary marker of 'authentic' Aboriginality according to dominant discourses concerning what constitutes 'real' Aboriginal tradition. It cannot be a real Aboriginal painting if it does not have a Dreaming story. It cannot be a real Aboriginal dance if it is not a

---

20   Cowlishaw 2009 (in press): 16.
21   Taylor 2005; Beckett 1996; Merlan 2006; Macdonald 2004; Everett 2009.

Dreaming dance. People are not really Aboriginal unless they 'have' Dreaming stories. So, if 'having Dreaming' contributes to the 'authenticity' of a given group of Aboriginal people, then the interpretation of what counts as Dreaming becomes less an analytical problem than a political one. That is, academic arguments including those of Rumsey, Merlan, Maddock, Turner, and Austin-Broos among others, concerning what, precisely 'counts' as myth and what constitutes history are less important in the context of Gwalan than the political advantage that Gwalan gain from calling their 'stories' Dreaming stories.[22] In other words, if Aboriginal peoples can convince the wider Australian society that they have Dreaming, that is, that they are spiritual, they are thought to be 'authentic'. This is because dominant Australian discourses 'essentialise' Aboriginality and conceptualise it as the binary opposite of westernness. 'We' western thinkers cannot escape our own traditions of thought, which place 'real' Aboriginal people into the category of 'primitive'. Aboriginality is conceptualised as 'spiritual', while westernness is conceptualised as 'material' (or modern). This kind of binary opposition serves to substantiate the identity of Aboriginal peoples for the purposes of native title.

The irony of this is that the Gwalan people I work with know that they cannot win a native title claim under current law because they have tried and failed. But 'we' whites can afford to believe in Gwalan Dreaming precisely because we are not threatened by it. We know that they cannot win a native title claim for the same reason that Gwalan do. The political advantage that Gwalan gain from 'having Dreaming' is that it affirms their claims to identity as difference. Dreaming produces narratives which support claims to distinctive Aboriginal identity because these stories articulate the difference between Gwalan and non-Gwalan. In this way, Gwalan Dreaming affirms Gwalan 'authenticity'.

Of course, claims to authenticity are highly problematic. Even though the category 'authentic' is inherently flawed, power inflected and political because it is always the powerful that impose the category (or withhold it) from the less powerful, it still has the potential to damage legitimate claims and to support dubious ones.[23] The group of Gwalan I work with are fragile, marginalised and powerless, not only in relation to the wider Australian non-Aboriginal society, but also in relation to the other group of Gwalan to which I refer earlier. The other Gwalan group is larger and has the long-term support of a number of senior academics including linguists, archaeologists, biologists and historians who support their claims. These claims, as I have said, are based on evidence produced by western research, which, in turn, supports the careers of the other Gwalan group's academic supporters. The 'primitive', 'inauthentic' representations made by the Gwalan group I work with are regarded, by the

---

22   Rumsey 1994; Merlan 1995; Maddock 1988; Turner 1988; Austin-Broos 1994.
23   Cf Everett 2008: 147.

other group and their supporters, as a threat to the 'authenticity' of all Gwalan. They are consequently denied by the other Gwalan group, and it seems, by just about everyone except those who practise them.

Indeed, the Gwalan stories I recount above defy categorisation. They do not fit into anthropological, historical or mythological analysis. They fail, necessarily, to live up to the criterion demanded to reach the status of myth proper or Dreaming story. Yet they also, necessarily, perform the same kinds of effects. Thus, what is important in my view is that Gwalan call these stories Dreaming stories. Whether this is right or wrong from the point of view of anthropological theory, and whether anthropology can ever understand these stories better by calling them something else, does not affect the cultural and political power of these stories to articulate Gwalan identity.

Conclusion

Gwalan claim that the Burial Tree Ceremony involves acts which are considered essential for the spirits of the recently dead to pass from the earthly realm into the spiritual realm of their ancestors, the 'sky people'. This enacts other transformations, transitions and confirmations including the transformation of the tree into an emblem of Gwalan identity as dendroglyph. Practices and stories related to the cult of Baiame invoke the ancestral spirits of Gwalan land and relationships between Gwalan and non-Gwalan and facilitate the relationships between Gwalan ancestors and Gwalan. As this chapter demonstrates, this is sometimes done before the eyes of those who not only deny the 'authenticity' of the acts and the reality of their effects, but the very presence of ceremony and people performing it.

Histories of extermination, internment, assimilation and self determination of Australian Aboriginal peoples have been well documented. Accounts of ceremonies and various kinds of cultural practices saturate the literatures of various disciplines. In the context of claims to land, courts hear countless representations of Aboriginal traditions, customs and culture. Advertisements, news stories and documentaries constantly present images of Aboriginal people as pristine primitives, troublesome rebels, or tragic wrecks. Aboriginal academics and authors challenge these representations and make their own. Aboriginal artists have gone some way to represent their culture in their own terms. What is less documented and less recognised is that the representations of the majority of Aboriginal people, urban people, are often not recognised or recorded at all.

References

Primary sources

Everett, Fieldnotes, July, September 2003, Euroka Clearing.

Everett, Fieldnotes, April 2005.

Everett, Video, Euroka Clearing, July 2003.

Secondary sources

Altman, J and J Niewenhuysen 1979, *The Economic Status of Australian Aborigines,* Cambridge University Press, Cambridge.

Aplin, Graeme 1988, *A Difficult Infant: Sydney Before Macquarie,* University of New South Wales Press, Sydney.

Austin-Broos, Diane 1994, 'Narratives of the encounter at Ntaria (Aboriginal histories, Aboriginal myths)', *Oceania* 65(2): 131.

Barwick, Diane 1962, 'The self conscious people of Melbourne', in *Aborigines Now,* M Reay (ed), Angus and Robertson, Sydney.

Beckett, Jeremy 1996, 'Against nostalgia: place and memory in Myles Lalor's oral history', *Oceania* 66(4): 312.

Berndt, Catherine 1962, 'Mateship or success: an assimilation dilemma', *Oceania* 33(2): 88.

Berndt, Ronald 1947, 'Wiradjeri magic and clever men', *Oceania* 17: 334.

Broome, Richard 1996, *Historians, Aborigines and Australia*, Allen & Unwin, Sydney.

Cameron, ALP 1885, 'Notes on some tribes of New South Wales', *Journal of the Anthropological Society of Great Britain and Ireland* 14: 364.

Collins, David 1975[1788], *An Account of the Colony in New South Wales Vol. 1,* University of Chicago Press, London.

Cowlishaw, Gillian 2009, *The City's Outback*, University of New South Wales Press, Sydney.

— 2009 (in press), 'Suburban mythology', *The Australian Journal of Anthropology*.

Eades, Diana 1976, *The Dharawahl and Dhurga Languages of New South Wales South Coast*, Australian Institute of Aboriginal Studies, Canberra.

Elkin, AP 1975, *The Aboriginal Australians*, Longmans, London.

Everett, Kristina 2008, 'Too much information: when the burden of trust paralyses representation', in *Indigenous Biography and Autobiography*, Peter Read, Frances Peters-Little and Anna Haebich (eds), Aboriginal History Monograph 17, Aboriginal History Inc, Canberra: 147–157.

— 2009, 'Welcome to Country – not', *Oceania* 79(1): 53–65.

Gale, Fay 1977, 'Aboriginal values in relation to poverty in Adelaide', in *Aborigines and change: Australia in the '70s*, RM Berndt (ed), Australian Institute of Aboriginal Studies, Canberra: 45–52.

Geertz, Clifford 1993, *The Interpretation of Cultures,* Fontana Press, London.

Goodall, Heather 1995, 'New South Wales', in *Contested Ground: Australian Aborigines Under the British Crown*, A McGrath (ed), Allen & Unwin, Melbourne: 62–74.

Howitt, AW 1904, *The Native Tribes of South East Australia,* Macmillan, London.

Jacubowicz, Andrew (ed) 1994, *Racism, Ethnicity and the Media,* Allen & Unwin, St Leonards, New South Wales.

Kolig, Erich 1989, *Dreamtime Politics: Religion, World View and Utopian Thought in Australian Aboriginal Society,* Dietrich Reimer Verlag, Berlin.

Lang 1899, 'Australian gods: a reply', *Folklore* 10(1): 1–46.

Lane, KH 1978, 'Carved trees and initiation ceremonies on the Nambucca River', in *Records of Times Past: Ethnohistorical Essays on the Culture and Ecology of the New England Tribes*, Isabel McBryde (ed), Australian Institute of Aboriginal Studies, Canberra: 222-234.

Macdonald, Gaynor 2004, 'Photos in Wiradjuri biscuit tins: negotiating relatedness and validating colonial histories', *Oceania* 73(4): 225.

Maddock, Kenneth 1982, *The Australian Aborigines: a Portrait of their Society,* Penguin, Ringwood.

— 1988, 'Myth, history and a sense of oneself', in *Past and Present: the Construction of Aboriginality*, Jeremy Beckett (ed), Australian Institute of Aboriginal Studies, Canberra: 42–57.

Manning, J 1882, 'Notes on the Aborigines of New Holland', *Journal and Proceedings of the Royal Society of New South Wales* 16 : 170.

Mathews, RH 1905, *Ethnographical Notes on the Aboriginal Tribes of New South Wales and Victoria*, Government Printer, Sydney.

Merlan, Francesca 1995, 'The regimentation of customary practice: from Northern Territory land claims to Mabo', *The Australian Journal of Anthropology* 6(1-2): 167–183.

— 2006, 'Explorations towards intercultural accounts of socio-cultural reproduction and change', *Oceania* 75(3): 64–83.

Nash, Manning 1989, *The Cauldron of Ethnicity in the Modern World*, University of Chicago Press, Chicago.

Ortner, Sherry 1995, 'Resistance and the problem of ethnographic refusal', *Comparative Studies in Society and History* 37: 173–193.

Povinelli, Elizabeth 2002, *The Cunning of Recognition: Indigenous Alterities and the Making of Australian Multiculturalism*, Duke University Press, Durham and London.

Reay, Marie 1964, *Aborigines Now*, Angus and Robertson, Sydney.

Reynolds, Henry 1989, *Dispossession: Black Australians and White Invaders*, Allen & Unwin, St Leonards, New South Wales.

— 1998, *This Whispering in our Hearts*, Allen & Unwin, St Leonards, New South Wales.

Rowley, CD 1972, *The Destruction of Aboriginal Society*, Penguin, Ringwood.

Rumsey, Alan 1994, 'The dreaming, human agency and inscriptive practice', *Oceania* 65: 116.

Sissons, Jeffery 2005, *First Peoples: Indigenous Cultures and their Futures*, Reaktion Books Ltd, London.

Stanner, WEH 1968, *White Man Got No Dreaming*, Australian National University Press, Canberra.

Sutton, Peter 2001, 'The politics of suffering: Indigenous politics in Australia since the 1970s', *Anthropological Forum* 11: 125.

Swain, Tony 1993, *A Place for Strangers: Towards a History of Australian Aboriginal Being*, Cambridge University Press, Melbourne.

Taylor Luke 2005, 'Manifestations of the mimih', in *The Power of Knowledge: the Resonance of Tradition*, L Taylor, G Ward, G Henderson, R Davis and L Wallis (eds), Aboriginal Studies Press, Canberra: 34–50.

Tench, Watkin 1996[1788], *1788*, T Flannery (ed), The Text Publishing Company, Melbourne.

Troy, Jakelyn 1990, *Australian Aboriginal Contact with the English Language in New South Wales: 1788–1845*, Pacific Linguistics, Australian National University, Canberra.

Walsh, M 1993, 'Language contact in early colonial New South Wales', in *Language and Culture in Aboriginal Australia*, M Walsh and C Yallop (eds), Aboriginal Studies Press, Canberra: 64–76.

— 1993, 'Introduction', in *Language and Culture in Aboriginal Australia*, M Walsh and C Yallop (eds), Aboriginal Studies Press, Canberra: 4–12.

13. *Island Home Country*: working with Aboriginal protocols in a documentary film about colonisation and growing up white in Tasmania

JENI THORNLEY

*Well, how do you become responsible? Well it's simple.
It's like the old traditions where when one Aboriginal group
visited another, they waited at the borderline, the boundary of
that cultural country, until they were invited in.*[1]

*It is through image and fantasy – those orders that figure
transgressively on the borders of history and the unconscious –
that Fanon most profoundly evokes the colonial condition.*[2]

---

1   Everett 2008.
2   Bhabha 1986: xiii.

Fig 1. My white Irish Celtic family, Deddington (meenamatta country), Tasmania c1910

'We have been very happy here in the territory of the Nuenone people. Has any one of us paused to do a reckoning?'[3] In the midst of the 'History Wars' of the early 2000s, these words by historian Cassandra Pybus spoke to me. Born in the late 1940s into an Irish Celtic family, I grew up white in 1950s Tasmania, and knew no Tasmanian Aboriginal people and little of their culture.[4] Now, more than five decades later, it was time to do my own reckoning. I wanted to penetrate the 'silence' around my childhood imaginary of this island, and then connect it, somehow, to the reality of colonisation – the attempted genocide of the Tasmanian Aboriginal people – and that community's resilient and dynamic struggle to re-establish sovereignty of their country.

So, in 2004 I set off to make a documentary film about these issues. As a filmmaker, I knew film offered ways to consider the past other than simple

---

3   Pybus 1991: 7.

4   I was of convict stock, transported for theft and dumped by the British into Gadigal country in 1788. The traditional owners of the Sydney City region are the Cadigal band of Port Jackson. Their land stretches from South Head to Petersham. Sam Watson's comments provided a compass to my learning about country: 'Find out the history of the land on which you are living – just find out. And don't use white academic sources, use Aboriginal sources as your primary sources, and find out whose country your on and find out exactly what happened to that mob. Find out what the dreaming stories are, the dances and songs. Then, when you know, that's the first step on the journey of enlightenment'. Watson 2005.

reliance on the historical record. Film's textual strategies can strongly evoke feeling and emotion, 'affect'. I was mindful of Deleuze's comment: 'if we want to grasp an event we must not show it … but plunge into it, go through all the geological layers that are its internal history'.[5] I eventually finished the film, *Island Home Country* (52 minutes), in 2008. I produced it independently, as part of a Doctorate of Creative Arts degree at the University of Technology, Sydney. ABC Television licensed the film on completion for three broadcasts during 2009–12. Thus, the making of the film was framed by the 'history wars' at the outset and the government's national *Apology to Australia's Indigenous Peoples*, made by Prime Minister Kevin Rudd in February 2008 at its close.

Filming with my own white family and Tasmanian Aboriginal community members involved ethics and protocols.[6] As words on paper these might seem clear and direct, but in practice observing proper protocols became a sometimes ambiguous process involving relationship, dialogue, responsibility, trust, and in some situations, lack of trust. This essay discusses how the ensuing 'ethical encounter' with Aboriginal protocols in the filmmaking process affected the film I finally made.

This 'eerie' silence … of a secret self[7]

In developing this film project, it became necessary to dig deep into how the idea of a peaceful island, both when I was growing up and later, screened out the reality of Britain's colonial race policies. I needed to think about the amnesia that pervaded Tasmania for so long.

Years prior to making *Island Home Country,* I saw an eclectic collection of films produced by post-war European filmmakers which explored Nazism, the trauma of the Holocaust, and its repercussions on national identity.[8] In particular the New German Cinema of the 1960s–1980s erupted into the numbness of post-Holocaust Germany. In *Stranded Objects: Mourning, Memory and Film in Postwar Germany*, Eric Santner draws on Freud's notion that absence is the 'real cause of traumatisation', as he considers the textual strategies these filmmakers developed to 'recuperate affect', to speak into numbness.[9] He also drew on A and M Mitscherlichs' 1975 psychoanalytic study of the repression of memory

---

5   Deleuze 1989: 254–255.

6   Everett 2004: <http://www.arts.tas.gov.au/> is the principal protocol document for this project, along with SBS 2004 (draft) Indigenous Protocols, updated by Janke 2009: <http://www.screenaustralia.gov.au/about_us/pub_indig_protocols.asp> As a DCA at University of Technology Sydney, the project engaged in an approvals process with the UTS Human Research Ethics Committee and Jumbunna, Indigenous House of Learning.

7   Nandy 1999: 308.

8   *Night and Fog* 1955; *Hitler: A Film from Germany* 1977; *Germany Pale Mother* 1980; *Heimat* 1984; *Shoah* 1985.

9   Santner 1990: 155.

of the Holocaust in post-war Germany, a study which laid the groundwork for subsequent research by psychoanalysts, historians and cultural theorists, linking psychoanalytic insights to nation states.[10]

The Mitcherlichs' 'inability to mourn' thesis, I thought, might provide insight into the potential of my film to be a 'work of mourning'. Other scholars have also used the Mitscherlichs' work to help them think about Australian difficulties in coming to terms with the past. Ross Gibson applies it to the repression of 'the bloody past of Australia's colonized frontier', while Bain Attwood suggests that the Australian nation is like Freud's patient who 'resisted having a history'.[11] Felicity Collins and Therese Davis both utilise psychoanalysis to explore 'shock, recognition and trauma' in Australian films 'after *Mabo*'.[12] Their work also contributed to my own process, examining resistance or 'blind spots', in my earlier 'pre-Mabo' documentaries.[13]

Psychoanalysis also played a part in producing *Island Home Country,* not only as a theoretical contribution, but affectively, in my attempts to 'work through' family patterns of madness and recognise in them echoes of Australia's 'Colonial Horror Story'.[14] Perhaps this 'working through' allowed less detritus from my own 'dirty history' to leach into the film's protocols process, or maybe my own family madness generates some kind of porosity, an opening to the colonial nightmare? Such porous private-public-national borders are germane to Aileen Moreton-Robinson's analysis in *Duggaibah or 'Place of Whiteness': Australian Feminists and Race.*[15] She investigates how growing up in uncertain, liminal spaces, or amidst cultural difference, may impact on subjectivity, particularly for those interviewees raised in households where a parent's mental illness dominates daily life. Moreton-Robinson suggests that the capacity 'to deploy different subject positions in order to function' may contribute to a more aware inter-cultural subjectivity.[16] Perhaps, then, my dogged perseverance in the complex inter-cultural space of the film's protocols process was fired in a family member's madness?

Working with Aboriginal protocols

Non-Aboriginal people have made an enormous number of films about Aboriginal people – ethnographic, documentary and fiction film.[17] Many of

---

10   See Najeeb 2002; Rose 2003, 2007; Gilroy 2005; Volkan 2006.
11   Gibson 2002: 50; Attwood 2007: 64.
12   Collins and Davis 2004: 8–9.
13   *Maidens* 1978, *For Love or Money: A History of Women and Work in Australia* 1983.
14   Russell 1999: 40.
15   Moreton-Robinson 2000a: 248–250.
16   Moreton-Robinson 2000a: 249.
17   In 1988 Michael Leigh, filmmaker and film archivist, established that more than 6000 ethnographic films had been made about Aboriginal people since the 1890s, the majority by churches and missions, Leigh

these were made with scant regard for the wishes of the Aboriginal people and communities depicted in them, who increasingly objected. Over time verbal agreements developed into formal written protocols.[18] At the 1978 Ethnographic Film Conference, held at the Australian Institute for Aboriginal Studies (later AIATSIS), Aboriginal participants turned the tide with a statement of demands for participation in film production, training and distribution, the right to self-representation and a proposed code of ethics.[19] Later Marcia Langton referred to Eric Michael's 1986 'Primer on restrictions on picture-taking in traditional areas of Aboriginal Australia' as 'the first clear statement of Aboriginal rules on authority over images and the rights to representation'.[20] Protocols were further developed in 1987 with the Northern Lands Council Protocol, *Guess Who's Coming to Dinner in Arnhem Land?*[21] Since then protocols have become mandatory across filmmaking, art, anthropology, archaeology and sociology and in Indigenous based media organisations. In 2009, after extensive consultations with many communities and organisations across Australia, a new film protocol document *Pathways & Protocols* was published, updating earlier film and television protocols.[22]

Protocols have proved to be complex and contentious, and over the last three decades, various commentators have discussed them. During the 1980s both Marcia Langton[23] and Eric Michaels[24] considered the intricate issues around representation and the defining of 'Aboriginality', with Langton stressing 'intersubjectivity, when both the Aboriginal and the non-Aboriginal are subjects, not objects … Can we decolonise our minds? Probably not. But we can try to find ways to undermine the colonial hegemony'.[25] Recently, Noonuccal-Quandamoopah researcher, Karen Martin, argues for the potential of protocols:

> A different relationship to self as researcher is articulated in the reframing and redefining of research agreements to give greater agency

---

1988: 79. There have been many other kinds of film, both documentary and fiction, by non-Aboriginal and Aboriginal filmmakers. As well as the extensive collection of 6000 video titles and 6,500,000 feet of film at AIATSIS: <http://www.aiatsis.gov.au/collections/collections.html>, the National Film and Sound Archive has 8319 film and television items about Aboriginal people and 7472 Torres Strait Islander items. The ABC has the largest collection of Aboriginal and Torres Strait Islander footage shot since 1959.

18   Bryson documents the evolution of film protocols at the Australian Institute for Aboriginal Studies (AIAS), with Research Officer Nicholas Peterson's 1969 report detailing his verbal agreements with Aboriginal people and the filming of secret ceremonies. Bryson 2002: 44.

19   Bryson 2002: 65.

20   Langton 1994[1986]: xxxi.

21   Mackinolty and Duffy 1987 reprinted in Langton 1993: 91–92.

22   Janke 2009.

23   Langton 1993.

24   Michaels 1994: 21–27.

25   Langton 1993: 32, 8.

to the Aboriginal research participants ... This stronger dialogic and self-reflexive researcher role works towards addressing, if not neutralising, issues of power of researcher over researched.[26]

Jennifer Deger develops the concept of *intercultural regard* in her media collaboration with the Yolngu community in Gapuwiyak.[27] In her critical, self-reflexive analysis of the 'anthropology of indigenous media' she examines her own role, as well as discussing contributions by anthropologists, filmmakers and theorists, including David MacDougall, Eric Michaels and Faye Ginsburg who have worked collaboratively with Aboriginal communities over many years.[28] Others have, however, been more critical. Indigenous filmmaker Frances Peters-Little doubted the use of protocols for film production, suggesting they 'are almost impossible to follow', and Mitchell Rolls sustained a polemical attack on them calling them 'the Messrs Goody-Two-Shoes of Research practices'.[29]

Yet without them, what do critics propose? A return to the previous unregulated practice of anything goes? If the producers of the controversial documentary *The Last Tasmanian* (1978) and Tasmanian Aboriginal communities had negotiated agreed protocols, then the documentary may have been less damaging to the community, or in fact, not made at all. Instead, the film re-enacts what Moreton-Robinson calls 'White possession'.[30] It perpetuates the 'ugly' re-assertion that the British genocide of Tasmanian Aboriginal people was achieved, thus evading any discussion of the ongoing 'politics of Aboriginal sovereignty' in Tasmania.

Contrast this film with *Black Man's Houses* (1992), made 15 years later in Tasmania. Steve Thomas produced the documentary with the Flinders Island Aboriginal Association, and together they make a very different film from *The Last Tasmanian*. During this film's process, the filmmaker and community seem to have negotiated a collaborative, ethical approach to tell the story of Tasmanian Aboriginal continuity and survival from an Islander perspective. Towards the close of the film, the community re-enact a night funeral at Wybalenna, the transit camp on Flinders Island where so many of their 'Old Ones' died. In the slow, dignified movement of the mourners in the firelight, the drum beating out their loss and pain, we can sense how 'texts must be performed to be experienced'.[31] This re-enactment and the naming of each gravesite in the Wybalenna Cemetery turn the genocidal thesis of *The Last Tasmanian* on its head. The repetitive hammering of the grave-stakes into the earth is performative – bringing to consciousness the reality of what happened, at the same time as recuperating

---

26 Martin 2008: 146.
27 Deger 2006: 220.
28 Deger 2006: 34.
29 Peters-Little 2002: 7; Rolls 2003: para 5.
30 Moreton-Robinson 2006: 391.
31 Bruner 1986: 7.

the 'Old Ones' into the present, in a restored genealogy. Not only does *Black Man's Houses* 'recuperate affect' it seems to have been accepted by community members as a good film.

Black Man's Houses shares a structuring method with Claude Lanzmann's documentary on the Holocaust, *Shoah* (1985), where the living survivors bear witness to the past in the present. There were clues in both these films for me, suggesting ways I might develop a documentary film about Tasmania from the position of a white settler-invader. Despite the many films made about Aboriginal people across Australia, I could find few where non-Aboriginal filmmakers have considered their own agency as 'white' or as 'newcomers'. Anthropologist and ethnographic filmmaker Eric Michaels, in his collection of essays, *Bad Aboriginal Art: Tradition, Media, and Technological Horizons,* based on media work with Warlpiri Aboriginal communities of western Central Australia, offers an insightful, theoretical and practice based account of the ethnographer as 'other' and issues around reflexivity.[32] Rolf de Heer, in his documentary, *The Balanda and the Bark Canoes* (2006) and anecdotal essay, 'Personal Reflections on Whiteness and Three Film Projects', examines his own attempts to negotiate the complexities of cross-cultural filmmaking.[33] Although *Balanda's* narrative strategies, including de Heer's narration, consolidate his identity as the strong auteur in control, while the 'other' remains 'other', something of the intricacy or density of the inter-cultural encounter is conveyed.

Aboriginal control

Protocols involve communication, negotiation and relatedness, and may be complex and lengthy. All these features of protocols were present in my own filmmaking process. The principal protocol document for me was *Respecting Cultures, Working with the Tasmanian Aboriginal Community and Aboriginal Artists.*[34] Several Tasmanian Aboriginal community members, who participated in this project, interpreted the protocols in *Respecting Cultures.* During the making of the film from 2004 to 2008, as I began to examine my own unconscious assumptions, I realised I had to let go of my control of the project into a process of negotiation and dialogue. There is an inevitable letting go of any imagined or actual 'script' in documentary filmmaking, but this felt different. The process required me to question my ingrained assumptions.

In hindsight, the protocols *Aboriginal Control* and *Continuing Cultures* in the Tasmanian *Respecting Cultures* document, really pushed me to question my motives, further de-centering my control. I had to learn to wait for negotiations

---

32   Michaels 1994.
33   de Heer 2007.
34   Everett 2004.

to unfold in their own time.[35] In this contested site, as if in the midst of the 'politics of sovereignty',[36] I was no longer able to hold the film in my mind. It was slipping away into quicksand. It was not that it was becoming an Aboriginal film; it was more the challenge of *whose story is being told here, and who is the storyteller*? The protocol process requires time to develop trust in working relationships; it also needs an appropriate film budget, which I did not have.[37] And why should I be trusted? In the colonised-colonising spaces of Tasmania, this was a challenge – and for good reason, as Tasmanian Aboriginal artist Julie Gough so clearly articulates:

> Given our post invasion history of near extinction, Aboriginal people in Tasmania have not been especially keen to share knowledge, information, places, skills, stories with outsiders. We absenced ourselves and were simultaneously removed by the mainstream from everyday Tasmania. We were positioned as doomed or dead – definitely past ... Our shared cross cultural history is an uncomfortable one. Here the grieving and the celebratory avoid each other.[38]

As the years passed by, the reality of the film as a finished work seemed increasingly remote. I sensed a loss of control and a feeling of instability that forced me to shift the gaze further towards myself as 'other'. Fiona Nicoll reflects on a similar process: 'I unlearn what I think I know when I am knocked off my perch ... and hit the ground with a thud ... it does help me to understand Australian race relations *within my skin*, rather than presuming to know them from some point outside it'.[39]

An important moment in the process occurred in 2006 when Julie Gough, whose interview and artworks are in the film, provided a detailed shot-by-shot critique of the film's first edit as part of the protocol, *Communication, Consultation and Consent*.[40] Julie also suggested I return to Tasmania to film with more community members. The following year, after further filming with Tasmanian Aboriginal elders Jim Everett and Aunty Phyllis Pitchford, and revised film edits during

---

35 The *Aboriginal Control* protocol states, 'Projects involving Aboriginal cultural expression must be negotiated with the owner(s) or Aboriginal community-based organisations, as appropriate'. The *Continuing Cultures* protocol recommends that, 'An Aboriginal perspective should be sought on all issues surrounding the project...Projects must acknowledge the owner(s) of the cultural heritage and/or expression and satisfy the Tasmanian Aboriginal community on any concerns about the project. These may include: the aims and outcomes; the methodology – the way it will be done; how the results are to be interpreted – the finished/end result; and how it will benefit the Aboriginal community', Everett 2004: 21–24.

36 Moreton-Robinson 2006: 391.

37 A lengthy protocols process is challenging for any 'no-budget film'. *Island Home Country* took five years requiring a bank loan to complete.

38 Gough 2009.

39 Nicoll 2004: 30.

40 'Sufficient time should be allocated for consultation and responses. Permission needs to be obtained prior to use of stories, images or creations that might infringe on artists' and communities' ownership or copyright', Everett 2004: 22.

2007–08, Everett commented: 'I think the storyline should be more yours – looks too much like our story'.[41] This observation precipitated a turn to my 'white story'. I became the 'unsettled' settler. Finding an embodied visual metaphor to express this white 'other', as well as working through how to 'name' myself, or my family, in speech – in narration – became a challenge.

What to call 'us'? The Tasmanian Aboriginal people I liaised with were direct – 'you can't call yourselves settlers, because you aren't'. Anthropologist WEH Stanner uses the term 'newcomers',[42] while filmmaker Rachel Perkins describes the colonists as 'strangers' in the *First Australians* (2008). Germaine Greer turns to the notion of 'Aboriginality as a nationality' for all Australians: 'I was born in an Aboriginal country, therefore I must be considered Aboriginal'.[43] Other writers have suggested that a move to 'belonging' if grounded in responsibility and shared ethics, may offer a way to be *here* in 'country'.[44] This is clearly different from belonging to one country, one nation. I wondered which of these terms to adopt for myself. Eventually, through dialogue, internal process and film edit process, I opened the film with – *I am white, born on a stolen island* – a reflexive sentence of eight words, which took five years to articulate and texturally create in sound and image. This issue of 'naming' is also posed later in narration: *What to call us? Invaders, settlers, newcomers? I've heard that Aboriginal Australians called us ghosts.*

I am white, born on a stolen island

As I sought a way to turn the film's gaze onto the interior space of my own colonised-colonising mind, the visual metaphor of myself as a *white ghost of Australian history* emerged – a floating-fleeing signifier of the traumatic 'affect' of colonisation. This image partly evolved from sensing a thread to PennyX Saxon's eerie, white ghost soldier in her painting, *The Hand's of White Man's Destruction,* reproduced later in the film.[45]

---

41   Everett, pers comm, 2007.
42   Stanner 1979: 144.
43   Greer 2003: 15.
44   Graham 1999: 107; Read 2000: 2; Rose 2004: 190; Everett 2008.
45   Saxon 2006 (detail from her larger painting).

Fig 2. PennyX Saxon, (detail) *The Hands of White Man's Destruction*, 2006

This British soldier is half man, half boy. His eyes are vacant, glassy, his mouth fallen – as if he is both witness and accomplice to the inexpressible, to 'the silence'. The British adrift, neither here, nor there, yet enacting white possession, coloniser and colonised, imbricated in each other's minds. I sought out descriptions of white people by Aboriginal writers, as if to experience 'whiteness' through their gaze. Re-reading Mudrooroo Narogin's *Dr. Wooreddy's Prescription for Enduring the Ending of the World,* it was as if I was reading a description of Saxon's ghost soldier and by implication, my own ghost-self:

> The ghost's face, round like the moon, though unscarred, shone pink like the shoulder skin of the early morning sun. Sharp, sea-coloured eyes sought to bridge the gap between them. The ghostly eyes showed such an avid interest in him that he evaded those eyes by staring at the strange skin on the ghost's head. From under it, his hair showed rust-coloured like a vein of red ochre in grey rock.[46]

The opening image of the film thus contains several layers, suggesting the ghostly return of the never-faced 'Possession', or perhaps the ancestral ghost, some say Aboriginal people assumed white-fellas to be. These phantoms imply a restless, uncanny presence, provoking the 'edgy, disturbed, questioning' history discussed by historian Greg Dening.[47] This ghost exists in a liminal non-space, a floating signifier of un-settlement. Like Freud's 'uncanny' *unheimliche*, it evokes no-belonging – being an outsider.[48] Isaac Deutscher writes about this outsider as a 'non Jewish-Jew':

> They lived on the margins or in the nooks and crannies of their respective nations. Each of them was in society and yet not in it, of it and yet not of it. It was this that enabled them to rise in thought above their societies, above their nations, above their times and generations, and strike out mentally into wide new horizons and far into the future.[49]

I think about WEH Stanner's 'analysis of the Australian conscience' where he offers Aboriginal perspectives on the 'ugly deeds' of colonising Australians:[50]

46 Narogin 1983: 29–30.
47 Dening 1998: 220.
48 Freud 1953[1919]: 217–256. See also Ken Gelder and Jane Jacobs for a discussion of 'the post-colonial uncanny' and 'ghost stories' in the Australian context: Gelder and Jacobs 1988: 23.
49 Deutscher 1968: 27.
50 Stanner 1979: 188–189.

From their point of view we were men from Mars ... we are 'like sharks',
meaning that we pursue land, money and goods as sharks pursue little
fish; some of it is perhaps very near the bone – as one old man said to
me: 'You are very clever people, very hard people, plenty humbug.'[51]

It is as if Stanner is articulating a 'non-Australian' Australian, like Deutscher's
'non Jewish-Jew' or John Docker's 'strangers amongst the nations'.[52] Martin
Nakata in *Disciplining the Savages, Savaging the Disciplines* takes it further –
outsiders must 'feel what it is like *not* to be a 'knower' of this world'.[53] As any
solidity in knowing slips away, I experience *un-possession* – ghostly unsettlement
– on this dislocated colonial-neo-colonial island.

Facing challenges

One challenge to my white researcher assumptions was Julie Gough's discussion
about my possible use of Bishop Nixon's (c1858) photograph of Tasmanian
Aboriginal Elders at Oyster Cove.[54] What right do I have to use this photograph?
The photograph is stark and confronting. The Elders carry a defiant gaze, as if to
refute Nixon's camera. In the film, I show the photograph to my Aunty. In a later
sequence Gough discusses ethics and the protectiveness the community feels
towards the Elders and inappropriate use of these photographs.[55] I'm between a
rock and a hard place. This is a 'messy text'.[56] I can't control it. I want to make
a film about being a whitey growing up in Tasmania encountering the reality of
colonisation, but I'm clumsy and keep putting my foot in it. More than that, the
process pushes me to examine my assumptions every step of the way.

There are other challenges, too. During the *Colonialism and its Aftermath
Conference* in Hobart in 2004, another moment shakes my edifice. I present the
film's research process in the context of a 'work of mourning'. In the discussion,
I was asked: 'What makes you think you're welcome at our mourning sites?' I
was surprised. Did I deliver the paper with that assumption? Had I assumed
newcomer Australians should somehow be welcomed with open arms at
massacres sites?[57] This direct question really challenged me to think through

51   Stanner 1979: 235.
52   Deutscher 1968; Docker 2001: 262.
53   Nakata 2007: 217.
54   Frances Russell Nixon, the first Anglican Bishop of Tasmania, experimented with the newly invented
glass plate camera, photographing surviving members of the Tasmanian Aboriginal community, who had been
removed from Flinders Island to Oyster Bay, near Hobart in 1847. The photographs are held in the State Library
of Tasmania: <http://images.statelibrary.tas.gov.au/> and have been used to signify competing paradigms of
Tasmanian history, from the 'doomed race' thesis, as in the documentary film *The Last Tasmanian* 1978, and
more recently as an expression of resilience and sovereignty in the documentary series *First Australians* 2008.
55   Gough 2008. See also Gough 2004.
56   Marcus 1994: 567.
57   Ryan's *The Aboriginal Tasmanians* (1981) was an important early influence on my learning about
Aboriginal resistance to Britain's violent possession of Tasmania and the imposition of Martial Law in 1828.

the whole premise of this project. It is as if I assumed that the film, as a 'work of mourning', was a worthwhile activity. I had not considered how this might be presumptuous or invasive to the community. I am reminded of the Aboriginal funeral in *Jindabyne* (2006) when the uninvited whites barge in. I see the comment with fresh insight – we newcomer Australians think we possess the country, the story, and now we want to be in on the mourning sites. Is it an unconscious need for redemption – a case of white 'settlers' trying to make bad settlement history good?

By now, in the film's production process, engaging with protocols is having an intense impact on my childhood memories. The Tasmanian pastoral idyll is breaking down; I understand the land 'grants' and possession of the island as theft in a way I never did as a child. Back then, the island was simply 'home'. In this breakdown of idealised memories, many layers are interacting. There is the impact of the 'revisioning' of Tasmanian history by historians like Lyndall Ryan and Henry Reynolds and their accounts of Tasmanian Aboriginal resistance.[58] Yet, more powerful is the profound body of work by Tasmanian Aboriginal writers, poets and artists that rush in and 'affect' me. Their collective works offer a way of seeing – a philosophical articulation of 'country' – what Everett writes about as a place in the mind, 'beyond the colonial construct'.[59] Ricky Maynard, too, in his photographs and film, *Portrait of a Distant Land,* communicates this sense of place – a genealogy of thousands of years – embedded in the way he places his camera in country.[60]

To a white Tasmanian knowing so little of Tasmanian Aboriginal culture or history, these works are like a lightning bolt on the mind. Since reading Ryan's *The Aboriginal Tasmanians* in 1981 – I had learnt *something* – and it drew me to make this film. Yet, everything seemed indirect, unlike Sam Watson's counsel to 'use Aboriginal sources as your primary sources'.[61] Subsequently, I read Mollie Mallet and Ida West's autobiographies, Aunty Phyllis Pitchford's poetry, Jim Everett's poetry, essays and political writing, and Greg Lehman's essays.[62] I also felt a connection with Julie Gough's art works and essays, PennyX Saxon's art works and Ricky Maynard's photography.[63] Alongside this creative force, were the works of cultural recovery and continuity, documented in *Keeping Culture:Aboriginal Tasmania* – a collection of essays, art, craft, poetry and song – which expressed the resilience of the Tasmanian Aboriginal community culturally and their fundamental relationship to country.[64] Coursing through

58   Ryan 1996[1981]; Reynolds 1999, 1995.
59   Everett 2006a: 92.
60   Maynard 2008.
61   Watson 2005.
62   Mallet 2001; West 1984; Pitchford 2006; Everett 2006a, 2006b, 2006c; Lehman 1996, 2006.
63   Gough 1998, 2004, 2005; Saxon 2006; Maynard 2008.
64   Reynolds 2006.

all this, like a raging river, is the ongoing political activism of the Tasmanian Aboriginal Council (TAC) around land rights, repatriation, compensation, languages and sovereignty. It is when all these layers meet 'protocols' – in dialogue with those Tasmanian Aboriginal community members who are prepared to take this white filmmaker on – that I have to confront the question of Who's telling whose story here, and what is 'my story'?

When Julie Gough made her sustained critique of the film's edit,[65] she showed me images from her installation *Whispering Sands* – haunting, ghostly figures of nineteenth century British collectors of Tasmanian Aboriginal people and culture.[66]

I wondered, am I like one of those collectors? Maybe she is suggesting I am. I feel paranoid now. Was I collecting Aboriginal stories, like filmmaker Chris Marker's 'bounty hunter' in his essay film *Sans Soleil* (1983), yet without the ironic distance that Marker deploys to get himself both in and out of his own film? My unstable feelings around being a white person making this film take a greater hold. I try and work this instability back into the fabric of the film.

My attempt to defer narrative authority in a multi-vocal film had become increasingly difficult with Jim Everett's injunction that I tell my story, not theirs. Later Aunty Phyl suggests, 'just make sure it's your voice speaking, so it's really clear it's a film about you'.[67]

I am thrown further into myself as a white 'other'. Yet in this process, a shift is also taking place – from the project as an imaginary artefact in my own mind, or words on a page – to relationships with people in the present. To be present and grounded in what is happening seems to involve a shift from introspection, to what Aboriginal philosopher and lawyer Irene Watson describes as 'a meditation on discomfort', to considering questions such as the lawfulness of settler Australia.[68] The focus of the project shifts from being a 'mourning work' towards articulating an intense experience of Australia's race relations *within my skin*.[69]

---

65 Gough, pers comm, 2006.
66 Gough 1998.
67 Pitchford, pers comm, 2008.
68 Watson 2007: 30.
69 Nicoll 2004: 30.

Fig 3. Julie Gough, *The Whispering Sands (Ebb Tide)*, 1998

On the borders of history and the unconscious

Literature, art and film ... can be particularly useful to critical race theory because their images, tones, and, textures often perform subtle emotional work that richly engages the nonreflective aspects of white privilege.[70]

The invisibility of whiteness was laid down so deep in my unconscious that it was not until my direct 'engagement with an Indigenous critical gaze' in the film's protocols process, that it was exposed.[71] To dig into unconscious patterns is not easy. Resistance is rife. Cathryn McConaghy discusses the reactions of a class of student teachers to a screening of *Rabbit Proof Fence* (2002).[72] McConaghy explores what happened in the classroom in the context of Freud's 'repetition compulsion' and his notion of 'mourning and melancholia' and 'intergenerational trauma' in both survivors and perpetrators.[73] One third of the students walk out. The screening is intensified by the presence of Veronika B, a Stolen Generation survivor who introduces the film and links it to her own experience. McConaghy observes one non-Indigenous student's response as profoundly ambivalent, an 'excess of trauma ... split between being the accuser and the accused, between reproach of others and self-reproach'. The presence of Veronika B. connects this student 'with her fears about being engulfed by the trauma of Australian existence'.[74]

There is a connection here to Homi Bhabha's discussion of the way Franz Fanon's 'psychoanalytic framework illuminates the 'madness' of racism' – lying unexamined in the psyche.[75] His notion that the imaginary and the performative offer ways to work through the effects of colonial-post-colonial political power, assists my own 'deliberate act of mental decolonisation'.[76]

'Images recuperate affect'[77]

Across time, space, and cultures Julie Gough's *'Transmitting Device'* surfaces.[78]

---

70 Sullivan 2006: 1.
71 Moreton Robinson 2000b: xxiii.
72 McConaghy 2004: 15.
73 Freud 1953[1922], 1953[1917].
74 McConaghy 2004: 18–19.
75 Bhabha 1986: x.
76 Hamilton 1993: 6.
77 Santner 1990: 155.
78 Gough 2005.

Fig 4. Julie Gough, *Transmitting Device*, 2005

This delicate sculpture, constructed from *Lomandra longifolia* and limpet shells made into a headdress, carries echoes of a mourning cap. Beyond words, the artist reaches back and 'transmits', across time, the living presence of her culture. Gough invents a metaphor, an artefact for now and the future: a listening device, a ceremonial container to protect the internal mind of her culture – as sovereign space. It transmits what the 'white possession' tried to annihilate, yet what is always in a continuous process of becoming.

We can sense this force of 'continuous process' in Darlene Mansell's charged words in her interview in the documentary series *First Australians* (2008).[79] Mansell's piercing address, direct to camera: 'There will *never ever* be no Tasmanian Aboriginal people, *never, ever'*, transmits 'affect' way beyond the square frame of any television screen. 'Affect' moves, it touches us. It is mysterious, trembling – alive. Mansell challenges the 'western' screen of denialism, colliding past into present – asserting sovereignty.

Homi Bhabha discusses the 'houses of racial memory' and 'the unspoken, unrepresented pasts that haunt the historical present'.[80] In Tasmania, as I filmed, the past seemed to be present in absence. As I searched the ruins of my own memory, I scrutinised old photographs for clues, like the one of my sister and me in fancy dress:

I'm the pixie, my sister in – 'black face'. Who is she supposed to be and who dreamt up that costume? The photograph carries a 'trace' of the real – a hint of race. Sitting with this photograph – being with it, in duration, a process starts. We may call it 'affect', 'memory shock', or 'aura', whatever, but something is taking place, an invocation to the act of looking – Roland Barthes' 'punctum'.[81] The photograph 'pricks' me. It disturbs, unsettles. As I edit it into the film – there is a sudden rush of memories into the present – yet no space in the film edit for the narrative detail this photograph evokes so intensely from the past.[82]

---

79 Mansell 2008.
80 Bhabha 2007: 18.
81 Barthes 1981: 27.
82 Sitting with particular photographs may precipitate a stream of memory and affect, as in Barthes' response to the photograph of his mother: Barthes 1981: 67–72. See also Annette Kuhn's *Family Secrets*, a study of photographs and the performative nature of remembering: Kuhn 1995: 158.

Fig 5. St Georges Church Fete, Launceston 1954

Memories

There was a fancy dress competition every year at Nana's church. We carried our trays, with the sweets spread out – Turkish delight, pink and white coconut roughs, bright red toffee apples. We walked through the crowd, selling our baskets for 3d each. The string around the tray was rough and chafed my neck. It was hot and noisy in the crowd and the faces were red and their eyes bulgy. They pinched our cheeks between their fingers and said, 'Ila's dear grand-daughters'. My sister had a black sheer stocking over her face with black woollen hair sewn in curly rings. Was she dressed as an Aboriginal person? I think she felt strange wearing it, because through her stocking face she never smiled. The stories of the Tasmanian Aboriginal people were never spoken then – not by a soul. Yet there she was in this costume. And still the silence. The secret. Then she won first prize for best costume and they took the photograph. Everyone was saying smile, but she couldn't. It was hot and my mouth was dry and I felt I might cry. All I wanted was a ginger beer in a bottle with a paper straw. It had a spicy taste, but was nice.

We grew up behind a hedge, keeping history out

Fig 6. The Midlands Tasmania c1952

January 1981. Uncle R said to me, while on a visit to the sheep farm, 'What are you going to Cape Barren for? There's nothing there'. His words were delivered hard, like his weathered, red face. The words were code. *Don't you go digging around. Don't mess with history. Tasmania's white. There are no blacks (left)*. This moment in the sunroom, the pale winter's light filtering through the drawn blinds – the emerald green hedge surrounding the farmhouse like a barricade – is a memory I can touch with my fingers. Aunty is about to push the trolley down the corridor with afternoon tea and cake. Everything hangs suspended in space, adrift, time standing still. The distant, denuded barren hills, the dying sheep farm, the phosphate-layered soil – a dead weight around my neck, strangling me. This moment holds my childhood on the island. Keep your mouth shut. Your mind shut. This is amnesia, forced forgetting. *Woe betide if you break the lock*. Outside in the car, my closely read copy of Lyndall Ryan's just published, *The Aboriginal Tasmanians*. The next day, on Flinders Island, at Wybalenna, sitting with Lyndall, she reads from her book:

> For Flinders Island was now a ration station to a remnant group of people from whom the most able and the most healthy had been removed. Supply ships still failed to arrive at regular intervals, many of the Aborigines still could not stomach salt meat, and on a clear day a number of women would sit on Flagstaff Hill and look across to the north-east coast of Van Diemen's Land ninety kilometres away and lament the loss of their country … At night they performed ceremonial dancing and by day they went hunting for mutton birds and shellfish without … permission.[83]

In that moment my mind opened up to 'the secret' on this island where I was born. I knew that I would try and make a film about the fissure revealed then – this mighty space between past and present. 'Deep history'.[84]

The narcissism of white

Ann Curthoys, in her 1999 article *Expulsion, Exodus and Exile in White Australian Historical Mythology*, prises the scab off the white wound to get a good look at the messy knot of complex emotions layered beneath the surface. She writes about the victim mentality in the white settler community's sense of homeland and the way victimological narratives take form: 'the trauma of expulsion, exodus, and exile obscures empathetic recognition of indigenous perspectives, of the trauma of invasion, institutionalisation, and dispersal'.[85] I read this early on in the film's research phase. It offered ways to think about

83   Ryan 1996[1981]: 196–197.
84   Lehman 2006. See also Dening 1998.
85   Curthoys 1999: 18.

the 'subject position' of the white settler – how being a victim occupied centre stage in the 'white Australian' historical narrative. It resonated, too, with my own family in Tasmania – no one ever talked about Aborigines, and there was an ingrained sense of our own hardship.

If unconscious, the white wound bleeds relentlessly, as Curthoys discusses – in the white nation's foundation myths – the suffering on the land, the white child lost in the bush, the heroic but failed explorers, the wounded soldier, the pain of Gallipoli,[86] and now my own narrative construction – *anxious white filmmaker*.[87] Ghassan Hage intimates, when 'Whiteness is ... a field of accumulating Whiteness', there is a danger.[88] He suggests whiteness reinforces its own 'mastery', perpetuating 'a fantasy of White supremacy'.[89] In narrating my own whiteness as a ghostly performance I am aware of Sara Ahmed's penetrating analysis, that such declarations may be 'unhappy performatives'.[90] Anti-racism, she argues, is not performative, it may simply reproduce white privilege: 'What does such an anxious whiteness do?'[91]

The instability of whiteness is a fluid, uncertain space – uncomfortable – a space where change might happen, or not. It is a space where this privileged, consolidated white colonial invader-settler is pushed into unsettlement, into being strange, into becoming 'other' – to what Judith Butler calls, 'the strange fecundity of that wreckage'.[92] I did not set off to make a film about myself; I wanted originally to examine Tasmanian historical amnesia. Yet the protocols process around *Communication, Consultation, Consent* and *Aboriginal Control* push the film irrevocably to come from my speaking position – whiteness.

Borderline

This place of *being strange* is a place to inhabit, to feel, to listen from and to be speech-less. As Ahmed explores, 'To hear the work of exposure requires that white subjects inhabit the critique, *with its lengthy duration*'.[93] In deconstructing 'possession' another 'possession' is forming – these words on the page now, the film itself – both forms of possession, holding the reins of story. Despite

---

86 Curthoys 1999: 3–13.
87 Katrina Schlunke made this observation in her capacity as co-doctoral supervisor to the project: Schlunke, pers comm, 2008. It helped me link my performance of 'anxious whiteness' to the white victim analysis developed by Curthoys.
88 Hage 1998: 58
89 Hage 1998: 18.
90 Ahmed 2004: para 50.
91 Ahmed 2004: para 6.
92 Butler 2003: 469.
93 Ahmed 2004: para 57.

my attempts to be self-reflexive and explicate something of the negotiated protocols process in the film, Ahmed's questions reverberate. Does the film *'block* hearing'?[94]

I sit and listen to Vernon Ah Kee's passionate critique as he talks the audience through his powerful art works, which deconstruct anthropologist Norman Tindale's colonist gaze.[95]

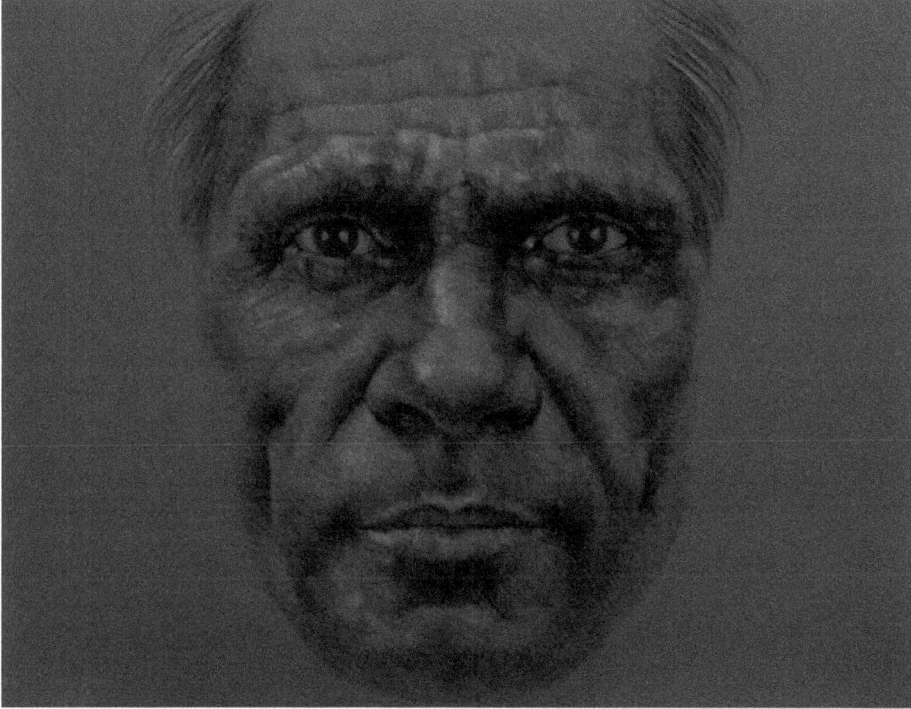

Fig 7. Vernon Ah Kee, George Sibley, 2008

Acrylic, charcoal and crayon on canvas, 180x240cm, Private collection, Brisbane. Courtesy the artist and Milani Gallery, Brisbane

I try to stay open to his rage. Sometimes I close my eyes to hear the ebb and flow in his voice – now gentle, insightful about his art practice – then Ah Kee shifts to another register, anger spilling out against white privilege. To listen and stay open I have to separate out my pain around Dad's angry violence in our family, from Ah Kee's intense feelings around white racist oppression.

94   Ahmed 2004: para 56.
95   Ah Kee 2008a.

we pondered whether black folks and white folks can ever be subjects together if white people remain unable to hear black rage ... A black person unashamed of her rage, using it as a catalyst to develop critical consciousness, to come to full decolonized self actualisation.[96]

At the borderline of becoming 'other' emerges exposure, inside this white skin, learning to listen, stay open and *pass through* 'anxious whiteness'. Ahmed writes about a 'double turn ... for white subjects ... to stay implicated in what they critique ... their role and responsibilities in these histories of racism ... to turn away from themselves and towards others'.[97] In this unsettling process, there is a shift from the personal, the individual – towards community.

Conclusion

Thinking about this *Island Home Country* project, then, *not* as 'some creativity capacity of the mind', as Stephen Muecke puts it, but more as 'the *practice of visiting* country and its associated ethics ... a visitor in Aboriginal country', I am reminded of the 'visiting protocols' I encountered along my way in Tasmania.[98] 'It's simple', says Jim Everett, 'It's like the old traditions where one Aboriginal group visited another, they waited at the borderline, at the boundary of that tribal country until they were invited in'.[99]

In this unsettling space of becoming 'other', while at the same time working through the protocols *Benefit to Community* and *Proper Return*s, there are challenges.[100] The term *reckoning* does not fit this 'double turn'. As in Jacques Derrida's ruminations on 'there shall be no mourning',[101] in 'post Apology' Australia *there shall be no reckoning* – not any time soon – while we newcomers learn to be in what Irene Watson calls, 'a meditation on discomfort'.[102] This is not a passive process. It is about listening, along with responsibilities in the here and now. As 'newcomers', this uncomfortable meditation may move us to face the implications for our actions in the present and the future of 'our' illegal sovereign status.

---

96   bell hooks 1995: 12, 16.
97   Ahmed 2004: para 59.
98   Muecke 2008: 80–81, 84.
99   Everett 2008.
100   A percentage of *Island Home Country*'s returns go to the Tasmanian Aboriginal Land and Sea Council's, Aboriginal Land Management Team. Returns to the Tasmanian Aboriginal artists whose work is in the film were paid from the ABC license fee. The ATOM Study Guide and DVD provide an educational resource to secondary and tertiary sectors and is available at: <http://www.jenithornley.com> and The Education Shop: <http://www.theeducationshop.com.au>
101   Derrida 2001: 211–242.
102   Watson 2007: 30.

Acknowledgments

A heartfelt thanks to Aunty Phyllis Pitchford, Jim Everett, Julie Gough and PennyX Saxon for sharing protocols process with me; Vicki Grieves for lively discussions around history and Indigenous philosophy; a special thanks to UTS doctoral supervisors Sarah Gibson, Katrina Schlunke, Heather Goodall, production supervisor Toula Anastas; and to Judy Spielman, Stephen Ginsborg and my family for their involvement.

References

Ah Kee, V 2008a, 'Framing Race Politics and Identity in the Visual Arts', Jumbunna Indigenous House of Learning Annual Lecture, October 2008, University of Technology Sydney, Sydney.

— 2008b, 'What is an Aborigine', (installation of 12 paintings), Cockatoo Island, 16th Biennale of Sydney.

Ahmed, S 2004, 'Declarations of whiteness: the non-performativity of anti-racism', *Borderlands e-journal* 3: 2, accessed 29 December 2008: <http://www.borderlands.net.au/vol3no2_2004/ahmed_declarations.htm>

Attwood, B 2007, 'The Australian patient: traumatic pasts and the work of history', in *The Geography of Meanings: Psychoanalytic Perspectives on Place, Space, Land and Dislocation,* MT Savio Hooke and S Akhtar (eds), International Psychoanalytical Association, London: 63–78.

Barthes, R 1981, *Camera Lucida: Reflections on Photography,* Farrar, Straus & Giroux, New York.

bell hooks 1995, *Killing Rage: Ending Racism,* Henry Holt & Co, New York.

Bhabha, H 1986, 'Foreword, Remembering Fanon: self, psyche, and the colonial condition', in *Black Skin, White Masks,* F. Fanon, Pluto Press, London: vii–xxxv.

— 2007, *The Location of Culture,* F Fanon, Routledge, London.

Bruner, E 1986, 'Experience and its expressions' in *The Anthropology of Experience,* VW Turner and EM Bruner (eds), University of Illinois Press, Urbana: 3–32.

Bryson, I 2002, *Bringing to Light: A History of Ethnographic Film-Making at AIATSIS,* AIATSIS Press, Canberra.

Butler, J 2003, 'Afterword: After loss, what then?' in *Loss, The Politics of Mourning,* D Eng and D Kazanjian (eds), University of California Press, Berkeley: 467–473.

Curthoys, A 1999, 'Expulsion, exodus and exile in white Australian historical mythology', *Journal of Australian Studies* 61: 1–18.

Collins, F and T Davis 2004, *Australian Cinema After Mabo,* Cambridge University Press, Cambridge.

Colonialism and Its Aftermath: An Interdisciplinary Conference 2004, University of Tasmania, Hobart.

Deger, J 2006, *Shimmering Screens: Making Media in an Aboriginal Community,* Visible Evidence 19, University of Minnesota Press, Minneapolis.

Deleuze, G 1989, *Cinema 2: The Time Image,* University of Minnesota Press, Minneapolis.

Dening, G 1998, *Readings/Writings,* Melbourne University Press, Melbourne.

de Heer, R 2007, 'Personal reflections on Whiteness and three film projects', *Australian Humanities Review* 42, accessed 9 December 2008: <http://www.australianhumanitiesreview.org/archive/Issue-August-September%202007/Deheer.html>

Derrida, J 2001, 'Jean-Francois Lyotard (1924–98) all-out friendship', in *The Work of Mourning,* PA Brault and M Naas (eds), University of Chicago Press, Chicago: 211–241.

Deutscher, I 1968, *The Non-Jewish Jew and Other Essays,* Merlin Press, London.

Docker, J 2001, *1492 Poetics of Diaspora,* Continuum, London.

Everett, Jim 2004, *Respecting Cultures: Working with the Tasmanian Aboriginal Community and Aboriginal Artists,* Aboriginal Advisory Committee, Arts Tasmania, Hobart, available at: <http://www.arts.tas.gov.au/>

— 2006a, 'This is Manalargenna country', in *Keeping Culture: Aboriginal Tasmania,* A Reynolds (ed), National Museum of Australia Press, Canberra: 89–97.

— 2006b, *Meenamatta Water Country Discussion,* with J Kimberley, Bett Gallery, Hobart.

— 2006c, 'Dispossession' in *Memory, Moments and Museums,* M Lake (ed), Melbourne University Press, Melbourne: 215–227.

— 2008, Interview in *Island Home Country* (DVD), Anandi Films, Sydney.

Fanon, F 1986, *Black Skin, White Masks,* Pluto Press, London.

Freud, S 1953[1917], *Mourning and Melancholia,* SE 14, Hogarth Press, London: 243–258.

— 1953[1919], *The Uncanny,* SE 17, Hogarth Press, London: 217–256.

— 1953[1922], *Beyond the Pleasure Principle,* SE 18, Hogarth Press, London: 7–64.

Gelder, K and J Jacobs 1998, *Uncanny Australia: Sacredness and Identity in a Postcolonial Nation,* Melbourne University Press, Melbourne.

Gilroy, P 2005, *Postcolonial Melancholia,* Columbia University Press, New York.

Gibson, R 2002, *Seven Versions of an Australian Badland,* University of Queensland Press, St Lucia, Queensland.

Gough, J 1998, *The Whispering Sands (Ebb Tide)* (installation), Sculpture by the Sea, Eaglehawk Neck Bay, Tasman Peninsula.

— 2004, 'Voices and sources – making art and Tasmanian Aboriginal history', *Colonialism and Its Aftermath, An Interdisciplinary Conference,* University of Tasmania, Hobart.

— 2005, *Transmitting Device* (sculpture), Gallery Gabrielle Pizzi, Melbourne.

— 2008, Interview in *Island Home Country,* (DVD), Anandi Films, Sydney.

— 2009, 'Living in the past. An Aboriginal artist's experience of being Tasmanian', Perspectives on Urban Life: Connections and Reconnections, AIATSIS National Indigenous Studies Conference, Australian National University, Canberra, 29 September–1 October, accessed 21 February 2010: <http://www.aiatsis.gov.au/research/conf2009/papers/R1.2.html>

Graham, M 1999, 'Some thoughts about the philosophical underpinnings of Aboriginal worldviews', *Worldviews: Environment, Culture and Religion* 3: 105–118.

Greer, G 2003, 'Whitefella jump up: The shortest way to nationhood', *Quarterly Essay* 11: 1–78.

Hage, G 1998, *White Nation: Fantasies of White Supremacy in a Multicultural Society,* Pluto Press, Sydney.

Hamilton, A 1993, Foreword, in '*Well, I heard it on the Radio and I saw it on the Television…*', M Langton, Australian Film Commission, Sydney: 5–6.

Janke, T 2009, *Pathways & Protocols: A Filmmaker's Guide to Working with Indigenous People, Culture and Concepts*, Screen Australia, Sydney, available at: <http://www.screenaustralia.gov.au/about_us/pub_indig_protocols.asp>

Khun, A 1995, *Family Secrets: Acts of Memory and Imagination*, Verso, London.

Langton, M 1993, '*Well, I heard it on the Radio and I saw it on the Television…*': *An essay for the Australian Film Commission on the politics and aesthetics of filmmaking by and about Aboriginal people and things*, Australian Film Commission, Sydney.

— 1994[1986], 'Introduction', in *Bad Aboriginal Art, Tradition, Media, and Technological Horizons*, E Michaels, University of Minnesota Press, Minneapolis: xxvii–xxxvi.

Lehman, G 1996, 'Life's quiet companion', *Island* 69: 54–61.

— 2006, 'Beneath the Still Waters: connecting with Tasmania's deep history in Sullivans Cove', *Conversations in the Cove*, Sullivans Cove Waterfront Authority, Hobart: 2–8.

Leigh, M 1988, 'Curiouser and Curiouser', in *Back of Beyond: Discovering Australian Film and Television*, Australian Film Commission, Sydney: 78–89.

McConaghy, C 2004. 'Linda C. and the Terrors of the Rabbit-Proof Fence', *English Studies in Canada* 30(2): 13–20.

Mackinolty, C and Duffy 1987, *Guess Who's Coming to Dinner in Arnhem Land?*, Northern Land Council, Darwin.

Mallet, M 2001, *My Past, their Future: Stories from Cape Barren Island*, Blubber Head Press and Riawunna Centre for Aboriginal Education, Sandy Bay, Tasmania.

Mansell, D 2008, Interview in *First Australians*, Episode 2 (documentary series), Blackfella Films, Sydney.

Marcus, GE 1994, 'What comes (just) after "Post"? The case of ethnography', in *The Handbook of Qualitative Research*, NK Denzin and YS Lincoln (eds), Sage, Thousand Oaks, CA: 563–574.

Martin, K 2008, *Please Knock Before You Enter: Aboriginal regulation of Outsiders and the Implications for Researchers*, Post Pressed, Teneriffe, Queensland.

Maynard, R 2008, *Ricky Maynard: Portrait of a Distant Land* (exhibition of 60 photographs), Museum of Contemporary Art, Sydney.

Michaels, E 1994[1986], *Bad Aboriginal Art: Tradition, Media, and Technological Horizons*, University of Minnesota Press, Minneapolis.

— 1994[1986], 'Primer on restrictions on picture-taking in traditional areas of Aboriginal Australia', in *Bad Aboriginal Art: Tradition, Media, and Technological Horizons*, University of Minnesota Press, Minneapolis: 1–18.

Mitscherlich, A and M 1975, *The Inability to Mourn: Principles of Collective Behaviour,* Tavistock, London.

Moreton-Robinson, A 2000a, 'Duggaibah or "Place of Whiteness": Australian feminists and race', in *Race,Colour and Identity in Australia and New Zealand*, J Docker and G Fischer (eds), University of New South Wales Press, Sydney: 240–255.

— 2000b, *Talkin' Up to the White Woman: Aboriginal Women and Feminism,* University of Queensland Press, Brisbane.

— 2006, 'Towards a new research agenda?: Foucault, Whiteness and Indigenous sovereignty', *Journal of Sociology* 42(4): 383–395.

Muecke, S 2008, 'A chance to hear a Nyigina song', in *Joe in the Andamans: and other Fictocritical Stories,* Local Consumption Papers, Sydney: 80–93.

Najeeb, S 2002, 'Circles in the Dust', *Psychoanalysis Down Under* 2, accessed 21 September 2009: <http://www.psychoanalysisdownunder.com/downunder/backissues/issue2/112/circles_in_dust>

Nakata, M 2007, *Disciplining the Savages, Savaging the Disciplines,* Aboriginal Studies Press, Canberra.

Nandy, A 1999, 'The invisible holocaust and the journey as an exodus: the poisoned village and the stranger city', *Postcolonial Studies* 2(3): 305–329.

Narogin, M (C Johnson) 1983, *Dr. Wooreddy's Prescription for Enduring the Ending of the World,* Hyland House, Melbourne.

Nicoll, F 2004, 'Reconciliation in and out of perspective: white knowing, seeing, curating and being at home in and against Indigenous sovereignty', in *Whitening Race*, A Moreton-Robinson (ed), Aboriginal Studies Press, Canberra: 17–32.

Nixon FR (Bishop) c1858, *Aborigines of Tasmania* (photograph), Allport Library and Museum of Fine Arts, State Library of Tasmania, Hobart.

Peters-Little, F 2002, 'On the impossibility of pleasing everyone: the legitimate role of white filmmakers making black films', *Art Monthly* 149: 5–9.

Pitchford, P 2006, '"Our tally": a day's birdin' through the eyes of a child', in *Keeping Culture: Aboriginal Tasmania,* AJ Reynolds (ed), National Museum of Australia Press, Canberra: 59–67.

Pybus, C 1991, *Community of Thieves,* Minerva, Melbourne.

Read, P 2000, *Belonging: Australians, Place and Aboriginal Ownership,* Cambridge University Press, Cambridge.

Reynolds, AJ (ed) 2006, *Keeping Culture: Aboriginal Tasmania*, National Museum of Australia Press, Canberra.

Reynolds, H 1995, *Fate of a Free People,* Penguin, Melbourne.

— 1999, *Why Weren't We Told? A Personal Search for the Truth about Our History,* Viking, Ringwood, Victoria.

Rolls, M 2003, 'Why I don't want to be an "ethical" researcher: a polemical paper', *Australian Humanities Review,* Jan-March, accessed 29 December 2008: <http://www.australianhumanitiesreview.org/archive/Issue-Jan-2003/rolls1.html>

Rose, DB 2004, *Reports from a Wild Country: Ethics for Decolonisation,* Universiy of New South Wales Press, Sydney.

Rose, J 2003, *On Not Being Able to Sleep: Psychoanalysis and the Modern World,* Princeton University Press, Princeton.

— 2007, *The Last Resistance*, Verso, London.

Rudd, K 2008, 'Apology To Australia's Indigenous Peoples', House of Representatives, Parliament House, Canberra, accessed 13 February 2008: <http//:://www.aph.gov.au/house/Rudd_Speech.pdf>

Russell, C 1999, *Experimental Ethnography: The Work of Film in the Age of Video*, Duke University Press, Durham.

Ryan, L 1996[1981], *The Aboriginal Tasmanians*, Allen & Unwin, St Leonards, New South Wales.

Santner, E 1990, *Stranded Objects: Mourning, Memory, and Film in Postwar Germany*, Cornell University Press, Ithaca.

Saxon, PX 2006, *The Hands of White Man's Destruction* (painting), 'Walk on the Dark Side' (exhibition), School of Fine Arts, University of Newcastle, New South Wales.

Stanner, WEH 1979, *White Man Got No Dreaming: Essays 1938–1973*, Australian National University Press, Canberra.

Sullivan, S 2006, *Revealing Whiteness: The Unconscious Habits of Racial Privilege*, Indiana University Press, Bloomington.

Volkan, V 2006, *Killing in the Name of Identity: A Study of Bloody Conflicts*, Charlottesville, Pitchstone Publishing, Virginia.

Watson, I 2007, 'Settled and unsettled spaces: are we free to roam?', in *Sovereign Subjects: Indigenous Sovereignty Matters*, A Moreton-Robinson (ed), Allen & Unwin, Crows Nest, New South Wales: 15–32.

Watson S 2005, 'The politics of Indigenous resistance in Australia', *3rd Asian Pacific International Solidarity Conference*, 26 March 2005, Sydney.

West, I 1984, *Pride against Prejudice*: *Reminiscences of a Tasmanian Aborigine*, Australian Institute of Aboriginal Studies, Canberra.

Films

The Balanda and the Bark Canoes 2006, M Reynolds, T Nehme, R de Heer, Film Australia, Sydney.

Black Man's Houses 1992, S Thomas, Ronin Films, Canberra.

First Australians 2008, R Perkins and D Dale, Blackfella Films and SBS Australia, Sydney.

For Love or Money: a history of women and work in Australia 1983, M McMurchy, M Oliver, M Nash and J Thornley, Ronin Films, Canberra.

Heimat 1984, E Reitz, Facets Multimedia, Germany.

Hitler, A film from Germany 1977, HJ Syberberg, Germany, Facets Multimedia.

Germany Pale Mother 1980, H Sanders-Brahms, Facets Multimedia, Germany.

Island Home Country 2008, J Thornley, Anandi Films, Sydney and The Education Shop, Victoria.

Jindabyne 2006, R Lawrence, Sony, Australia.

The Last Tasmanian 1978, T Haydon, Ronin Films, Canberra.

Maidens 1978, J Thornley, Anandi Films, Sydney.

Night and Fog 1955, A Resnais, Criterion, France.

Portrait of a Distant Land 2008, M Cummins, Roar Films, Hobart.

Rabbit Proof Fence 2002, P Noyce, Orchard, Australia.

Sans Soleil 1983, C Marker, Criterion, France.

Shoah 1985, C Lanzmann, New Yorker Video, France.

Ten Canoes 2006, R de Heer, Vertigo Productions, Australia.

Part five: the Stolen Generations

14. Reconciliation without history: state crime and state punishment in Chile and Australia

PETER READ

Chile in the 1990s struggled to confront the brutal oppression of the left during the Pinochet years (1973–1990). In the same period, Australia struggled to confront the brutal persecution of its Indigenous minority, especially the Stolen Generations (1788–1970s). My paper asks: did the enquiries into state repression by the two nations encourage or impede national understandings of their pasts? Did they lead to national reconciliation? Do we expect too much of Truth and Reconciliation Commissions?

Re-establishing the republic after state violence: the *via Chilena*

The psychologist Elizabeth Lira and the political scientist Brian Loveman examined a number of formal and informal strategies developed in Chile over two centuries to re-stabilise the nation after a period of state violence, a set of procedures for reconciliation after political cataclysm. The measures are partly constitutional, partly informal, but each helps to allow the government, and the nation, to function again with the approval of a majority of its citizens. The measures include commutation of prison sentences for crimes committed by police and military, the return of exiles sometimes with restitution of property or pension, one-off payments to sufferers on both sides of the recent conflict, and special laws for named individuals for purposes of reparation, and symbolic measures like public memorials. They also include the creation of new political coalitions involving some of the losers in the conflict, redefinition of key actors, parties and worker organisations to carry on under new names, re-incorporation of some of the politically defeated into cabinet, universities or bureaucracy, and constitutional and legal reforms to ratify the re-establishment of the 'Chilean family'. Though few Chileans surviving a coup d'etat or revolution believed that political forgetting was possible, Chileans held it to be necessary periodically to 'start again'. Such attempted reconciliation did not necessarily signify forgiveness, more that certain violent measures taken by the state in a period of crisis were not later to be openly discussed. Measures of reconciliation demanded that officials of a new political regime avert their gaze from certain events; citizens who refused to do so were held to be in bad taste, or worse. Lira and Loveman argue that such measures have been to a point enacted by post-Pinochet left-centre governments as well as in earlier periods.[1]

A key element of this strategy for national survival, then, was what was left unsaid. Two Chilean Commissions, known as the Rettig and the Valech Reports, examined the violence of the Pinochet period.[2] Neither achieved what its supporters hoped for: Rettig examined the history of the political assassinations and the disappeared, Valech the experiences of the tortured. Neither investigated the circumstances leading to Pinochet's coup of September 1973 in any detail. Neither named any but a very few of the perpetrators or violators of human rights, nor discussed the wider historical context in which these events took place. Critics noted similarities with other recent Latin American enquiries into state violence. Argentina's and Guatemala's showed an implied preference for catharsis and forgiveness over punishment.[3] All tended towards the story rather than the explanation, the narrative rather than the forensic. They affirmed as truth the testimony of the victims. They presented history less as a collective conflict of interests or ideas, more as violations of individual human rights beyond the constitutional or legal laws of each country. Resistance, especially collective resistance, was not a major theme of any of the reports. Each tended to avoid the deep structural, racist or economic issues that had led to the violence. They largely eschewed naming any guilty individuals or political parties. They did not explicitly require subsequent governments to exact any punishment except – if the government chose – against a few named individuals. In this way, the privileging and validating of the individual experience of trauma and healing had turned the focus away from the inequities of the social structure.

Despite the non-punitive nature of the recommendations, the Guatemalan and Argentinean governments distanced themselves from the final reports, while for successive centre-left Chilean governments the powerful military has been

---

1   Lira and Loveman 2007: 42–76.
2   The Rettig Report, or the 'Report of the National Commission for Truth and Reconciliation': 'Rettig Report', Wikipedia, <http://en.wikipedia.org/wiki/Rettig_Report>; Valech: National Commission on Political Imprisonment and Torture Report, 2004, 'Valech Report', Wikipedia, <http://en.wikipedia.org/wiki/Valech>
3   The editors of the 2007 special edition of *Radical History Review* criticised *Memory of Silence*, the 12-volume Guatemalan Report of 1991 which followed 34 years of internal conflict and 200,000 dead, for narrowing the narratives through which the past is understood. The editorial claimed that the Report merely individualised violations of human rights and neglected to identify victims also as social actors or activists for social change. Grandin and Klubock 2007: 3–7.

a constant reminder that the internal stability of the country depends on its continuing good will. Pinochet supporters have always maintained that they did nothing wrong: they merely saved the republic from the cancer of communism.[4]

The Chilean people have developed a strategy for punishing those whom the state refuses to name but whose identity is public knowledge. As long as the Chilean state declines to punish the murderers and torturers of the Pinochet regime, runs the popular reasoning, then the people will have to do it. This public spectacle is known as the *funa*, a public denunciation of a former official of the regime who has so far remained unpunished.

The *funa* occurs outside the home or workplace of the accused. In preparation for each such denunciation, the 'Funa Commission of Chile' posts on the web the chosen starting-point, usually a street corner. The exact destination, however, is not divulged. The crowd – it may be 50, it may be many hundreds – assembles with placards, flags and loudhailers. At this point, the destination, perhaps 20 minutes march away, is now revealed. The procession begins. Marching, or ambling, to the dwelling or workplace, the leader shouts

Si no hay justicia… [If there is no justice…]

And the crowd roars in response

Hay funa! [There is *funa*]

While the invocation literally translates 'If there is no justice, there is *funa*' it carries the deeper implication that 'for as long as there is no justice carried out by the state, then there is the *funa* of the people'. Arrived and assembled, the crowd joins in the public denunciation of the named killer or torturer, whom the Chileans call the '*condenado*', the 'condemned'. The *funa* concluded, the participants then disperse.[5]

Such a conclusion may seem rather anti-climactic, but granted the limitations in which successive post-Pinochet Chilean governments move (or choose to move) against notorious Pinochet officials, the *funa* is grounded in a sound sense of the possible. Only a handful of very senior Pinochet officials have been prosecuted and imprisoned by a government whose formal investigations have worked very energetically to name the victims and their sufferings, but refused to move against all but a very few of the most infamous perpetrators.

Funa originated in Argentina, and first were led by the survivors or close family of the disappeared. Some lasted for a week, the '*funistas*' camping outside the dwelling. Argentineans sometimes describe the Chilean version, some of which

---

4   Read and Wyndham 2008: 81.
5   For a detailed description of a *funa* of lesser importance, see Read 2009: 45–51.

last not much more than an hour, as feeble in comparison. Yet some *funa* are not without danger for the participants. Any major *funa* in the Santiago central business district will be closely observed by busloads of police, water cannon and tear gas ready. In August 2007 an Argentinean cameraman covering a *funa* was arrested for 'public disorder', and only released on a promise to leave the country.[6]

Like the measures identified by Lira and Loveman, the *funa* is, perhaps, useful for everyone – the left, the government and the armed forces of the right. The revolutionary Chilean left, once so strong, is now disunited and has nowhere to go. At *funa,* the crowd sings the Internationale, condemns the United States' government for its imprisonment of Cuban political prisoners, and applauds speeches in praise of Chavez. Much fury is expressed over the Bachelet government's social policies, its failure to name the perpetrators of state violence, and its handling of Indigenous issues. The military itself may find the *funa* useful. Since Pinochet's death, and as younger officers continue to assume the higher commands, an attitude may be developing that from now on the old guard will have to look after itself, provided that the army itself is not humiliated by state-driven public trials and prison sentences.

The huge and passionate *funa* of the killer of Victor Jara shows how far angry Chileans are prepared to usurp the role of the state to punish individuals irrespective of official enquiries. A popular left-activist singer-song writer enjoying something of the status and position of Pete Seeger, Jara was killed in the first days after the coup. Ignoring his family's pleas, he insisted on attending what was to have been a function led by Allende at the Technological University of the State on the 11 September 1973. Next day with hundreds of others he was arrested and taken to Estadio Chile – now the Victor Jara Stadium – where he was recognised by a tall, blond Chilean known as '*el principe'*, the prince, who reportedly said, 'This one's for me'. Jara was horribly tortured, especially by *el principe,* for several days before being murdered. But it was not until 2006 that *el principe* was identified as Dimter Bianchi, 'mad Dimter', a senior bureaucrat of a government department working in the Central Business District of Santiago. A massive *funa* was arranged. Such were the grief and fury of the *funistas* (the people who carry out the *funa*) on that day that the film of the *Funa* of Victor Jara can still reduce an audience to shocked silence.[7]

Early in the video, we see the planning taking place, including the crucial question of who amongst the *funistas* will enter the building to ascend to the high-level office where Bianchi will be at work. The procession begins. Camera

---

6   Ernesto Carmona, 'Detención illegal de documentistas en Chile', Argentina Centro de Medios Independientes, 23 August 2007, <http://argentina.indymedia.org/news/2007/08/541832.php>
7   *The Funa of Victor Jara* 2007. Excerpts can be seen on YouTube under this title.

following, some 20 people push their way through. They form a crush so tight that the leader of the *funa*, designated to carry out the formal accusation, cannot squeeze in. He ascends his podium in the passage outside to begin his formal, ten-minute denunciation. Those inside the office surround and jostle Bianchi. Amidst the uproar of shouts and execrations, we see Bianchi at his desk, trying to rise. Perhaps in the commotion, the camera is bumped or loses focus for a few seconds, for next we see him still in his neat trousers, white shirt and tie, now lying on his back on his desk, legs waving in the air like a cockroach. Everywhere the *funistas* are screaming or brandishing huge photographs of Jara. Bianchi tries to shield his face from the faces and the cameras with his arms and hands. In panic, he seizes the nearest poster that a protester is pushing into his face. It is a huge photograph of his victim centimetres from his nose. Someone pushes open the window, possibly to allow the huge crowd waiting below to hear the commotion. Above the tumult, outside in the passageway, another camera follows the cantor calmly reading the official denunciation. No one can hear a word. After 20 minutes the *funistas* leave the building and the cantor, now mounted on his ground-level ladder, repeats the denunciation through a megaphone to the people outside who, their texts at the ready, follow and recite the denunciation word by word. We can now understand better, in the light of the *via chilena*, how *el principe* happened to be working as a senior government bureaucrat in 2000, and, equally, why the crowd was so enraged that Bianchi had not been punished by the state. Of Jara's murder the state enquiries to this point had said very little.

In the widest sense, *funa* may represent a trend in the western world towards civil governance, in which 'the people' act in the name of human rights wherever government is perceived to be quiescent or unwilling. Whistle-blowers, local citizenry and investigative reporters converge on the belief that the defence of human rights is no longer a state responsibility alone. Indeed, a democratic state may sometimes oppose the exercise of certain rights, and for a variety of reasons. The *funa* too is a recognition that in modern civil society justice must sometimes be administered in many forms and by several interest groups, even by individuals. But as we shall see, *funa* is practised best by those citizens whose political culture has prepared them to expect state violence, and state denials of that violence, and to take their own measures of retribution beneath the shadow of military power.

Little by little, we are inching towards setting Australians' confrontation with their own violent past against the events of the South American dictatorship. For while Chileans since 1990 were confronting the executions, tortures and disappearances of the 17 years of Pinochet terror, Australians were grappling with understanding the long persecution of Indigenous people. Indeed, the similarities between the history of these Truth and Reconciliation Commissions, and Australia's recent enquiries are intriguing. The Australian equivalents of the Rettig and Valech Reports were the 1993 Royal Commission into Aboriginal Deaths in Custody, the 1990 Enquiry into the Stolen Generations *Bringing Them Home* and the Final Report of the Council for Aboriginal Reconciliation.[8]

First was the 1987 Royal Commission into Aboriginal Deaths in Custody. The Commission investigated 99 cases of Aboriginal prison or institutional deaths over a ten year period, the individual findings of which were published in separate, and often horrifying, reports. The major five volume findings included recommending fundamental changes in official procedures from prison design to arrest procedures, but no recommendations for further judicial inquiries into the behaviour of individuals.[9] *Bringing Them Home,* the so-called 'Stolen Children' Report of 1997, was carried out by the national Human Rights and Equal Opportunity Commission under a small budget. It took an enormous quantity of mainly oral evidence about how and why the children were removed and their subsequent history in institutions or private homes. The Enquiry produced important recommendations, but again called for no prosecutions. The Council for Aboriginal Reconciliation, established in 1990, received a ten-year brief to present its Recommendations as to how the nation might best reconcile with its Indigenous people. It consisted of some 30 members, half of them Indigenous, and was led throughout its life by an Indigenous Chairperson and a non-Indigenous Vice-Chairperson. While theoretically independent, its meetings were monitored by a government observer, and its funding remained in government hands. It presented its Final Report and Blueprint for the Future at a huge ceremony at the Sydney Opera House in May 2000. While not specifically enjoined to investigate the past, clearly the Council was predicated on the need to ameliorate the historically bad relations between invaders and invaded.

It may be wondered, given the different purposes and methodologies of each, to what extent the three Commissions can be seen as forming a national soul-searching. While it is true that each followed different procedures, the most persuasive consideration is that each addressed historic violence against Aboriginal people over a short or long period. Each was commissioned by less conservative governments after public pressure to reassess a violent past against an identified minority section of the population, and to provide blueprints for the

---

8   Aboriginal Deaths in Custody. The Royal Commission and its Records, <http://www.naa.gov.au/naaresources/Publications/research_guides/pdf/black_deaths.pdf>; *Bringing Them Home*, The Stolen Children's Report (1997), <http://www.hreoc.gov.au/social_justice/bth_report/index.html>

9   The Royal Commission produced a number of reports, including individual reports for each death investigated. These were presented separately as they were completed. The Commission also produced an Interim Report, which was presented on 21 December 1988. The final report, signed on 15 April 1991, made 339 recommendations, mainly concerned with procedures for persons in custody, liaison with Aboriginal groups, police education and improved accessibility to information. Many of the reports are available at: <http://www.austlii.edu.au/au/other/IndigLRes/rciadic/>

future. Each made Final Reports within the same decades as the Latin American experiences. Each set of Commissioners had to decide how to balance individual rights with collective rights, what weight to give to international protocols of human rights, how much to investigate patterns of abuse rather than a series of specific events, how much, in the perceived national interest, to weigh an exposition of past evil against a program of future reform. Though some states had conducted their own inquiries into specific allegations of wrongdoing, the national commissions of the 1980s and 1990s may be said to have been brought about by pressure from informed and articulate *general* criticism of both policies and bureaucratic action. Like Chile's 'Rettig Report', neither the Royal Commission into Black Deaths in Custody nor the *Bringing Them Home* Commissioners recommended prosecutions against any individuals responsible for policy decisions or criminal acts. The fate of all three, so disappointing to their proponents in terms of government response, together form an argument that the three Enquiries were the nearest Australia was able to come, or likely ever to come, to a Truth and Reconciliation Commission into its own historic past.

Again we may pause to ask, granted that the three Australian Enquiries can in some senses be placed together, in what ways are they comparable to investigations into the Pinochet regime. There may indeed be closer analogies. Children of Argentinean 'subversive' parents, for instance, were much more specifically targeted by the military junta than Chile's.[10] Clearly, there were obvious differences between officials removing Aboriginal children and Pinochet's secret police torturing and killing Chilean leftists. On the other hand, I am here discussing the role of the *state,* not its agents, and the malevolent attitude of state governments intent on putting an end to the childrens' Aboriginality for over 100 years is the point at issue, not the individual motives that certain well meaning officials may have had. While comparisons of absolute numbers of deaths and instances of great cruelty between any two nations can be distracting, the violence inflicted upon Aboriginals on the frontier, and later by the police, and the administrative violence visited upon adults on reserves and children in institutions, seem to me to be comparable with the Chilean experience. Surely, it was this awareness of very deep injustices that caused the Labor government to establish the Council for Aboriginal Reconciliation.

Valech's naming of the 30,000 individual tortured Chileans achieved some senses of recognition and validation of the victims' experience. Especially in the context of *Bringing Them Home,* we may ask – was the unearthing of the story of the stolen children cathartic, traumatic, painful or healing for the victims? The consensus seems to be, broadly, healing. Did exploring and presenting some

---

10   The enforced adoptions, sometimes like Australia's policies, were intended to re-socialise the children of murdered mothers by 'responsible' elements of society; see Arditti 1991: 1.

historical truths achieve the national reconciliation that it has failed to do in Chile? I would answer, for the stolen children themselves, yes, but for the wider issue of dispossession, no. To the Recommendations of the Royal Commission into Aboriginal Deaths in Custody the Labor government was sympathetic, but it implemented few of its recommendations. The succeeding conservative government of John Howard distanced itself decisively from *Bringing Them Home* first by refusing to apologise to the Stolen Generations, then acceding to very few of its 64 Recommendations. Howard stated 'I do not believe, and have always strongly rejected, notions of intergenerational guilt'.[11]

As we shall see, Howard did not have much sympathy either for the 2000 Final Report of the Council for Aboriginal Reconciliation.

An implied question for the members of the Council for Aboriginal Reconciliation was, like Chile's: to what extent is a reconciled future contingent upon the acknowledgement of an evil past? Or might such a presentation actually be counter-productive? Might a thorough, and therefore necessarily horrific, exposure of a national past actually work against building the metaphoric bridges that the Council for Aboriginal Reconciliation was recommending to the nation? In short, how much history is necessary, or desirable, for national reconciliation in the future? The answer to that question lies in the view of national history that is accepted by the population. Both the Reconciliation Council and the Black Deaths in Custody Commission avoided strong general condemnation of the national context in which historic evils had occurred. The Stolen Children enquiry labelled the removal policy 'genocide' and opened a hornet's nest.[12]

I propose, then, that apart from the more or less accepted narrative of the Stolen Generations, Australians still have no accepted public discourse of significant wrongdoing towards Aborigines. We may judge the force of my argument by considering the findings of the Canadian Royal Commission into its historical relationship with Indigenous people:

> A careful reading of history shows that Canada was founded on a series of bargains with Aboriginal peoples – bargains this country has never fully honoured. Treaties between Aboriginal and non-Aboriginal governments were agreements to share the land. They were replaced by policies intended to
>
> ...remove Aboriginal people from their homelands
>
> ...suppress Aboriginal nations and their governments

11   Commonwealth Parliamentary Debates, House of Representatives, 30 October 1996: 6158; quoted in Goot and Rowse 2007: 141.
12   For instance, 'Sir Ronald Wilson Should Apologise', <http://www.ipe.net.au/nltr8.html>

...undermine Aboriginal cultures

...stifle Aboriginal identity.[13]

History and the Council for Aboriginal Reconciliation

If the Chilean Commissioners thought it wiser to present just one side of the Pinochet oppression, what of the Reconciliation Council? In truth, while an important self-elected task for the Council was to inform the public, it did not produce much historical material in its ten-year existence.[14] The public seemed to have remained resistant to what it did produce; indeed a whole generation of publications highly critical of settler and government actions, by historians, Indigenous autobiographers, and a mountain of oral history, seemed not to have made much difference outside universities and schools.[15] The television personality and member of the Reconciliation Council Ray Martin recalled that on the very first Council meeting in 1990, each member explained their own life experiences: 'All the whitefellers walked away shocked – we thought, if only the rest of Australia could hear this'.[16] Michelle Grattan concluded from an unenthusiastic response that Australians found it too painful to see through the eyes of victims, to comprehend that their democracy had a serious flaw, that collective responsibility was hard to accept. Both the national education system and the folk culture had written the Indigenous people out of the national story.[17] While Chileans knew far better what had happened to the Allende supporters, many justified their repression as a necessary preemptive strike against a Castro-style dictatorship. Australians like Howard remained several misapprehensions behind, following a fairy-story of fundamentally peaceful interaction between invaders and invaded. Inga Clendinnen asked

> Why construct a single, simple and therefore necessarily false tale and call it Australia's history? Why not a cornucopia of true stories that will tell us what really happened? Why deny the courage of the early settlers? ... What most surely unites Aborigines now – what leads them

---

13   Highlights from the Report of the Royal Commission on Aboriginal Peoples, <http://www.ainc-inac.gc.ca/ap/pubs/rpt/rpt-eng.asp#chp3>

14   Only one of Council's 'Issues Papers' dealt specifically with history. The Issues were: Key Issues Papers; Understanding Country, Improving Relationships Valuing Cultures, Sharing History, Addressing Disadvantage, Responding To Custody Levels, Agreeing On A Document, Controlling Destinies, Addressing The Key Issues For Reconciliation; <http://www.austlii.edu.au/au/other/IndigLRes/car/pubs.html#publish>

15   A reviewer of this paper queried whether I am underestimating the support for the idea of a critical history. I do not think so. Though clearly national perceptions have changed in relation to the stolen children, ethnic origins may play a significant part in perceptions about the original dispossession; I suspect also that historical knowledge is not always sufficiently distinguished by pollsters from opinion. In research amongst Australians of Greek, Ghanean and Chinese origin, especially, I found little sympathy for dispossession and a wider failure to link dispossession with national policy. See Read 1997: 87–96.

16   Ray Martin, quoted in Grattan 2000: 7.

17   Grattan 2000: 38.

to define themselves as Aborigines, whatever the percentage of blood –
is their shared historical experience of dispossession at the hands of the
whites, and that is a history that we, who are their fellow citizens, know
too little about. It happened, but we were looking the other way. They
know it in their bones because it happened to their grandmothers, their
uncle, their brother – because it happened to them.[18]

Clendinnen's powerful rhetoric perhaps put it too simply, but a visit to
Reconciliation Place in Canberra shows how powerful was the drive of
'Reconciliation-without-history' in the Howard years. This site in the heart of
the capital, extending over 100 metres, is described officially as 'a place which
recognizes the importance of understanding the shared history of Indigenous
and non-Indigenous Australians'. There is not much history to be seen, and very
little of that is confrontational. Some of the monuments are simply wordless
rock engravings, while others do not advance beyond 'feel-good' statements
by Aboriginal elders such as Wenten Rubuntja: 'All of us have to live in this
country, look after each other, share this country'.[19] Amidst the platitudes, only
one monument strikes a decisive dissonance. By far the strongest invocation
of 'this is what really happened' (the wording of which does not appear on
the Reconciliation Place website) is the Stolen Generations memorial. It is the
only one actually planned by any of the victims of government policies, and
the only one created independent of government monitoring. Its construction
followed the public display of plans for a bowdlerised memorial to children
deeply insulting to the memory of the victims of the separation policy.[20] Its
stern but heartfelt invocation resounds against the historical vacuity for what
passes as 'Aboriginal reconciliation' in the rest of the memorials.

> We the separated children of Australia would urge you to look through
> our eyes and walk in our footsteps, in order to understand our pain. We
> acknowledge all Australians to acknowledge the truth of our history to
> enable us to move forward together on our journey of healing because it
> is only the truth that will set us all free.[21]

Short on history as it may have been, the Reconciliation Council was by no
means timid in its Blueprint for the Future. Its 2000 Final Declaration included
the proposition 'Our nation must have the courage to own the truth, to heal
the wounds of the past so that we can move on together with ourselves'.

---

18   Clendinnen 2000: 252–253.
19   National Capital Authority nd, <http://www.nationalcapital.gov.au/downloads/visiting/ reconciliation_
place/Reconciliation%20Place_A_lasting_symbol_of_our_shared_journey.pdf>
20   The design implied the removal of Aboriginal children was merely another example of how children are
socialised into an adult world. The memorial was constructed in defiance of strong Aboriginal disapproval
and stands today adjacent to this second, 'counter-stolen generations memorial' quoting testimonies in strong
condemnation of the policy of child removal. See Read 2007: 98–107.
21   'Stolen Generations', Memorial, Reconciliation Place, Canberra.

Though the nature of the 'wounds' was not enunciated, the carefully-worded proposals included 'an agreement or treaty through which unresolved issues of reconciliation might be resolved'.[22] It also courageously proposed, given the political climate, that one part of the nation should formally apologise and express 'its sorrow and sincere regret for the injustices of the past', while the other part accept 'the apologies and forgives'.[23] Howard's government comprehensively rejected all of the six Proposals except number five, which dealt with measures of 'practical reconciliation'. He claimed that the government was already working hard on that.

Criticism from conservatives of the Declaration was expected, but some non-conservatives were unhappy that the Council did not go beyond broad non-specifics like 'building bridges', at the cost of marginalising issues which did not fit, like sovereignty and land rights. Nor, perhaps by reasons of its funding, did the Council criticise the conservative position of the federal government.[24] Nor were the proposals without Indigenous criticism. Heidi Norman found it 'extremely limiting and problematic' that reconciliation came to be linked with the Stolen Generations, and that 'sorry' came to be linked with them; 'the reconciliation movement had embraced the Stolen Generations not only in language but also as an over-riding understanding of Indigenous peoples' unjust treatment'.[25]

Sovereignty and a treaty proposal were not the only casualties. Having 'the courage to own the truth' could mean everything – or nothing. Ready to trip any would-be reconciler was the stumbling block of history, as Aboriginal people understood it, and its relationship to natural, restorative or even transitional justice. The failed Joy Williams and the Cubillo and Gunner cases indicated that none of the perpetrators of acts of inhumanity against them would ever be punished, even after a 2007 Australian Court found for the first time that a removed Aboriginal child was entitled to compensation.[26]

---

22 Council for Aboriginal Reconciliation 2000, Final Report of the Council for Aboriginal Reconciliation, Recommendation 6, <http://www.austlii.edu.au/other/IndigLRes/car/2000/16/text10/htm>. The Council was of course well aware of the government's implacable opposition to a treaty.

23 Council for Aboriginal Reconciliation 2000, 'Australian Declaration Towards Reconciliation', <http://austlii.edu.au/au/other/IndigLRes/car/2000/12/pg3.htm>

24 Gunstone 2005: 18–19.

25 Norman 2002: 13, 16. Heidi Norman had a point. Prime Minister Rudd's 'Apology' speech contained only two words about Aboriginal history generally before beginning on the main theme of separation: 'We reflect on their past mistreatment. We reflect in particular on the mistreatment of those who were stolen generations – this blemished chapter in our nation's history'; 'Rudd's apology to indigenous Australia', The Daily Telegraph, 12 February 2008.

26 The Bruce Trevorrow case: see Penelope Debelle and Jo Chandler, 'Stolen generation payout', The Age, 1 August 2007. The South Australian government proposes to appeal the amount of compensation, but not the factual findings of the Court.

Does the truth, as the Stolen Generations memorial asserted, set us all free? Even if the world has agreed that there should be no more Nurembergs, then Truth Commissions that identify pain but not perpetrator, act but not issue, may lay false trails towards future reconciliation. The historian Mary Nolan, discussing Truth and Reconciliation Commissions generally, asked, what kinds of truth can such enquiries produce. Is truth justice – or is it an *alternative* to judges, forensic courts and punishments.[27] What priority will Commissioners who are asked both to investigate the past, and to make recommendations about the future, allot to reparations to those injured, as it were, last year, compared to ameliorating the structural or attitudinal inequalities, of next year? At best, Truth Commissions may merely reduce the number of lies in circulation; they will never cleanse the nation.[28]

We can begin to see how the *Bringing Them Home* Commissioners, anxious to acknowledge past injustice, produced an official and (to some) irrefutable depiction of a terrible past, but one which perhaps necessarily depoliticised and decontextualised the historical circumstances and hence did not advance an understanding of the nation's history beyond cataloguing the types of abuse and identifying bad policy and cruel agents. By contrast historians well understand that the repression of Aboriginal people since 1788 may be explained in very wide contexts indeed – as a product of human nature, the imperatives of imperialism and colonialism, or the inevitable clash between agrarian and hunting economies. Other explanations might include the exigencies of an unyielding environment, the excesses of venture capitalism, masculinity, social elites, ideological movements, political parties, and, finally, of individuals acting malevolently on behalf of or independently of government. These all may be valuable contextual truths of one kind or another, but to an Aboriginal person the hard fact remains, 'My father was shot dead by a white man', or 'I was taken screaming from my mother, and put in a home and I have never recovered from the trauma. Why don't you admit that and say you're sorry?'

Herein lies the tricky nexus faced by all Truth and Reconciliation commissions, between doing justice to victims of great evil and the compiling of a wider history to which contextualising historians can assent. We can begin to see the utility of the *via chilena*, in enacting measures of individual and collective reparation without the state's necessary admitting why the measures are needed. Post-dictatorship Chile has achieved something close to what many had thought to be the minimum goal, that is, conciliation with neither reconciliation nor serious punishment of the guilty parties. The country is again governed by assent. Democracy of a kind has been restored. A few of the most notoriously guilty have been punished by one means or another. Most of the survivors and

---

27 Hayner 2002; Nolan 2007: 145–146.
28 Nolan 2007: 146.

their families have received some kind of compensation. The ceremony of the *funa* also clearly belongs to those forms of 'people's reconciliation' which makes the victims of state violence, while not openly challenging state authority or disrupting public order very much, feel that they have exacted significant justice.

A *funa* in Australia?

Yet the kinds of truths to be uncovered, any proposed punishment, and any restitution to the injured, in the last resort depend on the political culture of a particular state. Howard's sentiments perhaps reflected those of the wider Australian nation when he said,

> I do not believe it is accurate or fair to portray Australia's history since 1788 as little more than a disgraceful record of imperialism, exploitation and racism. Such a portrayal is a gross distortion and deliberately neglects the overall story of great Australian achievement that is there in our history to be told'.[29]

That is the political culture into which fell *Bringing Them Home* and the Reconciliation Council's *Australian Declaration Towards Reconciliation*.[30] It is now clear that the hundreds of books and thousands of articles and tens of thousands of hours of oral history have been insufficient to steer the nation away from perhaps its most deeply ingrained conviction that 'we couldn't have been all that bad'. Only the older Aborigines who 'know it in their bones' and the bush workers, historians, linguists and anthropologists who understand it in their hearts, know just how terrible has been the early – and continuing – history of the Indigenous people of Australia at the hands of the invaders.

Such a comprehensive rejection of *Bringing Them Home* and the Reconciliation Council's Final Report by a conservative government might have sponsored, as it did in Chile, a series of *funas* directed against individuals for committing crimes or acts of inhumanity or against government ministers for failing to punish them. Yet that seemed barely possible in an Australian context. The first obstacle, as we have seen, was the somewhat self-serving historical narrative accepted by the

---

29 John Howard, 'Practical Reconciliation', quoted in Grattan 2000, 88–90. The furthest that Howard moved towards acknowledgement of Indigenous injustice was 'And yet it is not possible, it is not possible for any of us, for any of us, to reflect upon the desirability of moving forward without acknowledging the impact that European civilization had on the people of this country and on the culture of the indigenous people. [We should] acknowledge the tragedies and sadness and the pain and the hurt and the cruelty of the past. To accept the ongoing trauma of that.'

30 Council for Aboriginal Reconciliation 2000.

nation's citizens. Many Australians remain profoundly uninformed, unmoved or uninterested in the iniquities of the Aboriginal past, and certainly unprepared to accept a national narrative such as Canada's.

Secondly, Australian political culture was against it. The traditional Australian mechanisms of balancing competing interests have not anticipated reconciling deep-seated racial injustice. Unlike South Africa, no continuing Commission or Court exists to enquire into how and why Aboriginal people lost their land.[31] The Racial Discrimination Act investigates uncontextualised cases brought by an individual against another individual. Australian mechanisms for public stability such as the former Wage Tribunal and Arbitration Court and Howard's Australian Workplace Agreements were developed out of British notions that the elements to be reconciled in society were those of capital and labour, worker and boss, not 'sectional' interests such as women's and Indigenous rights. Australian freedoms are the free speech of an individual, parliamentary privilege, and an impartial Governor General, or the collective balance between claims of state and federal government, or interest-based political parties. Historically these mechanisms have protected the nation well against the tensions they were intended to address.

Measures to protect Indigenous collective interests have been grossly inadequate, decisively unable to protect their interests, because the cultural legacy of the British *did not anticipate that such divisions would ever arise in a British society and therefore would not need to be redressed*. Chileans expect civil strife and the need for reparations, they utilise their established measures to re-stabilise the nation. By contrast, Australian governments have never admitted the wrongs they had inflicted on the Aborigines. They squirmed at the findings of Commissions or the High Court, and in the absence of established mechanisms, enacted few measures to confront what seemed to be irrefutable collective wrongs. Prime Minister Rudd apologised handsomely to the Stolen Generations but unaccountably offered no further measures of reparation.[32] Many Native Title claims, while stoking bitter inter-family Aboriginal rivalries, remain mired in legal difficulties almost the equal of Jarndyce and Jarndyce in Charles Dickens' *Bleak House*. Aboriginal people enjoy very few of the ad-hoc Chilean measures informally and formally to achieve a *modus vivendi* after great trauma.[33]

---

31 See also Reynolds 2000: 56–57.
32 Again, Rudd's failure to consider such measures stands in strong contrast to measures adopted by the Canadian government, based on Boven 1996: 2.
33 One of the few is the Indigenous Land Fund, which restores land to Aboriginal groups not through appropriation but by purchase from existing owners. It is close as Australians have come to the *via chilena*'s 'one-off payments to sufferers on both sides of the recent conflict'. Other Chilean measures of conciliation include a memorial to a policeman killed by anti-Pinochet forces, state sponsored memorials to the disappeared at the former Santiago prisons of Villa Grimaldi, Jose Domingo Cañas and Londres 38, and whole-of-life pensions paid to families of the disappeared.

Could Australians ever adopt that other interesting measure of the *via chilena* – the *funa*? The most spectacular expression of public disapproval of the government's position in the decade occurred as the Council of Reconciliation presented its Final Report in Sydney in May 2000. Australia's most senior Aboriginal public servant, Charles Perkins, sacked some years earlier from the Aboriginal Affairs Ministry, shouted at the Prime Minister in the packed Sydney Opera House, 'Say sorry you bastard!' Next day perhaps 300,000 people walked across the Sydney Harbour Bridge as a declaration of support for the Indigenous cause while a skywriter wrote the enormous letters of SORRY above them.[34] The invitation had not been not cast as a castigation of the Prime Minister.[35] Yet many saw it as an opportunity to punish him, for as the Chileans put it, 'as long as there is no justice carried out by the state, then there is the *funa* of the people'. While the Prime Minister was not stretched on his back like a cockroach, there was no doubting the intention or the intensity of the public denunciation. Perhaps Australia had achieved its first *funa*.

Chile had made its gestures towards reconciliation, and perhaps realists could have expected no better. Some Australians had higher hopes, but were disappointed. Yet reconciliation is more than present time. A less tense meeting of minds may well be possible in a generation or two in Chile when memories fade and records newly unsealed reveal how grandchildren of left and right may join hands to mourn together a hateful past. That can't be done without oral and historical records made as exhaustively and as fearlessly as possible shortly after the event. Thus Australians movingly reunited in 2000 at the site of the 1838 Myall Creek Massacre because plentiful records were collected at the time for the trial of the perpetrators. Many more Aborigines were killed at Waterloo Creek not far away in place or time, but because no proper investigation was carried, no reconciliation has ever, and probably never will, take place.[36]

Exhaustive historical enquiries are indeed essential both for the living victims of state violence and generations of the future who wish to reconcile. Perhaps we should not expect too much of them in the present.

Acknowledgements

I am grateful to Dr Marivic Wyndham for valuable comments on a draft of this paper.

---

34 See *Sydney Morning Herald* and *The Australian*, 27 May 2000; Gadigal Information Service, Aboriginal Corporation, 'Bridge Walk', <http://www.gadigal.org.au/GadigalInfo/Bridge_Walk.aspx?Id=6>

35 'On Sunday May 28 [2000] you are invited to join thousands of Australians on an Historic People's Walk for Reconciliation across the Sydney Harbour Bridge': 'Harbour Bridge Walk', pamphlet, Council for Aboriginal Reconciliation collection, AIATSIS.

36 Indeed, Aboriginal communities of the north-west of New South Wales rarely speak of it, and young people seem unaware of it; Serene Fernando, pers comm, 2009.

References

Primary sources

Harbour Bridge Walk, pamphlet, in Council for Aboriginal Reconciliation collection, Australian Institute of Aboriginal and Torres Strait Islander Studies, Canberra.

van Boven, T 1996, Revised set of basic principles and guidelines on the right to reparation for victims of gross violations of human rights and humanitarian law prepared by Mr. Theo van Boven pursuant to Sub-Commission decision 1995/117, U.N. Doc. E/CN.4/Sub.2/1996/17, 24 May 1996.

Newspapers

The Australian

Sydney Morning Herald

Secondary Sources

Arditti, Rita 1991, *Searching for Life*, University of California Press, Berkeley.

Australian Human Rights Commission, *Bringing Them Home*, The Stolen Children's Report (1997), accessed 23 May 2010: <http://www.hreoc.gov.au/social_justice/bth_report/index.html>

Carmona, Ernesto 2007, 'Detencion illegal de documentistas en Chile', Argentina Centro de Medios Independientes, 23 August 2007, accessed 23 May 2010: <http://argentina.indymedia.org/news/2007/08/541832.php>

Clendinnen, Inga 2000, 'True Stories and What We Make of Them', in *Essays on Australian Reconciliation*, Michelle Grattan (ed), Black Inc, Melbourne: 242–253.

Commonwealth Parliamentary Debates, House of Representatives, 30 October 1996: 6158.

Council for Aboriginal Reconciliation 2000, 'Australian Declaration Towards Reconciliation', Corroboree 2000: Towards Reconciliation, accessed 23 April 2010: <http://austlii.edu.au/au/other/IndigLRes/car/2000/12/pg3.htm>

Council for Aboriginal Reconciliation 2000, 'Final Report of the Council for Aboriginal Reconciliation', Recommendation 6, accessed 20 April 2010: <http://www.austlii.edu.au/other/IndigLRes/car/2000/16/text10/htm>

Council for Aboriginal Reconciliation Archive, Publications, Key 'Issues' papers, AustLII, accessed 20 April 2010: <http://www.austlii.edu.au/au/other/IndigLRes/car/pubs.html#publish>

Debelle, Penelope and Jo Chandler, 'Stolen Generation payout', *The Age*, 1 August 2007.

Gadigal Information Service, Aboriginal Corporation, 'Bridge Walk', May 2000, accessed 23 April 2010: <http://www.gadigal.org.au/GadigalInfo/Bridge_Walk.aspx?Id=6>

Goot, Murray and Tim Rowse 2007, *Divided Nation*, Melbourne University Press, Melbourne.

Grandin, Greg and Thomas Miller Klubock 2007, 'Editorial introduction', *Radical History Review*, 97, Winter: 3–7.

Grattan, Michelle (ed) 2000, *Essays on Australian Reconciliation*, Black Inc, Melbourne.

— 2000, 'Public Opinion on Reconciliation', in *Essays on Australian Reconciliation*, Michelle Grattan (ed), Black Inc, Melbourne: 33–54.

Gunstone, A 2005, 'Unfinished Business: the Australian Reconciliation Process from 1991 to 2000', *Journal of Australian Indigenous Issues* 8(September-December): 16–32.

Hayner, Priscilla 2002, *Unspeakable Truths. Facing the Challenges of Truth Commissions*, Routledge, New York.

Indigenous Law Resources: reconciliation and Social Justice Library, Royal Commission into Aboriginal Deaths in Custody, AustLII, 29 April 1998, accessed 23 May 2010: <www.austlii.edu.au/au/other/IndigLRes/rciadic/>

Lira, Elizabeth and Brian Loveman 2007, 'Truth, justice, reconciliation and impunity as historical themes: Chile, 1814–2006', *Radical History Review* 97: 42–76.

Nagle, Peter and Richard Summerrell 2002, *Aboriginal Deaths in Custody, The Royal Commission and its Records, 1987–91*, Research Guide no 2, National Archives of Australia, Canberra, accessed 23 May 2010: <http://www.naa.gov.au/naaresources/Publications/research_guides/pdf/black_deaths.pdf>

National Capital Authority nd, 'Reconciliation Place: A lasting symbol of our Shared Journey', National Capital Authority, Department of Families, Community Services and Indigenous Affairs, Canberra, accessed 23 May 2010:

<http://www.nationalcapital.gov.au/downloads/visiting/reconciliation_place/Reconciliation%20Place_A_lasting_symbol_of_our_shared_journey.pdf>

Nolan, Mary, 2007 'The elusive pursuit of truth and justice', *Radical History Review* 97: 143–154.

Norman, Heidi 2002, 'An examination of the limitations of Reconciliation as a framework for Aboriginal social policy development', *Journal of Australian Indigenous Issues* 5(2): 10–17.

Read, Peter 1997, 'Pain, yes, racism, no. The response of non-British Australians to Indigenous land rights', in *The Resurgence of Racism*, G Grey and K Winter (eds), Monash Publications in History, 24, Monash University Press, Melbourne: 87–96.

— 2007, 'The Truth that Will Set Us All Free: National Reconciliation, *Oral History* 35(1): 98–107.

— 2009, 'Following the *Funa*: punishing the state in Chile', *Arena Journal* 32: 45–51.

— and Marivic Wyndham 2008, 'Putting site back into trauma studies: a study of five detention and torture centres in Santiago, Chile', *Life Writing* 5(1): 79–96.

'Rettig Report', Wikipedia The Free Encyclopedia, 22 December 2009, accessed 23 April 2010: <http://en.wikipedia.org/wiki/Rettig_Report>

Reynolds, Henry 2000, 'A Crossroads of Conscience', in *Essays on Australian Reconciliation*, Michelle Grattan (ed), Black Inc, Melbourne: 53–64.

Royal Commission on Aboriginal Peoples 1996, *People to People, Nation to Nation: Highlights from the Report of the Royal Commission on Aboriginal Peoples*, Indian and Northern Affairs Canada, 11 March 2008, <http://www.ainc-inac.gc.ca/ap/pubs/rpt/rpt-eng.asp#chp3>

'Rudd's apology to Indigenous Australia', *The Daily Telegraph*, 12 February 2008.

'Sir Ronald Wilson Should Apologise', accessed 23 May 2010: <http://www.ipe.net.au/nltr8.html>

The Funa of Victor Jara, 2007, video, Nèlida D Ruiz de los Paños and Christian R Villablanca (dirs), Parallel 40 and Televisió de Catalunya, Spain.

15. Overheard – conversations of a museum curator

JAY ARTHUR, WITH BARBARA PAULSON AND TROY PICKWICK

I am a curator at the National Museum of Australia, a social history museum that opened in 2001. I work in the Aboriginal and Torres Strait Islander Program. One of my tasks in 2007 was to re-vamp an older exhibit on one of the key threads in Indigenous history, the removal of Aboriginal children from their communities. The exhibit includes the story of Link-Up, the organisation that reunites Aboriginal families dismembered by the policies of child removal. In this chapter, I track this task from a curatorial perspective, outlining some of the questions I have faced over the past three years.[1]

I locate myself on one side of the historical fracture that I see running through any episode of Australian history – that of the colonisation of Aboriginal Australia. I am on the colonising side of that fracture and my clients, whose story I am telling, are on the other. So I always understand my task as *telling someone else's story*. I did not have this 'location' when I was working in the environmental history section of the Museum.

What is an 'Aboriginal object'?

As a museum curator, my working premise is that objects 'hold' history. Objects that have been part of a human experience or event are able to communicate something of that experience to us; by preserving and displaying these objects, we make a connection with this event or experience.

The focus of the first version of the Stolen Generations exhibit had been a moving and powerful artwork centred on the original gates from the Bomaderry Aboriginal Children's Home. This item was due to be returned. I needed new objects for the exhibit.

---

1   Readers should think of this article as a primary source, rather than as a compendium of contemporary theory of museology.

The Museum, however, had very few relevant objects that I could use. The majority of its Indigenous collection consists firstly of traditional artefacts and secondly of artworks, particularly bark paintings, of which it has the most extensive collection in the world. My other area of interest as a curator is the post-contact history of Aboriginal people's lives in missions, reserves, settlements, and camps. Again, the Museum has some artworks that tell this story – such as works by Elaine Russell and Lin Onus – and some material belonging to former missionaries, but very little else. The Museum has very little of the material culture that arises from the ways the majority of Aboriginal people in Australia spent the greater part of the twentieth century.

My search for new objects, both for the Stolen Generations exhibit and for other exhibits, led me to question how we traditionally define what constitutes an Aboriginal object. I visited a central Queensland Aboriginal township with fellow curator and Munnuntjarli-Gungarri woman, Barbara Paulson. When we talk to the local community about collecting objects that would tell the story of their community within the Museum, people immediately began to bring out painted boomerangs, clapsticks, and children's art in the style of Arnhem Land rock art. They apologise for having so little to show. Yet lying in the grass in the local sportsground were two giant stew pots, probably left over from the coastal whaling industry. Once they had been used to feed the whole community. These stewpots told the story of that period of incarceration – both the negative aspects of repression, police-state policies – and the positive of community bonds that existed despite the repression, and partly because of it. Yet the community was not interested in giving one of these stewpots to the Museum – for them it was both their object and not an Aboriginal object.

The notion of an Aboriginal object is also challenged and expanded by one of the other objects in the Museum's collection – two sets of seats from the old Ray-Mond Theatre, Bowraville, northern New South Wales that have recently come into the Museum's collection. One set of five is wooden; the other set of three faded red plush. The Ray-Mond theatre, like many other country cinemas, was segregated until it closed in 1965. The wooden seats were for the Aboriginal patrons; the plush seats for everybody else. Aboriginal patrons entered through a special door after the film had begun. This theatre was one of those targeted by the Freedom Ride in 1965. These seats by their physical structure and their implicit relationship, side by side, tell the story of segregation in Australia at that time.

As a curator, and looking at what is in its collection, I wonder if the Museum had unknowingly taken on the construction held by the wider community, both Aboriginal and non-Aboriginal, that only certain kinds of objects are 'Aboriginal objects'. Objects that are not visually immediately identifiable as 'Indigenous' have not been as extensively collected as those that are.

Fig 1. Plush seats from Ray-Mond Theatre, Bowraville

National Museum of Australia

Barbara Paulson and I talk about the Aboriginal attitude to mundane (as opposed to sacred) objects. Barbara sees how Aboriginal communities often perceive everyday objects differently. An object such as a spear or a football jerscy is usually not valuable *in itself*. An object is part of a complex web of human relationships and it is only its continued existence within that web of relationships that gives it any meaning. Who is using it now? Who gave it to that person? Who might that person pass it on to? Who knows how to make it? So far so good, but at this point the cultures diverge. Take a 'community' away from the object's *continuing* interaction with people and the object becomes meaningless. Meaning does not attach to an object; meaning is shone upon it in a series of projections by its temporal situation within those relationships. As a curator, I take away that meaning by removing it from that continuing relation.

Christine Hansen, another curator at the Museum and doctoral student, found the same thing. For her thesis, she chose to work with a south-eastern Aboriginal community, to make a collection of objects so that their story could be told in a Museum exhibit. The response of the community was quite different from the one she expected. For that community, objects did not hold history.

Objects move in and out of their lives, but they do not accrete meaning through that process. Their history was held in their stories and photographs. However, Christine also found that the community really wanted to have their story told in the Museum and they, like the central Queensland community Barbara and I visited, were prepared to act on her cultural assumptions and to provide objects and artefacts for the Museum. They were prepared to tell their story in the 'language' of the Museum: that is, the language of objects as history.

If this is how Aboriginal people often see objects, how do they see the Museum?

Working with Indigenous communities presents a cultural complexity that challenges my assumptions and which I confront in my work. I ask Troy Pickwick, another Indigenous curator, about the Aboriginal response to museums and he replies

> Aboriginal people – they look at the Museum and they think 'Oh that's whitefella business'. Nothing to do with them.

I visit an Aboriginal elder who had recently donated one of the few items of mission cultural history we have in the Collection – a piece of ripple iron from the former Hollywood reserve near Yass – and saw him tossing an invitation to a Museum exhibition opening in the bin. He comments:

> Yeah, we'll come to the Museum one day – just waiting for something we want to see.

He appreciates the Museum's role of keeping history and of telling it to the future. He is acutely aware that the history he has taken part in is little valued by his non-Indigenous local community. He also knows that his local Indigenous community is in general not interested in museum ways of preserving the past. His anxiety to preserve that past however has resulted in his donation to the Museum – but he still sees the Museum as in some sense still irrelevant.

I ask Barbara what Aboriginal people in general might think of museums. She replies

> Ask the average Aboriginal person in the street – 'What do you think of museums?' and they'll say 'That's where they've got all those old bones – the ones they stole from the graves'.

Therefore, there is not only irrelevance to consider when I am working with Aboriginal clients but also violence, a cultural rape that locates the Museum in opposition to the Aboriginal community.

I take an Aboriginal visitor on a tour of the Museum. She is a relative of Troy's. We pass an open doorway through which we can glimpse racks of spears and shields. The woman hastily averts her eyes. 'Looks like men's business in there', she comments. She does not trust the Museum to keep her safe, to keep to cultural protocols – even though she has a relative on the staff. The room in fact is a display area showing traditional artefacts from both men and women.

These encounters make me more concerned to tie the object to the person who gave it, to try to ensure the meaning that it has for that person at the moment of donation remains attached to that person. This meaning may be different from the provenance that museums require. Rather, it is the meaning for that person at that moment in time. I have begun using video recordings of people with the object they have donated recording them, as they talk about it, touch it, explaining what it meant to them when they gave it.

The legacy of colonising violence means that I feel I am bound to an implied unwritten contract of trust with the Aboriginal people I work with. The 'contract' between us implies that if they tell me their stories I will then re-tell them in the Museum in the way that best represents their histories as they see them. I send all the text of the labels to them. If they do not like it, I change it and send it back again. I have told all the people I have mentioned that their stories will be included in this paper. I do this because I am the heir to all that bad faith between Aboriginal people and museums. It does not mean that I include anywhere material that I consider inaccurate or distorted history, or that I abandon my professional responsibilities, but I keep faith in attempting to represent their stories as they see them.

The Stolen Generations exhibit

This question of trust is particularly acute when working with Stolen Generations material. It is raw. In Australia, the story of the removal of Aboriginal children is 'new' history – still unfolding – still affecting the lives of living people. The Stolen Generations people who are willing for me to present their personal stories in the Museum know that some visitors will not believe them. These clients may not have read Andrew Bolt's columns on the 'myth' of the Stolen Generations, but they still understand that their story is contested.[2] The 2008 Apology to the Stolen Generations by the Australian government has given them more assurance than they had previously, but they still have a basic distrust of governments and the non-Indigenous community.

It is my task to attempt to tell the Stolen Generations story in the museum. This story is of course complex. There are different responses to the experience of

---

2   For example, Bolt 2004.

removal – despair, anger, resolve to succeed despite all, a triumphant return to Aboriginality, a denial of Aboriginality. There are different kinds of loss – personal, communal, cultural. People were not only denied the experience of family life, of a relation with parents, siblings and extended family, but the transfer of cultural knowledge. There are the various institutions – church or government – who took and cared for removed children, the foster homes or adoptive families who took removed children. There is the role of the government policy and of Link-Up to be explored.

I had first to collect some new objects. The only significant appropriate item already in our Collection was an artwork, *Matters of Her Heart*, by Pamela Croft, which explores her personal story as a removed child. It is a powerful assemblage of documents that relate to her personal experience – adoption papers, marriage and divorce certificates, letters to her birth mother and adoptive mother, and photographs of herself and her families. These are contextualised with a large painting of a riven heart and face fractured into jigsaw pieces and a heart-shape decorated with ochre and human hair.

To this painting, I added a booklet, another painting by a former inmate of an Aboriginal orphanage, a boomerang, a hatband and bracelet in Aboriginal colours, an old Namatjira print, and two scrapbooks. I could at least begin to tell that complex story.

The booklet is by Peter Read, first published in 1981. It marks the first use of the term Stolen Generations and is a document which can speak to the government policies that underlay so many of the removals. The painting, *Matters of Her Heart,* is by Cecil Bowden, incarcerated from the age of ten in the notorious Kinchela Aboriginal Boys Training Home. His painting shows three heads behind what appear to be prison bars and is titled 'There only crime was: born Aborignal' [sic]. The boomerang was donated by Barbara Nicholson. She was removed from her community at aged four and returned to it as an adult. Her father, who died before she returned, left this boomerang for her.

The hatband and bracelet were made by Joy Williams to celebrate her discovery of her Aboriginality. Joy was removed from her mother as a baby and put in a 'white' orphanage because the authorities thought she could 'get away' with being white. It never occurred to the authorities that she might, later in her life, choose to identify as Aboriginal. Her family is one of the prominent Aboriginal families of the Wiradjuri community of central New South Wales. The battered print of Namatjira also belongs to Joy. She bought it because Namatjira was the only Aboriginal person she had ever heard of. The scrapbooks were hers too – they contain clippings of newspaper articles about Aboriginal matters. We did not display them because of the problems associated with the exposure of such light-sensitive items as newspaper.

Fig 2. Cecil Bowden's reflection on his experience as a member of the Stolen Generation

National Museum of Australia

I also had on loan a book of Bible stories, loaned by Marie Melito-Russell. Only her foster sister, who gave her this book, made her deeply unhappy foster home bearable. We also have a poem written by Marie, and displayed in her own handwriting, responding to her finding and meeting with her mother, when Marie was in her 60s. The artworks by Cecil Bowden and Pamela Croft, and Marie Melito-Russell's poem together give the exhibit an emotional resonance that is essential in the presentation of this story.

We have no objects from parents – just as the *Bringing Them Home* report, which recorded many hundreds of hours of testimony from people involved in the experience of child removal, has almost no testimony from parents.[3] It seems the experience as a parent of having a child, or indeed a whole family, removed, is so unbearable as to make it unspeakable.

---

3   Human Rights and Equal Opportunity Commission 1997.

Fig 3. Jack Tattersall's boomerang and the text panel that accompanies it

National Museum of Australia

Object as witness

From my conversations with many members of the stolen and their families, they seem overwhelmingly *to want to be believed*. To have their story validated.

That is why they have a relationship with the museum through me as curator. So while they may still have ambivalent responses to the museum, for them the museum is an authorised space. They know it is a space that non-Aboriginal people believe in. Furthermore, this is not *a* museum; it is the *national* museum. The men from Kinchela Aboriginal Boys Training Home, a notorious institution that closed in 1970, tell me 'We want the story told. We don't want it swept under the carpet.' They are looking for manifestation of their experience in a public place in the nation's museum.

Therefore, the objects that we take into the Museum for the people of the Stolen Generations are to be witnesses to them, to their version of history. It is object as witness.

This notion of object as witness influences the way we display the objects. If we were a traditional ethnographic museum, we might label Barbara Nicholson's boomerang:

> Mulga wood boomerang, probably from far western NSW, incised with marks, significance unknown. Origin unknown.

But this is how we actually describe it in the text panel next to the object:

> *This is all I have left from my father.*

> Barbara Nicholson was taken from her father when she was four years old. She never saw him again. Her father left her this boomerang, but Barbara has no idea where it came from or what the marks on it mean. Link-Up can help find people's families and reconnect them with their Aboriginal community but some things can never be recovered.

Jack Tattersall left this boomerang for his daughter Barbara who had been taken away at aged four. When she found her way back to her community, he had died. She has no other memorabilia of him. Barbara Nicholson does not know what the marks on the boomerang mean, where it came from, or what it meant to her father. The boomerang represents the cultural loss experienced by members of the Stolen Generations. There are undoubtedly experts in the Museum who would know something of this boomerang. Barbara does not want us to tell her this kind of information because it should have come from her father. *Nor have we investigated this possibility* so the label on the object represents only what Barbara herself knows.

So for my clients and me, the objects I have collected are one-dimensional. They are mute voices of the Stolen Generations. That is why they are there. Other Museum objects may have a multifaceted nature – containing in themselves a variety of stories, even though initially collected for one association. The boomerang is 'Jack Tattersall's boomerang' only – it has not been collected for display in any other association with boomerangs. Clearly, this is only a partial and temporal situation, which will change with time as both Barbara and I are forgotten. However, in the present it is what they are – objects as witness to a particular story that I have called as testimony to this particular historical memory.

This account is the telling of history and memory that is placed in a particular context – that of a colonising relation. In the future, the imposition by me of this context on the task of telling may seem irrelevant, essential, erroneous, enlightening or even corrupting. But for me in this time it is the ethical basis of my work.

References

Bolt, Andrew, 'The Stolen Generations ... a dangerous myth', *Herald-Sun,* 25 February 2004.

Human Rights and Equal Opportunity Commission 1997, *Bringing Them Home: a guide to the findings and recommendations of the National Inquiry into the Separation of Aboriginal and Torres Strait Islander Children from Their Families*, National Inquiry into the Separation of Aboriginal and Torres Strait Islander Children from Their Families (Australia), Human Rights and Equal Opportunity Commission, Sydney.

16. On the significance of saying 'sorry': Apology and reconciliation in Australia

ISABELLE AUGUSTE

As an observer of Aboriginal politics over the past ten years, I have followed closely the outcome of three federal elections wondering if a change of leadership in Australia would really result in an apology. Last year, I was privileged to witness a significant moment in Australian history. On 13 February 2008, I was on the lawns of Parliament House in Canberra, with some Aboriginal people and some other Australians, when Prime Minister Kevin Rudd said 'sorry' to the Indigenous peoples of the country.

The Australian Apology has already paved the way for other important gestures worldwide. On 6 June 2008, the Japanese Parliament, in a bipartisan motion, recognised the Ainou people as the Indigenous peoples of Japan and promised to improve their living conditions.[1] A few days later, on 11 June, in another part of the world, Canadian Prime Minister Stephen Harper apologised to the Aboriginal people of the country for Canada's role in the Indian residential school system and the harm, the disastrous effects, it created. There is indeed a growing international trend to apologise for past wrongs, notably for past human rights abuses.[2] An apology, nevertheless, is far from being an easy gesture nor an insignificant one, as American scholar Aaron Lazare shows in his book *On Apology*. It requires an individual, a group or an institution to acknowledge an offence or grievance and accept responsibility for it. An apology has a dual role. It responds, on the one hand, to the need of the victims for recognition, and on the other, it offers the offenders the opportunity to make amends for their misdeeds.[3] As a sign of regret, in the political discourse in particular, it presents this ideal, of redressing past injustices and of laying a foundation for

---

1 'Le Japon reconnaît enfin le peuple aïnou', *Libération*, 4 June 2008.
2 See, for example Barkan and Karn 2006; Brooks 1999. On the political uses of official apologies in the United States, Australia, Canada and New Zealand, see Nobles 2008.
3 Lazare 2004.

better relationships between the two parties. The dual role of the apology is exemplified in the Australian Apology. But why did Australia apologise? What was the Apology about? Why was it significant to say 'sorry'?

In this essay, I will provide some historical background to the Apology. More specifically, I will deal with the place the Apology takes in the reconciliation process and offer an account of what happened on 13 February 2008 to show its significance in the Australian context.

Some background on the reconciliation process

Reconciliation, if we look at its core definition, is derived from the Latin word *'conciliare'* which means bringing together. The most basic meaning of the word is 'restoring friendly relations between'. We can also summarise reconciliation as Hamber and Kelly have in their study of Northern Ireland as a process of 'addressing conflictual and fractured relationships'.[4] In Australia, the conflict that opposes Indigenous Australians – the Aboriginal and Torres Strait Islander people – to the Australian settler-state finds its origins in the colonisation of the country. Australia, as we all know, is the homeland of the Aboriginal and Torres Strait Islander people. They have lived there since time immemorial, at least 40,000 years according to some scientific evidence, since the Dreaming or Dreamtime, which is the time of creation, according to their own beliefs.[5] When the British arrived in 1788, the Indigenous people were dispossessed and then became subject to discriminatory policies of segregation and assimilation. More recently, Australia, like other settler societies such as Canada, has attempted to adopt a new relationship with its Indigenous population. As Short says, 'the peacemaking language of Reconciliation has been the preferred rhetorical device for such endeavour' in those countries.[6]

In Australia, the 1967 Referendum can be considered as the starting point of reconciliation. On 27 May 1967, a referendum was held in order to amend two sections of the Constitution considered discriminatory to Aboriginal people. Many myths surround that event, as historians Andrew Markus and Bain Attwood have argued in their book *The 1967 Referendum or when the Aborigines did not get the Vote* (1997). The 1967 Referendum *per se* was not about citizenship rights such as voting rights as we could still read in some Australian newspapers in 2007. It was about repealing section 127, which reads: 'in reckoning the numbers of the people of the Commonwealth or of a State or other part of the Commonwealth, Aboriginal natives shall not be counted', and amending section 51 (26) to give powers to the Commonwealth to legislate for

---

4 Hamber and Kelly 2004.
5 Broome 1994: 9–10; Kohen 1993: 3; Willmot 1987: 9.
6 Short 2005: 267.

Aboriginal people. It is true that the reformists of the 1960s, notably FCAATSI, the Federal Council for the Advancement of Aborigines and Torres Strait Islanders, which had fought for more than ten years for such a referendum to take place, had transformed the 'Yes Vote' into a campaign for equal rights, for the end of discrimination, better conditions of life and full citizenship for Aboriginal people. This is probably what they expected would result as they believed that federal control of Aboriginal Affairs would be beneficial to the Aboriginal people in the country. Nevertheless, whether one voted for one reason or another, people became aware there was a wrong to be put right and what makes the event significant is the symbol of changes it represents. The least one can say is that FCAATSI and their supporters brilliantly succeeded in rallying the Australian population to the Aboriginal cause. Indeed, a massive 90 per cent of the population voted 'yes' to the 1967 Referendum.[7] This sweeping vote should have put strong pressure on the Commonwealth government to act as it was expected to play a much greater role in Aboriginal Affairs. But, the changes were slow and it was not until 1972 and the election of a new Labor government headed by Gough Whitlam that the Aboriginal cause became a national issue and new measures were introduced as part of a self-determination policy. This marked the beginning of a new approach in Indigenous Affairs in Australia and a new period which saw the development of some land rights policies, the creation of some Aboriginal-specific structures and the elaboration of some special socio-economic programs at the federal level.

The word reconciliation itself did not actually appear in political discourse until 1983 when Minister for Aboriginal Affairs Clyde Holding stated in his presentation of the Labor program to Parliament that there should be some form of reconciliation by the bi-centenary of the colonisation of the country. He did not give further explanation of what it meant, nor how to get there, nor the form it should take.[8] In 1988, nothing came out but some Aboriginal protests in Sydney where the motto was, 'We have survived'. Prime Minister Robert Hawke did promise then to sign a Treaty with Aboriginal people,[9] and it is arguable that the formal process of reconciliation that his government set up was a way to delay the whole issue. In the meantime the end of the 1980s were marked by a number of inquiries highlighting the plight of Aboriginal people. Notably, the Royal Commission into Aboriginal Deaths in Custody (RCIADIC) became one of the most extensive inquiries conducted on the conditions of Aboriginal people in Australia. Among the 339 recommendations, Commissioner Johnston put forward the idea that 'the reconciliation of the Aboriginal and non-Aboriginal communities must be an essential commitment of all sides if change is to be

---

7   Auguste 2008: 41–44.
8   Holding 1983: 3487.
9   See the 'Barunga Statement' of 1988 which is now hung in Parliament House.

genuine and long term'.[10] Robert Tickner, the third of Bob Hawke's Ministers for Aboriginal Affairs, is the one who formalised this notion of reconciliation. He managed to obtain support from some Aboriginal organisations and from the opposition for his project.[11] And for the first time in eight years of Labor government, a legislation concerning Aboriginal people passed with bi-partisan support.[12] The *Council for Aboriginal Reconciliation Act* was voted in 1991 and set up an organisation comprising some Aboriginal representatives and some delegates of different political affiliations to promote reconciliation for ten years. The Council for Aboriginal Reconciliation (CAR), first headed by Patrick Dodson, envisioned for the centenary of Federation, the anniversary of the Australian nation, 'a united Australia which respects this land of ours; values the Aboriginal and Torres Strait Islander heritage and provides justice and equity for all'.[13] This was the beginning in Australia of a formal process of reconciliation.

The issue of an Apology became associated with the reconciliation process six years afterwards with the release of a report on the Stolen Generations.

Stolen Generations, Apology and reconciliation 'off-track'

In the words of Peter Read who coined the term with Jay Arthur:

> We Stolen Generations are the victims of Australia-wide policies which aimed to separate us from our parents, our family, our neighbourhood, our community, our country and our rightful inheritance as Aboriginal citizens of Australia.
>
> We are the victims of a policy which – if it had been successful – would have put an end to Aboriginality forever. Not just ours – everyone's. And we are still hurting.[14]

The issue of forcible removal, already condemned in the 1920s by Fred Maynard and the Australian Aboriginal Progressive Association,[15] was not much talked about in the 1980s when the pamphlet on the Stolen Generations was released and when its authors Peter Read and Coral Edwards set up Link-Up, an association to help reunite families. But a growing awareness of it emerged. In presenting the policy of the Hawke government in 1983, Minister for Aboriginal Affairs Clyde Holding referred to the deliberate policy of governments to separate children

---

10   Royal Commission into Aboriginal Deaths in Custody 1991: recommendation 339, chapter 38.
11   This does not mean that there was no opposition to the process of reconciliation. For some comments, see for example Moores 1995.
12   Tickner 2001: chapter 2.
13   Council for Aboriginal Reconciliation 1994: viii.
14   Read 1999: xi.
15   Attwood and Markus 1999: 66–67.

from their families with a view to assimilating them, and promised to 'restore the rights of Aboriginal families to raise and protect their own children'.[16] In 1991, The Royal Commission Into Aboriginal Deaths In Custody showed that among the 98 cases studied, 43 persons had been separated from their families.[17] In 1995, the Keating government finally set up an inquiry because of an 'increasing concern that the general public's ignorance of the history of forcible removal was hindering the recognition of the needs of its victims and their families and provision of services'.[18]

The inquiry was conducted by Human Rights and Equal Opportunity Commission President Sir Ronald Wilson and by Aboriginal and Torres Strait Islander Social Justice Commissioner Mick Dodson whose mission was to trace the history of separation past and present, but also to examine principles for compensation. As the inquirers stated, it is 'no ordinary report'. It goes to the heart of personal stories, testimonies of separation, institutionalisation, abuses and denigration. Five-hundred and eighty-five Aboriginal persons courageously came forward to talk about their painful experiences, a violation of their human rights that the inquirers compared to an act of genocide. It was not only established that this practice of forcible removal began with colonisation but that it was still happening in the 1970s. No Indigenous family seems to have escaped from its effects.[19]

It is from the disturbing findings of this particular inquiry that a call for an apology emerged. An acknowledgement from the perpetrators of the wrongs separation caused and an apology to the victims and their families were seen as central to a healing process. The Commission received many submissions along these lines. For the Commission, 'the first step in any compensation and healing for victims of gross violations of human rights must be an acknowledgement of the truth and the delivery of an apology'. This apology was also seen as an elementary condition of and a first step towards reconciliation.[20]

The *Bringing Them Home* Report was released in May 1997 while the Council for Aboriginal Reconciliation was holding a major convention in Melbourne. The convention, as Sir Ronald Wilson stated, had the effect of merging the two issues of reconciliation and the stolen generation into one.[21] The issue of an Apology became inextricably intertwined with the process of reconciliation from then on. Bringing to light this hidden aspect of Australia's history caused dismay and there was a massive positive response from State Parliaments, Churches,

---

16   Holding 1983: 3486.
17   Royal Commission into Aboriginal Deaths in Custody 1991: para 2.2.9.
18   Human Rights and Equal Opportunity Commission 1997: introduction.
19   Human Rights and Equal Opportunity Commission 1997: introduction.
20   Human Rights and Equal Opportunity Commission 1997: chapter 14.
21   Wilson 1998.

community groups, ethnic organisations and local governments that supported the stance of apologising.[22] Since the first Sorry Day in 1998, thousands of people have signed sorry books across the country to express their grievances.[23]

By contrast, the Howard government refused to formally apologise. It ignored the recommendations of an apology and compensation when it responded to the *Bringing Them Home* Report in December 1997.[24] Before the federal election of 1998, Howard explained that his motives did not involve a fear of compensation but a belief that, if you express regrets for things, 'you are collectively and in a direct sense responsible', and he did not think 'that applies to the current generation of Australians'.[25] In that sense, he was faithful to a position he had taken on Indigenous issues when he was leader of the opposition in the 1980s: 'guilt is not hereditary'. In August 1999, he did move a motion in which he expressed his deep and sincere regret 'that Indigenous Australians suffered injustices under the practices of past generations'.[26] But his motion and his speech did not even mention the Stolen Generations and it was not the long awaited formal apology. In May 2000 when CAR released the Documents of Reconciliation, John Howard responded with his own version of reconciliation in which he excluded the Apology. Those documents CAR developed in the course of its three mandates, in consultation with the Australian population, provide a definition of reconciliation for Australia.

The Australian Declaration Towards Reconciliation, which has the touch of writer David Malouf and historian Jackie Huggins, is a strongly worded document offering a vision of a reconciled Australia. It refers in particular to the need to recognise Aboriginal people as the Indigenous component of Australia – their unique status, their cultural identity, the necessity to sign a treaty, a recognition of past mistreatment, and the right to self-determination within the life of the nation. This Declaration is supported by a Road Map to Reconciliation embracing four National Strategies: to sustain the reconciliation process, to recognise Aboriginal and Torres Strait Islander Rights, to achieve Economic Independence, and to overcome Disadvantage. The Strategies include symbolic as well as practical actions to respond to the 'unfinished business' of reconciliation and are addressed to all levels of government, to the private sector, and to the community at large. And to give effect to these actions, CAR called in its last annual report for a Constitutional reform to recognise and protect the specific status of Aboriginal people in Australia.[27]

---

22 Dodson 1997.
23 National Sorry Day Committee 2008.
24 Herron 1997.
25 Quoted in Read 1999: ix.
26 Howard 1999: 9205.
27 Council for Aboriginal Reconciliation 2000: recommendation 5–6.

It is, however, this idea that Aboriginal people can have special rights because of their indigeneity which has been most problematic. As in 1967, there was another massive popular response to reconciliation, exemplified in May 2000 in the Sydney Harbour Bridge walk, gathering together a quarter of a million of Australians. Nevertheless, the government response did not follow. In December 2000 when he received the final report of CAR from Evelyn Scott, second and final chair of the Council, Prime Minister Howard stated that he would consider the recommendations of the Council but that his position on some points was unchanged.[28] He did not have to be more precise and he was not. John Howard had made his position clear on Indigenous issues in the 1980s when he was leader of the opposition on such matters as a Treaty, self-determination, and 'inter-generational guilt'.[29] And he kept to this line when he became Prime Minister in 1996. Throughout his mandate, he repeated in a number of motions his commitment to genuine reconciliation.[30] Nevertheless, his government and the Liberal Party had a different vision of reconciliation from CAR. They made a distinction between the practical and what they referred to as the symbolic. The practical is about overcoming disadvantage and true reconciliation for them was limited to a socio-economic issue. The symbolic embraced anything to do with the recognition of the Aboriginal as the Indigenous component of Australia and a recognition of past mistreatment – in other words, the Apology. As a result, the reply of the government to the recommendations made by CAR was not surprising. In the Commonwealth Response, all the recommendations dealing with special rights were not considered by the government whose focus was on 'practical reconciliation'. There is a sentence which is quite significant:

> The Prime Minister indicated at the time of release of the Declaration that though there were significant areas of agreement, the Government could not give its full support. Consequently, on May 11th 2000, the Government presented a revised Declaration to which it offered its full support.[31]

In other words, they were in favour of reconciliation but on their own terms. What may be surprising is the time the government took to give its answer. The Aboriginal and Torres Strait Islander Social Justice Commissioner Bill Jonas was among those who expressed concern about the slowness of the government response to the documents. In his *Social Justice Report* of 2001, he recommended that the matter be inquired into.[32] It was at the genesis of the Senate Legal and

---

28   Howard 2000.
29   Liberal Party of Australia 1988: 96.
30   See for example Howard 1996: 6155, 1999: 9205.
31   Commonwealth Government 2002: recommendation 2.
32   Aboriginal and Torres Strait Islander Social Justice Commissioner 2001: recommendation 11.

Constitutional References Committee inquiry which started in August 2002, a month before the answer of the government. The title of the report says it all: *Reconciliation Off Track*. The first page gives the thrust of the inquiry:

> This inquiry has clearly established that the Commonwealth Government's practical reconciliation approach is failing Indigenous people. Indicators of Indigenous disadvantage are not improving in many areas. There has been a very minimal response to the symbolic issues outlined by the Council for Aboriginal Reconciliation. There is no legislation to enact a treaty process and no timeframe or process to resolve 'unfinished business'. The Government's emphasis on areas of perceived agreement leaves many important issues off the agenda, to the detriment of Indigenous people. In short, there is a failure of national leadership on this, one of the most critical issues in the definition of the nation.[33]

The organisers recognised the work done by many agencies for reconciliation, in particular Reconciliation Australia (RA), the foundation which took over the mission of CAR in 2001.[34] Overall for the committee, however, 'the process is now off track. There is a sense that momentum is being lost. People are becoming disheartened and reconciliation is slipping off the national agenda'.[35]

The 40th anniversary of the 1967 Referendum in 2007 echoed this dismay. It was a bittersweet commemoration. The veterans of the referendum campaign expressed mixed feelings about achievements since the 1960s. For Faith Bandler, there have been changes which cannot be denied:

> Of course there have been some changes as a result of [the 1967 Referendum]. No one can possibly dispute it. Before that, the people were just locked away on reserves, deprived of a voice to speak out by whoever controlled the reserve, usually one white person. It was a grim situation.[36]

But for an angry Lowitja O'Donoghue, 'conditions for Aboriginal people are not improving but going backward'.[37] I will not try here to compare the situation of Aboriginal people in the 1960s and today, I have done it elsewhere.[38] The least one can say is that the condition of Aboriginal people is deplorable compared to other Australians. This was dealt with for instance in a report by the National

---

33   Senate Legal and Constitutional References Committee 2003: v.
34   Senate Legal and Constitutional References Committee 2003: chapter 3.
35   Senate Legal and Constitutional References Committee 2003: v.
36   Quoted in Rintoul 2007.
37   Quoted in Rintoul 2007.
38   Auguste 2008: chapter 4.

Aboriginal Community Controlled Health Organisation and Oxfam which came out before 27 May.[39] The focus has notably been on health, on closing the 17-year life expectancy gap.

For a more balanced view of the past 40 years we can turn to Mick Dodson and Fred Chaney from Reconciliation Australia:

> Forty years of reconciliation can at best be described as having mixed outcomes. If reconciliation is about developing a relationship that works better between Aboriginal and Torres Strait Islander peoples and other Australians, if it's about ending indigenous disadvantage, we have certainly not achieved it … On the other hand, it's important in this anniversary year that we recognise and build on developments that could not have been imagined 40, or even 20 years ago.[40]

Such hopes were expressed before 21 June. That day, Prime Minister Howard and Minister for Indigenous Affairs Mal Brough called a special press conference to announce a national Emergency Intervention in the Northern Territory. This was officially to respond to the *Little Children are Sacred* report made public a few days before.[41] The Commonwealth government accused the Northern Territory government of reacting too slowly to this report bringing to light some serious issues of child abuse in communities, and decided to interfere in their jurisdiction. No one could of course argue against the gravity of the matter. But some scepticism arose about the motives of the government. Why has child abuse and violence in communities become an emergency issue all of a sudden when numerous reports over the years have called for action? What has the scrapping of the Permit System allowing the Aboriginal people of the Northern Territory to control access to their land to do with responding to the problem?[42] These were among the first questions to emerge and they were dealt with extensively in the Senate when the government decided to enshrine its measures into laws two months later. At that time, words such as 'paternalism' and assimilation were aired without reserve.

To describe the intervention, Jon Altman and Melinda Hinkson have used the notion of 'coercive reconciliation' as the title of a book which came out in October 2007. Australia then appeared to be going backward in her relationship with her Indigenous people at a particular time when the Declaration on the Rights of Indigenous Peoples was voted at the United Nations Assembly –

---

39   National Aboriginal Community Controlled Health Organisation and Oxfam Australia 2007.
40   Dodson and Chaney 2007.
41   Wild and Anderson 2007.
42   See for example a special edition of *Living Black*, SBS Television, 8 July 2007.

Australia being one of the four countries to vote against it. Nevertheless, the federal election which took place on 24 November 2007 brought some new prospects for reconciliation in Australia with the promise of an apology.

Sorry – a first step towards reconciliation?

ALP candidate Kevin Rudd promised, like his predecessors, to apologise to the Stolen Generations if elected. Right after the election, on 26 November, the new Prime Minister Rudd announced that an apology would be delivered at the next sitting of Parliament. The official date was known at the end of January as well as the absence of compensation. On 12 February, the 42nd Parliament was sworn in, after an Aboriginal ceremony. It was the first time in Australian History that Aboriginal people had taken part in the opening of Parliament. The following day, 'sorry' resonated throughout the country.

Thousands of people, Aboriginal and non-Aboriginal, Australians and non-Australians, had gathered in the main square of capital cities, in the outback, or on the lawns of Parliament. Others followed the event on television or on the radio. Some even woke up in the middle of the night overseas to watch the Apology on the internet. It was a really emotional moment. Many had travelled by bus from as far away as the Northern Territory to be in the capital city for the first time. Many Aboriginal persons thought an Apology would never happen in their lifetime. Some brought with them pictures of family members who did not have that chance.

According to Aaron Lazare, the success or failure of an apology depends on four major components: the acknowledgement of the offence, the explanation, the expression of shame and remorse, and reparation.[43] Kevin Rudd's Apology contains those ingredients. Rudd began his speech by relating a personal story, that of Nana Fejo, a member of the Stolen Generation. It was a way for him to put his words into context and explain that he was not talking about 'intellectual curiosities' but human beings, human lives. He then explained the significance of the moment for those still in doubt, for his opponents, for everyone. He was cautious in the way he acknowledged the offence. In 2000, a survey commissioned by CAR found that 40 per cent of Australians agree and 53 per cent disagree that, 'On behalf of the community, governments should apologise to Aboriginal people for what happened in the past'.[44] Rudd specified that those individuals who implemented the laws were not responsible. Those who were responsible were governments and the Parliament of the nation in what was one of the 'darkest chapters of Australia's history: the forced removal of Aboriginal children on racial grounds':

43 Lazare 2004.
44 Newspoll 2000.

Therefore, for our nation, the course of action is clear, and therefore, for our people, the course of action is clear: that is to deal now with what has become one of the darkest chapters in Australia's history. In doing so, we are doing more than contending with the facts, the evidence and the often rancorous public debate. In doing so, we are also wrestling with our own soul. This is not, as some would argue, a black-armband view of history; it is just the truth: the cold, confronting, uncomfortable truth – facing it, dealing with it, moving on from it. Until we fully confront that truth, there will always be a shadow hanging over us and our futures as a fully united and fully reconciled people. It is time to reconcile. It is time to recognise the injustices of the past. It is time to say sorry. It is time to move forward together.[45]

A jubilant crowd applauded at the first sorry. It was amplified when in a powerful manner the Prime Minister addressed his direct apologies to the Stolen Generations and detailed the hurt caused, recalling Prime Minister Keating in his Redfern Speech in 1992:

To the stolen generations, I say the following: as Prime Minister of Australia, I am sorry. On behalf of the government of Australia, I am sorry. On behalf of the Parliament of Australia, I am sorry. I offer you this apology without qualification. We apologise for the hurt, the pain and suffering that we, the parliament, have caused you by the laws that previous parliaments have enacted. We apologise for the indignity, the degradation and the humiliation these laws embodied. We offer this apology to the mothers, the fathers, the brothers, the sisters, the families and the communities whose lives were ripped apart by the actions of successive governments under successive parliaments. In making this apology, I would also like to speak personally to the members of the stolen generations and their families: to those here today, so many of you; to those listening across the nation – from Yuendumu, in the central west of the Northern Territory, to Yabara, in North Queensland, and to Pitjantjatjara in South Australia.[46]

Rudd recognised the difficulty of forgiveness but called for reconciliation and a new beginning, putting forward a number of proposals for the future, even taking Brendan Nelson, the leader of the opposition, by surprise in calling for a joint-policy commission.

Nelson was of course in an uncomfortable position if we consider the line taken by his party in the previous ten years. Nevertheless, despite some obvious dissensions, the coalition offered its in-principle support at the beginning of

---

45   Rudd 2008.
46   Rudd 2008.

February and on 13 February, Brendan Nelson stood up to 'speak strongly in favour of the motion'. Nelson, however, while recognising the hurt suffered by Aboriginal people, tried to justify the policies of the time. His decision to repeat numerous times words such as 'good intentions' or 'rescued' was not well received. It added to the pain of some who were listening to him. Tears of joy were replaced by tears of sadness. In the crowd I was in I saw many aunties bursting into tears. Anger also arose.

Talking to people afterwards, I realised that many who watched the event on television thought that the crowd turned their back on the opposition leader right from the start without even listening, an impression created by the news reports. This was not the case. After a while Nelson's speech became so unbearable for many that they turned their back to the screens as occurred in Canberra, or they chose to leave. In Perth, they switched off the television.

Nevertheless, as Tom Calma, Aboriginal and Torres Strait Islander Social Justice Commissioner, said, what is to be remembered of that historic day is that:

> It's the day our leaders – across the political spectrum – have chosen dignity, hope and respect as the guiding principles for the relationship with our first nations' peoples;
>
> Through one direct act, Parliament has acknowledged the existence and the impacts of the past policies and practices of forcibly removing Indigenous children from their families;
>
> And by doing so, has paid respect to the Stolen Generations. For their suffering and their loss. For their resilience. And ultimately for their dignity.[47]

The image of the Prime Minister and the leader of the opposition walking hand in hand towards the members of the Stolen Generations is the image that will remain. To the 'sorry', some Aboriginal people have responded with tears of joy and 'thanks', 'apologies accepted', through the shirts they were wearing.

Forty-one years after the 1967 Referendum, eleven years after the *Bringing Them Home* report, seven years after the end of the Council for Aboriginal Reconciliation, Australia apologised to her Indigenous population for past mistreatments. Like an echo of the Declaration of Reconciliation, we could say that one part of the nation apologised and expressed its sorrow and sincere regret for the injustices of the past, while the other part accepted the apologies and forgave. This picture is ideal and can even be perceived as naïve. The

---

47   Calma 2008.

Apology was nonetheless significant – if not for everyone, it was at least, and importantly, meaningful for those Stolen Children and their families who were waiting for some acknowledgement of what had occurred.

The Apology of course cannot be and was not meant to be the panacea for the problems affecting the Indigenous peoples of Australia. Nevertheless, it signalled some changes in Indigenous Affairs policy in the country. It had, in particular, the effect of putting the idea of reconciliation 'back on track'. Considering that the Documents of Reconciliation are also part of the many electoral promises of the Australian Labor Party,[48] there remains another problematic and controversial issue raised at the 2020 Summit: the Treaty.[49] Together with 'sorry', it was referred to in the press in 2000 as the 'other dirty word' the government would never agree on.[50] If 'sorry' was the first step, can the Treaty be the final one?

References

Aboriginal and Torres Strait Islander Social Justice Commissioner 2001, *Social Justice Report 2001*, Human Rights and Equal Opportunity Commission, Sydney.

Altman, Jon and Melinda Hinkson (eds) 2007, *Coercive Reconciliation, Stabilise, Normalise, Exit Aboriginal Australia,* Arena Publications Association, Melbourne.

Attwood, Bain and Andrew Markus 1997, *1967 Referendum or when Aborigines did not get the vote,* Aboriginal Studies Press, Canberra.

— 1999, *The Struggle for Aboriginal Rights, A Documentary History,* Allen & Unwin, Sydney.

Auguste, Isabelle 2008, *L'administration des Affaires Aborigènes en Australie depuis 1972: l'autodétermination en question,* l'Harmattan (Collection Lettres du Pacifique), Paris.

Australian Government 2008, *2020 Summit,* accessed 11 August 2009: <http://www.australia2020.gov.au>

Australian Labor Party 2007, 44th National Conference, Aboriginal and Torres Strait Islanders, accessed 11 August 2010: <http://www.alp.org.au/platform/chapter_13.php>

---

48   Australian Labor Party 2007: section 48.
49   Australian Government 2008.
50   Jopson 2000.

Barkan, Elazar and Karn Alexander (eds) 2006, *Taking Wrongs Seriously: Apologies and Reconciliation*, Stanford University Press, Stanford.

Brooks, Roy (ed) 1999, *When Sorry isn't Enough: The Controversy over Apologies and Reparations for Human Injustice*, New York University Press, New York.

Broome, Richard 1994, *Aboriginal Australians: Black Response to White Dominance 1788–1994*, 2nd edn, Allen & Unwin, Sydney.

Calma, Tom 2008, 'Let the healing begin – response to government to the national apology to the Stolen Generations', Members Hall, Parliament House, Canberra, 13 February 2008.

Commonwealth Government 2002, *Response to the Council for Aboriginal Reconciliation Final Report – Reconciliation: Australia's Challenge*, AGPS, Canberra.

Council for Aboriginal Reconciliation 1994, *Walking Together, the First Steps – Report of the Council for Aboriginal Reconciliation 1991–1994*, AGPS, Canberra.

— 2000, *Reconciliation: Australia's Challenge – Final Report to the Prime Minister and the Commonwealth Parliament*, available at: <http://austlii.edu.au/au/other.IndigLRes/car/2000/16>

Dodson, Michael 1997, 'We all bear the cost if apology is not paid', *The Age*, 18 December 1997.

— and Fred Chaney 2007, 'The stage is set for closing the gap', *The Weekend Australian*, 5–6 May 2007, The Inquirer.

Hamber, B And G Kelly 2004, 'Reconciliation: a working definition', Democratic Dialogue, accessed 10 May 2010: <http://www.democraticdialogue.org>

Herron, John 1997, 'Bringing Them Home': Commonwealth initiatives, Press Release, Minister for Aboriginal and Torres Strait Islander Affairs, 16 December 1997.

Holding, Clyde 1983, 'Aboriginal Affairs', *Commonwealth Parliamentary Debates*: 3485–3494.

Howard, John 1996, 'Racial Tolerance', *Commonwealth Parliamentary Debates*: 6155.

— 1999, 'Motion of Reconciliation', *Commonwealth Parliamentary Debates*: 9205.

— 2000, 'Address at the presentation of the final report to Federal Parliament by the Council for Aboriginal Reconciliation', Canberra, 7 December 2000.

Human Rights and Equal Opportunity Commission (HREOC) 1997, *Bringing Them Home: National Inquiry Into the Separation of Aboriginal and Torres Strait Islander Children from their Families*, HREOC, Canberra.

Jopson, Debra 2000, 'The other dirty word', *Sydney Morning Herald*, 3 June 2000.

Kohen, Jim 1993, *The Dharug and Their Neighbours*, Dharug Link and Blacktown Historical Society, Sydney.

Lazare, Aaron 2004, *On Apology*, Oxford University Press, New York.

Liberal Party of Australia 1988, *Future Directions – It's Time for Plain Thinking*, The Parties, Canberra.

Moores, Irene (comp) 1995, *Voices of Aboriginal Australia: Past, Present and Future*, Butterfly Books, Springwood.

National Aboriginal Community Controlled Health Organisation and Oxfam Australia 2007, *Close the Gap, Solutions to the Indigenous Health Crisis facing Australia, a Policy Briefing*, Oxfam, Melbourne.

National Sorry Day Committee 2008, accessed 10 May 2010: <http://www.nsde. org.au>

Nelson, Brendan 2008, 'Apology to Australia's Indigenous peoples', accessed 10 May 2010: <http://www.aph.gov.au/house/Nelson_speech.pdf>

Newspoll 2000, 'Quantitative Research into Issues Relating to a Document of Reconciliation', prepared for the Council for Aboriginal Reconciliation, accessed 10 May 2010: <http://www.austlii.edu.au/au/other/IndigLRes/ car/2000/3/quant.pdf>

Nobles, Melissa 2008, *The Politics of Official Apologies*, Cambridge University Press, Cambridge.

Read, Peter 1999, *A Rape of the Soul so Profound: The Return of the Stolen Generations*, Allen & Unwin, Sydney.

Rintoul, Stuart 2007, 'Veterans of the referendum campaign look back with mixed feeling', *The Weekend Australian*, 19–20 May 2007, The Inquirer.

Royal Commission Into Aboriginal Deaths in Custody 1991, *National Report*, AGPS, Canberra.

Rudd, Kevin 2008, 'Apology to Australia's Indigenous peoples', accessed 10 May 2010: <http://www.aph.gov.au/house/rudd_speech.pdf>

Senate Legal and Constitutional References Committee 2003, *Reconciliation Off Track*, the Senate, Canberra.

Short, Damien 2005, 'Reconciliation and the problem of internal colonialism', *Journal of Intercultural Studies* 26(3): 267–282.

Tickner, Robert 2001, *Taking a Stand, Land Rights to Reconciliation*, Allen & Unwin, Sydney.

Wild, Rex and Patricia Anderson 2007, *Ampe Akelyernemane Meke Mekarle 'Little Children are Sacred'*, a Report of the Northern Territory Board of Inquiry into the Protection of Aboriginal Children from Sexual Abuse, Northern Territory Government, Darwin.

Willmot, Eric 1987, *Australia: The Last Experiment*, ABC Boyer Lectures, Sydney.

Wilson, Ronald (Sir) 1998, 'Native Title and Reconciliation: a People's Movement', an address to the nation, National Press Club Canberra.